THE COLLECTED COURSES OF THE ACADEMY OF EUROPEAN LAW



# VOLUME XXVIII/4

# Global Rights?

# Human Rights in Complex Governance

# THE COLLECTED COURSES OF THE ACADEMY OF EUROPEAN LAW

Edited by: Professor Neha Jain, Professor Claire Kilpatrick, Professor Sarah Nouwen, and Professor Joanne Scott

Assistant Editor: Joyce Davies

The Academy of European Law is housed at the European University Institute in Florence, Italy. The Academy holds annual advanced-level summer courses focusing on topical, cutting-edge issues in Human Rights Law and The Law of the European Union. The courses are taught by highly qualified scholars and practitioners in a highly interactive environment. General courses involve the examination of the field as a whole through a particular thematic, conceptual, or philosophical lens or look at a theme in the context of the overall body of law. Specialized courses bring together a number of speakers exploring a specific theme in depth. Together, they are published as monographs and edited volumes in the Collected Courses of the Academy of European Law series. The Collected Courses series has been published by Oxford University Press since 2000. The series contains publications on both foundational and pressing issues in human rights law and the law of the European Union.

OTHER TITLES IN THE SERIES INCLUDE:

**Human Rights in Transition**
Edited by Nehal Bhuta

**The Emergence of European Society through Public Law**
**A Hegelian and Anti-Schmittian Approach**
Armin von Bogdandy

**Revisiting the Fundamentals of the Free Movement of Persons in EU Law**
Edited by Niamh Nic Shuibhne

**Data at the Boundaries of European Law**
Edited by Deirdre Curtin and Mariavittoria Catanzariti

**Legal Mobilization for Human Rights**
Edited by Gráinne de Búrca

**The UK's Withdrawal from the EU**
**A Legal Analysis**
Michael Dougan

**Justifying Contract in Europe**
**Political Philosophies of European Contract Law**
Martijn W. Hesselink

**Contemporary Challenges to EU Legality**
Edited by Claire Kilpatrick and Joanne Scott

**Reframing Human Rights in a Turbulent Era**
Edited by Gráinne de Búrca

# Global Rights?

## *Human Rights in Complex Governance*

*Edited by*

NEHAL BHUTA
RODRIGO VALLEJO

OXFORD
UNIVERSITY PRESS

OXFORD
UNIVERSITY PRESS

Great Clarendon Street, Oxford, OX2 6DP,
United Kingdom

Oxford University Press is a department of the University of Oxford. It furthers the University's objective of excellence in research, scholarship, and education by publishing worldwide. Oxford is a registered trade mark of Oxford University Press in the UK and in certain other countries



Published in the United States of America by Oxford University Press
198 Madison Avenue, New York, NY 10016, United States of America

British Library Cataloguing in Publication Data

Data available

Library of Congress Control Number: 2024947774

ISBN 978–0–19–894016–6

DOI: 10.1093/oso/9780198940166.001.0001

# Contents

# Notes on Contributors

**Anna Beckers** is Professor of Private Law and Social Theory at the Faculty of Law at Maastricht University. She has published widely on topics related to corporate social responsibility and the law, business and human rights, global value chains, and the regulation of digital technologies. She is the author of two monographs, *Enforcing Corporate Social Responsibility Codes* (Hart Publishing, 2015) and *Three Liability Regimes for Artificial Intelligence* (Hart Publishing, 2021, co-authored with Gunther Teubner) and numerous articles on these topics. Anna is also the Principal Investigator of the research project CHAINLAW—Responsive Law for Global Value Chains (2023–2028, ERC Starting Grant) which aims to develop a conceptual and normative legal language for capturing the phenomenon of global value chains.

**Nehal Bhuta** holds the Chair of Public International Law at the University of Edinburgh and is Co-Director of the Edinburgh Centre for International and Global Law. He previously held the Chair of Public International Law at the European University Institute (EUI) in Florence, where he was also Co-Director of the Institute's Academy of European Law. He is a member of the editorial boards of the *European Journal of International Law*, the *Journal of International Criminal Justice*, and *Constellations* and a founding editor of the interdisciplinary journal *Humanity*. He is also a series editor of the Oxford University Press (OUP) series in *The History and Theory of International Law*. Prior to the EUI, he was on the faculty at the New School for Social Research in New York, and at the University of Toronto Faculty of Law. Before entering academia, he worked with Human Rights Watch and the International Center for Transitional Justice.

**Michael Fakhri** is a Professor at the University of Oregon School of Law. He is the Special Rapporteur on the Right to Food (2020–2026), although he writes in this collection in his personal capacity.

**Matthias Goldmann** is Professor of International Law at EBS University (Wiesbaden) and a Senior Research Fellow at the Max Planck Institute for Comparative Public Law and International Law (Heidelberg). He has published on questions of international law and European law, particularly in the fields of international organizations, sovereign debt and finance, and international law's colonial history. He has advised UNCTAD (United Nations Trade and Development) on issues of sovereign debt. He was co-editor-in-chief of the *German Law Journal* from 2017 to 2022 and received a Freigeist Fellowship of the Volkswagen Foundation in 2015.

**Eliav Lieblich** is Professor of International Law at Tel-Aviv University's Buchmann Faculty of Law, and the Hans Kelsen Visiting Professor for the History and Theory of International Law at the Institute for International Peace and Security Law, Faculty of Law, University of Cologne. He teaches and researches public international law, with a focus on the laws of war, the use of force, just war theory, international humanitarian law, and the history and theory of international law. He has previously been a visiting professor at the schools of law at Columbia University and Northwestern University and has taught at the European University Institute's Academy of European Law. He is also general editor of the *Yearbook of International Humanitarian Law*.

**Guy Fiti Sinclair** is an Associate Professor and the Associate Dean (Pacific) at the University of Auckland Faculty of Law. He holds first degrees in law and history, and a Doctor of Juridical Science (JSD) degree from New York University School of Law. He publishes widely in public international law, with a focus on international organizations, international economic law, law and global governance, and the history and theory of international law. His first book, *To Reform the World: International Organizations and the Making of Modern States* (Oxford University Press, 2017) won the European Society of International Law Book Prize in 2018. In 2023, he was granted a five-year Rutherford Discovery Fellowship from the Royal Society of New Zealand.

**Rodrigo Vallejo** is Assistant Professor at Amsterdam Law School and researcher at the Amsterdam Centre for Transformative Private Law and the Sustainable Global Economic Law network. He specializes on the interactions between economic law, socio-political theory, and regulatory policies at the national and international levels. Rodrigo has been recently granted a Marie Sklodowska-Curie fellowship to develop a research project on transnational law and market valuations at the Centre for Private Governance of Copenhagen Law School. He was previously an affiliate researcher to the projects on European Regulatory Private Law (European University Institute) and Global Administrative Law (New York University) under a Hans Kelsen and a Fulbright scholarship respectively.

# 1

# Human Rights in Global Governance

*Nehal Bhuta and Rodrigo Vallejo*

## 1. Introduction: Post-National Human Rights?

The place of international human rights law (hereinafter, 'human rights law') in the governance of global governance is more perplexing than it ought to be.

The rise of complex legal and administrative governance beyond the state is no longer a novel phenomenon—and indeed, has arguably been a secular trend in international and transnational affairs since 1945 (notwithstanding the entry into common usage of the term 'global governance' in the early 1990s).[1] But the plausible intuition that the emerging 'post-national constellation' of institutions, processes, and actors that perform governance activities beyond and between states can threaten the realization of human rights goes hand in hand with the equally plausible intuition that human rights law can and should provide a framework for the normative governance of global governance.[2] Indeed, in some influential accounts, human rights law qua cosmopolitan legal order provides the baseline for the legitimacy and authority of institutions purporting to exercise global governance functions.[3] Surely, a global legal order such as that of human rights law is fit for the purpose of constraining, reforming, and redirecting the plethora of actors, institutions, and processes which govern the globe?

The answer to this problem is surprisingly complex, even after years of analysis and reflection. In the first instance, the *de jure* application of human rights *law* to and by global governance institutions and actors (e.g. as international organizations, or transnational corporations) remains beholden to what Alston described in 2005 as the 'Not-a-Cat syndrome'.[4] This refers to the limitation of the formal, *de jure* application of human rights law only to states or, at most, state-like authorities. Despite several decades of *intellectual* dissatisfaction with the view that human rights law is directly applicable to and creates direct duties *only* upon states, the

[1] See M. Zürn, *A Theory of Global Governance: Authority, Legitimacy, and Contestation* (2018).

[2] See e.g. the reflections in E. Benvenisti, *The Law of Global Governance* (2014). See also Habermas, 'Remarks on Legitimation through Human Rights', in M. Pensky (ed. and tr.), *The Postnational Constellation: Political Essays* (2001).

[3] Buchanan and Keohane, 'The Legitimacy of Global Governance Institutions', 20 *Ethics & International Affairs* (2006) 405.

[4] P. Alston, *Non-State Actors and Human Rights* (2005) ch. 1.

Nehal Bhuta and Rodrigo Vallejo, *Human Rights in Global Governance*. In: *Global Rights?* First Edition. Edited by: Nehal Bhuta and Rodrigo Vallejo, Oxford University Press. 
DOI: 10.1093/oso/9780198940166.003.0001

contrary view—that other kinds of legal persons might also be direct duty bearers under, and guarantors of, human rights law—remains heavily contested (not the least by states, international organizations, and corporations themselves). Human rights law, then, is not straightforwardly a law for the governance of global governance, except insofar as states themselves are agents of such governance.

But there is a deeper puzzle beyond *de jure* application. Human rights *law*, as a treaty architecture and system of international legal norms, acts on, in, and through the state legal order. It is a profoundly *statist* legal order in the sense that it functions as a complement to and corrective of the state's authority over people and territory. Rather than replace the state legal order, human rights law *presupposes it* as the means through which guarantees set out in human rights treaties are to be made concrete and effective for a given people in a given place. The *de jure* status of the state as a direct duty bearer under human rights law brings with it an important corollary at the level of legal concepts: the material content of the legal concepts (e.g. a right to a fair trial, freedom from arbitrary detention, the right to health, or the right to social security) rests upon historical types of state institutions (e.g. courts, police services, health ministries, and welfare agencies) and their expected behaviour. Thus, from a historical perspective, the possibility of human rights assumes the state or a similar kind of political order that is symbolically and materially capable of sustaining and ensuring human rights' legal recognition and materialization as values. As Arendt famously put it, human rights have always presupposed a 'right to have rights' that is generally ascertained through some category of political membership or citizenship.[5]

The 'birth' of human rights law after 1945 and its progressive *legal–institutional* development at the international level after 1950 initially twinned the emergence and high-water mark of the 'neo-corporatist state' in the advanced capitalist world and the developmental state in the developing world.[6] Some version of Gunnar Myrdal's 'welfare world'—a globe of national welfare states coordinating internationally to enhance each state's economic and social welfare—is the imaginary underlying economic and social rights, while civil and political rights rest on an ideal of the integrated 'positive state' of equal citizenship and liberal constitutional order.[7] Perhaps the greatest historical irony is that this modular template of strong states and managed capitalist economies presupposed by the postwar human rights legal order, would begin to be dismantled from 1970 onwards with the

[5] H. Arendt, *The Origins of Totalitarianism* (1973) 266–268. In this sense, see Bhuta, 'The Frontiers of Extraterritoriality—Human Rights Law as Global Law', in N. Bhuta (ed.), *The Frontiers of Human Rights* (2016) 1.

[6] In their many national configurations: Schmitter, 'Still the Century of Corporatism?', 36/1 *The Review of Politics* (1974) 85; and M. Conway, *Western Europe's Democratic Age: 1945–1968* (2020). On the United States, see the compelling N. Lemann, *Transaction Man: The Rise of the Deal and the Decline of the American Dream* (2019).

[7] See Kjaer, 'What Is Transformative Law?', 1 *European Law Open* (2022) 760, at 773–774.

electoral, policy, and ideational-discursive success of neoliberalism in the North, and rigorously imposed austerity in the South.[8]

The emergence of 'globalization' and 'crack up capitalism',[9] and their diffuse processes and agents of global governance, parallels not the birth of human rights law per se but rather its emergence as a salient legal–political lingua franca to characterize political and economic harms and injustices. Many of these harms and injustices continued to be committed by states, to be sure, but the motility of human rights as a language of critique and condemnation meant that it could and would be extended to harms flowing from the policies of international organizations and the conduct of corporations: austerity, capital account liberalization, the dismantling of welfarist policies and institutions, and the intensifying exploitation and insecurity of workers. The perplexity raised by such an extension was that these harms arose as a consequence of the erosion, weakening, or absence of the neo-corporatist 'social state' and its regulatory capacities, and human rights law on its own could hardly restore or create them *de novo*.

The phenomenon of human rights *in* global governance and *beyond* the state thus leads to the question of what happens to human rights when they are extracted from their constitutive presumptions. This goes beyond a mere practical or causal question regarding how or when these rights are protected in global governance regimes. It goes deeper into a distinctively conceptual question: when human rights are purportedly safeguarded in global governance, what kind of entitlement are we safeguarding? What happens to these human rights without the backstop of a state legal order? What does it mean to have a human right vis-à-vis a global governance agent such as an international organization or multinational corporation? It is an essential premise of this volume that these questions can only be answered by examining the uses of human rights law concepts in specific global governance contexts. This takes us well beyond debates about *de jure* application and into an inquiry about the meaning and nature of human rights law beyond the state and within institutional environments—such as international organizations—where the dynamics and presuppositions of the institution's legal order are quite different to the legal order of a state.

A commonplace of contemporary studies in global (governance) law is that 'transnational' or 'post-national' legal orders develop around specific functional imperatives, forms of technical expertise, and domain-specific value rationalities.[10]

[8] G. Gerstle, *The Rise and Fall of the Neoliberal Order: America and the World in the Free Market Era* (2022).

[9] Q. Slobodian, *Crack-Up Capitalism: Market Radicals and the Dream of a World Without Democracy* (2023); Q. Slobodian, *Globalists: The End of Empire and the Birth of Neoliberalism* (2018).

[10] See the helpful overview and analysis from the perspective of legal theory in D. Roth-Isigkeit, *The Plurality Trilemma: A Geometry of Global Legal Thought* (2018). From an empirical perspective, see Halliday and Shaffer, 'Transnational Legal Orders', in T. C. Halliday and G. Shaffer (eds), *Transnational Legal Orders* (2015) 3: inductively drawing upon several case studies to note that 'a transnational legal order seeks to produce *order* in a domain of social activity or an issue area that relevant actors have

Such legal orders (including, e.g., the internal legal order of transnational corporations) are constructed around what Maurice Hauriou called 'directing ideas' (*ideé directrice*), which articulate the purposes to be achieved by agents of that order, but also articulate the (permeable) boundaries of each order *and* qualify what counts as a relevant source of law in that order.[11] 'Directing ideas' can be found in constitutive charters and documents (e.g. founding treaties or articles of association), but do not remain fixed in their meaning: they are constantly reworked and rearticulated by the jurists and laypeople working with and through these concepts in order to enable the institution to act and react to its political, economic and social environment. Social function and legal form do not exist in a strictly determined, one-way relationship of dependence, one upon the other; rather they are made and remade through processes of negation, adaptation, and reformation. 'Functional–rational' imperatives underlying a given legal order are susceptible to revision by the reworking of the directing ideas through which such rationalities must be conceptualized and articulated in order to become a basis for intentional, meaningful action.[12]

Santi Romano's account of legal order, which he developed to dissolve any categorical distinction between state and non-state *law* but also to capture the *dynamics* of the interaction between legal orders deriving from different *types* of institutions, is helpful to our reflection.[13] Romano observes that a legal order is a unity, but not exclusively a unity of norms. It is, at any given moment, a unity of norms *and* social relationships, which together make up what he calls 'an institution'.[14] An institution is a legal order, and a legal order is an institution.[15] An institution is, in essence, a *mode of existence* of a human collectivity which is united as 'a social organization' in and through law:

> If law [can only] materialize and take shape within the institution, and if, conversely, all that is socially organized and is subsumed under the institution as one of its elements takes on a legal character, we obtain the following corollary: the

construed as a "problem" of some sort or another' and how 'an order connotes some regularity of behavioural orientation, communication and action'.

[11] Hauriou, 'The Theory of the Institution and the Foundation: A Study in Social Vitalism [1925]', in A. Broderick (ed.), *The French Institutionalists: Maurice Hauriou, Georges Renard, Joseph T. Delos* (1970) 93.

[12] For a contemporary illustration in the realm of global governance, see Arato, 'Treaty Interpretation and Constitutional Transformation: Informal Change in International Organizations', 38 *Yale Journal of International Law* (2013) 289. See also, more generally, H. Lindahl, *Authority and the Globalisation of Inclusion and Exclusion* (2018) ch. 2: advancing in this vein the notion of 'institutionalised authoritative collective action' (IACA) as a model of law within and beyond the state; and Koskenniemi, 'The Politics of International Law—20 Years Later', 20 *European Journal of International Law* (2009) 7: stressing the relevance of 'institutional biases'.

[13] S. Romano, *The Legal Order [1917]*, tr. M. Croce (2017).

[14] Ibid. 13.

[15] Ibid. 16–21.

> law is the vital principle of any institution, that which animates and holds together the various elements that compose it, which determines, fixes and preserves the structure of immaterial entities. In its turn, the institution is always a legal regime. While in a way it might be correct to think of the institution as the body, the scaffolding, the framework of law, the law is as inseparable from the institution, either materially or conceptually, as life from the living body. They are not two phenomena standing in a given relationship to one another, or that follow one another; instead, it is the same phenomenon.
>
> ... The primary and fundamental aspect of law is given by the institution in which it materializes, and not by the norms or generally the precepts through which it operates.... Hence, law's first occurrence is not determined by the norm, which is a late and subsidiary manifestation. On the other hand, there can be no law before and outside the institution, precisely because there is no organization that makes the norm legal. The law cannot just be the norm established by the social organization ...; for it is the social organization that, among its manifestations, also establishes the norm. It is true that the legal character of the latter is conferred by the social power that issues it, or at least sanctions it, it follows that this character must be already present in the institution, which could not assign such a legal character to the norm if it did not have it itself.[16]

As Croce concisely glosses:

> Romano never gets tired of saying that there is no distinction between the existence of an institution and the establishment of a legal order ... the law provides an *intelligibility condition* for one to conceive an entity as that particular entity... In its turn, the ostensible phenomena one accounts for (that is, the entity which is being described from a juristic point of view) provide the *existence condition* for law. ... The law is nothing but a complicated interaction between the factual existence of a normative entity (existence condition) and that normative entity's accounting for its own existence with reference to its internal law (intelligibility condition)—this activity of accounting of course requires mediators, that in Romano's minds are the jurists.[17]

This account of law as institution, and institution as law, leads to the apperception of a plurality of legal orders standing in a wide variety of relationships to one another—vertical, horizontal, orthogonal, adjacent, and interleaved. This theoretical account allows a variety of legal orders to be perceived, including transnational legal orders which emerge across and between state legal orders. Most interesting for our purposes is that this account opens the path to think about the dynamics

[16] Ibid. 24–25.

[17] Croce, 'Afterword', in S. Romano, *The Legal Order*, tr. M. Croce (2017) 111, at 122.

by which legal orders standing orthogonally or adjacent to each other become *relevant* to one another and the role of juristic labour in forging and negotiating this *relevance*.

The problem of *de jure* (non-)application of human rights law to specific kinds of global governance institutions can be recast as a problem of the *relevance* of the human rights legal order to the legal order of those institutions. *Relevance*, in Romano's account, refers to the ways in which legal orders open up to, or become effective within, other legal orders; legal orders all maintain boundary conditions, which distinguish them from other legal orders. But these boundary conditions are themselves the product of the juristic labour of articulating the purpose, nature, and meaning of the legal order and its norms, in interaction with its wider social, political, and legal environment (which could include other legal orders). Hierarchies of supremacy and subordination between legal orders are, seen through this lens, just specific kinds of *relevance*, which could reflect the particular origins of one legal order as derivative (genealogically speaking) of another, or the granting of supremacy on certain questions by one legal order to another through the creation of an all-encompassing legal order (e.g. a federal state created by constituent units).[18]

The 'not-a-cat' syndrome of human rights law described by Alston, which rejects the *de jure* application of human rights norms to international organizations, transnational corporations, and other kinds of non-state collectivities that can reasonably be understood as constituting their own legal order, can be productively understood in terms of what Romano calls *relevance*. Ergo, if the human rights legal order does not directly bind these other legal orders, it does not have a (formal) legal title to make its norms directly effective through those orders—it is, in other words, *not relevant* in the sense of hierarchy and supremacy vis-à-vis those orders. But the valuable insight derived from Romano's construction is that the relationship of *relevance* between orders can take a variety of modes and forms, not limited to the statist analogue of superiority and subordination in a vertical relationship. Rather, specific relationships of *relevance* can emerge or be crafted between dimensions or extensions of different orders that stand alongside each other or hover over one another (without necessarily determining one another in a vertical relationship). Romano expresses examples of the relationship of *relevance* of legal orders to one another in a topological register:

> ... In this sense, international law hovers over state law, but it can neither suppress nor invalidate it. At any rate, when two orders are in such a position, it is evident that this is a legal title whereby one is relevant to the other *in various degrees and with various effects* ... [A]n order could [also] be the presupposition of

[18] See Romano (n. 13) 66–67, 69–71.

> another. ... In this sense, the international community presupposes the states that belong to it. This means that international law presupposes state law, just like the law of the federal state presupposes the member states' law and so on. ... It might also be the case that an order, without being forced to do so, spontaneously subordinates some features of its content or of its effectiveness to another order from which it is totally independent but that in this way becomes relevant to it.[19]

*Relevance* is a juridical relationship between legal orders that can take a wide variety of forms and modalities: it can be the product of rigorously decisionist legal acts (a declaration to adhere to certain norms from another legal order through self-binding), or it may be a gradual, casuistic, and subtle process of 'inter-legality'[20] or modes of 'legal entanglement'[21] through which orders open on to each other and are partially interpellated and interleaved through administrative reception of the form or substance of particular norms, or an acceptance in one legal order of the juridical relevance of certain meanings and concepts gestated in another legal order. But *relevance* is not reducible to the transposition or application of a norm or concept from one order into another; such transposition is a modality of *relevance*, but other modalities of *relevance* could entail a significant shift in the meaning or application of a concept as it is juristically assimilated and developed into a different legal order which rests on different kinds of presuppositions and modes of existence.[22]

In this way of thinking about human rights *in* global governance, one must look for the modalities of *relevance* of the human rights legal order in other legal orders over which it does not necessarily claim a direct application. Such a starting point requires an examination of juristic concepts and other doctrinal constructions but cannot limit itself to those. As the several chapters of this volume demonstrate, one must also look into how this law becomes relevant *in action*, with socio-legal inquiries establishing a baseline for further theory and doctrine concerning the place of human rights law in global governance. The landmark pointillist style used by Paul Klee in the 'Ad Parnassum' painting selected as the volume's cover image evokes this kind of interaction between the micro and the macro when analysing the specific ways through which human rights law is entering into relationships of *relevance* (in Santi Romano's sense) with diverse global governance regimes.

According to some chapters in the volume, this modality of *relevance* of human rights law seems to be voluntary (as in the case of the World Bank and

[19] Ibid. 70–71.

[20] J. Klabbers and G. Palombella (eds), *The Challenge of Inter-Legality* (2019).

[21] N. Krisch (ed.), *Entangled Legalities Beyond the State* (2021).

[22] This phenomenon resonates with the notion of 'legal transplants' and other modalities of 'legal change' that have become one of the hallmarks of the noticeable developments that comparative law has been experiencing within contemporary legal studies. See, in general, M. Siems, *Comparative Law* (3rd ed., 2022) ch. 10; and Michaels, 'Transnationalizing Comparative Law', 23 *Maastricht Journal of European and Comparative Law* (2016) 352.

the Food and Agriculture Organization), but this belies a complex process of orchestration and world-making by jurists and activists who have insisted upon the *de jure* application or *de facto* significance of human rights concepts within these international organizations. The chapters by Guy Fiti Sinclair, Michael Fakhri, and Matthias Goldmann in particular show that the modalities by which human rights act—both juristically and politically—within the legal order of an international organization cannot be easily reduced to questions of bindingness or non-bindingness—or even to considerations of direct and indirect effects. Instead, what emerges is the transmission, circulation, and salience of human rights concepts through assemblages of actors and agents, including but not only lawyers. The picture that emerges is, to be sure, a *very attenuated* modality of legal *relevance*, but this dynamic nonetheless owes much to juristic efforts to insinuate the human rights legal order into the 'directing ideas' of these international organizations and thus to attempt to reshape their own understanding of their intelligibility conditions.[23]

In other cases, such as the emerging trend for states to mandate human rights due diligence obligations for corporations domiciled in their territories, but maintaining extensive extraterritorial subsidiary operations and supply chains analysed in the chapter by Anna Beckers, the relationship of *relevance* between human rights and the internal legal order of the corporation (and its extraterritorial private law relationships) is a result of the state's legal order's enactment of its interpretation of its obligations under human rights law and the extension of some of these obligations to the domiciled corporation—under the shadow of liability before that state's courts. The state and its courts create an aperture for the *relevance* of human rights law for the legal order of the corporation within that state's territory. But this relationship of *relevance* is extended through the private-ordering legal acts of the corporation and its agents into the legal order of other states and other corporations. In this indirect way, multiple 'wormholes' of *relevance* of human rights legal norms are insinuated in a multiplicity of legal relationships in diverse legal orders, most of them of a private law nature. However, what remains to be discovered and understood is what *happens* to the content of the human rights concept of 'due diligence'—or indeed substantive human rights norms such as 'the right to fair and just working conditions'—when they are determined principally through the ordering effects of private law instruments (e.g. contracts), within and between private legal orders (corporations or industry associations). As the chapter by Anna Beckers underscores, some initial empirical research suggests that the concepts from human rights law become highly malleable

[23] For a recent study of the role of lawyers in the life of the World Bank that vividly highlights these tensions within this global governance institution, see D. Van den Meersche, *The World Bank's Lawyers: The Life of International Law as Institutional Practice* (2022).

once stripped of their relationship with state law frameworks of accountability and enforcement.[24]

## 2. The Permutations of Human Rights in Global Governance

The contributions to this volume rise to the theoretical and methodological challenges of grasping modalities of the *relevance* of human rights law in a diverse range of global governance institutions and contexts. The chapters develop in-depth studies of the permutations of human rights throughout the contemporary landscapes of different global governance regimes. These regimes include the global governance of sovereign debt (Matthias Goldmann), food (Michael Fakhri), transnational commerce through global supply chains (Anna Beckers), development assistance as channelled through the World Bank complex (Guy Fiti Sinclair), and the transnational use of force against non-state actors (Eliav Lieblich).

This set of specialized studies brings to the fore a wide spectrum of theoretical and methodological frameworks for the study of international law and global governance. These frameworks encompass actor–network (or 'assemblage') theory (Guy Fiti Sinclair), systems theory and polycontextural governance (Anna Beckers), doctrinal analysis (Eliav Lieblich), genealogical studies (Matthias Goldmann), and political economy (Michael Fakhri). In all their rich analytical diversity, these studies reaffirm the prominent place and role that human rights have attained in each of these global governance regimes. At the same time, these studies illuminate the power, transfigurations, untapped potentials, and constraints that human rights evidence in these diverse global governance contexts.

### A. Historiographical Permutations: Human Rights in the Global Governance of Sovereign Debt

The chapter by Matthias Goldmann traces the role of human rights in the global governance of sovereign debt. As Goldmann documents, references to human rights of an economic and social nature have lately become prominent in different fora within this regime. These references have been mostly used to normatively contest the type of austerity measures imposed by global financial authorities on indebted states and their populations as part of their sovereign debt restructuring processes. Austerity measures render themselves particularly susceptible to critique from the perspective of economic and social rights protection because these measures often entail stringent modes of fiscal discipline that affect established

[24] In this vein, see also Sarfaty and Deberdt, 'Supply Chain Governance at a Distance', *Law & Social Inquiry* (2023) 1.

socio-economic entitlements to ensure future debt repayment, including ample cuts in social expenditures and an impulse towards marketization of public services. The chapter thus notes how the Polanyian frictions between 'the economic' (dis-embeddedness) and 'the social' (re-embeddedness) that pervade much of contemporary law and policymaking also underpin the referred tensions between austerity and human rights in the global governance of sovereign debt.

Goldmann draws upon genealogical methods to situate these tensions in historiographical perspective. The restructuring processes of sovereign debt have a long history, which in many ways outdates the emergence and uses of human rights. The chapter thus essentially aims to trace 'when and how' human rights have attained such a prominent place within the sovereign debt regime. Through this analysis, the chapter also traces some shifting meanings of human rights informing institutional action within this regime. On these bases, Goldmann challenges certain established dogmas regarding the place and role of human rights in contemporary political economies and suggests more nuanced insights into their permutations within the global sovereign debt regime.

This historiographical examination is deployed through two axes of analysis. The first axis is outward-looking. It contrasts human rights with other concepts that have been also used by stakeholders to normatively contest austerity measures (axis 1). As Goldmann explains, these concepts are varied. They include economic terminologies (e.g. the 'new international economic order', the notion of 'human needs', or of 'social welfare'), political terminologies (e.g. 'sovereignty or self-determination'), or religious/moral grounds ('odious debt'). Through this axis of analysis, the chapter thus seeks to distil the place and role of human rights vis-à-vis other lexes of socio-political struggle against austerity measures in the sovereign debt regime.

The second axis is inward-looking. It explores the different conceptions of economic and social rights within the sovereign debt regime (axis 2). The chapter builds in these respects upon the distinction between 'sufficientarian' and 'egalitarian' conceptions of economic and social rights that has been influentially advanced by Samuel Moyn. This distinction is used by Goldmann to delineate which conception informs predominant uses of human rights in the global governance of sovereign debt.

On these analytical bases, the chapter advances a periodization regarding the role of human rights within the sovereign debt regime sustained upon four distinctive paradigms. After their relative muteness in contesting austerity measures during the 1950s–1960s, which Goldmann explains as part of the functionalism pervading that period, human rights entered the debate by the end of the 1970s under a 'collective, structuralist paradigm'. Driven by the rising debt crisis and a shift towards starker austerity measures, under this paradigm human rights tend to coalesce in complex and often implicit ways with parallel economic and political lexes of a 'new international economic order' and 'self-determination'. These lexes played alongside a mainstream developmental discourse that was largely centred upon safeguarding 'human needs' (axis 1). According to Goldmann, this blending of human rights discourses with modernizing regulatory processes and proliferating socio-political struggles for decolonization rendered appeals to human rights within the sovereign debt regime during the 1970s as distinctively aligned with an egalitarian conception committed with several types of redistributive policies (axis 2).

During the 1980s paradigm, these notions of human rights became largely neutralized and replaced by a predominant socio-economic discourse centred upon enhancing 'human capital' (rather than 'human needs', or political 'self-determination'). This was operationalized through a distinctive set of marketization policies aligned with the developmental templates of an emergent 'Washington Consensus' (axis 1). The appeal of human rights was thereby defused during the 1980s by ideals of efficiency, economic growth, and social welfare largely represented through econometric terms. As Goldmann suggests, these ideals reduced human rights to some 'sufficientarian' conception—if anything (axis 2).

This 'sufficientarian' conception of human rights within the sovereign debt regime became finally entrenched during the 1990–2000s paradigm. This paradigm was characterized by the revitalization of human rights discourses among civil society institutions to contest an expanding pace of austerity measures imposed on peripheral countries driven by programmes of 'structural adjustments' (axis 1). At the same time, this revitalization operated alongside a concurrent sidelining of these human rights discourses. Instead of tackling the root causes of the social hardships generated by those proliferating 'structural adjustment' programmes, during this period human rights discourses became largely functional to these policy programmes. This is because the appeal of human rights was generally recast as a way to add a human/social dimension to these policy programmes focalized on ensuring certain minimums that contributed to alleviate poverty rather than relying on redistributive, egalitarian agendas (axis 2). The legalistic strategy of using human rights to contest austerity measures through litigation, even when marginally successful, only reaffirmed their structural sidelining.

One of the most provocative contributions of the chapter is the articulation of a new paradigm that has been taking shape since the financial crisis (2010–to date). Goldmann aptly characterizes it as a 'political paradigm'. This is because human rights concerns are no longer channelled mainly through judicial fora but consistently come to infuse and sustain a renewed political process within the sovereign debt regime (axis 1). As Goldmann explains, this qualifies as a new paradigm because these global policymakers within this regime are making recurrent references to human as a basis to overcome 'structural adjustment' parameters, prompting a new model that is centred upon objectives of environmental sustainability and social justice (axis 2). The conceptualization of this new paradigm is not merely descriptive. It also entails a normative intervention that seeks to guide current and future political processes and social action within the sovereign debt regime. In a recollective move that intriguingly transcends the historiographical arc used so far, Goldmann concludes the analysis by linking this new paradigm with the visions of social rights and social constitutionalism that once informed progressive political and regulatory programmes during the Weimar Republic a century ago.

This is not the only contribution of the chapter. Goldmann's study of human rights within the sovereign debt regime offers at least three additional contributions. One additional contribution concerns our understanding of the role of human rights within the global governance of sovereign debt. By underscoring how shifting paradigms of human rights informed regulatory processes, the chapter adds some relevant nuance to the generalized impression that human rights arrived 'too late' and have done 'too little' to address social hardships imposed by the sovereign debt regime.[25] At the same time, the chapter also seeks to challenge visions of human rights as inherently aligned with the dogmas of neoliberalism.[26] Through this historiographical analysis, Goldmann thus seeks to revitalize a belief in the emancipatory power of human rights by showing their capacity to become the political ground for institutionalizing progressive policy programmes aligned with established traditions of social justice in legal and political thought.

The second additional contribution is to human rights theory and history more generally. The chapter, in these respects, problematizes some received frameworks in human rights discourses. One framework is the tendency to align human rights with 'the social' against 'the economic'. The second framework is to place growing concerns about economic and social rights as the somehow inevitable result of a certain historical progression between different generations of rights. Conversely, the historiographical analysis advanced in the chapter shows that there have been different ways of representing the social beyond the vocabularies of human rights (axis 1) and how 'fluctuating paradigms of human rights law' in the sovereign debt regime impair any linearities in their developments (axis 2). As with other chapters in this volume, the chapter by Goldmann could thus be read as an invitation to engage in more granular analyses of the role of human rights in global governance processes through a careful examination of the relevant primary sources informing these processes and archival material related to their respective historical contexts.

The third additional contribution concerns the permutations of human rights in the global governance of sovereign debt. The chapter departs from a vision of human rights in global governance that reduces their nature and significance to judicial mechanisms of protection. The chapter in fact evidence how judicialization

[25] The reference is made to the influential account signalling that impression by M. Guzman, J. A. Ocampo, and J. E Stiglitz (eds), *Too Little, Too Late: The Quest to Resolve Sovereign Debt Crises* (2016).

[26] The references are to the works of N. Klein, *The Shock Doctrine: The Rise of Disaster Capitalism* (2007) and J. Whyte, *The Morals of The Market: Human Rights and the Rise of Neoliberalism* (2019), among others.

strategies may be at times futile or even functional to the depoliticization of human rights. The *relevance* of human rights in global governance (in Santi Romano's sense) is better grasped when expanding the analytical and historical purview beyond courtrooms, tracing their influence as catalysts of institutional action and contestation throughout socio-political processes in global governance. Goldmann's study of the global governance of sovereign debt shows how economic and social human rights have played these catalyst roles, prompting policy agendas and counter-agendas that have marked the shifting paradigms of the global governance of sovereign debt and that are likely to keep on shifting alongside the spirals of history.

## B. Institutionalist Permutations: Human Rights in the Global Governance of Commerce

The chapter by Anna Beckers takes us into the salient role that human rights have attained within transnational commercial relations through the ubiquitous structures of global value chains, which are usually recast under the rubrics of corporate social responsibility (CSR) or 'business and human rights'. This salient role is nowadays marked by a multilevel set of statutory or soft law initiatives that have integrated human rights within the governance processes of multinational corporations and their global supply chains. These include initiatives at the national level (e.g. the French *Loi di Vigilance* or the UK Modern Slavery Act 2015), regional level (e.g. the EU's Timber or Conflict Minerals Regulation), international level (as the proposed Treaty on Business and Human Rights), and transnational level (e.g. the OECD Guidelines for Multinational Enterprises). As the chapter highlights, John Ruggie's 2008 'Protect, Respect, and Remedy' framework has played an influential role in fostering this scenario; a framework that later crystallized in the 2012 UN Guiding Principles of Business and Human Rights (UNGP) that has taken a leading role in the global governance of CSR.

The chapter opens by relating this contemporary salience of human rights in global corporate processes to previous editions of the Academy of European Law summer courses led by Philip Alston and Andrew Clapham that had already taken up this theme. After contrasting their differing predictions on the topic—Alston denying and Clapham upholding the possibility that corporations may be subject to international legal obligations concerning human rights— paradoxically, Beckers notes how these contemporary developments reaffirm and, at the same time, defy Alston's and Clapham's differing visions.[27] The chapter by Beckers is

[27] As Beckers explains:

> Clapham's vision of a stronger responsibility for companies under international human rights law appears to have become reality, yet in a different form than he envisaged. Instead of a

thus driven by three puzzles or guiding questions: (i) how to make sense of the novel role that transnational corporations have attained in human rights protection throughout their supply chains; (ii) what this novel role entails for our understanding of human rights and human rights law in the global governance of commerce; and (iii) whether these developments ought to be normatively welcomed or rather resisted.

The chapter assigns a prominent role to the figure of John Ruggie and his work on new governance theory as an answer to the first question. It charts how Ruggie's account of polycentric governance in the Polanyian tradition of 'embedded liberalism' infused the novel model advanced by the UNGP, albeit in ways that exacerbate the authority of transnational corporations to implement international human rights law vis-à-vis their home states. This is expressed in the UNGP's second pillar that largely aligns human rights with established processes of business management by recasting corporate responsibilities for human rights as procedural obligations to be operationalized through vocabularies that are already standard within corporate practices, such as the 'social license to operate' or 'due diligence'. This is also expressed in the UNGP's first pillar that largely relegate home states to a background role of enabling these corporate governance processes for human rights protection. This is done through fostering contestation from relevant stakeholders (e.g. consumers, shareholders, workers) that can prompt businesses own 'social acculturation', while restraining the state's regulatory and enforcement powers in substance and territorial scope. Beckers explains this inclination taken by the UNGP in Ruggie's own 'principled pragmatism' that prompted him to 'build on consensus among the many actors involved' in a way 'to achieve "the maximum reduction in corporate-related human rights harm in the shortest possible period of time" and to adopt "whatever measures work best, in creating change where it matters the most"'.

Beckers' answer to the second question provides some distinctive and moving insights into the transfiguration that human rights have experienced throughout this uploading into transnational corporate governance processes and global value chains. Drawing upon a wide-ranging set of empirical studies on the phenomenon, the chapter by Beckers shows how this uploading has entailed some significant transformations in our established understandings of human rights in international law. This transformation comprises three dimensions: (i) *what* rights are protected; (ii) *how* are they protected; and (iii) *why* are they protected. Due to the significance of these insights to our study on human rights in global governance, we briefly elaborate on each of these dimensions.

gradual evolution of international corporate personality or international human rights obligations through state practice and soft law, corporations are now included in international human rights documents as governance actors. In this sense, as predicted by Alston, the idea of including non-state actors in international law with a formal role and responsibility has not succeeded, but there is a formal, ambiguous, role that focuses on codified responsibilities of corporations to make use of private governance structures.

Drawing upon empirical evidence, regarding the first dimension, Beckers shows that this corporatization of human rights is circumscribing the scope of human rights solely to those that are relevant to businesses' 'stakeholders' (e.g. health and safety in the workplace, labour rights, equality as non-discrimination). Regarding the second dimension, Beckers shows how human rights protection has been incrementally transformed into an 'obligation of means' in corporate governance, rather than an 'obligation of result' as in international human rights law, in ways that have significantly impacted our established understandings of access to a remedy for human rights violations. Finally, regarding the third dimension, Beckers shows how, from a civic–humanitarian justification as universal moral/legal obligations, when translated into corporate governance structures, human rights protection has become grounded upon socio-economic justifications, usually associated with the tradition of philanthropy or established templates for risk management in corporate operations. In this sense, the chapter by Beckers provides one of the most eloquent illustrations of the type of permutations of human rights in global governance by showing how the business rationality that pervades corporate governance processes is contributing to human rights de-formalization.

This is the basis upon which Beckers tackles the third guiding question towards the conclusion of her chapter. Beckers addresses this question in a careful and nuanced way (only as a 'tentative conclusion'). She outlines two leading positions within contemporary legal thought in this regard. The first position is represented by the towering figures of Gunther Teubner and Hans Lindahl who understand these developments as the inevitable/desirable result of the accelerated legal pluralization processes that we are currently witnessing and posit these transformations as the germ of a growing, agonistic re-politicization of global corporate processes. The second position is represented by the towering figures of Phillip Alston and Hugh Collins who largely resist this 'merger & acquisition' of international human rights law by corporate governance and seek to preserve the distinctive rationality and normative commitments that have respectively characterized the fields of human rights law and private law.

Beckers distances herself from these positions and align her outlooks with the prospects of human rights in corporate governance and global value chains with those authors who have articulated the middle ground between them. This middle ground entails expanding the purview beyond human rights law and socio-political processes surrounding corporate governance by exploring the ways that other legal fields, such as private international law, consumer law, company law, or tort law, may contribute to 'provide related rules that bind companies to human rights protection'. This entails re-ascribing a pivotal role to private law (*qua* state law) in its capacity to shape socio-economic relations to meet these growing societal expectations for safeguarding human rights throughout global value chains.[28]

[28] As Beckers states: 'If this option is relied upon, the future of transforming human rights in corporate governance structures may still be found in the state and its judicial system.'

Yet Beckers is cautious in warning that this process of legal evolution should not be regarded as necessarily feasible or desirable.[29] We take this warning as a call for attentive scrutiny of these legal evolutions as they keep moving along. The chapter by Beckers thus shows how the business rationality that characterizes compliance processes within corporate governance have rendered a reductionist, deformalized account of human rights, while underscoring the potential that private law could have in institutionalizing a scheme to ensure their due safeguard and prompt novel modalities for their re-formalization throughout global value chains.

## C. Post-Institutionalist Permutations: Human Rights in the Global Governance of Development Assistance by the World Bank Complex

The studies by Goldmann and Beckers show how the contents, mechanisms of protection, and the very meaning of human rights are inevitably shaped by the distinctive rationalities or structures informing the respective global governance organizations/regimes. In the chapter by Beckers, this is the result of the strategic rationality and managerialist structure that characterizes commercial relations and corporate governance processes alongside global value chains. The chapter by Goldmann enlarges this vision towards the broader zeitgeist that global governance regimes are respectively embedded in a certain historiographical period. Whether these structures are endogenous or exogenous to the respective global governance regime, or more or less historically contingent, the contributions from Goldmann and Beckers could thereby be characterized as broadly aligned with an 'institutionalist' approach to human rights in global governance.

In its analysis of how human rights impinge on the development policies pursued by the World Bank, the chapter by Guy Fiti Sinclair transcends this institutionalist approach to human rights in global governance. Sinclair focuses the analysis on the pivotal role that the World Bank Inspection Panel (WBIP) has had in this regard. The WBIP was created within the World Bank in 1993 in response to growing apprehensions and controversies concerning the human rights

[29] As Beckers concludes:

> However, the question remains of whether a project of turning these private law rules for the regulation of private relations upside-down from a facilitative towards a regulatory attitude to corporate governance structures and including human rights is possible at all. ... It further remains to be seen how far existing legal fields, such as human rights law and private law, may depart from their own distinct heritage and enter into new legal fields. Can international human rights standards become part of private law without compromising its very heritage? The fact that there is a list of past legal fields in which such two-way traffic has proved to be successful—ranging from the protection of consumers between contract law and competition and economic law to the evolution of environmental law between tort law and administrative law—provides ground for hope, but is no panacea.

impacts of some of the development projects that were sponsored by the World Bank. Although the WBIP became pioneering among international organizations as an instance through which stakeholders could raise complaints against an organization, it is important to stress that the competence of the WBIP does not extend to directly enforcing international human rights norms. The WBIP only provides an internal review mechanism, whose competence is limited to monitoring whether the Bank has complied with its own internal policies and procedures during the design, evaluation, or implementation of a relevant project. Nevertheless, as Sinclair documents, throughout its nearly 30 years of activities the WBIP has been largely understood as institutionalizing an accountability mechanism for the safeguarding of human rights within the World Bank operations.

This pivotal role of the WBIP in institutionalizing human rights within the World Bank has generated contrasting evaluations. Most commentators and activists tend to see the WBIP as an instance that either has or could enhance human rights protection within the World Bank despite some acknowledged limitations. This is typically due to salient cases where the monitoring and recommendations issued by the WBIP (usually in the application of the prominent 'environmental and social safeguard policies' of the World Bank) have prompted more awareness of human rights considerations or some relevant adaptations, and even the withdrawal, of development projects that were generating significant human rights impacts.

Yet there are critical accounts as well. Among other authors, the chapter highlights the work of Galit Sarfaty who notes how the deontological rationality of human rights (as universal, absolute, inalienable entitlements) has largely become subservient to the economic/managerial rationality of a consequentialist nature that prevails within the World Bank (based on calculative models driven by perfect markets, rational actors, and resource constraints). In this latter view, which is aligned with the 'institutionalist' approaches to human rights in global governance advanced in the chapter by Beckers, human rights tend to become captured and thereby instrumentalized by this economic/managerial rationality informing the World Bank's operations.

Sinclair eloquently diagnoses how underlying both of these leading positions is a distinctive 'accountability frame'. This frame entails conceiving the WBIP and World Bank as two distinct, solid entities that are continuously engaged in asymmetrical and oppositional dynamics of control exercised by an account holder (the WBIP) towards a power-wielder (the World Bank management). The frame also assumes human rights represent relatively fixed and stable parameters of control for these accountability purposes and thereby attributes human rights with a certain normative solidity. More importantly, as Sinclair notes, implicit in this framework are the 'deeply state-centred and hierarchical normative assumptions of the human rights project' that, in a more or less conscious way, lead international lawyers to assimilate international organizations with administrative agencies in a national setting and thereby 'to measure the "success" or "failure" of the WBIP against an imagined archetype of judicial review'.

While acknowledging the accountability functions that the WBIP certainly plays within the World Bank, the chapter by Sinclair seeks to overcome this entrenched 'accountability frame' and the methodological nationalism underpinning it as a pathway to examining the place and role of human rights within international organizations and global governance. This breakthrough is pursued through a key analytical shift: the move 'from institutions to assemblages' in the way we conceive international organizations, by drawing upon the apparatus of the actor–network theory or—as the author prefers to term it—'assemblage theory' usually associated with the work of Bruno Latour. According to this theory, instead of unified, solid (albeit transformable) institutions, organizations can be disaggregated into complex, circumstantial assemblages of shifting interactions among an array of heterogenous 'actants' (whether human or non-human, material or non-material) that constantly interact to uphold, modify, or revert these fragile modes of socio-political ordering. As Sinclair explains, this interaction happens through recursive practices of 'problematization', '*interessment*', 'enrolment', and 'representation' of relevant aims or values that are articulated by these different actants through diverse modes of 'translation' and 'inscription devises'. The chapter then uses this apparatus to analyse the way that human rights are 'translated' into the activities of the World Bank by the WBIP through the World Bank-financed China: Western Poverty Reduction Project (CWPRP) as a specific case study.

The analysis elicits several innovative accounts of human rights in global governance. On the one hand, the CWPRP case study read through the lens of assemblage theory challenges the deontological notion of human rights as abstract, resolvable, and inalienable entitlements that usually accompany established visions of legality in international organizations and the 'accountability frame' underpinning them. Echoing the chapter by Goldmann, this analysis shows that human rights are just one register among other technical, moral, political, and legalistic registers that channel the interactions between the WBIP and the World Bank on certain development projects and the practices of constant assembling and reassembling surrounding them. Instead of a relatively standardized parameter of accountability, this insight reveals how human rights rather operate as mechanisms of persuasive authority that contribute to shape, but also become themselves shaped through, these different registers in ways that are reciprocally productive. As Sinclair explains: 'the translation of claims from expert, moral, or legal registers into and through the register of human rights itself performs and constructs human rights—as well as those other registers—as distinct and different. Furthermore, the transformation of a human rights claim by its revoicing in another register will always retain a remnant of the original, and vice versa.'

On the other hand, the CWPRP case study also challenges the institutionalist position advanced by Sarfaty and other authors in this volume who see human rights as usually subservient to some distinctive rationality informing the operation of a certain global governance regime. Conversely, Sinclair argues, assemblage theory reveals how human rights have much more fluid, flexible, and multivalent roles in the lives of international organizations. Drawing upon the CWPRP case, as Sinclair explains, within the World Bank: 'on the one hand, human rights often appear as a source of ethical principle and morality; on the other hand, they link to expert processes as an expression of due process and a guide to administrative procedure. ... [T]he success of efforts by advocates and others to incorporate human rights claims into WBIP requests depends crucially on their ability to move fluidly along this continuum between different registers.'

In this sense, the chapter reads as an appeal to overcome our prejudices and any received understanding of the place and roles of human rights in global governance. As Sinclair concludes, the CWPRP case analysed through assemblage theory reveals that 'the WBIP is neither simply an accountability mechanism nor an instrument or mask for the World Bank's managerial ends'. The chapter by Sinclair can thus be understood as advancing a post-institutionalist approach to human rights in global governance that is in line with the latest turn to practices in international law.[30] This is because the chapter reads as an invitation to bracket any transcendental characterization of global governance institutions and immerse ourselves in the routinary practices of these organizations through the purview of assemblage theory to develop a wider, finer, and ultimately richer understanding of the 'multiplicity of ways that the language and normativity of human rights can be channelled, absorbed, and translated into the life of global governance'.

## D. Materialist Permutations: Human Rights in the Global Governance of Food

With all its distinctive and refreshing insights into the role of law in a diverse set of socio-political processes and the socio-technical bases of lawmaking, the turn to practices in international law has not been exempt from critical appraisals. Its revitalization of a law-in-action agenda driven by the impetus of mapping shifting relations among several 'people with projects' or other relevant 'actants', risks representing social practices as 'flat ontologies' of merely contingent relations that tend to overlook the asymmetries of power and distributive settings that condition or are prompted by those relations. The chapter by Michael Fakhri, while in general sharing the referred post-institutionalist approach to the study of human rights in global governance, also signals a way to overcome those limitations through the integration of political economy into the analytical matrix. The chapter illustrates

[30] See e.g. N. M. Rajkovic, T. E. Aalberts, and T. Gammeltoft-Hansen (eds), *The Power of Legality: Practices of International Law and their Politics* (2016).

this through an examination of the place and role of the human right to food within the global geographies of food production, exchange, and their regulation.

As with the previous studies in this volume, Fakhri's analysis of the human right to food transcends its merely formalistic representations. It does not primarily centre on questions of legal hermeneutics or its justiciability at the national/international levels. The analysis rather takes a socio-legal perspective by focusing on the uses of the right to food to advance certain political agendas within the global political economy of food. As Fakhri explains from the very outset of the study, in this sense 'the right to food is better understood as part of the global politics of food and the socio-economy of growing, gathering, hunting, and herding'. These practices involve salient social, economic, and political dimensions that are governed by a multipolar global governance landscape comprising several stakeholders that nowadays coalesce institutionally around the Food & Agriculture Organization (FAO), the World Trade Organization (WTO), and the UN Committee for World Security (CFS).

As in the previous chapter by Sinclair, Fakhri thoroughly documents how this landscape is driven by a range of shifting assemblages among several players and the significant role that invocations of the human right to food have played in these respects. Yet political economy informs the analysis through the scrutiny of 'the distribution of power and wealth generated by the institutions, practices, legal rules, and social organizations surrounding (or laying claim to) the right to food'. As the human right to food is not seen as subservient to certain structures, this largely aligns Fakhri's chapter with the post-institutional approach to human rights in global governance advanced by Sinclair, albeit with the referred political economy twist.

Through the reconstruction of the social origins and effects of the human right to food amid this multipolar global governance landscape, the chapter provides a roadmap through the shifting geographies of power within the food regime. Several transnational social movements take a protagonist role in the analysis, most notably La Vía Campesina that has nowadays grouped with other social movements in the International Planning Committee for Food Sovereignty (IPC). The main aim of the chapter is to highlight how the human right to food may be tactically deployed to alter those loci of power towards emancipatory aims.[31] In this sense, theoretically the chapter aligns with the strategic uses of law that have been informing current approaches to critical legal studies.[32]

[31] As Fakhri explains: 'I then imagine this study as tracking and learning from the tactical manoeuvrings of this cunning citizen who wants to start with understanding what mechanisms of power and wealth are already at play because that will determine what they understand their interest to be, conditions what goals they want to achieve, and determines what tactics are available.'

[32] In its more general articulation, see Christodoulidis, 'Strategies of Rupture', 20/1 *Law and Critique* (2009) 3; and, more recently, E. Christodoulidis, *The Redress of Law: Globalisation, Constitutionalism and Market Capture* (2021) pt IV.

Through this analysis, the chapter elicits at least three distinctive contributions. The first is a revisionist account of the role that the human right to food has had in these global landscapes of food production and their regulation. As Fakhri explains, when analysed from a socio-legal perspective, the developments of the human right to food do not really fit recent historiographies of international human rights (Samuel Moyn) or the specific historiographies of economic and social rights (Aoife Nolan and Joe Wills, among others). It also challenges entrenched narratives that give the General Agreement on Tariffs and Trade (GATT)/WTO a focal place and role in the contemporary global regulation of food production and exchange alongside the 1994 Agreement on Agriculture. Conversely, throughout the historiographical analysis, the chapter shows that trade has had other meanings than free trade and that the regulation of food production and exchange has been (and still is) the mark of a much wider range of global governance institutions. Fakhri particularly highlights the key role that the FAO has had as a trade and development institution for the regulation of food production and exchange (and nowadays has even in a heightened way), to the extent that 'one cannot understand the right to food today without understanding the history of the FAO'.

This revisionist historiography that the chapter advances of the global governance of food renders a richer account of the shifting legal meanings and modes of political (dis-)empowerment that the human right to food produces in this global governance setting. As Fakhri explains, throughout this historiography these shifting roles of the human right to food within its global governance regime have mainly coalesced around two leading and interrelated conceptions: 'food security' and 'food sovereignty'. Although embroiled in the configuration of the FAO during the 1940s–1950s, during the 1960s the human right to food was pioneeringly instigated within the FAO under the leadership of B. R. Sen (an eminent Indian diplomat) as part of his 'freedom from hunger' campaign. This contributed to reconfiguring the place and role of the FAO from a mere statistical provider to a trade and development organization with an active policy agenda to address this global political concern, which also infused the definition of the human right to food in the International Covenant on Economic, Social and Cultural Rights (ICESCR). But this reconfiguration failed to gain significant traction in an agricultural trade and development scenario which by that time was governed through International Commodity Agreements (ICAs) under the purviews of the International Trade Organization (ITO) and the UN Conference on Trade and Development (UNCTAD), which were largely devoid of human rights vocabularies.

The human right to food entered mainstream registers of policymaking in international agriculture during the 1970s through the emergent notion of 'food security'. Striking problems of hunger and famine throughout the Third World and the 1972–1975 'world food crisis', prompted the elaboration of new policy programmes to meet food demand beyond food surplus management. This is the context where the human right to food became mainstream and was used to sustain a policy agenda to ensure 'food security'. This is relevant because 'by including human rights within the concept of food security, this ensured that food would always be understood as a matter of hunger and not strictly as a commodity (as was done in ICAs)'. Yet, the institutional landscape shows how diverging approaches of how to ensure 'food security' took shape surrounding fragile assemblages of different institutions that respectively emerged from the World Food Conference (the World Food Council and the International Fund for Agricultural Development), the GATT (in its Tokyo Round), and UNCTAD (the New International Economic Order—NIEO).

The commodity and oil crises and the overall recession that these events triggered between 1979 and 1986 marked a turning point. Alongside the emerging 'Washington Consensus', the NIEO and the Third World project collapsed, and the GATT became the focal place for trade and development policymaking through the doctrine of free trade. As Fakhri explains, from the perspective of the human right to food, 'This could be interpreted as an attempt to delink food security from its human rights origins by treating food more as a commodity. It was, however, more likely part of the emerging trend in human rights discourse writ large towards a "trade-related, market-friendly" framework.'

The chapter adds two relevant components to this transformative period. One is how the FAO aptly navigated these changing political winds and managed to remain as a site for the cultivation (however attenuated) of alternative conceptions of trade and development related to food, mainly through the establishment of enduring links with Third World countries (now the Global South). The second element is how a transnational social movement began to take shape during the 1990s to counteract the grounds and effects of these free trade policies, which were prompting an overall industrialization of agriculture and food production processes and thereby undermining the rural lifestyle of small-scale farmers and producers. Led by La Vía Campesina, the motto of this transnational social movement became to reclaim their 'food sovereignty'. This concept signified a decisive strategy of political rupture. As Fakhri explains, the movement 'sharpened the difference by highlighting how food security frames hunger as a problem of distribution (with a focus on access and commerce). Food sovereignty instead asks the question: who controls the systems of production and consumption? The tactic was to wrestle the right to food away from food security towards food sovereignty, thereby delegitimizing food security and its beneficiaries (agribusiness).'

From their grassroots origins, the chapter then documents how the movement significantly expanded during the 2000s, establishing important links to several key players in the global governance of food. These players include especially the FAO, which the movement contributed to reposition as a focal international agriculture organization. The human right to food played a pivotal role in establishing these assemblages. As Fakhri stresses, 'the FAO, La Vía Campesina, and right-to-food NGOs used the right to food to work together and align their interests ..., while at the same time deploying it against the WTO to try and get the WTO out of agriculture entirely'. The chapter documents how the securitization of food has returned to the global agenda alongside the food and financial crisis that hit the globe over 15 years ago. While several global governance assemblages sought to seize the juncture to advance their own food policy agendas (including the G8 and the UN High-Level Task Force on the Global Food Security Crisis), Fakhri posits how this pivotal role of the right to food prompted a revitalization of the UN's CFS by the G77 under the auspices of the FAO that was better prepared to step up to the challenge and position itself nowadays as a powerful cluster for new agricultural policies. In this sense, Fakhri's chapter echoes the previous chapters by Sinclair and Goldmann in noting how the human right to food has operated as a salient mechanism of persuasive authority for the marshalling of powerful agendas centred around conflicting accounts of 'food security' and 'food sovereignty'.

This leads us to the final contribution of the chapter concerning the role of law. Fakhri concludes his chapter diagnosing that an incipient new order in the global governance of food is taking shape, centred around the CFS/FAO and driven by new political imaginaries of socio-economic practices of food production and distribution signified by the concept of 'agroecology'. Yet Fakhri also diagnoses some challenges ahead. One challenge is how to consolidate these progresses within a multipolar governance landscape.[33] The second challenge comes from an entrenched scepticism about whether the use of the language and encoding techniques of international law may be useful or lead to some regression. As Fakhri explains, this is why La Vía Campesina and other social movements that have been advancing this agroecological transformation have maintained a cautious and ambivalent relationship to the language of human rights.[34] The chapter intervenes in this setting underscoring the key role of law in formalizing this socio-political transformation: 'you cannot avoid fighting over legal forms in these political struggles, [because] law is too powerful a terrain to ignore or cede. Law, for better or for worse, remains a common form of national and international institutional power

[33] 'As the CFS gains credibility through increased participation by private sector actors and philanthropic foundations, the food sovereignty movements have to ensure they maintain what gains they have made while at the same time reconfiguring themselves to ensure that they can still enact parts of their agenda through the CFS—all while the CFS's authority continues to be challenged by other fora and institutions like the G8/G20' because (and this is an aspect where the post-institutionalist approach followed by Fakhri comes in) 'these sorts of spaces and the right to food are always the product of undulating matrices of power, authority, and legitimacy. That means that institutional and normative gains and losses are always temporary.'

[34]

> The price you pay for using international law—or any law—is losing a bit of yourself to its authority. ... This is always the worry about using human rights as well as international law. While human rights provide a powerful platform to articulate one's claim in universal terms, it often curtails agendas aimed at radical reconfigurations of power. This has always been clear to La Vía Campesina, which has 'dealt with both the conceptual and strategic limitations of the human rights framework, in an attempt to keep intact the subversive potential of its rights-based claims'.

to legitimate and implement ideas.' While originally departing from formalistic approaches to law and the human right to food, Fakhri thus ends by stressing how an enduring material and symbolic role of human rights within the global governance of food largely depends on their legal re-formalization.

Fakhri contends that this legal re-formalization does not mainly or necessarily depend on some renewed, lofty notion of a human right to food. It is rather achieved through 'site-specific, contextual, and diverse' reconfiguration of the legal infrastructures that sustain the social and economic practices of food production and distribution—such as received notions of 'property' or 'family'—and thereby can shape them towards their required 'agroecological' transformation. As Fakhri argues:

> the meaning and internal cohesion of the right to food is not the principal issue. ... The hard work is in ensuring that legal tactics always serve the long-term strategy of creating more equitable socio-economic relations amongst beings within the biosphere. ... This would lead to reimagining the right to food's legal form to include the multitude of ways that people socially and politically organize themselves around food along with their concomitant notions of authority and legitimacy—all grounded in the everyday practices around procuring and making food.

In this sense, the key insight that stems from this thorough study of the trajectories of the human right to food is that there is no socio-political transformation without its legal institutionalization beyond the narrow realm of human rights *law*.

## E. Doctrinal Permutations: Human Rights in the Global Governance of the Use of Force

The importance that Fakhri places on legal forms for the institutionalization of emergent socio-political orders is echoed in the chapter by Eliav Lieblich concerning the legitimate use of force against non-state actors across state borders. As Lieblich explains, since 11 September 2001, there has been a new order taking shape in international warfare in this respect. While traditionally the use of force was only under certain conditions legitimate among states, this new order is marked by the traumatic experience and exponential awareness of the devastating consequences that attacks from foreign non-state groups may generate. This has concurrently triggered growing resort to the use of force from affected states against these non-state groups located in foreign territories to safeguard the security of their own populations. Lieblich signifies this new order as a transition from an international to a *transnational* paradigm of the legitimate use of force that is nowadays taking shape.

From the perspective of international relations, the chapter also highlights how these instances of the transnational use of force are also fringe moments where global governance is at 'vanishing point' because 'collective security mechanisms break down, and bilateral relations are insufficient to resolve the issue'. Lieblich conceives these proliferating instances of the transnational use of force as 'a radical, residual form of governance, in which public authority is both challenged and exercised violently across state borders'. From an international law perspective, the legality of such transnational uses of force has been the object of an intense forensic and scholarly debate, where the only consensus is probably that 'the law is nowadays in flux'. The aim of the chapter is to intervene in this legal debate by addressing the question of when and why the use of force against non-state actors that are positioned in another state may be legally justified on grounds of self-defence.

The chapter deploys a doctrinal method to answer this question. It starts with a review of the relevant legal norms/doctrines and the overall literature on the topic. On this basis, it analytically distinguishes two main positions on the question. The first position is the one that requires the host state's *fault* as a condition for valid transnational self-defence, whether due to its actions or omissions. The second position is one that foregoes that requirement, justifying recourse to the transnational use of force on grounds of self-defence to safeguard the victim's autonomy and integrity. As the chapter explains, some have raised concerns that this latter position would be problematic. This is because it would authorize the use of force within the territory of states that are largely 'innocent', as the belligerent activities of these non-state groups cannot be attributed to their actions or omissions, and thereby affect an essential component of their 'sovereign rights' or 'sovereignty'. This 'myth of the innocent state'—as the chapter is titled—is the legal argument that Lieblich specifically seeks to debunk, by arguing that 'the mere lack of state fault carries limited normative weight in ascertaining whether there is a just cause for self-defence'.[35]

The chapter aptly applies a doctrinal playbook for these purposes.[36] It proceeds through two moves. First, it challenges the vision of the sovereign state that is implicit in this argument. As Lieblich explains, underlying this innocent state argument is an anthropomorphic representation of the state and its sovereign rights. Unless the host state incurs a certain *fault*, its territory is regarded as inviolable because the state is 'equated to an autonomous individual, and its territory to

[35] As Lieblich explains: 'This is important, since of all the existing objections to transnational self-defence, the argument on fault is the one that if accepted, poses an insurmountable barrier to transnational self-defence against attacks where attribution—or at least a lesser form of responsibility—is lacking.'

[36] For a recent overview of this playbook, see P. Schlag and A. J. Griffin, *How to Do Things with Legal Doctrine* (2020).

something akin to a physical body'. Drawing upon just war theory, Lieblich claims that this representation is unjustified.[37] In the case of transnational attacks from non-state groups, the territory of the innocent host state, Lieblich argues, should be conceived as a mere 'thing' or 'object' that is being used by these armed groups to launch their attacks and thereby better analogized to the legal status of physical 'property'. This renewed account of the rights or interests at stake is, in turn, the basis for Lieblich's second doctrinal move that places these rights or interests in an ascertained order of values. Lieblich argues: 'as rights to "things" seems generally secondary to the right to life, in such scenarios the former should be overridden, regardless of fault or its absence'.

The key to any appealing doctrinal argument, with all their (re-)descriptive–prescriptive implications, is that it needs to be analytically sound and, at the same time, entail good policy. Lieblich does not shy away from this latter aspect to sustain his position. While the chapter acknowledges that such doctrine entails expanding the hypothesis of the legitimate use of force that can be manipulated by powerful states or give more leeway for the international order of peace and security to be jeopardized, it argues that 'the theoretical approach offered here might also support limitations on the right to self-defence in opposite cases: for instance, when the non-state actor's attack does not implicate individual rights, but only state rights, and on the other hand, a forcible response will harm innocent individuals in the territorial state'.

The chapter concludes by asserting how this account of a transnational right to self-defence can be legally crystallized in a reformed test in the international laws of war to determine when an attack from non-state actors can be considered an 'armed attack'. As Lieblich explains, this test should centre on the type and magnitude of the harm to the population rather than its scale or scope.[38] In turn, he affirms that even if the attack from this non-state group crosses the threshold, established modes of proportionality analysis in the international laws of war would

[37] Lieblich advances an essentialist argument to sustain his position that is worth quoting in full:

> On these *revisionist* views, a state is in essence an organized group of individuals, and therefore, the moral rights of states cannot exceed the aggregate of the moral rights of its individuals. Simply put, individuals, coming together as a state, cannot create an entity that enjoys transcendental rights that they do not possess as individuals. If this is true, the territory of the state cannot be put on the same plane as the physical bodies of individuals harmed by the non-state actor's attack. Rather, the territory of the state is simply an *object*, in relation to which the state *qua* collective enjoys some rights.

[38] The author elaborates:

> One example can be the launch of mortar rounds by non-state actors that hit open areas in another state. In such cases, it is unclear why self-defence on the territory of the territorial state would be *automatically* justified. To sum up this point… for a non-attributable attack by non-state actors to amount to an armed attack, it should pose a grave and immediate threat to the life and limb of individuals (or harm objects or infrastructure essential for the survival of individuals). Attacks that merely implicate a state's territory should not, in general, be presumed to cross this threshold.

also apply to assess its legality.[39] In line with the insights of Fakhri and Beckers regarding the significance of legal forms to institutionalize emerging socio-political orders, in this sense, the chapter by Lieblich can be read as taking an active part in that endeavour by contributing to the formalization of a new norm that can authorize and at the same time delimit these modes of *transnational* use of force that are changing the landscapes of global warfare.

What is the vision of human rights in the global governance of war and the use of force conveyed by this chapter? The chapter sets the analysis within changing landscapes of global warfare and focuses on a fringe instance of 'radical, residual form of governance' as the use of force against non-state actors located in foreign territory. The chapter here charts a competing set of rights/interests at stake, including the sovereign right to territorial integrity of the host state and the interest to ensure the security of its population from the affected state. Strictly speaking, the human rights involved are the individual rights to life and physical integrity of the victims of these attacks from non-state groups. The chapter places these human rights at the highest order of moral and political value to sustain the establishment of a right to self-defence that would delimit the legitimate use of force from the affected state against these non-state groups located beyond its borders.

## 3. Conclusion

Romano's account of law as an institution that ontologically conveys diverse *modes of social existence* and Hauriou's account of how the 'directing ideas' informing these institutionalized legal orders (contingently) structure the relational *ethos* and *telos* of their participants are relevant because they also entail a theory of crisis. According to this account, moments of socio-political crisis arise when those purportedly 'directing ideas' lose normativity or significance, which is to say that these ideas no longer have the capacity to inspire or generate allegiance by the participants in these institutionalized practices. These moments of socio-political crisis usually evoke a societal sense of estrangement from the institution and mistrust among its participants, triggering an eventual institutional decay unless some 'directing idea' informing the institution is revitalized or replaced by a new one.[40]

[39] As Lieblich explains:

> It is here that the question of state fault might be significant. If a state is 'innocent' (unable), the necessity threshold should be higher, *in particular* when the armed attack is not ongoing. Conversely, if the state is *responsible* for the attack, say, by supporting or harbouring a non-state actor, this indeed might implicate our perceptions on the necessity of a transnational response. Beyond that, if the state is *culpable* (the attack is attributable), this can affect the scope of permissible response under proportionality.

[40] For a contemporary instantiation of these dynamics in relation to the perceived crisis of the European Union as a political project, see Weiler, 'United in Fear—The Loss of Heimat and the Crises

To the extent that prevalent imaginaries informing contemporary human rights praxis emerged as 'the last utopia',[41] that is as a replacement of anti-colonial vocabularies of self-determination and largely driven by the neo-functional differentiations of renewed forms of advanced capitalism, human rights would currently be experiencing its own modes of legitimation crisis.[42] This suggests a moment of reckoning for human rights movements[43] and the necessary quest for a new or reinvigorated 'directing idea' for human rights *law* to avoid its decay.[44] The specialized studies in this volume add significant insights and nuances to this scenario by charting and scrutinizing the *relevance* of human rights in several global governance regimes. With their contextual focus as well as their diverse methodological and substantive approximations to the roles of human rights in global governance, the chapters in this volume represent a refreshing contribution to the contemporary developments of human rights theory, the law of global governance, and transnational legal studies.

of Europe', in L. Papadopoulou, I. Pernice, and J. H. H. Weiler (eds), *Legitimacy Issues of the European Union in the Face of Crisis* (2017) 359; F. de Witte, *Re:Generation Europe: Ten Proposals for Another Europe* (2019); and J. Komárek (ed.), *European Constitutional Imaginaries: Between Ideology and Utopia* (2023).

41 S. Moyn, *The Last Utopia: Human Rights in History* (2012).

42 J. Habermas, *Legitimation Crisis [1973]* (1975).

43 Kennedy, 'The International Human Rights Regime: Still Part of the Problem?' in R. Dickinson *et al.* (eds), *Examining Critical Perspectives on Human Rights* (2012).

44 For some contemporary efforts in this regard, see S. Wheatley, *The Idea of International Human Rights Law* (2019); G. de Búrca, *Reframing Human Rights in a Turbulent Era* (2021); and Bhuta, 'Recovering Social Rights', 1 *Institute of International Law and Justice Working Papers* (2023) 2, https://www.iilj.org/wp-content/uploads/2023/04/Bhuta-IILJ-WP-HTIL-2023.pdf (last visited 5 November 2023).

# 2

# Contesting Austerity

## Genealogies of Human Rights Discourse

*Matthias Goldmann**

### 1. Introduction: Human Rights and Austerity

Since the emergence of sovereign statehood in early modernity, there have been sovereign debt crises.[1] Their resolution has regularly involved hardship for the population of the debtor state due to adjustments in fiscal and economic policy known as austerity. Addressing such hardship as human rights problems is, however, a rather recent phenomenon. This chapter seeks to explain the reasons for the lack of human rights perspectives on austerity in the past and tracks crucial junctures in austerity debates. It turns out that, in the 1970s, important actors came close to framing austerity as a human rights issue, despite the relative disillusionment with human rights prevailing at the time. The international financial institutions (IFIs), however, managed to push through a slight, but decisive, semantic shift from 'human needs' to 'human capital'. The latter concept came to dominate austerity debates in the following years. Framing austerity as a human rights problem gained broader traction again only in civil society circles in the 1990s, but it took until after the global financial crisis for international institutions and courts to begin recognizing austerity as a human rights issue. Curiously, therefore, the rise of human rights to the level of foundational global constitutional principles—to nothing less than the 'last utopia'[2]—which began towards the end of the Cold War, reached the perception of austerity only with a delay of several decades. It seems that human rights came late and helped little—a trope all too familiar to anyone

* For helpful discussions I am indebted to Nehal Bhuta, Juan Pablo Bohoslavsky, Julia Dehm, Anuscheh Farahat, Silvia Steininger, Margot Salomon, Ingo Venzke, the students attending the human rights course of the AEL in June 2017, and participants in the AEL conference at the EUI in February 2018 and at the Conference on Contingency in the Course of Human Rights at UvA in May 2018. Thanks to Hannah Kull and Seoyoung Shin for research assistance. A prior, abbreviated version of this chapter appeared in I. Venzke and K. J. Heller (eds), *Contingency in International Law: On the Possibility of Different Legal Histories* (2021) 297.

[1] For defaults during early modernity, see C. M. Reinhart and K. S. Rogoff, *This Time Is Different. Eight Centuries of Financial Folly* (2009) 86–87.

[2] S. Moyn, *The Last Utopia* (2010).

Matthias Goldmann, *Contesting Austerity*. In: *Global Rights?* First Edition. Edited by: Nehal Bhuta and Rodrigo Vallejo, Oxford University Press. © Matthias Goldmann 2024. DOI: 10.1093/oso/9780198940166.003.0002

involved in the tragedy of sovereign debt restructuring.[3] Moreover, one cannot explain this delay by simple reference to the progressive expansion of human rights from the first to the second and third generations of human rights, as the trajectory set out in this chapter illustrates regressive phases.

This has important implications for the history of human rights. Far from reflecting progress, its history reveals fluctuating paradigms of human rights law. There is thus no single understanding and, accordingly, no single historical trajectory of human rights. Rather, the closest one can come to a comprehensive history of human rights is by mapping the alternations of different human rights paradigms.[4] This chapter therefore uses the concept of human rights paradigms to track and explain the evolution of human rights discourse in the context of austerity. Each paradigm of human rights discourse is situated at a certain point on the scale of broader social struggles spanning from the 'economic' to the 'social'. In this account, the 'economic' stands for the market logic of economic liberalism, i.e. the maximization of profits in a competitive environment characterized by a high degree of division of labour and the guarantee of property rights. In other words, the term 'economic' as I use it here refers to modern capitalism's inherent tendency to 'disembed' social relations and undermine solidarity.[5] Conversely, the 'social' stands for the preconditions that create social cohesion and solidarity, for institutions, policies, and rules that reduce the disruptive power of modern capitalism and seek to re-embed economic relations in their wider social context.

Sovereign debt crises are complex challenges to the relationship between the economic and the social. The financial shortfall somehow has to be redistributed among old and new creditors who have to accept cuts to their returns on the one hand, and the debtor state and its citizens who regularly become subject to adjustment programmes commonly known as austerity on the other. Sovereign debt restructurings, therefore, bring the conflict between the economic (or 'market justice') and the social (or 'social justice') to a culmination.[6] If market justice prevails, sovereign debt crises might follow a pattern which Naomi Klein has called 'disaster capitalism':[7] adjustment programmes can entrench the interests of creditors in the long term, reaching far beyond an acute crisis, for example by privatizing public services, reducing public expenditure, and adopting debt and budget deficit limits to ensure future debt repayment. If social justice prevails, it collides with thick layers of economic, political, legal, and religious thinking and practices that reaffirm the duty to repay one's debts.[8]

[3] Cf. M. Guzman, J. A. Ocampo, and J. Stiglitz (eds), *Too Little, Too Late: The Quest to Resolve Sovereign Debt Crises* (2016).

[4] On the concept of paradigm, see generally T. S. Kuhn, *The Structure of Scientific Revolutions* (1962). In a legal context, see Habermas, 'Paradigms of Law', 17 *Cardozo Law Review* (1995) 771.

[5] K. Polanyi, *The Great Transformation: The Political and Economic Origins of Our Time* (1944) ch. 2.

[6] W. Streeck, *Buying Time: The Delayed Crisis of Democratic Capitalism* (2014) 58.

[7] N. Klein, *The Shock Doctrine: The Rise of Disaster Capitalism* (2007) 10.

[8] From a critical perspective: D. Graeber, *Debt: The First 5000 Years* (2012) 13ff; K. Dyson, *States, Debt, and Power: 'Saints' and 'Sinners' in European History and Integration* (2014) 37.

Given the complexity of such struggles, the two concepts of the economic and the social obviously represent ideal types. Each human rights paradigm, just like each plan for the resolution of a debt crisis, reflects a particular entanglement between market justice and social justice. Nevertheless, I believe that the simplification implied in this dichotomy is justified as it allows me to demonstrate how human rights discourse has interacted with the struggle between the economic and the social.

This interaction is less than straightforward. As the chapter will elaborate, there is no seamless alignment of human rights with 'the social'. Rather, one can break down the relationship between human rights and the struggle between the economic and the social in the sovereign debt context into two different, but intersecting, axes of discursive evolution. For each human rights paradigm, one needs to determine the position on these axes.

The first axis maps the dynamic relationship between human rights discourse and *other concepts* for articulating 'the social' in the context of austerity. Throughout the last century, human rights discourse was not the only game in town. For much of that period, advocates of 'the social' refrained from recurring to human rights, challenging austerity on economic terms by proposing heterodox macroeconomic policies, on legal terms by emphasizing sovereignty and self-determination, or on religious or moral terms overlapping, but not identical with, human rights. As the chapter will show, the specific context of austerity and human rights discourse during the last four decades explains when and how human rights discourse replaced alternative normative grounds for challenging the relationship between the economic and the social. The chapter therefore lends little support to the claim that human rights are the Fifth Column of neoliberalism,[9] irrespective of the difficulty involved in establishing such causalities.[10]

The second axis tracks the position of human rights *within* the struggle between the economic and the social. Human rights, like fundamental rights, their constitutional brethren, are not natural allies of 'the social', or a particular vision thereof. Rather, as Samuel Moyn has masterfully shown, human rights oscillate between a sufficientarian understanding of the relationship between the economic and the social, characterized by formal equality, an emphasis on economic rights, and only minimum guarantees of social protection, and a more egalitarian understanding based on a substantive concept of equality, which requires government

[9] Klein (n. 7) 144ff. On the emergence of a specific neoliberal concept of human rights: J. Whyte, *The Morals of the Market: Human Rights and the Rise of Neoliberalism* (2019). On epistemological affinities: Odysseos, 'Human Rights, Liberal Ontogenesis and Freedom: Producing a Subject for Neoliberalism?', 38 *Millennium* (2010) 747. For a balanced view, see Nolan, 'Human Rights and Market Fundamentalism in the Long 1970s', in N. Frei (ed.), *Toward a New Moral World Order? Menschenrechtspolitik und Völkerrecht seit 1945* (2013) 172.

[10] Moyn, 'A Powerless Companion: Human Rights in the Age of Neoliberalism', 77 *Law & Contemporary Problems* (2014) 147, at 156ff.

intervention to realize economic prosperity and social welfare.[11] The former position reaches back to the emergence of fundamental and human rights in the context of predominantly liberal constitutions of the eighteenth and nineteenth centuries. The latter view also looks back at a considerable pedigree, notably at the crucial role assigned to fundamental and human rights for social integration in transformative constitutions adopted in a period spanning from the interwar years (Mexico 1917, Germany 1919) to constitutions belonging to the third wave of democratization (Colombia 1991, South Africa 1997).[12] It therefore all depends on the understanding given to human rights in a particular context, or rather, on the *dominant* understanding that informs institutional action, in particular the conditionalities imposed by the IFIs.

As it turns out, human rights paradigms prevalent in thinking about debt crises and austerity have shifted markedly over time. These shifts broadly reflect the genealogies of human rights law in the postwar era.[13] Four different paradigms emerge. During the 1970s, the decade preceding the debt crisis of the 1980s, the idea of austerity as a response to debt crises was contested by the basic (human) needs approach and by the proposal of a New International Economic Order (NIEO). Both strands of thought showed some affinity with human rights law, although not without ambiguity, understanding self-determination as a structural requirement for economic, social, and cultural (ESC) rights enjoyment. Hence, human rights lent themselves as a comprehensive framework for contesting austerity (axis 1) in the name of redistributive equality (axis 2) (Section 2).

Counterintuitively, the debt crisis in the Global South beginning in the 1980s and the related wave of more and more intrusive austerity nearly silenced, rather than provoked, any form of human rights-based critique. While it prompted UNICEF and other international organizations to contest structural adjustments proposed by the International Monetary Fund (IMF) out of their concern for basic (human) *needs*, the IMF managed to refocus the debate on human *capital*, bringing economic growth and efficiency into focus in line with the emerging Washington Consensus. It seemed that the earlier structuralist paradigm of human rights as claims to national independence did not easily morph into one of human rights as a yardstick for international organizations. Hence, the debate

[11] S. Moyn, *Not Enough. Human Rights in an Unequal World* (2018) 3–4. For a resounding defence of sufficientarianism: L. Shields, *Just Enough: Sufficiency as a Demand of Justice* (2016).

[12] On the Jacobin legacy of the latter view, see Moyn (n. 11) 12. On social rights in transformative constitutions, see Menéndez and Goldmann, 'Weimar Moments: Transformations of the Democratic, Social, and Open State of Law', Max Planck Institute for Comparative Public Law and International Law (MPIL) Research Paper No. 12 (2022), https://dx.doi.org/10.2139/ssrn.4141137 (last visited 17 November 2023).

[13] On the different genealogies of human rights discourse: Hoffmann, 'Einführung: Zur Genealogie der Menschenrechte', in S.-L. Hoffmann (ed.), *Moralpolitik. Geschichte der Menschenrechte im 20 Jahrhundert* (2010) 7, at 26.

about austerity used purely economic language (axis 1), and the call for more efficiency allowed sufficiency to prevail over greater redistributive equality (axis 2) (Section 3).

When the Iron Curtain fell, concerns for development became more acute as states from the Global South would then have to stand on their own feet economically. This led to cautious changes in the framework of sovereign debt restructurings to the benefit of the debtor states. But the latter had to pay with ever more intrusive forms of austerity, including structural conditions such as the domestic implementation of civil and political rights. This 'governance paradigm' of human rights was countered by a transformative paradigm of human rights in which civil society articulated its critique of austerity (axis 1). The IFIs avoided the issue of human rights but reacted by adding 'social' components to austerity that aligned with their focus on efficiency and growth and further entrenched sufficiency (axis 2) (Section 4).

After the global financial crisis, when austerity hit the European periphery, Europe's constitutional context and the experience of the fight against terrorism created new inroads for human rights discourse. While litigation against austerity had only mixed success and stumbled over structural obstacles of human rights discourse, the crisis aftermath saw enormous progress in the political recognition of human rights as a relevant standard for austerity. This has given rise to a new political paradigm (Section 5).

This history of human rights in the context of austerity yields a number of sobering, yet not hopeless, insights about the role and potential function of human rights discourse. On the one hand, from a historical perspective, concern for the social has been articulated in terms other than human rights. Human rights are only one possibility of addressing the social, and austerity may be more or less intrusive with or without explicit reference to human rights. Even where reference to human rights is made, much depends on the specific understanding of human rights underlying appeals to the social. On the other hand, in the context of economic constitutionalism, a transformative, political concept of human rights can rebalance the scales between the economic and the social by providing incentives for rethinking economic orthodoxy. Their significance for contesting authority lies in their capacity to defy and challenge economic expertise from an external standpoint and thereby re-empower progressive politics. It therefore does not follow that human rights should keep out of the socio-economic field entirely as they would only raise unrealistic expectations.[14] While there is no guarantee for the success of human rights discourse, there is no evidence that the relationship between the economic and the social would be more balanced and more egalitarian without it (Section 6).

[14] Moyn (n. 10) 151.

## 2. The 1970s as a Turning Point

### A. Debt and Conditionalities in the Postwar Period

Economically, the aftermath of the Second World War was characterized by strong growth in most countries and consequently saw debt-to-GDP ratios fall.[15] Nevertheless, it would be misleading to conclude from this that sovereign debt had not been an issue. On the one hand, developing countries struggled to escape responsibility for old, pre-independence debt.[16] On the other hand, to develop their economies, they incurred considerable new external debt, mostly in the form of bilateral loans.[17] This rendered them vulnerable, as the Final Act of the first UN Conference on Trade and Development (UNCTAD) in 1964 amply testifies.[18] Due to its bilateral nature, the restructuring of such debt primarily took place in the relatively predictable framework of the Paris Club, established in 1956. Even though Paris Club restructurings were less than generous in that period, granting the debtor state only maturity extensions and interest rate reductions,[19] they have required since the very beginning that the debtor state commits to a stabilization programme supported by the IMF.[20]

The IMF has required such stabilization programmes, or adjustment programmes, since 1951.[21] A stabilization programme is only necessary in case a Member State's drawings exceed the so-called gold tranche, the amount corresponding to the member's contribution to the fund, and the IMF demands substantially more onerous commitments of the debtor state if drawings exceed the so-called first credit tranche (corresponding to 125 per cent of the member's quota).[22] Hence, only few, comparatively heavily indebted countries were exposed to harsh austerity during the early postwar period.

[15] Eichengreen *et al.*, 'Public Debt through the Ages', IMF Working Paper No. 6 (2019) 21.

[16] J. King, *The Doctrine of Odious Debt in International Law: A Restatement* (2016) 79–80.

[17] Eskridge Jr, 'Les Jeux Sont Faits: Structural Origins of the International Debt Problem', 25 *Virginia Journal of International Law* (1985) 281, at 328ff; Pahuja, 'Technologies of Empire: IMF Conditionality and the Reinscription of the North/South Divide', 13 *Leiden Journal of International Law* (2000) 749, at 761; Goldmann, 'Staatsverschuldung und Entwicklung', in P. Dann, S. Kadelbach, and M. Kaltenborn (eds), *Entwicklung und Recht* (2014) 377, at 383.

[18] Proceedings of the United Nations Conference on Trade and Development, Geneva, 23 March–16 June 1964, vol. I: Final Act and Report, UN Doc. E/Conf.46/141, vol. I.

[19] Cf. Hudes, 'Coordination of Paris and London Club Reschedulings', 17 *International Law and Politics* (1984–1985) 553; Weiss, 'The Paris Club and International Debt Relief', Congressional Research Service, RS 21482 (2013).

[20] Grard, 'Le Club de Paris et les Dettes Publiques des Etats', in D. Carreau and M. N. Shaw (eds), *La Dette Extérieure* (1995) 197, at 208ff.

[21] Dreher and Vaubel, 'The Causes and Consequences of IMF Conditionality', 40 *Emerging Markets Finance & Trade* (2004) 26, at 32; C. Payer, *Lent and Lost: Foreign Credit and Third World Development* (1991) 47; the term 'conditionality', however, only seems to have surfaced in 1964, see Gold, 'Conditionality', IMF Pamphlet Series No. 31/2 (1979).

[22] Gold (n. 21) 4ff.

For the IMF, stabilization and adjustment have always meant some form of austerity. This point of view goes back to its monetary policy model, which has remained, by and large, the same. It considers exports and domestic credit growth as the two main exogenous variables determining the balance of payment problems.[23] To increase exports, 'internal devaluations' such as wage reductions have been the means of choice, given that exchange rates used to be fixed and exchange-rate manipulations are now prohibited. To increase domestic credit, it was believed that public debt should be reduced because it would prevent private credit growth.[24]

But there are vastly different forms, degrees, and temporal horizons of austerity. Adjustment programmes prior to the 1970s mostly comprised macroeconomic performance criteria.[25] Such requirements could be quite intrusive for the sovereignty of the debtor state,[26] and they usually favoured reliance on markets instead of government interventions.[27] For example, Argentina's 1958 and 1960 stand-by-arrangements, the instrument defining the terms for granting the debtor state access to the Fund's resources, required Argentina to ensure the free fluctuation of the peso. In its letter of intent accompanying the stand-by arrangement, Argentina committed, for example, to reduce its outstanding debt and deficit by laying off government employees, increasing railroad prices and the cost of electricity, raising taxes, abolishing specified price controls, and discontinuing the practice of the central bank ensuring exchange-rate risks.[28] Performance criteria made progress on adjustment programmes measurable and concretized the threat that the IMF would withdraw funding in the case of non-performance.

Measured by today's standards, one cannot deny the human rights relevance of conditionalities in this early period. However, lending and conditionalities were still short-term and mostly comprised one-off measures, staying clear of demanding profound structural reforms of the debtor states' economic policies. The goal of conditionality was to quickly recalibrate the balance of payments.[29] It was still a far cry from the policy reform programmes of today.[30] This might be one of the reasons why the Final Act of the 1964 first UNCTAD conference does not mention them.

[23] Polak, 'The IMF Monetary Model at Forty', IMF Working Paper No. 49 (1997).

[24] M. Blyth, *Austerity: The History of a Dangerous Idea* (2013) 164.

[25] E. Denters, *Law and Policy of IMF Conditionality* (1996) 89; see also IMF decision No. 102-(52/11) of 13 February 1952 and decision No. 2603-(681132) of 20 September 1968, reprinted in Appendix II.

[26] Pahuja (n. 17) 770.

[27] J. M. Boughton, *Silent Revolution. The International Monetary Fund 1979–1989* (2001) *passim*.

[28] See Western Hemisphere Department, IMF, 'Argentina—Request for Stand-by Arrangement' (1958), http://www.bcra.gov.ar/Pdfs/Institucional/01-SB-58.pdf (last visited 17 November 2023); Western Hemisphere Department, IMF, 'Argentina—Request for Stand-by Arrangement' (1961), http://www.bcra.gov.ar/Pdfs/Institucional/04-SB-61.pdf (last visited 17 November 2023).

[29] Pahuja (n. 17) 760; Meller, 'IMF and World Bank Roles in the Latin American Foreign Debt Problem', in P. Meller (ed.), *The Latin American Development Debate: Neostructuralism, Neomonetarism, and Adjustment Processes* (1991) 169, at 169.

[30] See Gold (n. 21) 2–3.

Thereafter, conditionalities increased and intensified over several decades in a 'two steps forward, one step back' mode of interaction between the staff and the executive board on the one hand, and the Member States on the other. As the Bretton Woods system of fixed exchange rates approached its decline, the IMF broadened its activities and expanded into development issues. Part of this expansion was an increased focus on debt. Worried about the increasing flow of capital to developing countries, a 1967 decision defined external debt limitations as new performance criteria to be included in stand-by arrangements.[31] Member States pushed back with the first guidelines on conditionality dating from 1968, which restricted the use of performance criteria to macroeconomic issues, also with a view to ensuring equal treatment even though Member States borrowed at widely different levels of their tranches.[32]

The crisis-struck decade of the 1970s reversed the tide. The Global South compensated for the decline in official development aid from industrial countries by massively expanding their commercial borrowings, fuelled by, among other things, the excess liquidity of internationally operating banks thanks to increased oil revenue in the Organization of the Petroleum Exporting Countries (OPEC) ('petrodollars'). With progress in growth and development stalling and debt problems quivering on the horizon, the question emerged whether the IMF should expand its narrow focus on macro issues and tackle development issues more broadly. In 1971, it began advising on external debt, including debt ceilings, in the frame of its Article VIII and XIV consultations.[33] This resonated with the interests of lenders, who wanted to avoid any intermingling of the development aid they were providing with sovereign debt issues.[34] In 1974, the Fund established the Extended Fund Facility, a new lending functionality providing longer-term finance to overcome debt crises. Conditionalities included performance instruments, which went considerably beyond the erstwhile performance targets. The amendment of Article IV of the Articles of Agreement earlier that year provided the legal basis for the inclusion of more stringent conditionalities in adjustment programmes.[35] The structural character of such conditionalities considerably increased their impact on domestic policies.

[31] IMF Doc. SM/67/96.

[32] Dreher and Vaubel (n. 21) 32; Gold, 'The Rule of Law in the International Monetary Fund', IMF Pamphlet Series No. 32 (1980) 75–77; Denters (n. 25) 96.

[33] Sgard, 'How the IMF Did It—Sovereign Debt Restructuring between 1970 and 1989', 11 *Capital Markets Law Journal* (2016) 103, at 107.

[34] Minutes of the Executive Board meetings 71/33 and 71/34 of 21 and 23 April 1971; IMF Doc. SM/71/80; cf. Pahuja (n. 17) 766.

[35] UNCTAD, Report of the Trade and Development Board on the first part of its fifteenth session held at the Palais des Nations, Geneva, 5–16 August 1975, A/10015/Rev.1 (1976), paras 161–163; Pahuja (n. 17) 769; Dreher and Vaubel (n. 21) 32.

## B. The Twofold Emergence of a Structural Human Rights Paradigm

In the postwar era up until the 1970s, criticism of the austerity induced by adjustment programmes was hardly articulated in terms of human rights, even though their influence on the economic policies of debtor states was growing. Only at the end of the 1970s, did the possibility of a human rights critique come within reach.

Several factors compounded this process. Despite the inclusion of social rights in the 1948 Universal Declaration of Human Rights, ESC rights discourse barely got off the ground in the industrialized economies during the '*trente glorieuse*', the period of growth from the mid-1940s to roughly the 1970s. The new historiography of human rights has explored the reasons for this silence in some detail.[36] In particular, the lack of ESC rights discourse had nothing to do with linear progress in human rights law, a common, self-gratulatory narrative according to which classical liberal rights devised the path which the development of ESC rights could follow in a second step. Rather, it seems that ESC rights had already, in substance, entered the legal and political vocabulary of the twentieth century during the interwar period. The decline of nineteenth-century bourgeois constitutionalism and the shift to mass democracy in many industrialized countries during the first half of the twentieth century indeed brought with it explicit constitutional recognition for social concerns. The classic, paradigmatic examples are the 1917 Mexican Constitution and the 1919 Weimar Constitution, to which one might add the 1931 Spanish Constitution, Roosevelt's 1941 Four Freedoms, or the 1948 Italian Constitution.[37] These fundamental charters articulated social concerns not necessarily in terms of rights, but often in the form of programmatic provisions that would set in motion societal and political processes to build up the welfare state and balance the diverging interests of various segments of society.[38] Although constitutional rights adjudication (against the administration, not the legislature) in some cases goes back to this period,[39] the enforcement of ESC rights against the legislature was not part of this constitutional agenda at this period, just as constitutional rights adjudication generally was still in its infancy in most jurisdictions.

After the Second World War, the framing of the social question remained essentially the same in Western democracies. The memories of the Great Depression and the Cold War lent some urgency to the establishment and expansion of the

36 For references, see J. R. Slaughter, 'Hijacking Human Rights: Neoliberalism, the New Historiography, and the End of the Third World', 40 *Human Rights Quarterly* (2018) 735, at 741ff.

37 Goldmann and Menéndez (n. 12).

38 Stolleis, 'Die Soziale Programmematik der Weimarer Reichsverfassung', in H. Dreier and C. Waldhoff (eds), *Das Wagnis der Demokratie. Eine Anatomie der Weimarer Reichsverfassung* (2018) 195; R. Gargarella, *Latin American Constitutionalism, 1810–2010: The Engine Room of the Constitution* (2013) 101ff.

39 Dreier, 'Grundrechtsrepublik Weimar', in H. Dreier and C. Waldhoff (eds), *Das Wagnis der Demokratie. Eine Anatomie der Weimarer Reichsverfassung* (2018) 175.

welfare state.[40] Domestically, this period therefore coincided with the steep rise of the welfare state. Health care, the improvement of working conditions, and the expansion of secondary and tertiary education are visible signs of the profound entanglement between the economic and the social in the period. Soon enough, the Philipps curve dominated labour market policies, leading to macroeconomic policies that sought to achieve a balance between unemployment and inflation.[41] The welfare state was part of a larger project of an international economic order that should have embedded capitalism to avoid a recurrence of the Great Depression and the war. Never again should the risks to international peace arising from uncoordinated, unchecked economic interests be allowed to materialize.[42]

This context of embedded capitalism at the domestic and international levels explains why ESC rights gained little significance as *rights* in industrialized countries even after the adoption of the Universal Declaration of Human Rights (UDHR).[43] Protecting social rights was a task for national welfare systems. Considering the context of its creation, and particularly the influence of Latin American constitutionalism,[44] one needs to understand the UDHR as setting out a programme for domestic welfare states, rather than as a compendium of judicially enforceable individual social rights.[45] ESC rights were more of a shibboleth for a new concept of the state, of a state that endorsed mass democracy and put the welfare of the people first. It is in line with this thinking that human rights discourse in the Global South saw the struggle for national independence become aligned with the realization of human rights.[46]

The transnational dimension of welfare was formulated in an analogous language of development, breathing the air of modernization theories, not of rights discourse.[47] Development became the means of choice to overcome global

[40] For Europe: Kjaer, 'The Transnational Constitution of Europe's Social Market Economies: A Question of Constitutional Imbalances?', 57 *Journal of Common Market Studies* (2019) 143, at 147ff.

[41] Cf. Samuelson and Solow, 'Analytical Aspects of Anti-Inflation Policy', 50 *The American Economic Review* (1960) 177.

[42] Ruggie, 'International Regimes, Transactions, and Change: Embedded Liberalism in the Postwar Economic Order', 36 *International Organization* (1982) 379.

[43] Moyn (n. 11) 57ff; Moyn, 'The Universal Declaration of Human Rights of 1948 in the History of Cosmopolitanism', 40 *Critical Inquiry* (2014) 365.

[44] Glendon, 'The Forgotten Crucible: The Latin American Influence on the Universal Human Rights Idea', 16 *Harvard Human Rights Journal* (2003) 27.

[45] Moyn (n. 11) 55. As Moyn emphasizes, a UNESCO publication of 1948 reveals great scepticism about the future of human rights. See further M. Goodale (ed.), *Letters to the Contrary: A Curated History of the UNESCO Human Rights Survey* (2020).

[46] Burke, '"The Compelling Dialogue of Freedom": Human Rights at the Bandung Conference', 28 *Human Rights Quarterly* (2006) 947, at 962; Okafor, 'The Bandung Ethic and International Human Rights Praxis', in L. Eslava, M. Fakhri, and V. Nesiah (eds), *Bandung, Global History, and International Law: Critical Pasts and Pending Futures* (2017) 515, at 517. Likewise, the Soviet vision of human rights relied on independent nation states: E. D. Weitz, *A World Divided: The Global Struggle for Human Rights in the Age of Nation-States* (2019) 281, 295.

[47] Cf. Kößler, 'Development—Analytical Value and Ideological Bagge of an Elusive Term', in U. H. Bittlingmayer *et al.* (eds), *Education and Development in Afghanistan—Challenges and Prospects* (2019) 47, 48.

economic asymmetries, whereas ESC rights as entitlements would have raised more pressing questions of redistribution. Even states with autocratic leaders could participate in development, allowing developed democracies to cooperate with them under the premise of assisting them to 'mature' into fully-fledged democracies. Besides, ESC rights discourse would have exposed the failures of the colonial powers.[48] That the asymmetry of the international economic order would undermine the plan of building up domestic welfare states was overlooked by many, with the exception of Gunnar Myrdal, who called for international welfare coordination.[49] But even Myrdal's highly egalitarian ideas rested much more on an idea of the state and of social morals than on rights as individual entitlements.[50] The welfare state should remedy the suffering caused by the Great Depression and the ensuring Great War.[51]

In fact, some saw rights as too individualistic to be relied upon for societal change. This position is reflected in John Galtung's 1969 definition of peace research. He advocates a broad notion of peace that includes social justice and considers starvation as a form of 'violence', whether structural or personal.[52] In a highly revealing footnote, Galtung concedes that the requisite standard of social justice may be found in international human rights agreements. However, he rejects using the notion of human rights because he believes them to enshrine at best personal entitlements, not the structural causes leading to distributive unfairness. ESC rights would not challenge the power disparities responsible for unfair distribution.[53]

The welfare-state focus of postwar development cooperation began to fade in the 1970s with the realization that the recipe of development through growth had reached an impasse. Despite economic growth, unemployment and inequality soared.[54] The rising debt crisis and related harsher austerity prompted two parallel, different but related discourses in international organizations that sought to reframe the relationship between the economic and the social during debt crises. While each of these discourses is fraught with ambivalence about the role of human rights for economic policy, each of them reflects to some extent a new paradigm of human rights that notably differed from Galtung's view by emphasizing the structural significance of human rights to challenge austerity.

48 Whyte (n. 9) 120.

49 Calling for the international coordination of welfare planning: G. Myrdal, *An International Economy: Problems and Prospects* (1956) 51ff; cf. Moyn (n. 11) 104ff.

50 G. Myrdal, *Beyond the Welfare State: Economic Planning and Its International Implications* (1960) 95, at 277–279. In fact, he mentions rights only once on p. 277 near the end in a general, passing way, referring to the right to life, liberty, and the pursuit of happiness as part of the essence of the welfare culture.

51 Moyn (n. 11) 48.

52 Galtung, 'Violence, Peace, and Peace Research', 6 *Journal of Peace Research* (1969) 167, at 171.

53 Ibid. 181 fn. 18.

54 Jolly, 'The World Employment Conference: The Enthronement of Basic Needs', 9 *Development Policy Review* (1976) 31, at 76; D. J. Shaw, *World Food Security: A History since 1945* (2007) 223.

The first of these discourses emerged from the call for an NIEO. This initiative derived from heterodox, structuralist critiques of the postwar economic order prevalent particularly in Latin America. Sensing the risks implied in trade liberalization for developing countries, Raul Prebisch, the first Secretary-General of UNCTAD, advocated targeted measures of protectionism to allow for industrial development and diversification with a view to substituting imports and redistributing the benefits of development.[55] These efforts culminated in the NIEO proposal, an intellectually influential challenge to the economic hegemony of the industrialized countries.[56]

This proposal ushered in a new perspective on austerity in the Global South. During the 1960s, a lot of attention had been absorbed by the question whether the newly independent states would inherit the debt of colonial powers incurred for the benefit of their territory, and under which circumstances the former could dismiss such debt as odious.[57] In the context of rising indebtedness and the NIEO initiative, the Global South shifted its focus in the 1970s towards improving international debt restructuring practice to reduce the need for austerity and the related abyss of despair by alleviating the debt burden in the first instance. A sequence of resolutions sought to establish this desire on the international agenda. The second UNCTAD conference in 1968 emphasized the shortcomings of ad hoc frameworks for debt restructuring.[58] The Paris North-South Conference of 1974 on the NIEO gave rise to the UNCTAD Ad Hoc Group of Governmental Experts on the Debt Problem of Developing Countries. With this group, for the first time since the war, an international body came up with a series of recommendations for a broad-based, effective institutional framework for debt restructuring, recommendations which have lost little of their practical relevance.[59] A few years later, Tanzania proposed that the international debt commission should be competent to consider issues of social fairness when deciding on a debt restructuring.[60] This process culminated in Resolution 222 (XXI),[61] which specifies in its annex the 'Detailed features for

[55] Lustig, 'From Structuralism to Neostruturalism: The Search for a Heterodox Paradigm', in P. Meller (ed.), *The Latin American Development Debate Neostructuralism, Neomonetarism, and Adjustment Processes* (1991) 27.

[56] Moyn (n. 11) 113ff; Q. Slobodian, *Globalists: The End of Empire and the Birth of Neoliberalism* (2018) 219ff.

[57] International Law Commission, First Report on Succession of States in respect of rights and duties resulting from sources other than treaties, by Mr Mohammed Bedjaoui, Special Rapporteur, UN Doc. A/CN.4/204, 5 April 1968, 2 *Yearbook of the International Law Commission* 95, 109–110. For cases, see King (n. 16) 79–80; see also Frey, 'A Revolutionary Process? Decolonialization and International Law', in N. Frei (ed.), *Toward a New Moral World Order? Menschenrechtspolitik und Völkerrecht Seit 1945* (2013) 122.

[58] UNCTAD, *Beyond Conventional Wisdom in Development Policy. An Intellectual History of UNCTAD (1964–2004)* (2004) 33.

[59] UNCTAD, Report of the Trade and Development Board 10 March–2 October 1975, UN Doc. A/10015/Rev. 1, Annex A, Document submitted by the Group of Seventy-seven and Romania on proposed additional policy measures for incorporation into the International Development Strategy for the Second United Nations Development Decade, para. 22.

[60] Sgard (n. 33) 108.

[61] UNCTAD Trade and Development Board, Res. 222 (XXI), 27 September 1980.

future operations relating to the debt problems of interested developing countries'. The document constitutes a compromise. It dangles the prospect of debt relief in front of the debtor states while falling short of institutionalizing a formal debt restructuring mechanism.[62]

Even though the resolution does not mention human rights, the context of the NIEO and its relationship with human rights suggests that these efforts within UNCTAD might indeed be understood as a genuine human rights perspective by another name, as a structuralist human rights paradigm that sought to safeguard them by rebalancing the relationship between the economic and the social at a global level.

This understanding follows from the role of human rights in the NIEO initiative, although that relationship was not free from ambiguity. On the one hand, it did not go without saying that supporters of the NIEO would endorse a language of rights, as the implementation of this agenda, a variety of Keynes-inspired development economics, required in the first place a strong state, rather than individual entitlements.[63] Moreover, the NIEO debate mirrored certain general tensions between decolonization and human rights.[64] Democracy had been short-lived in some newly independent states. Not all states backing the NIEO initiative showed a high level of respect for democracy and human rights internally, which made their invocation a controversial issue. A case in point is the scepticism expressed towards civil and political rights at the Teheran Conference on Human Rights in 1968.[65] Some authors from the period also recognized the neo-imperialist potential inherent in human rights discourse, even though these concerns emerged in full only with the rise of Western human rights discourse in the subsequent decades.[66] It is probably for these reasons that the international documents setting out the NIEO hardly mention human rights. In fact, the NIEO Declaration contains only one reference to human dignity while placing emphasis on sovereignty and the construction of domestic welfare states.[67] The subsequent Charter of Economic Rights and Duties of States at least mentions the duty of states to comply with international human rights norms.[68]

[62] E. Cosio-Pascal, *The Emerging of a Multilateral Forum for Debt Restructuring: The Paris Club* (2008) 11.

[63] Baxi, 'The New International Economic Order, Basic Needs and Rights: Notes Towards Development of the Right to Development', 23 *Indian Journal of International Law* (1983) 225; Moyn (n. 11) 117.

[64] J. Eckel, *Die Ambivalenz des Guten. Menschenrechte in der Internationalen Politik seit den 1940ern* (2014) 260ff.

[65] R. Burke, *Decolonization and the Evolution of International Human Rights* (2010) 99ff.

[66] Galtung, 'The New International Economic Order and the Basic Needs Approach', 4 *Alternatives* (1979) 455, at 462; Mutua, 'The Ideology of Human Rights', 36 *Virginia Journal of International Law* (1995) 589.

[67] UN General Assembly, Declaration on the Establishment of a New International Economic Order, UN Doc. A/RES/S-6/3201, 1 May 1974.

[68] GA Res. 3281 (XXIX) Charter of Economic Rights and Duties of States, UN Doc. A/RES/29/3281,12 December 1974, ch. 1, lit. k.

On the other hand, the struggle for independence in the Global South, which provided the context for the idea of an NIEO, was closely aligned with a structural understanding of human rights as reflected some decades earlier in the Bandung Conference.[69] Accordingly, sovereign equality and independence were considered as crucial prerequisites for realizing human rights by way of economic development.[70] This framing of human rights is reflected in the first article of each of the two international covenants. Similarly, the 1968 Proclamation of Teheran emphasizes national liberation, anti-racism, and economic development as key challenges for human rights.[71] In the light of this, some go as far as to claim that the connection between human rights, self-determination, and development had become so strong that the Global South monopolized human rights discourse and made it unattractive for industrialized economies to engage in human rights discourse up until the rediscovery of human rights during the 1970s.[72]

Exemplary for the affinity between the NIEO and a structural human rights paradigm are the debates surrounding the emergence of the right to development—a collective right expressing the desire for national economic self-determination rather than an individual entitlement.[73] The human rights practice of the United Nations during the 1970s—the incubation period of the right to development—reflects this understanding of human rights and its close alignment with the NIEO. Notably, General Assembly Resolution 32/130 of 1977 outlines a comprehensive set of 'alternative approaches and ways and means within the United Nations system for improving the effective enjoyment of human rights and fundamental freedoms'. The resolution stipulates that human rights questions require a global perspective, thereby shifting the focus from individual entitlements to collective plight characterized by structural Western dominance, including apartheid, colonialism, threats to national sovereignty, and sovereignty over natural resources. It goes on to declare the realization of the NIEO as

[69] See n. 46 and accompanying text.

[70] Anand, 'Sovereign Equality of States in International Law—II', 8 *International Studies* (1966) 386, at 406; Reus-Smit, 'Human Rights and the Social Construction of Sovereignty', 27 *Review of International Studies* (2001) 519; Simpson, 'Self-Determination, Human Rights, and the End of Empire in the 1970s', 4 *Humanity* (2013) 239; Moyn (n. 11) 104, 111–112; Slaughter (n. 36); Mende, 'Are Human Rights Western—and Why Does It Matter? A Perspective from International Political Theory', 17 *Journal of International Political Theory* (2021) 38; Burke (n. 65) 37. This connection between sovereign equality and development recalls the Kantian idea of formal freedom and equality, which Kant believed to bring about social justice, see Rauscher, 'Kant's Social and Political Philosophy', *The Stanford Encyclopedia of Philosophy* (2022), https://plato.stanford.edu/entries/kant-social-political/ (last visited 17 November 2023).

[71] United Nations, Final Act of the International Conference on Human Rights (22 April–13 May 1968) UN Doc. A/CONF.32/41, ch. II 'Proclamation of Teheran'.

[72] Eckel, 'Symbolische Macht. Antikolonialismus und Menschenrechte in den Vereinten Nationen', in N. Frei (ed.), *Toward a New Moral World Order? Menschenrechtspolitik und Völkerrecht seit 1945* (2013) 134, 138, 142–143. On the rebirth of human rights discourse in the West, see Moyn (n. 2) 120ff.

[73] Cf. Declaration on the Right to Development, UN Doc. A/RES/41/128, 4 December 1986.

essential for promoting human rights.[74] In this sense, UNCTAD Resolution 222 (XXI) on the problems of developing countries, a brainchild of the NIEO, is but part of the mosaic in the broader struggle for economic independence understood as a struggle for human rights.

The second discourse challenging austerity became known as the basic (human) needs approach. It began to thrive in virtually all international organizations charged with development issues since about 1970. The concept received a decisive impulse from the International Labour Organization (ILO), at the time also grappling with the realization that growth alone would not lead to equitable development, peace, and stability in the developing world. To bring redistribution to the table, it shifted its focus to basic (human) needs.

The turns and twists of the debate about the basic (human) needs approach are too many to recount in detail here.[75] Suffice it to say that it was never fully resolved whether basic (human) needs implied a 'thick', egalitarian concept of welfare, or whether they amounted to ensuring only minimal requirements. On the one hand, the 1976 Tripartite World Conference on Employment, Income Distribution and Social Progress and the International Division of Labour had already suggested in its title that it aimed for more ambitious levels of redistribution. Consequently, its Programme of Action explicitly extended the notion of basic needs beyond those necessary for survival, and stipulated that full and fair employment should not only provide income, but also self-respect and dignity.[76] It therefore advocated a participatory approach that drew on multiple influences, including heterodox economic policy approaches in China and Tanzania.[77] Accordingly, the concept of basic *human* needs was associated both with minimum floors and with income ceilings.[78] Contrariwise, the World Bank's basic needs approach launched by President McNamara set itself less ambitious objectives by focusing on poverty, hence on those most in need.[79] This emphasis on efficiency and the alleged lack of respect for self-determination inherent in the basic needs approach drew criticism from representatives of the Third World[80] but remained nevertheless influential through the institutional prowess of the World Bank.

[74] GA Res. 32/130, 16 December 1977, para. 1(d), (e), and (f); see Baxi (n. 63) 227; Dehm, 'Highlighting Inequalities in the Histories of Human Rights: Contestations over Justice, Needs and Rights in the 1970s', 31 *Leiden Journal of International Law* (2018) 1, at 11ff.

[75] See Green, 'Basic Human Needs: Concept or Slogan, Synthesis or Smokescreen?', 9 *The IDS Bulletin* (1978) 7; Bequele and Freedman, 'Employment and Basic Needs: An Overview', 118 *International Labour Review* (1979) 315; Dehm (n. 74) 4.

[76] World Employment Conference, Declaration of Principles and Programme of Action, UN Doc. E/5857, 5 July 1976, paras 4–5.

[77] Green (n. 77) 8; see also Mouly, 'Employment: A Concept in Need of Renovation', 116 *International Labour Review* (1977) 1; Bequele and Freedman (n. 77) 318.

[78] Green (n. 77) 10.

[79] Moyn (n. 11) 131, 190. Background on the World Bank discussions in Dehm (n. 74) 8.

[80] Galtung (n. 66) 461ff.

Given the ambiguity inherent in the basic (human) needs approach, some established a connection with human rights to tilt it towards a 'thick', egalitarian meaning. Such a shift was almost an obvious choice as the 1968 Teheran Proclamation had popularized the framing of development issues in human rights language.[81] One striking example is the Declaration of Principle of the 1976 World Employment Conference. Characterized by highly egalitarian aspirations, this hallmark document of the basic (human) needs approach makes explicit reference to the UDHR and specifically to the right to work and trade unions' rights.[82] In fact, this Declaration prompted Philip Alston to highlight commonalities and differences between basic (human) needs and human rights, merging the two discursive strands with egalitarian objectives in mind.[83] Similarly, Upendra Baxi argued that the basic (human) needs approach reflected an egalitarian concept of ESC rights.[84] The association of basic (human) needs with human rights therefore represented a discursive strategy to vindicate the social against the economic in the ongoing rethinking of development economics. Once more, the understanding of human rights emerging in this context expresses a structural paradigm. Rather than guaranteeing individual entitlements, the Declaration emphasizes states' sovereign rights to determine their economic policies.[85] Human rights are meant to facilitate quality development, including fair and full employment, going significantly beyond sufficiency.

Hence, at the end of the 1970s, both the UNCTAD debt debate and the basic (human) needs approach, the two discourses relevant for framing debt and austerity at the international level during this period, were in various respects aligned with, and informed by, a structural idea of human rights that gave human rights a role to play in the relationship between the economic and the social (axis 1). Each of these discourses showed a certain affinity for more egalitarian forms of redistribution (axis 2). The NIEO debate followed an inchoate idea of human rights and only focused on the aggregate impact of the international order on the economic situation of states and groups. The basic (human) needs approach was caught up in disputes between equality and sufficiency. Nevertheless, despite these ambiguities, in retrospect it seemed possible for a structuralist understanding of human rights in one form or another to become a highly relevant standard for the governance of sovereign debt crises and austerity.

[81] United Nations, Final Act of the International Conference on Human Rights, 22 April–13 May 1968, UN Doc. A/CONF.32/41, Proclamation of Teheran, paras 12 and 13.

[82] See n. 76, preamble and paras 9, 15, 38.

[83] Alston, 'Human Rights and Basic Needs: A Critical Assessment', 12 *Human Rights Journal* (1979) 19, at 21.

[84] Baxi (n. 63) 228–233.

[85] See n. 76, paras 82ff.

## 3. From Human Needs to Human Capital in the 1980s

### A. Structural Adjustment in the 1980s

The potential alignment between the governance of sovereign debt crises and human rights discourse did not materialize in the subsequent decade, although the start was promising. The IMF's expansion of its lending activities during the 1970s had provoked a reform in 1979 that sought to scale back conditionalities. It reflected a pending dispute between the IMF Executive Board pressing for greater respect for self-determination, and the staff concerned about the economic success of its countries, which it increasingly saw best safeguarded by the neoliberal policy mix of liberalization and structural reform.[86] While the IMF had always inclined towards austerity,[87] the structural element of its conditionality that aimed at institutional reform constituted a novelty as genuine as it was controversial. Hence, the conditionality decision of 1979 required the Fund in rather broad terms to 'pay due regard to the domestic social and political objectives, the economic priorities, and the circumstances of members, including the causes of their balance of payment problems'.[88] The new guidelines restricted the use of performance criteria to the macroeconomic variables and to the extent necessary for evaluating the progress of the programme.[89]

The bulging debt crisis in the developing world, beginning with Mexico's default in 1982, quickly turned the discourse on austerity in the reverse direction and led to a steady increase in performance criteria, imposing tougher austerity on debtor states.[90] One could argue that this revival of austerity was unwarranted and counterproductive, given that the debt crisis resulted chiefly from major global developments like rising interest rates in the United States and falling commodity prices as developed countries made the transition from industrial to service economies. The debtor states were therefore not the only ones to blame for the crisis. However, the massive expansion of the IMF's lending activities created funding constraints on the part of the IMF that prompted it to impose tighter austerity to ensure timely repayment. In response to the crisis, the IMF opened two concessional lending windows, the Structural Adjustment Facility and the Enhanced Structural Adjustment Facility in 1986 and 1987, respectively.[91]

Another reason for the spread of austerity was ideological. The Baker Plan adopted in 1985 advocated the creed that debtor states should outgrow their debt

[86] Denters (n. 25) 141; on the IMF's neoliberal shift, Kentikelenis and Babb, 'The Making of Neoliberal Globalization: Norm Substitution and the Politics of Clandestine Institutional Change', 124 *American Journal of Sociology* (2019) 1720, at 1733.

[87] See n. 23 and accompanying text.

[88] IMF Decision No. 6056-(79/38), 2 March 1979, para. 4.

[89] IMF Decision No. 6056-(79/38), 2 March 1979, paras 1 and 9; Denters (n. 25) 96.

[90] J. P. Joyce, *The IMF and Global Financial Crises. Phoenix Rising?* (2013) 105ff.

[91] Dreher and Vaubel (n. 21) 37; Boughton (n. 27) 644ff.

crises in a grit-your-teeth-and-get-to-it mode. Harsh, shock-like adjustment and radical market orientation would ensure that growth would kick in soon and trickle down the echelons of the social hierarchy.[92] Baker's plan succeeded thanks to a supportive coalition comprising the governments of developed countries, international banks, and senior staff at the IMF.[93] This rendered resistance from the Global South futile.[94] Legally speaking, the guidelines on conditionality left the IMF enough interpretative leeway for such a profound reversal of the 1979 reform, not least because the distinction between macroeconomic and microeconomic criteria is all but clear-cut since many measures cause both macro and micro effects.[95]

As a result, the management of debt crises became a much more tightly regulated, internationally coordinated endeavour involving significant levels of austerity, i.e. contractionary fiscal policies.[96] Not only did the number of conditionalities increase, but their quality changed, too. Of particular significance was the introduction of structural benchmarks.[97] They require structural reforms, such as an overhaul of public financial management, aiming at long-term effects. This makes them highly intrusive from the point of view of sovereignty, but the hope was that such policies would send a powerful signal to creditors and restore that country's creditworthiness.[98] The cost of this new brand of structural adjustment came in the form of its huge impact on ESC rights, effectuated mainly through the cutting back of subsidies and public services and their simultaneous liberalization and privatization.

## B. A Crucial Shift

Against the background of the debates during the 1970s, one might have expected a human rights critique to come forward against increasingly severe levels of austerity. But it came otherwise. The most powerful critique, the one to which the IMF as the organization in charge of approving adjustment programmes finally reacted, was advanced by other international organizations in the language of (basic) human needs. The activities of the World Bank and UNICEF were instrumental in this regard.[99] UNICEF is a particularly interesting case. It was probably among the first organizations to notice the effects of the new forms of austerity on

[92] Boughton (n. 27) 417; Klein (n. 7) 155ff.
[93] See the meticulous reconstruction in Kentikelenis and Babb (n. 86).
[94] Reinhart and Rogoff (n. 1) 91–92; Pahuja (n. 17) 782ff.
[95] Denters (n. 25) 111.
[96] Cf. Blyth (n. 24) 161ff.
[97] Dreher and Vaubel (n. 21) 32; Boughton (n. 27) 417.
[98] Streeck, 'The Rise of the European Consolidation State', MPIfG Discussion Paper No. 15/1 (2015) 12.
[99] While reports by those involved on the side of UNICEF might overstate their role, the official IMF historian recognizes such external influences, see Boughton (n. 27) 694–695.

rising rates of malnutrition in children and the disproportionate impact of those rates on the situation of women and other groups with vulnerabilities.[100] A 1983 report recommended a mix of different measures. Some of them aimed at better ensuring the most basic needs by proposing simple strategies for using scarce resources more efficiently, which would be compatible with sufficientarian approaches.[101] Other proposed measures pursued more ambitious goals connected to the structural problems of the global economic order, including problems of female education, income inequality, and the divide between the North and the South.[102] The seminal 1987 UNICEF report 'Adjustment with a Human Face' featured a similar mix of sufficiency and equality. Like previous UNICEF reports, it avoids the term 'human rights' but, in substance, it was all about them.[103] The report begins with Tanzanian President Nyerere asking his now-famous rhetorical question: 'Must we starve our children to pay our debts?'[104] The report then recommends expanding the focus of adjustment from radical short-termism to medium-term recovery, requiring larger financial volumes and debt relief. While it recognizes the need to shield the vulnerable, it also considers measures that go beyond sufficiency, such as the idea of 'expansionary adjustment' to avoid deflation, or improving the income of the poorest parts of society to enable them to provide for themselves. One could therefore say that it combines a desire for greater efficiency to ensure minimal standards with awareness of the need for greater overall redistribution.

The IMF response to these proposals was at first brisk.[105] In contrast to the World Bank, the IMF had not at the time internalized the basic (human) needs approach. It still understood itself to be an organization with a macroeconomic mandate, not one of development economics. From its point of view, whether adjustment was the cause of the troubles or the cure was still an open question. In fact, it had studied the distributive impact of adjustment since the 1970s, and its research had not established whether adjustment worsened the distributive effects of a debt crisis compared to a scenario without an adjustment programme.[106] Subsequently, however, UNICEF and the Bretton Woods institutions entered into a policy dialogue on the matter at the request of the latter.[107]

[100] M. Black, *Children First. The Story of UNICEF, Past and Present* (1996) 158.

[101] UNICEF, *The State of the World's Children 1984* (1983) 5ff.

[102] Ibid. 23, 57ff, 67.

[103] UNICEF, *Adjustment with a Human Face*, published as part II of UNICEF, *The State of the World's Children 1987* (1986). In 1977, UNICEF adopted a policy on basic services that sounds minimalistic, see Alston (n. 83) 24. Nevertheless, by virtue of its different subject, this policy view did not address labour market issues and income distribution.

[104] UNICEF (n. 103) 95.

[105] See the account in Jolly, 'Adjustment with a Human Face: A UNICEF Record and Perspective on the 1980s', 19 *World Development* (1991) 1807.

[106] Ibid. 1811; Boughton (n. 27) 696.

[107] 'Report of the Executive Director', UNICEF Executive Board, E/ICEF/1987/2, 24 February 1987; Black (n. 100) 158.

This policy dialogue generated a remarkable result. The IMF Managing Director Jacques de Larosière in a much-noted, frequently quoted speech recognized the urgency of ensuring basic human needs on the one hand, but gave this notion a particular spin on the other hand. The relevant passage deserves to be quoted in full:[108]

> Programmes of adjustment cannot be effective unless they command the support of governments and of public opinion. Yet this support will be progressively harder to maintain the longer adjustment continues without some pay-off in terms of growth and while human conditions are deteriorating. Likewise, it is hard to visualize how a viable external position can be achieved if large segments of the work force lack the vocational skills—or even worse, the basic nutritional and health standards—to produce goods that are competitive in world markets. Human capital is after all the most important factor of production in developing and industrial countries alike.

Within one paragraph, de Larosière switched from human conditions (which one might consider as equivalent to human needs) to human capital. On the way, the structural orientation and egalitarian component once associated with the basic (human) needs approach as introduced by UNICEF got lost and basic (human) needs became a lever to push through market liberalization, as the speech further elaborates.[109] Hence, while income inequality goes unmentioned, the speech cultivates the image of the wasteful state. The recognition that cuts in investments can be detrimental provides little comfort as it is unclear whether it refers to private or public investments. In other words, this speech, given a few months after the

[108] Remarks of de Larosière before the UN Economic and Social Council, 4 July 1986, quoted in Jolly (n. 105) 1816. De Larosière continued as follows:

> But the fact that adjustment need not conflict with growth and protection of basic human needs does not mean either that the latter automatically result from the former. No. The extent to which adjustment is compatible with growth and with an improvement in living standards depends in large part on what form that adjustment takes. Adjustment that takes the form of increases in exports, savings, investments and economic efficiency will clearly be more supportive of growth than that which relies on cuts in investment and in imports. Similarly, adjustment that pays attention to the health, nutritional and educational requirements of the most vulnerable groups is going to protect the human condition better than adjustment that ignores them.
>
> This means, in turn, that the authorities will have to be concerned not only with *if* they close the fiscal deficit but also with *how* they do so. For example, safeguarding human needs may imply that employment in overstaffed and loss-making public enterprises or defense spending be reduced in preference to cutting an accelerated immunization and health care programme for children. Similarly, safeguarding human needs may imply that credit flows be managed so that small-scale producers are not crowded out by large enterprises and the public sector.
>
> The forms of adjustment that are most conducive to growth and to protection of human needs will not emerge by accident. They have to be encouraged by an appropriate set of incentives and policies. They will also require political courage.

[109] Ibid.

launch of the Baker Plan and the Structural Adjustment Facility, aligns the basic (human) needs approach with what was later called the Washington Consensus.[110] The shift was subtle but clear. The concept of basic (human) needs, which might have become a placeholder for an egalitarian idea of human rights, was bent in the direction of minimum requirements and bereft of its more egalitarian potential. The economic prevailed over the social.

This conceptual shift was paradigmatic for the austerity debates in the 1980s. It saw the near-complete abandonment of the structuralist paradigm of human rights familiar from the austerity debates in the 1970s. The void was not immediately filled by another human rights discourse or paradigm.

To explain the absence of the voice of human rights in the choir criticizing austerity, it is helpful to take into consideration the wider context within which these debates took place. For a number of reasons, it was not an obvious or even attractive choice for UNICEF or other actors to frame their scepticism of the new wave of austerity in the language of human rights.

To begin with, there is little evidence that the missing human rights-based critique of austerity resulted from the much-described rediscovery of human rights in the West towards the end of the 1970s in the context of the decline of the Soviet Union, the rise of neoliberalism, and terrorist threats, and the related rise of a new, old liberal paradigm of human rights as primarily individual, negative entitlements.[111] While I do not have reason to doubt the accounts of the rise of that paradigm, it seems unlikely that it would have motivated UNICEF to refrain from a human rights critique of austerity in the mid-1980s. At that point in time, the shift towards a liberal paradigm of human rights was still ongoing, and alternative understandings of human rights actually found quite some resonance in international organizations. The United Nations was in the midst of the emergence of a third generation of human rights.[112] One important outcome of this process was the previously mentioned right to development, endorsed in 1986.[113] UNICEF, for that matter, actively participated during those years in the drafting of the Convention on the Rights of the Child, an agreement bristling with second- and third-generation human rights reaching at least prima facie far beyond sufficiency.[114]

[110] Williamson, 'Democracy and the "Washington Consensus"', 21 *World Development* (1993) 1329.

[111] Eckel (n. 64) 343ff; Moyn (n. 2) 120ff; Moyn (n. 11) 70ff; on the neoliberal turn in human rights law, see U. Baxi, *The Future of Human Rights* (2007); Chimni, 'International Institutions Today: An Imperial Global State in the Making', 15 *European Journal of International Law* (2004) 1, at 11.

[112] Alston, 'A Third Generation of Solidarity Rights: Progressive Development or Obfuscation of International Human Rights Law?', 29 *Netherlands International Law Review* (1982) 307; Slaughter (n. 36) 753.

[113] UN General Assembly, Declaration on the Right to Development, UN Doc. A/Res/41/128, 4 December 1986.

[114] Documentation in OCHCHR, *Legislative History on the Convention on the Rights of the Child*, 2 vols (2007), https://resourcecentre.savethechildren.net/library/legislative-history-convention-rights-child-volume-1 (last visited 18 November 2023).

A different reason seems more plausible. There was simply no established practice of criticizing the operations of international organizations on the basis of their human rights record. In fact, international human rights emerged in the postwar period as protection against nation states and their governments, not against international organizations. In the 1960s, liberation movements invoked human rights to claim sovereign equality from other states, not from international organizations. As I have shown, the NIEO and the basic needs approaches understood international organizations as instruments for the promotion and realization of human rights. While it is one thing to debate how the IFIs should promote human rights, it is quite a different matter to claim that their operations threaten human rights. On the whole, the idea of international organizations as threats to human rights did not impose itself in the same way as it does today. This might reflect the legacy of functionalism, the mid-twentieth-century theory which had depicted international organizations as agents of peace through rational bureaucracy.[115] Imagining IMF-imposed austerity as a human rights problem might, therefore, seem much more obvious to us than it appeared to UNICEF and its contemporaries at the time. It may have helped that the IMF's mandate, as the official doctrine claimed, did not extend to 'non-economic' considerations.[116] The limits of the mandate were the bone of contention regarding structural performance criteria,[117] and adding human rights to the equation would have potentially undermined the position of those desiring a more restrictive exercise of the mandate. In any case, the IMF could react much better to economic rather than non-economic arguments.[118]

It is presumably for these reasons that there are very few scholarly critiques of austerity from a human rights perspective before the end of the 1980s.[119] Instead of

[115] Cf. Mitrany, 'The Functional Approach to World Organization', 24 *International Affairs* (1948) 350. On the emergence of the functionalist paradigm, see Klabbers, 'The Emergence of Functionalism in International Institutional Law: Colonial Inspirations', 25 *European Journal of International Law* (2014) 645; G. F. Sinclair, *To Reform the World: International Organizations and the Making of Modern States* (2017) 166ff. On the enduring legacy of functionalism, see Steffek, 'Max Weber, Modernity and the Project of International Organization', 29 *Cambridge Review of International Affairs* (2016) 1502.

[116] Gold (n. 32) 61. Hence, a Congressional Committee assumed in 1978 without further ado that membership rights could not be restricted by human rights, ibid. 62; F. Gianviti, *Economic, Social, and Cultural Human Rights and the International Monetary Fund* (2001). On the functionalist pedigree of this view: M. Darrow, *Between Light and Shadow: The World Bank, the International Monetary Fund and International Human Rights Law* (2003) 205–206. For an early deconstruction of this doctrine: Swedberg, 'The Doctrine of Economic Neutrality of the IMF and the World Bank', 23 *Journal of Peace Research* (1986) 377.

[117] Gold (n. 32) 66 on the overlap between economics and politics and the ensuing desire of the Board to restrict performance criteria to macroeconomic indicators.

[118] Gold, 'Financial Assistance by the International Monetary Fund: Law and Practice', IMF Pamphlet Series No. 27 (1979) 14–15; Boisson de Chazournes, 'The Bretton Woods Institutions and Human Rights', in W. Benedek, K. de Feyter, and F. Marrella (eds), *Economic Globalisation and Human Rights* (2007) 210, at 214.

[119] A rare example is Conklin and Davidson, 'The IMF and Economic and Social Human Rights: A Case Study of Argentina, 1958–1985', 8 *Human Rights Quarterly* (1986) 227. See also Mittelman and Donald, 'The International Monetary Fund, State Autonomy and Human Rights', 34 *Africa Today*

invoking human rights, scholars and international organizations exchanged economic arguments, debating the most desirable and efficient path to growth and development.[120] Paradigmatic is a conference convened by the ILO in 1987 bringing together many relevant stakeholders. Participants agreed on the devastating effects of the recent debt crises on employment and human conditions, but no one formulated their critique of austerity in terms of human rights. Instead, UNCTAD and a number of developing states like Tanzania recalled the NIEO framework when demanding more resources and better distribution, both within and between countries,[121] whereas the IMF and Western countries insisted on structural adjustment through liberalization as a path to growth. The conclusions of the conference combined a plea for basic needs with somewhat general concessions regarding procedures, stressing the need for a broad consensus on adjustment programmes in the debtor states.[122] Regional initiatives that had voiced analogous critiques experienced a similar fate, refuting the encroachment of neoliberal adjustment policies and proposing more heterodox approaches. With the Consenso de Cartagena, heavily affected Latin American countries called for additional funding and debt relief,[123] to which the capital-exporting countries responded with the Baker Plan. The UN Economic Commission for Africa's 1989 proposal for an African alternative adjustment framework made the case for a more holistic, long-term approach to adjustment that would allow the economies of the region to increase production and diversify, but was shrugged off by the IMF.[124]

The governments of crisis-ridden debtor states were often compromised with respect to human rights as their policies, including the implementation of austerity, quite often amounted to flagrant human rights violations.[125] The case of Chile in the 1970s had illustrated the potential impact of human rights campaigns on global public opinion.[126] Conversely, the political opposition developed an interest in presenting themselves as the better debtors, both before and after

(1987) 49 (focusing, however, on violations of civil and political rights committed by governments of debtor states forcing adjustment programmes upon their people).

120 ILO, High Level Meeting on Employment and Structural Adjustment, 23–25 November 1987, ILO Doc. WEP 2-46-04-03.

121 Ibid. para. 18

122 Ibid. 28 (para. 1) and 30 (para. 16); see Ngugi, 'Policing Neo-Liberal Reforms: The Rule of Law as an Enabling and Restrictive Discourse', 26 *University of Pennsylvania Journal of International Economic Law* (2005) 513, at 570.

123 'Consenso De Cartagena', 52 *El Trimestre Económico* (1985) 267; see also O'Connell, 'La coordinacion de los deudores Latinoamericanos: El consenso de Cartagena y el Grupo de los Ochos', 21 *Estudios Internacionales* (1988) 373.

124 United Nations Economic Commission for Africa, *African Alternative Framework to Structural Adjustment Programmes for Socio-Economic Recovery and Transformation* (1989); the ensuing common statement with the IMF reflects more disagreement than consensus, see Jolly (n. 105) 1817.

125 Abouharb and Cingranelli, 'IMF Programmes and Human Rights, 1981–2003', 4 *Review of International Organizations* (2008) 47.

126 Eckel (n. 64) 583ff; see also H. A. Bartilow, *The Debt Dilemma: IMF Negotiations in Jamaica, Grenada and Guyana* (1997); Jolly (n. 101) 1816.

ascending to power.[127] Calls for cancelling debt on the basis of its odious character only re-emerged with full force towards the end of the century.[128]

In the end, there was practically no one who could have been expected to invoke human rights during that period. The conflict about austerity in the 1980s happened to be framed as a dispute over competing economic approaches, and the powerful actors favoured the neoliberal response. Both the power of the purse deployed by the Baker Plan and the fact that the structural approach advocated by postwar Latin American development economists had foundered precisely with this crisis contributed to the ultimate success of their strategy.[129] The political left in Latin America and elsewhere found it difficult to formulate an alternative response to the growing neoliberal maelstrom.[130] Further difficulty arose from the fact that the debtor states did not agree on economic policies, with some of them even committing to austerity. It was certainly with the utmost delight that the Baker Plan quoted the Mexican president, saying: 'The only way to overcome our economic crisis is to tackle at their root the structural problems of our economy to make it more efficient and productive.'[131] Such views added pressure on countries like Ghana, Zambia, or Tanzania desiring in word or deed a different economic policy.[132]

[127] Cf. Bartilow (n. 126) 139.

[128] Klein (n. 7) 156ff reports an odious debt debate in Latin American states overcoming autocracies. However, apart from a few occasional mentions, there is relatively little evidence for an odious debt debate in civil society and academia before the mid-1990s. Exceptions include Frankenberg and Knieper, 'Legal Problems of the Overindebtedness of Developing Countries: The Current Relevance of the Doctrine of Odious Debts', 12 *International Journal of the Sociology of Law* (1984) 415. Discussions related to odious debt in the 1980s and early 1990s predominantly refer to old cases, such as Chinese bonds from 1911, e.g. Lewin, 'Legal Claims against China', *The New York Times*, 29 November 1983, Section D, p. 2. Only the use of the concept in the South African Truth and Reconciliation Commission's 1998 report and the debt relief granted to Iraq after the 2003 war triggered a rich debate on the odious character of dictatorship debts. See South African Truth and Reconciliation Commission, *Final Report*, vol. 4 (1998) para. 151; Buchheit, Gulati, and Thompson, 'The Dilemma of Odious Debts', 56 *Duke Law Journal* (2006) 1201, at 1220 (on past debates), 1230 (on Iraq). The debate critically revisited debt incurred by Argentina's military dictatorship, e.g. D. Harvey, *The New Imperialism* (2003) 159–160; E. Toussaint, *Your Money or Your Life!* (2003) 200ff; Michalowski, 'Repayment of Sovereign Debts from a Legal Perspective: The Example of Argentina', in J. Dine and A. Fagan (eds), *Human Rights and Capitalism: A Multidisciplinary Perspective on Globalisation* (2006) 303, at 303, 309. For a more cautious assessment, see Gelpern, 'What Iraq and Argentina Might Learn from Each Other', 6 *Chicago Journal of International Law* (2005) 391. The debate continues. On Chile, see J. P. Bohoslavsky, K. Fernández, and E. Lira (eds), *Complicidad económica con la dictadura Chilena. Un país desigual a la fuerza* (2019).

[129] Blyth (n. 24) 161; P. Franko, *The Puzzle of Latin American Economic Development* (2018) 70.

[130] Jolly (n. 105) 1817; Carr, 'The Mexican Left, the Popular Movements, and the Politics of Austerity 1982–1985', in B. Carr and R. Anzaldúa Montoya (eds), *The Mexican Left, the Popular Movements, and the Politics of Austerity* (1986) 1; Moyn (n. 11) 128ff.

[131] The Baker Plan is reproduced in D. C. Dicke (ed.), *Foreign Debts in the Present and a New International Economic Order* (1986) 290, at 294.

[132] On heterodox persistence, see Jolly (n. 105) 1817; on Ghana and Zambia, see further Baloro, 'African Responses to the Debt Crisis: The Relevance of Public International Law', 24 *Verfassung und Recht in Übersee/Law and Politics in Africa, Asia and Latin America* (1991) 28.

Unsurprisingly, one of the consequences of this debt crisis was the sidelining of UNCTAD as a relevant forum for debt issues, at least compared to its position during the 1970s. While it continued to monitor the debt situation, the momentum created by its earlier resolutions evaporated, and decisive impulses came from Western governments and the IFIs.

In conclusion, one might take from the development during the 1980s the insight that it is one thing to call for changes to the existing economic order in the name of human rights, but quite a different thing to operationalize human rights for a critique of adjustment programmes. Transiting from one paradigm to another requires a considerable shift in the function of human rights. The former view relies on state sovereignty; the latter view presupposes defining the role of human rights in global governance. The whole perspective on human rights had to shift, and for this to happen, there needed to be an actor possessing both the imagination and the situatedness to live up to the challenge. Absent this, human rights discourse did next to nothing to prevent the economic from prevailing over the social in austerity debates during the 1980s. It was simply unprepared for neoliberal globalization.

## 4. From Human Rights to Poverty Reduction in the 1990s and 2000s

### A. Debt Crises and Financialization after 1989

The Baker Plan of growing out of debt soon revealed its limits. Banks quickly restructured their portfolios and reduced their exposure so that they had less incentive to participate in yet another restructuring when growth kicked in more slowly than expected.[133] At the same time, the end of the Cold War ushered in a new period. It fundamentally altered the prospects for development as competition over the support of governments in the Global South in the form of development aid withered away and the former communist states suspended much of their official development aid.[134] This led to a profound revolution in the administration of debt relief that set in motion a number of initiatives and reforms over the subsequent years. They derived from the interest of capital-exporting countries in defining a new stability framework for the Global South to facilitate trade and minimize financial and economic risks. The Global South paid by exposing large parts of its domestic policies to international control. Hence, sovereign debt restructurings

[133] Boughton (n. 27) 478.

[134] Asmus, Fuchs, and Müller, 'Russia's Foreign Aid Re-Emerges', *AidData Blog*, 9 April 2018, https://www.aiddata.org/blog/russias-foreign-aid-re-emerges (last visited 18 November 2023).

were refocused on debt sustainability instead of debt repayment.[135] At the same time, conditionalities went through the roof. They pushed for market liberalization in debtor states, which came at higher sovereignty costs.[136]

One of the components of the new sustainability framework was debt relief. The Toronto terms, adopted by the Paris Club in October 1988, foresaw for the first time the partial cancellation of debt for the least developed countries. Subsequent terms were even more lenient. In 1989, the Brady Plan replaced the Baker Plan. Cooked up by the US government, it offered not only the good offices but also the financial guarantees of the G7 members and the IFIs to allow creditors to securitize suffering loans and sell them off as bonds to private investors.[137] Subsequently, the IMF modified its access policies to allow for lending to states with arrears to their private creditors.[138] Financialization and privatization, the principles governing the Brady Plan, were not accidental choices. Rather, they emerged from the contemporaneous efforts of fiscal consolidation in industrialized countries which imposed heavy austerity on their welfare states and compensated with private finance for the withdrawal of the state.[139]

In effect, however, the (re-)emergence of bonded debt only increased the pressure on debtor states, which now became much more difficult to handle due to the dispersed nature of their private creditors.[140] It made restructuring a lot more difficult, catalysing a large amount of thinking about facilitating efficient debt restructuring.[141]

Another important change occurred in the mid-1990s with the introduction of the Heavily Indebted Poor Countries Initiative (HIPC Initiative). Under this framework and the subsequent Multilateral Debt Relief Initiative, the poorest developing countries have received substantial debt relief from Paris Club members and private creditors.[142] The relief did come at a price—it required debtor states to

[135] Bohoslavsky and Goldmann, 'An Incremental Approach to Sovereign Debt Restructuring: Sovereign Debt Sustainability as a Principle of Public International Law', 42 *Yale Journal of International Law Online* (2016) 13.

[136] Polak, 'The Changing Nature of IMF Conditionality', 184 *Essays in International Finance* (1991) 63–64.

[137] Boughton (n. 27) 492ff (emphasizing at 492 the intention to avoid a public bailout of private money); Vásquez, 'The Brady Plan and Market-Based Solutions to Debt Crisis', 16 *Cato Journal* (1996) 233; Monteagudo, 'The Debt Problem: The Baker Plan and the Brady Initiative: A Latin American Perspective', 28 *The International Lawyer* (1994) 59.

[138] Boughton (n. 27) 277.

[139] Streeck (n. 6) 117ff.

[140] Gelpern, 'Sovereign Debt. Now What?', 42 *Yale Journal of International Law Online* (2016) 45, at 49.

[141] Buchheit and Gulati, 'Sovereign Bonds and the Collective Will', 51 *Emory Law Journal* (2002) 1317; Gelpern, 'Building a Better Seating Chart for Sovereign Restructurings', 53 *Emory Law Journal* (2006) 1119; Paulus, 'A Statutory Procedure for Restructuring Debts of Sovereign States', 49 *Recht der internationalen Wirtschaft* (2003) 401; Raffer, 'Sovereign Debt Workout Arrangements', in J. Weaver, D. Jacobs, and J. Baker (eds), *After Neoliberalism—Economic Policies That Work for the Poor* (2002) 88.

[142] L. F. Guder, *The Administration of Debt Relief by the International Financial Institutions* (2009); Institute for International Economics, 'The HIPC Initiative: Background and Critiques', https://piie.com/publications/chapters_preview/337/2iie3314.pdf (last visited 18 November 2023).

adopt poverty-reduction strategies that contained notable additions to standard IMF policy conditionalities. While the focus on poverty suggests a social orientation,[143] the HIPC Initiative in fact made debt relief dependent on economic, not on social, performance. The more successful a country was in generating growth and exports, the less debt relief it received.[144]

Outside the HIPC Initiative, structural adjustment programmes continued as before. By the time of the adoption of new Guidelines on Conditionality in 2002, conditionalities regularly included not only a set of macroeconomic benchmarks but also more and more structural performance criteria, defined either as requisite policy outcomes or as specific actions to be undertaken by the debtor state.[145] Structural adjustment policies touched upon sensitive issues of domestic policy, including law reform, the fight against corruption and money laundering, the reduction of subsidies, privatization and market liberalization of public services,[146] and even military expenditure.[147] Conditionalities ultimately became so intrusive and detailed that they gave rise to concerns about debtor states delaying necessary requests for assistance to avoid them.[148] The 2002 reform intended to streamline conditionalities, improving their focus and clarity and reducing the number,[149] but practical effects remained marginal.[150]

The impact of structural adjustment on human rights was enormous.[151] Countries may have benefited from debt relief, but not enough to make up for an increasingly crippling infrastructure that threatened growth and became more and more of a destabilizing factor. Perhaps the all-time low point was reached in Rwanda prior to 1994. A victim of the debt crisis raging in the Global South since the 1980s, Rwanda imposed severe austerity measures upon its population to get access to much-needed multilateral lending. These measures, which earned the Habyarimana regime praise from the IMF, hit the country heavily. Production stagnated, not least due to a lack of investment, while its population continued to grow, becoming increasingly impoverished. This development further undermined the

[143] Cf. UNCTAD, Least Developed Countries Report (2000) 141.

[144] Ibid. 146.

[145] IMF Guidelines on Conditionality, 25 September 2002.

[146] For a discussion of salient issues, see B. Bull, A. M. Jerfe, and E. Sigvaldsen, 'The World Bank's and the IMF's Use of Conditionality to Encourage Privatization and Liberalization: Current Issues and Practices. Report Prepared for the Norwegian Ministry of Foreign Affairs as a Background for the Oslo Conditionality Conference', SUM Report No. 13 (2006) https://www.duo.uio.no/bitstream/handle/10852/32692/Bull.pdf (last visited 18 November 2023).

[147] Polak (n. 136) 53.

[148] See the remarkable collection of quotes on this issue in M. Goldstein, 'IMF Structural Conditionality: How Much Is Too Much?', Revision of paper presented at NBER Conference on Economic and Financial Crises in Emerging Market Economies (2000) 1, at 1–3.

[149] IMF, 'Review of the 2002 Conditionality Guidelines', IMF Policy Paper, 3 March 2005, 6.

[150] Kentikelenis, Stubbs, and King, 'IMF Conditionality and Development Policy Space, 1985–2014', 23 *Review of International Political Economy* (2016) 543.

[151] There is a wealth of information on these effects. For an overview, see Stubbs and Kentikelenis, 'Conditionality and Sovereign Debt: An Overview of Human Rights Implications', in I. Bantekas and C. Lumina (eds), *Sovereign Debt and Human Rights* (2018) 359.

legitimacy of Rwanda's long-time ruler Habyarimana. The government therefore diverted funds received as loans from multilateral institutions to arms purchases and the creation of a militia.[152] The rest is history.

Despite such catastrophes, the idea of an institutional framework for debt restructuring faltered after a brief renaissance in the wake of the Asian crisis when the United States withdrew its support for Anne Krueger's proposal for an International Debt Restructuring Mechanism in 2003,[153] favouring market-based collective action clauses instead.[154] For the coming decade, free market forces would reign supreme, setting in motion a wave of sovereign debt litigation.[155]

## B. Liberal vs Transformative: Two Competing Human Rights Paradigms

This time, the catastrophic impact of austerity has triggered a human rights-based critique in civil society[156] and academic discourse,[157] at least since the mid-1990s. This wave of thinking about austerity as a human rights problem resulted from new human rights paradigms emerging at the time, which I seek to disentangle from other competing understandings.

One of these paradigms is the liberal paradigm, the one behind the much-described ascent of human rights as the 'last utopia' in Western societies at a time when the emerging victory of capitalism over communism suggested an end to century-old ideological controversies. The human rights-based backlash against the Pinochet regime, the Helsinki process, the emerging opposition in Central and Eastern Europe, the threat of terrorism, and the rise of Amnesty International are important pieces of this mosaic.[158] In the 1990s and the subsequent decade, this

[152] Cf. Chossudovsky and Galand, 'The 1994 Rwandan Genocide—The Use of Rwanda's External Debt (1990–1994). The Responsibility of Donors and Creditors' (2016) http://www.cadtm.org/The-1994-Rwandan-Genocide-The-Use (last visited 18 November 2023).

[153] A. O. Krueger, *A New Approach to Sovereign Debt Restructuring* (2002).

[154] Quarles, 'Herding Cats: Collective-Action Clauses in Sovereign Debt—the Genesis of the Project to Change the Market Practice in 2001 through 2003', 73 *Law and Contemporary Problems* (2010) 29.

[155] Fisch and Gentile, 'Vultures or Vanguards?: The Role of Litigation in Sovereign Debt Restructuring', 53 *Emory Law Journal* (2004) 1043; M. Waibel, *Sovereign Defaults before International Courts and Tribunals* (2011).

[156] E.g. the 1995 Oxfam report set out the severe impact of fiscal contraction and privatization on the right to education: Oxfam, *The Oxfam Poverty Report* (1995) 107.

[157] Skogly, 'Structural Adjustment and Development: Human Rights—an Agenda for Change', 15 *Human Rights Quarterly* (1993) 751; Bradlow, 'The World Bank, the IMF, and Human Rights', 6 *Transnational Law and Contemporary Problems* (1996) 47. For an early voice, see Diáz Müller, 'El Derecho al Desarrollo y los Derechos Humanos', 4 *Revista International de Derechos Humanos* (1986) 5. On the responsibility of the IMF, see S. Skogly, *The Human Rights Obligations of the World Bank and the International Monetary Fund* (2001), where this aspect takes up the largest part of the volume. Further literature is listed in Goldmann, 'Human Rights and Sovereign Debt Workouts', in J. P. Bohoslavsky and J. L. Cernic (eds), *Making Sovereign Financing and Human Rights Work* (2014) 79.

[158] Eckel (n. 64) 343ff; Moyn (n. 2) 120ff; Slaughter (n. 36); Mutua (n. 66).

discourse reached a new level. In theory, human rights were elevated to the rank of global constitutional standards,[159] together with democracy and the rule of law.[160] In practice, the 1990s saw the foundation or expansion of regional human rights courts and international criminal adjudication. Substantively, this new concept of human rights was the perfect match for the unfolding liberal international order. It placed the emphasis on civil and political rights, handing over the concern for the social to the market, seeing in the rules of liberal trade the same values at work as in human rights law.[161] A case in point is the 1990 Paris Charter of the Conference on Security and Co-operation in European (CSCE)/Organization for Security and Co-operation in Europe (OSCE), which stipulates democracy, human rights, and the rule of law as the foundational principles of the new order and places civil and political rights right at the centre of the new European order, while mentioning socio-economic rights only in passing.[162]

It is obvious that from the point of view of the liberal human rights paradigm, a human rights-based critique of austerity would have had a difficult time in emerging. Being interventionist to the bone, it seems difficult to use such an understanding of human rights for anti-interventionist purposes. This paradigm therefore parted ways with the close association between human rights and self-determination pervading much of the postwar era.

But the liberal paradigm of human rights competed with another, transformative one, which aspired to greater social justice, yet in ways markedly different from the old decolonization-era idea of human rights through self-determination. This transformative reading of human rights characterizes the constitutions of the third wave, which arose from democratic transformations chiefly in Central and Eastern Europe and in the Global South. The 1976 Portuguese Constitution arguably provided the first case.[163] Its catalogue of enforceable socio-economic rights makes it unique in the region.[164] The South African and Colombian Constitutions

[159] E.g. Tomuschat, 'Obligations Arising for States Without or Against Their Will', 241 *Recueil des Cours* (1994) 199, at 299, 309; Fassbender, 'The United Nations Charter as Constitution of the International Community', 36 *Columbia Journal of Transnational Law* (1998) 529, at 550; Kadelbach and Kleinlein, 'International Law—a Constitution for Mankind? An Attempt at a Re-Appraisal with an Analysis of Constitutional Principles', 50 *German Yearbook of International Law* (2007) 303. On the differences between this emerging substantive idea of international constitutional law and earlier, formal–institutional understandings of the international constitution, see Goldmann, 'Hopes of Progress: European Integration in the History of International Law', Max Planck Institute for Comparative Public Law & International Law (MPIL) Research Paper No. 26 (2018).

[160] Kumm, 'The Legitimacy of International Law: A Constitutionalist Framework of Analysis', 15 *European Journal of International Law* (2004) 907.

[161] Petersmann, 'The WTO Constitution and Human Rights', 3 *Journal of International Economic Law* (2000) 19; for a contextualization of Petersmann's thinking, see Slobodian (n. 56) 277ff.

[162] CSCE, Charter of Paris for a New Europe (1990), https://www.osce.org/files/f/documents/0/6/39516.pdf (last visited 18 November 2023).

[163] S. P. Huntington, *The Third Wave: Democratization in the Late Twentieth Century* (1993) 3.

[164] Brito Vieira and Carreira da Silva, 'Getting Rights Right: Explaining Social Rights Constitutionalization in Revolutionary Portugal', 11 *International Journal of Constitutional Law* (2013) 898.

popularized this type of constitution after 1990.[165] The transformative ambitions of these post-authoritarian constitutions compare to those of constitutions of the Weimar period, aiming at the break-up of traditional social stratification and the prevention of a relapse to the old regime. However, the means provided to achieve this end by the constitutions from the end of the twentieth century are profoundly different from those foreseen in earlier transformative constitutions. The success of constitutional adjudication in Western democratic states and the realization that parliaments in socially highly fragmented new democracies would be relatively weak, suggested attributing a strong role to the courts, especially constitutional courts, and consigning to them the power to adjudicate ESC rights.[166]

The emergence of the transformative paradigm in domestic constitutions resonated with attempts from human rights groups and scholars, particularly in the Global South, to use human rights for counter-hegemonic purposes,[167] replacing earlier needs-based approaches.[168] One significant example of this trend is the rights-based approach to development. While the right to development as such emerged from the structural view of human rights popular until the 1970s and 1980s, the rights-based approach to development refocused development cooperation on individual entitlements. It constituted a countermovement to the neoliberal paradigm of efficiency.[169] Compared to the former structural paradigm of human rights, it no longer aimed at revolutionizing the world economy by empowering developing countries, but at giving greater weight to social concerns within the existing order by empowering people in developing countries in line with a unified understanding of human rights that rejected categorical differences between different generations of human rights.[170] To align ESC rights with a development agenda, the International Committee for Economic, Social, and Cultural Rights (ICESCR) reconstructed several composite rights such as the

[165] Klare, 'Legal Culture and Transformative Constitutionalism', 14 *South African Journal on Human Rights* (1998) 146; Cepeda-Espinoza, 'Transcript: Social and Economic Rights and the Colombian Constitutional Court', 89 *Texas Law Review* (2010) 1699. For a comprehensive assessment and further case studies, see R. Gargarella, P. Domingo, and T. Roux (eds), *Courts and Social Transformation in New Democracies: An Institutional Voice for the Poor?* (2006).

[166] For a conceptualization of the transformative paradigm, see Gargarella, 'Theories of Democracy, the Judiciary and Social Rights', in R. Gargarella, P. Domingo, and T. Roux (eds), *Courts and Social Transformation in New Democracies* (2006) 13, at 27–29; A. von Bogdandy *et al.* (eds), *Transformative Constitutionalism in Latin America: The Emergence of a New Ius Commune* (2017).

[167] Rajagopal, 'Counter-Hegemonic International Law: Rethinking Human Rights and Development as a Third World Strategy', 27 *Third World Quarterly* (2006) 767, at 772ff.

[168] Miller, 'From "Rights-Based" to "Rights-Framed" Approaches: A Social Constructionist View of Human Rights Practice', 14 *The International Journal of Human Rights* (2010) 915, at 916.

[169] Cornwall and Nyamu-Musembi, 'Putting the "Rights-Based Approach" to Development into Perspective', 25 *Third World Quarterly* (2004) 1415.

[170] For an important milestone that marks the transition from the old, structuralist understanding to the new, individual one: UN Commission on Human Rights, 'The New International Economic Order and the Promotion of Human Rights, Realization of Economic, Social and Cultural Rights', Preliminary report prepared by Mr Danilo Türk, Special Rapporteur, UN Doc. E/CN.4/Sub.2/1989/19, 28 June 1989, paras 12–35.

right to water.[171] The developmental agenda behind the transformative paradigm of human rights brought new bearers of human rights duties into focus, including developed countries[172] and international organizations.[173]

This transformative paradigm opened completely new perspectives for a human rights-based critique of austerity. The United Nations Commission on Human Rights was quick to pick up the ball and articulate its criticism in a series of reports and documents at the dawn of the Cold War.[174] In fact, the 1989 report by Danilo Türk, arguably the first important international manifestation of the renewed interest in ESC rights, identifies structural adjustment as one of two key issues requiring a new approach to ESC rights, the other being poverty eradication,[175] and elaborates on the human rights responsibilities of the IMF.[176] This work later continued in the Human Rights Commission's Open-Ended Working Group on Structural Adjustment Programmes and Economic, Social and Cultural Rights established in 1997.[177] It appointed an independent expert in 2000[178] and intended to draft guidelines on structural adjustment programmes and economic, social, and cultural rights, but no such catalogue saw the light of the day before the great financial crisis.

On the surface, the transformative paradigm left the IFIs unperturbed, flatly denying their responsibility with questionable[179] reference to their supposedly apolitical mandate.[180] In substance, though, the IFIs were by no means immune to the plight of the people affected by austerity. For the IMF, the concern for the social gave rise to a series of policy innovations, some of which reach back to the

[171] ICESCR, General Comment No. 15: The Right to Water (Arts 11 and 12 of the Covenant), UN Doc. E/C.12/2002/11, 20 January 2003.

[172] De Schutter, 'Commentary to the Maastricht Principles on Extraterritorial Obligations of States in the Area of Economic, Social and Cultural Rights', 34 *Human Rights Quarterly* (2012) 1084.

[173] Nelson and Dorsey, 'At the Nexus of Human Rights and Development: New Methods and Strategies of Global NGOs', 31 *World Development* (2003) 2013.

[174] UN Commission on Human Rights, Foreign debt, economic adjustment policies and their effects on the full enjoyment of human rights and, in particular, on the implementation of the Declaration on the Right to Development, Res. 1989/15, 2 March 1989 (this resolution added the topic to the Commission's agenda). Cf. also UN Commission on Human Rights, The New International Economic Order and the Promotion of Human Rights, Draft resolution of the Sub-Commission on Prevention of Discrimination and Protection of Minorities, UN Doc. E/CN.4/Sub.2/1987/L.57, 28 August 1978 (this document marks the transition between the structural paradigm inherited from the NIEO and the new transformative paradigm. While not being specifically about debt, it mentions UNICEF's Adjustment with a Human Face report in para. 2);

[175] Türk (n. 170) paras 52ff. Türk begins by recognizing the connection between poverty and structural adjustment, ibid. para. 52.

[176] Ibid. paras 77ff.

[177] Cf. UN Commission on Human Rights, Report of the open-ended working group on structural adjustment programmes and economic, social and cultural rights on its first session, UN Doc. E/CN.4/1997/20, 10 March 1997.

[178] R. Balakrishnan, J. Heintz, and D. Elson, *Rethinking Economic Policy for Social Justice: The Radical Potential of Human Rights* (2016) 71.

[179] For an alternative reading of the concept of prosperity in the IMF Articles of Agreement, see E. Denters and A. Viterbo, *International Monetary Fund* (2nd ed., 2015) 83 (para. 206).

[180] Cf. Gianviti (n. 116).

preceding decade. These concepts comprise the creation of 'social safety nets' in adjustment policies, the introduction of the 'targeted approach' to social expenditure, the focusing of social policies on poverty alleviation, and the call for local 'ownership' of adjustment programmes to increase acceptance of the aforementioned closely interlinked policies. Beginning in 1989, the IMF encouraged measures to protect vulnerable sections of the population if so desired by the debtor state.[181] This approach was summarized in a comprehensive staff paper prepared for the 1995 World Summit for Social Development.[182] Later in the 1990s, the IMF began advocating social safety nets to dampen the short-term effects of structural adjustment.[183] For example, instead of cutting crucial subsidies instantly, adjustment programmes stipulated their phasing out, or provided for cash compensation for the most disadvantaged parts of society.[184] Apart from safety nets, however, social policy had to worship the primacy of the economic over the social. Hence, the IMF advocated that social expenditure should be targeted. States should only make expenditures where they were most efficient, benefiting recipients most in need.[185] Under this policy, debtor states had to discontinue subsidies for food and fuel, even though they were vital for many poor people, because the subsidies were granted across the board.[186] The targeted approach coincided with a turn to poverty alleviation, a concept reaching back to the World Bank's basic needs approach.[187] It now took a specifically numerical turn with the dollar-a-day formula for defining the upper bound of poverty.[188] Together with the World Bank, the IMF implemented this concept in the frame of the HIPC Initiative. Developing countries had to design Poverty Reduction Strategies to qualify for debt relief.[189] The sequencing of poverty-reduction strategies developed under the initiative put economic integration and growth first and expected poverty alleviation to ensue.[190]

[181] Denters (n. 25) 135–136.

[182] IMF, 'Social Dimensions of the IMF's Policy Dialogue', IMF Pamphlet Series No. 47 (1995) 1.

[183] Ibid. 11–23. Examples include progressive cuts in wages or pensions, which impose a higher burden on those with higher income, or cash payments to vulnerable segments of society to bridge acute crises.

[184] IMF, Review of Social Issues and Policies in IMF-Supported Programmes. Prepared by the Fiscal Affairs and Policy Development and Review Departments, 27 August 1999, 10–12.

[185] Ibid. 13ff.

[186] IMF Independent Evaluation Office, The IMF and Social Protection, 2017 Evaluation Report, 11.

[187] See n. 79 and accompanying text; on the history of the concept, see Finnemore, 'Redefining Development', in F. Cooper and M. Packard (eds), *International Development and the Social Sciences: Essays on the History and Politics of Knowledge* (1997) 203, at 203; Moyn (n. 11) 131.

[188] Konkel, 'The Monetization of Global Poverty: The Concept of Poverty in World Bank History, 1944–90', 9 *Journal of Global History* (2014) 276, at 297.

[189] Development Committee (Joint Ministerial Committee of the Boards of Governors of the Bank and the Fund on the Transfer of Real Resources to Developing Countries), Building Poverty Reduction Strategies in Developing Countries, DC-99/29, 22 September 1999.

[190] Craig and Porter, 'Poverty Reduction Strategy Papers: A New Convergence', 31 *World Development* (2003) 53; Ellis, 'The World Bank. Fighting Poverty—Ideology Versus Accountability', in K. N. Schefer (ed.), *Poverty and the International Economic Legal System: Duties to the World's Poor* (2013) 291, at 291, 295; Tan, 'The Poverty of Amnesia: PRSPs in the Legacy of Structural Adjustment', in D. Stone and C. Wright (eds), *The World Bank and Governance: A Decade of Reform and Reaction* (2007) 147, at 147, 151.

To ensure that debtor states would not revolt, the idea of 'ownership' became pivotal for adjustment programmes.[191] It had little to do with concern for the democratic legitimacy of the debtor state and the primacy of the social. Rather, it primarily served to shift the responsibility for adjustment from the IFIs to the debtor state. In reality, though, ownership has remained more a slogan than a reality. While poverty-reduction strategies have indeed been prepared by the debtor states, rather than by the IMF staff as in the case of other adjustment programmes, the IMF never took the bold step of taking a back seat to allow for flexible schedules, focusing on outcomes instead of prescribing instruments,[192] or scaling back its level of control over adjustment policies.[193]

What is common to these programmatic buzzwords is that they allow consideration of the social only within the four corners of the economic.[194] Social concerns may only matter under the proviso that they would enhance, or at least not compromise, the economic objectives of adjustment programmes. This dogma almost by necessity shifted the IMF's approach to the social towards sufficiency and minimum requirements.[195] States should spend resources where the need was greatest and spending was most efficient. Ownership provided little comfort given that it did not derogate from these requirements and the welfare model engrained in them. Again, the market was expected to fix social rights.[196]

After the turn of the century, this framework was entrenched by the rise of the Millennium Development Goals as the new focus of development policy. Hailed for their output focus and measurability, in the context of structural adjustment, they pale in comparison to more ambitious agendas from past decades. For example, while eradicating poverty and hunger and ensuring primary education are important and worthy objectives, they only require a modicum of equality and entrench sufficiency as the goal of development, consigning more far-reaching plans to oblivion. This minimalistic approach ultimately reached official United Nations endorsement in the financing of the development process. This process was intended to catalyse the resources necessary for implementing the Sustainable Development Goals. The 2002 Monterrey Consensus does not even mention ESC rights enjoyment as a reason for increasing the funds available for

[191] Boughton, 'Who's in Charge? Ownership and Conditionality in IMF-Supported Programs', IMF Working Paper No. 191 (2003).

[192] Khan and Sharma, 'IMF Conditionality and Country Ownership of Programs', IMF Working Paper No. 142 (2001); this was indeed suggested by Boughton (n. 191) 8.

[193] Cf. Eldar, 'Reform of IMF Conditionality: A Proposal for Self-Imposed Conditionality', 8 *Journal of International Economic Law* (2005) 509.

[194] Cf. IMF (n. 183).

[195] Young, 'The Minimum Core of Economic and Social Rights: A Concept in Search of Content', 33 *Yale Journal of International Law* (2008) 113, at 114.

[196] Cf. Fujita, 'The Challenges of Mainstreaming Human Rights in the World Bank', 15 *The International Journal of Human Rights* (2011) 374; Craig and Porter (n. 190); Pender, 'From "Structural Adjustment" to "Comprehensive Development Framework": Conditionality Transformed?', 22 *Third World Quarterly* (2001) 397.

development,[197] and the now-dominant concept of sovereign debt sustainability[198] is a purely economic one that disregards the human condition.[199] It also remains unclear whether necessary investments require private or public funding, not least because the document immediately stresses the importance of the financial sector and of microcredits.[200]

Why did the IFIs refuse to react to the human rights-based criticism of their activities? Why did the liberal paradigm of human rights prevail over the transformative one that made concern for the social a human rights obligation? Realists might argue that it was simply a matter of the superior power of the purse of the IFIs and developed states. While the relevance of this causal chain cannot be denied, factors intrinsic to human rights discourse impeded the materialization of the transformative paradigm.

One of these factors, probably not the least important one, was the fact that the IFIs adopted the liberal human rights paradigm. This became obvious soon after 1990. An important reference point on the way was the Craxi Report. Charged with exploring the causes and consequences of the protracted debt crisis in the developing world, Craxi recommended making debt relief conditional upon greater respect for human rights.[201] This would set the tone for subsequent steps by the IFIs, in particular the World Bank. Unabated by the prohibition of political activities in its Articles of Agreement, the latter ushered in the good governance paradigm with the 1991 World Development Report. This concept suggested that development required strong, representative domestic institutions and respect for the rule of law,[202] including (mostly) for civil and political rights.[203] No comparable importance was assigned to ESC rights. While the Bank soon recognized that its policies contributed to the realization of ESC rights,[204] the so-called Shihata

[197] On the neoliberal underpinnings of the Monterrey Consensus, see Soederberg, 'Recasting Neoliberal Dominance in the Global South? A Critique of the Monterrey Consensus', 30 *Alternatives: Global, Local, Political* (2005) 325.

[198] Bohoslavsky and Goldmann (n. 135).

[199] Monterrey Consensus on Financing for Development, final text of agreements and commitments adopted at the International Conference on Financing for Development, Monterrey, Mexico, 18–22 March 2002 (paras 4, 14, and 47 on debt sustainability).

[200] Ibid. paras 16ff.

[201] UN General Assembly, External Debt and Development, Report of the Personal Representative of the Secretary-General on Debt, the Honourable Bettino Craxi, UN Doc. A/45/380, 8 October 1990, para. 8. In the context of the transformations taking place around 1990, this position enjoyed quite some popularity. See e.g. Bradlow, 'Debt, Development, and Human Rights: Lessons from South Africa', 12 *Michigan Journal of International Law* (1990) 647.

[202] Weiss, 'Governance, Good Governance and Global Governance: Conceptual and Actual Challenges', 21 *Third World Quarterly* (2000) 795, at 801; D. Williams, *The World Bank and Social Transformation in International Politics: Liberalism, Governance and Sovereignty* (2012) 75ff.

[203] Kaufmann, 'Human Rights and Governance: The Empirical Challenge', in P. Alston and M. Robinson (eds), *Human Rights and Development: Towards Mutual Reinforcement* (2004) 352; Lateef, 'Evolution of the World Bank's Thinking on Governance', World Development Report Background Paper No. 3 (2016).

[204] W. Van Genugten, *The World Bank Group, the IMF and Human Rights: A Contextualised Way Forward* (2015) 4 (with many quotes).

formula stipulated that the World Bank could promote human rights only so long as they did not conflict with economic considerations.[205] Beneath this argument resided the well-established primacy of the economic over the social, the rationale that growth would secure ESC rights, and that strengthening the institutions of government while refraining from market interventions would boost growth—the programme of the Washington Consensus.[206] Granted, the World Bank reacted to criticism of its human rights record by establishing the Inspection Panel in 1994, but it is well known that this body may only apply the World Bank's own internal policies.[207] A proposal by General Counsel Roberto Daniño to put human rights first and reverse the focus of the Bank's policies accordingly never found the support of the institution.[208]

It now turned out that the liberal and the transformative paradigms were rather difficult to reconcile in the debates about austerity. This incompatibility, which is one in fact rather than in theory, derives from the dynamics of the debates about austerity. The promotion of (liberal) human rights in the debtor states by the IFIs, exposing the flaws in the human rights record and institutional frameworks of the latter, made the debtor states unlikely to invoke human rights, even in their transformative version, against the IFIs. For why should they invoke those international legal rules they had violated time and again while trying to stay in power, particularly while implementing IFI policies; rules that allowed unwelcomed IFI interference.[209]

This was not merely a theoretical concern, given the outcries among human rights NGOs caused by Pinochet's putsch and the Tiananmen massacre.[210] In fact, the latter created a veritable human rights backlash in Asia.[211] Some governments of the third wave may also have refrained from invoking human rights against the IFIs for fear that they would be held to account for their own austerity measures before their domestic courts—which they could not always prevent.[212] The case

[205] I. F. Shihata, *The World Bank in a Changing World: Selected Essays and Lectures*, vol. 2 (1991) 70ff.

[206] World Bank, *Development and Human Rights: The Role of the World Bank* (1998). The Monterrey Consensus fully succumbed to the liberal human rights paradigm, mentioning human rights only once in connection with good governance. See n. 199, para. 11.

[207] Fox, 'The World Bank Inspection Panel: Lessons from the First Five Years', 6 *Global Governance* (2000) 279.

[208] F. Maupain, *The Future of the International Labour Organization in the Global Economy* (2013) 75. On the congruence of the World Bank's mandate with human rights, see Dañino, 'The Legal Aspects of the World Bank's Work on Human Rights: Some Preliminary Thoughts' in P. Alston and M. Robinson (eds), *Human Rights and Development: Towards Mutual Reinforcement* (2005) 509, at 510.

[209] Ibhawoh, 'Structural Adjustment, Authoritarianism and Human Rights in Africa', 19 *Comparative Studies of South Asia, Africa and the Middle East* (1999) 158.

[210] Sarfaty, 'Why Culture Matters in International Institutions: The Marginality of Human Rights at the World Bank', 103 *American Journal of International Law* (2017) 647, at 655ff.

[211] Goodale, 'The Myth of Universality: The UNESCO "Philosophers' Committee" and the Making of Human Rights', 43 *Law & Social Inquiry* (2018) 596, at 597.

[212] On Colombia, see Landau, 'The Promise of a Minimum Core Approach: The Colombian Model for Judicial Review of Austerity Measures', in A. Nolan (ed.), *Economic and Social Rights after the Global Financial Crisis* (2014) 267, at 267. As the title suggests, the Constitutional Court did, though, stuck to a concept of sufficiency.

of Hungary stands out in this respect, where the Constitutional Court, invoking the rule of law rather than specific social rights, defended a socially transformative idea of the constitution against IMF-sponsored adjustment, much to the criticism of the court's liberal-minded founding president, who would have preferred the court to focus on poverty.[213]

Another factor for the marginalization of the transformative paradigm derived from its relative novelty and the lack of established doctrinal convictions concerning the status and content of ESC rights as enforceable individual entitlements. As has been shown, ESC rights in the postwar era were programmes to be implemented by government planning rather than by adjudication; and the decolonization movement considered them as collective rights to be ensured by newly independent states. This intellectual pedigree yielded few concrete criteria for courts and human rights activists to rely on when criticizing austerity. In fact, the idea of a minimum core content emerged only in this period, and its consolidation absorbed a considerable amount of energy and attention.[214] Even though many authors participating in this debate made it clear that the minimum core content did not exhaust the substance of ESC rights, they provided very few concrete indications of the limits that ESC rights would impose on government discretion. Of course, the new transformative paradigm lacked the structuralist dimension of earlier genealogies of human rights discourse and found it difficult to define an adequate, sufficiently concrete standard of redistribution.[215] The historical situatedness of the transformative paradigm therefore oriented it towards sufficiency, aligning it ultimately with the liberal paradigm and existing IFI policies.

One final factor that deserves elaboration concerns the debate in civil society at the time. Throughout the 1990s, there was a notable disconnect between the transformative and the liberal paradigms in human rights law. It persisted until well into the new century, when classical human rights NGOs joined the bandwagon and endorsed the rights approach to development.[216] Moreover, many NGOs with a focus on sovereign debt issues derived their intellectual framework from causes different from human rights. A 1989 German-language volume entitled 'Against

[213] Sajó, 'Social Rights as Middle-Class Entitlements in Hungary: The Role of the Constitutional Court', in R. Gargarella, P. Domingo, and T. Roux (eds), *Courts and Social Transformation in New Democracies* (2006) 83, at 83 (with case references).

[214] E.g. Alston, 'Out of the Abyss: The Challenges Confronting the New UN Committee on Economic, Social and Cultural Rights', 9 *Human Rights Quarterly* (1987) 332, at 352; Türk (n. 170) paras 30ff. The debate is still ongoing. Arguing for an absolute understanding of minimum core obligations: Tasioulas, 'Minimum Core Obligations: Human Rights in the Here and Now', World Bank Nordic Trust Fund Research Paper No. 23 (2017). For the opposite view, see Eide, 'Economic, Social, and Cultural Rights as Human Rights', in A. Eide, C. Krause, and A. Rosas (eds), *Economic, Social, and Cultural Rights: A Textbook* (2nd ed., 2001) 27.

[215] The capabilities approach is notable, see A. K. Sen, *The Idea of Justice* (2009); Nussbaum, 'Beyond the Social Contract: Capabilities and Global Justice', 32 *Oxford Development Studies* (2004) 3. As a principled approach, its concrete significance for austerity is not, however. always self-evident.

[216] Cornwall and Nyamu-Musembi (n. 169) 1423; Nelson and Dorsey (n. 173) 2013.

IMF and World Bank', bringing together a broad spectrum of critical voices from different parts of civil society, does not mention human rights as a strategy, but advocates a fundamental change in the world economy.[217] The Jubilee Campaign and its partners in various countries—such as Erlassjahr in Germany—is a faith-based NGO motivated by the obligation in chapter 25 of Leviticus to cancel all debts every 49 years.[218] It took inspiration from the South Africa Truth and Reconciliation Commission's referral to the odious debt doctrine.[219] The Comité pour l'abolition des dettes illégitimes (CADTM) has its roots in the anti-globalization movement. Over time, it adopted human rights as a normative reference point, but it never became a human rights NGO in the narrow sense.[220] Afrodad and Eurodad are networks of civil society organizations in the field of development cooperation. These organizations further share the goal of better, more sustainable, and more generous debt restructurings. From this perspective, austerity reveals itself as the consequence of odious debts and insufficient debt relief, not merely of a lack of respect for human rights.

In the end, there was hardly anybody left to advance a transformative idea of human rights for effectively opposing the creeping of austerity and the trend towards sufficiency. It was unclear whether the Gordian knot would ever be broken.

## 5. From Judicial Sobriety to Political Progress after the Financial Crisis

### A. The Constitutionalization of Austerity in Europe

The solution came from an angle that not many may have expected. The European debt crisis following the global financial crisis hit an unprepared Europe. Unlike the United States, European governments had hesitated to give up their monetarist dogmas and allow for greater European solidarity in fiscal matters. One of the reasons why Europe found it difficult to adjust to the changing circumstances, apart from path dependencies and cognitive frames on the part of some of the actors,[221] has to do with the constitutionalization of austerity. Although a global phenomenon,[222] it was particularly prevalent in the European Economic and

[217] R. Falk and A. Klörs (eds), *Gegen IWF und Weltbank. Beiträge vom internationalen Gegenkongress* (1989).

[218] M. Dent and B. Peters, *The Crisis of Poverty and Debt in the Third World* (2019) ch. 2.

[219] See n. 128 and accompanying text.

[220] CADTM, 'About CADTM: Presentation of CADTM International Affiliations', 8 November 2007, http://www.cadtm.org/About-CADTM (last visited 18 November 2023).

[221] M. K. Brunnermeier, H. James, and J.-P. Landau, *The Euro and the Battle of Ideas* (2016).

[222] E.g. on fiscal policy rules, Goldmann, 'On the Comparative Foundations of Principles in International Law: The Move Towards Rules and Transparency in Fiscal Policy as Examples', in C. Espósito, J. P. Bohoslavsky, and Y. Li (eds), *Sovereign Financing and International Law* (2013)

Monetary Union (EMU). In the postwar era, the balance between the social and the economic in European integration had been ambiguous, oscillating between government interventionism and a free market doctrine shining through, for example, in competition law.[223] After a first shift towards economic liberalization in the 1970s,[224] the establishment of EMU tilted the scales in favour of austerity by elevating price stability, fiscal consolidation, the no-bailout rule, and the prohibition of government monetary financing to the level of constitutional rules.[225]

When the no-bailout clause collapsed, austerity became entrenched even more deeply. Not only did the bailout fail to improve the financial situation of over-indebted Member States fast enough and to a satisfactory extent. It tied up any fiscal leeway and exposed their budgets to strict supranational scrutiny.[226] Ironically, the constitutional price for relaxing the no-bailout clause came in the form of stringent ex-post austerity, considered by European and domestic courts as a key ingredient of the new constitutional menu.[227]

Much has been written about the effects of this austerity and its immensely high impact on human rights. The effects on the welfare state of the affected countries reached far beyond the known constraints of the consolidation state.[228] The cuts threatened even the sheer minimum core content of human rights guarantees,[229] not to speak of the increase in inequality.[230] The ensuing destabilization of parliamentary democracy and their party systems has since recalled the Weimar

113, at 113; Biebricher, 'Neoliberalism and Law: The Case of the Constitutional Balanced-Budget Amendment', 17 *German Law Journal* (2016) 835.

[223] C. Joerges and F. Rödl, '"Social Market Economy" as Europe's Social Model?', EUI Working Paper Law No. 8 (2004); J. Bast and F. Rödl (eds), *Wohlfahrtsstaatlichkeit und Soziale Demokratie in der Europäischen Union. Europarecht Beiheft* (2013).

[224] Goldmann, 'The Great Recurrence: Karl Polanyi and the Crises of the European Union', 23 *European Law Journal* (2017) 272, at 277.

[225] Gill, 'European Governance and New Constitutionalism: Economic and Monetary Union and Alternatives to Disciplinary Neoliberalism in Europe', 3 *New Political Economy* (1998) 5; K. Tuori and K. Tuori, *The Eurozone Crisis: A Constitutional Analysis* (2014) 13ff; A. Hinarejos, *Euro Area Crisis in Constitutional Perspective* (2015) ch. 1.

[226] See e.g. the contributions in Bartl and Karavias, 'Austerity and Law in Europe: An Introduction', 44 *Journal of Law and Society* (2017) 1.

[227] CJEU, Case C-370/12, *Thomas Pringle v Ireland* (ECLI:EU:C:2012:756); BVerfG, Case 2 BvR 987/10, Judgment of 7 September 2011 (ECLI:DE:BVerfG:2011:rs20110907.2bvr098710), para. 11.

[228] Carmona, 'Alternatives to Austerity: A Human Rights Framework Foreconomic Recovery', in A. Nolan (ed.), *Economic and Social Rights after the Global Financial Crisis* (2014) 23, at 30ff. See also the report by Nils Muiznieks, Commissioner for Human Rights of the Council of Europe, following his visit to Spain, 3–7 June 2013, CommDH(2013)18, 9 October 2013, paras 9ff; Report of the Independent Expert on the effects of foreign debt and other related international financial obligations of States on the full enjoyment of all human rights, particularly economic, social and cultural rights on his mission to institutions of the European Union, Human Rights Council, 34th Session, 27 February–24 March 2017, UN Doc. A/HRC/34/57/Add.1, 28 December 2016.

[229] Kentikelenis *et al.*, 'Greece's Health Crisis: From Austerity to Denialism', 383 *The Lancet* (2014) 748.

[230] Mitrakos, 'Inequality, Poverty and Social Welfare in Greece: Distributional Effects of Austerity', 22 *Études helléniques/Hellenic Studies* (2014) 65.

period.[231] It took the European institutions years to question their approach and to finally adopt a more flexible slant to austerity,[232] which would also at least pay due regard to minimum standards of social rights.[233]

## B. Litigation Setbacks and Political Progress

### 1. The limits of the transformative paradigm before courts

The effects of this unprecedented wave of austerity almost immediately prompted a human rights debate. This time, human rights were at the centre of the critique.[234] Given the important role assigned to courts under both the liberal and the transformative paradigms, it did not take long for numerous legal disputes to arise before domestic and international courts. The relevant case law has been discussed in detail in the literature.[235] In these assessments, the impression prevails that anti-austerity litigation before domestic courts, the Court of Justice of the European Union (CJEU), and the European Court of Human Rights (ECtHR) has only had limited success. Beyond the idiosyncrasies of each individual case, the structure of sovereign debt governance and human rights discourse created a number of obstacles for the judicial scrutiny of austerity measures.[236]

[231] Haardt and Clark, 'Die Weimarer Reichsverfassung als Moment in der Geschichte', in H. Dreier and C. Waldhoff (eds), *Das Wagnis der Demokratie: Eine Anatomie der Weimarer Reichsverfassung* (2018) 9, at 37.

[232] Cf. Goldmann, 'Article 126 TFEU', in H. Siekmann (ed.), *The European Union. A Commentary on the Legal Foundations* (2021), margin notes 144ff.

[233] European Pillar of Social Rights, proclaimed at the Social Summit for Fair Jobs and Growth, 17 November 2017, https://commission.europa.eu/system/files/2017-11/social-summit-european-pillar-social-rights-booklet_en.pdf (last visited 18 November 2023).

[234] Krajewski, 'Human Rights and Austerity Programmes', in T. Cottier, R. M. Lastra, and C. Tietje (eds), *The Rule of Law in Monetary Affairs: World Trade Forum* (2014) 490, at 490; Fischer-Lescano, 'Troika in der Austerität: Rechtsbindungen der Unionsorgane beim Abschluss von Memoranda of Understanding', 47 *Kritische Justiz* (2014) 2; Christodoulidis, 'Europe's Donors and Its Supplicants: Reflections on the Greek Crisis', in J. van der Walt and J. Ellsworth (eds), *Constitutional Sovereignty and Social Solidarity in Europe* (2014) 241; A. Nolan (ed.), *Economic and Social Rights after the Global Financial Crisis* (2014); Salomon, 'Of Austerity, Human Rights and International Institutions', 21 *European Law Journal* (2015) 521. Sceptical about the crisis as a cause of austerity and hence the validity of the critique: Dowell-Jones, 'The Economics of the Austerity Crisis: Unpicking Some Human Rights Arguments', 15 *Human Rights Law Review* (2015) 193.

[235] Cf. Fabbrini, 'The Euro-Crisis and the Courts: Judicial Review and the Political Process in Comparative Perspective', 32 *Berkeley Journal of International Law* (2014) 65; Ragone, 'Constitutional Effects of the Financial Crisis at European and National Level: A Comparative Overview', 15 *Revista General de Derecho Público Comparado* (2014) 1; Fasone, 'Constitutional Courts Facing the Euro Crisis. Italy, Portugal and Spain in a Comparative Perspective', Max Weber Paper No. 25 (2014); Kilpatrick, 'Constitutions, Social Rights and Sovereign Debt States in Europe: A Challenging New Area of Constitutional Inquiry', in B. de Witte, C. Kilpatrick, and T. Beukers (eds), *Constitutional Change through Euro-Crisis Law* (2017) 279, at 279; C. Kilpatrick and B. De Witte (eds), 'Social Rights in Times of Crisis in the Eurozone: The Role of Fundamental Rights' Challenges', EUI Working Paper Law No. 5 (2014) 1.

[236] Cf. Salomon (n. 234).

The first structural obstacle relates to massive problems with standing.[237] It results from the two-level character of sovereign debt crisis measures. The problem with litigation before domestic courts is that domestic actors are not the real power yielders.[238] Conversely, attacking the Memorandum of Understanding might be pointless as it often sets out austerity measures only in general terms that require concretization and implementation by domestic law.[239] Thus, courts scrutinizing domestic implementing legislation found it difficult to identify human rights violations at the level of EU law.[240] The European Stability Mechanism (ESM) is officially not part of the EU and therefore, according to a controversial view of the CJEU, not directly bound by the fundamental rights applicable to the Union legal order.[241] When this view became untenable in light of burgeoning austerity, the CJEU took a detour and held in the *Ledra* case (ironically started by a creditor, not by a person affected by austerity), the Commission is always bound by the fundamental rights of the Union legal order, including when it participates in the work of the ESM on the basis of the respective treaty.[242] The IMF, however, has remained beyond the reach of human rights accountability mechanisms.

The second obstacle consists of the informality pervading the legal and institutional framework for the governance of sovereign debt crises. For a start, the Paris Club and private creditors' committees lack legal personality, and so does the Eurogroup.[243] Moreover, Memoranda of Understanding and Letters of Intent, the main normative instruments that stipulate austerity measures, are held to be non-binding, whether in the context of the IMF[244] or of the EU.[245] The gaping holes in the jurisdiction of the European Social Committee did not help to improve the situation.[246] So far, the CJEU has refrained from rethinking the notion of 'legal effects', the requirement for reviewing an act in accordance with Article 263(1)(1)

[237] Cf. Wills and Warwick, 'Contesting Austerity: The Potential and Pitfalls of Socioeconomic Rights Discourse', 23 *Indiana Journal of Global Legal Studies* (2016) 629, at 647.

[238] Poulou, 'Financial Assistance Conditionality and Human Rights Protection: What Is the Role of the Eu Charter of Fundamental Rights?', 54 *Common Market Law Review* (2017) 991, at 1024.

[239] Cf. CJEU, Case C-128/12, *Sindicato dos Bancários de Norte v Banco Português de Negócios SA* (ECLI:EU:C:2013:149); Case C-264/12, *Sindicato Nacional dos Profissionais de Seguros e Afins v Fidelidade Mundial* (ECLI:EU:C:2014:2036).

[240] Kilpatrick (n. 235) 314; Violante, 'Constitutional Adjudication as a Forum for Contesting Austerity: The Case of Portugal', in A. Farahat and X. Arzoz (eds), *Contesting Austerity: A Socio-Legal Inquiry* (2021) 173, at 173.

[241] CJEU, Case C-370/12, *Pringle v Ireland* (ECLI:EU:C:2012:756), paras 178–181.

[242] CJEU, Joined Cases C-8/15 P to C-10/15 P, *Ledra Advertising Ltd and Others v Commission and European Central Bank* (ECLI:EU:C:2016:701).

[243] ECJ, Joined Cases C-105/15 P to C-109/15 P, *Konstantinos Mallis and Others v Commission and European Central Bank* (ECLI:EU:C:2016:702).

[244] Gold (n. 21) 19.

[245] Markakis and Dermine, 'Bailouts, the Legal Status of Memoranda of Understanding, and the Scope of Application of the Eu Charter: Florescu', 55 *Common Market Law Review* (2018) 643, at 646.

[246] See Koukoulis-Spiliotopoulos, 'Austerity v Human Rights: Measures Condemned by the European Committee of Social Rights in the Light of EU Law', in J. Luther and L. Mola (eds), *Europe's Social Rights under the 'Turin Process'—Les droits sociaux de l'Europe sous le 'Processus de Turin'* (2016) 29.

of the Treaty on the Functioning of the European Union (TFEU), and to consider every exercise of public authority in whatever form to be in a position to produce at least indirect legal effects.[247]

Further obstacles for anti-austerity litigation derive from the dominant framing of the human rights discourse. As a result of the spread of the liberal human rights paradigm, many legal orders in the Western hemisphere simply lack a strong tradition of ESC rights adjudication. Even to the extent that the transformative paradigm left its mark on domestic constitutions and shaped social rights catalogues, years of international pressure towards liberalization combined with the constitutionalization of austerity at the European level influenced the jurisprudence of domestic constitutional courts and undermined the transformative potential.[248] The continuity between civil and political rights on the one hand, and ESC rights on the other, turned out to work more seamlessly in theory than in practice.[249] As a result, not only were there relatively very few austerity-related cases that revolved around specific social rights, such as the right to health, despite the undeniably heavy consequences of post-crisis austerity upon their enjoyment. Even to the extent that courts reviewed the impact of austerity on specific social rights, they tended to focus on minimum entitlements,[250] giving clear preference to sufficiency over equality.

A fourth, structural reason concerns the difficulty courts face in assessing austerity measures holistically from a systemic perspective. Recognizing the impact of austerity on equality in society requires precisely such a systemic perspective, rather than an isolated analysis of individual measures.[251] Courts sitting over individual complaints need to relate an isolated case to the entirety of austerity-related measures. Otherwise, their scope of review will necessarily shrink to checking violations of minimum requirements alone. In principle, proportionality review is a useful legal tool for such a relational, systemic review of austerity measures as it allows contextualizing an individual decision and exploring alternative options in dialogue with other branches of government.[252] However, proportionality review is not without risks. In particular, the rhetoric of an economic emergency and of the exceptionality of the situation works towards increasing the government's

[247] Cf.von Bogdandy and Goldmann, 'Sovereign Debt Restructurings as Exercises of Public Authority: Towards a Decentralized Sovereign Insolvency Law', in C. Espósito, J. P. Bohoslavsky, and Y. Li (eds), *Responsible Sovereign Lending and Borrowing: The Search for Common Principles* (2013) 39, at 39.

[248] See n. 214 and accompanying text; Michalowski, 'Sovereign Debt and Social Rights—Legal Reflections on a Difficult Relationship', 8 *Human Rights Law Review* (2008) 35.

[249] Cf. Christodoulidis, 'Social Rights Constitutionalism: An Antagonistic Endorsement', 44 *Journal of Law and Society* (2017) 123.

[250] Kilpatrick (n. 235) 290, 300–303.

[251] An example is Bohoslavsky, 'Economic Inequality, Debt Crises and Human Rights', 42 *Yale Journal of International Law Online* (2016) 181.

[252] Contiades and Fotiadou, 'Social Rights in the Age of Proportionality: Global Economic Crisis and Constitutional Litigation', 10 *International Journal of Constitutional Law* (2012) 660.

discretion, eclipsing the wider systemic effects austerity may have on equality.[253] This is what happened in some cases before the ECtHR. The *Koufaki v Greece* case, in which the Court began by diligently scrutinizing the proportionality of a Greek law leading to a wage reduction for public servants, is paradigmatic. However, at a critical juncture, it granted the Greek government a wide margin of appreciation to implement the adjustment programme, taking back its standard of review to the level of a check for obvious arbitrariness.[254] Other cases followed similar lines,[255] granting at best the essential minimum of protection.[256] The Court took a more systemic perspective in *Savickas v Lithuania* concerning salary cuts in the judiciary, in which it emphasized that the judiciary had not been singled out from the public sector, but failed to compare pay cuts in the public sector to the general wage level.[257] Compared to these substantive questions, the Court did much better in reviewing the formal and procedural requirements of austerity, such as the temporality of measures.[258] While a procedural perspective is not to be neglected from a transformative human rights perspective, it can hardly ensure equality alone.

The experience before domestic constitutional courts was similar. The Italian Constitutional Court restrained its review for the most part to ensuring the essential core of social rights. Its decision to hold pay cuts for judges to be in violation of the constitution was motivated by a concern for judicial independence, not for equality.[259] Spain's traditionally weak enforcement of social rights continued throughout the crisis, with the Constitutional Court ensuring only a minimum of health care.[260] The big exception in this regard has been the Portuguese Constitutional Court, which consistently measured austerity from a systemic perspective. The extensive social rights guarantees of the constitution may have contributed to this,[261] together with the possibility of reviewing legislative measures in the abstract, rather than in concrete cases. In addition, the court based its decisions

[253] Cf. Kilpatrick (n. 235) 293; Wills and Warwick (n. 237) 658ff.

[254] ECtHR, *Koufaki and ADEDY v Greece*, Appl. nos 57665/12 and 57657/12, Judgment of 7 May 2013; see also Kilpatrick (n. 235) 297. See Mola, 'The Margin of Appreciation Accorded to States in Times of Economic Crisis: An Analysis of the Decision by the European Committee of Social Rights and by the European Court of Human Rights on National Austerity Measures', *Lex social: revista de los derechos sociales* (2015) 174, at 182.

[255] ECtHR, *Valkov et al. v Bulgaria*, Appl. nos 2033/04 *et al.*, Judgment of 25 October 2011; *Da Conceição Mateus v Portugal and Santos Januário v Portugal*, Appl. nos 62235/12 and 57725/12, Judgment of 31 October 2013; *da Silva Carvalho Rico v Portugal*, Appl. no. 13341/14, Judgment of 24 September 2015.

[256] Cf. ECtHR, *McDonald v UK*, Appl. no. 4241/12, Judgment of 20 May 2014. One could also consider the case *NKM v Hungary*, Appl. no. 66529/11, Judgment of 14 May 2013, to fall in this category, in which the ECtHR held a 98 per cent tax on severance pay to be in violation of the right to property. Arguably, though, the tax needs to be understood as yet another highly controversial reform targeting the independence of the judiciary rather than as an austerity measure.

[257] ECtHR, *Savickas et al. v Lithuania*, Appl. nos 66365/09 *et al.*, Judgment of 7 November 2013.

[258] E.g. ECtHR, *Da Conceição Mateus v Portugal and Santos Januário v Portugal*, Appl. nos 62235/12 and 57725/12, Judgment of 31 October 2013.

[259] Fasone (n. 235) 17–18.

[260] Ibid. 20ff.

[261] Brito Vieira and Carreira da Silva (n. 164).

on general constitutional principles like legitimate expectations and equality, which invite systemic perspectives.[262] Thus, the court went to some length to review the impact of austerity on public employees with the cuts for the general population,[263] or to develop criteria for distinguishing legitimate pension reforms aimed at ensuring sustainable pension payments from one-off measures to reduce public expenditure.[264] Still, even the Portuguese Constitutional Court held that it was beyond its powers to decide whether the government should raise taxes rather than cut expenditure.[265]

This review of the case law shows the inherent limitations of human rights litigation in austerity. Austerity measures are systemic by design, but certain systemic questions are beyond the reach of human rights litigation, at least as it has been traditionally understood. The very problem of European labour markets, vexed by underinvestment and structural imbalances caused by austerity, among other factors, are beyond the reach of courts. This limitation might ultimately derive from, and be justified by, the doctrine of the separation of powers. While the liberal paradigm allows this doctrine to impose stricter self-restraint on judges than the transformative paradigm, even the latter cannot fully escape it. But if this is the case, one needs to recognize that human rights litigation has a very limited potential for promoting the social in the context of austerity. In particular, human rights litigation may not compensate for the lack of democracy in the design of austerity measures.

## 2. A new political paradigm?

In contrast to human rights litigation, the crisis strengthened the significance of human rights for policymaking. Under pressure from the exigencies of the crisis, international organizations eventually adopted policies that address the role of human rights for austerity, waking from hibernation a project that had been dormant in the United Nations for over a decade.

At the outset, the conceptual ground was still strikingly unprepared. Decades of writing in human rights law had not elaborated clear criteria for the legality of retrogressive measures.[266] For the liberal human rights paradigm, structural adjustment had been believed to bring a country back on a path of growth early enough to ignore supposedly temporary challenges for ESC rights. For the

262 Cf. Kilpatrick (n. 235) 294.

263 Canotilho, Violante, and Lanceiro, 'Austerity Measures under Judicial Scrutiny: The Portuguese Constitutional Case-Law: Portuguese Constitutional Court Decision 399/2010 (Surtax on Personal Income Tax 2010) Decision 396/2011 (State Budget 2011) Decision 353/2012 (State Budget 2012) Decision 187/2013 (State Budget 2013) Decision 474/2013 (Public Workers Requalification) Decision 602/2013 (Labour Code) Decision 794/2013 (40-Hour Work Week) Decision 862/2013 (Pensions Convergence) Decision 413/2014 (State Budget 2014) Decision 572/2014 (Special Solidarity Contribution 2014) Decision 574/2014 (Pay Cuts 2014-2018) Decision 575/2014 (Special Sustainability Contribution)', 11 *European Constitutional Law Review* (2015) 155, 163.

264 Ibid. 176.

265 Ibid. 162.

266 Wills and Warwick (n. 237) 653ff.

transformative paradigm, the first priority had been to establish human rights as a relevant standard, and doing so for the micro-perspective of project management may have been easier than for the macro-perspective of structural adjustment. As the great financial crisis began, it was therefore unclear whether and what kind of adjustment policies would be compliant with the obligation of states under Article 2 paragraph 1 ICESCR to promote ESC rights 'to the maximum of [their] available resources'—the key concept governing retrogressive measures. Two readings suggested themselves. The first one is static, restricting ESC rights enjoyment to the wiggle room left by presumably exogenous influences like austerity ('to the maximum of its *available* resources'); the second one is dynamic, reading the provision as a duty to increase the available resources as much as the situation permits ('to the *maximum* of its available resources').

Cephas Lumina, the special rapporteur for the Human Rights Council appointed in 2009, submitted his Guiding Principles on Foreign Debt and Human Rights to the Council in 2011.[267] The Guiding Principles are rather strict on the issue of retrogression, calling upon states to ensure that they avoid retrogressive measures and that debt service does not lead to retrogression.[268] They also stress the need to control the impact of adjustment policies on inequality.[269] Even though the Guiding Principles emphasize minimum requirements, it seems that they take a stand against sufficiency, in line with a dynamic understanding of Article 2 paragraph 1 ICESCR. Hence, human rights would oblige debtor states, international organizations, creditor states, and, through the backdoor of the obligation to protect, even private creditors to accept debt restructurings necessary to safeguard ESC rights.

The ESC Committee took a different position. In General Comment No. 3 of 1990, it had already specified that retrogressive measures were not entirely prohibited, although cautioning that such measures 'would require the most careful consideration and would need to be fully justified by reference to the totality of the rights provided for in the Covenant and in the context of the full use of the maximum available resources'.[270] This statement still left the issue of how to leave adjustment policies somewhat open. A 2012 letter by the chairperson, effectively the first statement from the sphere of the ESC Committee directly addressing adjustment programmes, set out rather permissive requirements. Accordingly,

[267] Human Rights Council, Guiding Principles on Foreign Debt and Human rights, Annex to the Report of the Independent Expert on the Effects of Foreign Debt and Other Related International Financial Obligations of States on the Full Enjoyment of All Human Rights, Particularly Economic, Social and Cultural Rights, Cephas Lumina (hereinafter Guiding Principles), UN Doc. A/RES/20/23, 10 April 2011, paras 10–20. The Human Rights Council endorsed the Guiding Principles by majority with Res. 20/10, 18 July 2012, UN Doc. A/HRC/RES/20/10.

[268] Guiding Principles on Foreign Debt (n. 267) paras 19–20.

[269] Ibid. paras 12–14.

[270] CESCR, General Comment No. 3, 'The Nature of States Parties Obligations (Art. 2, Para. 1, of the Covenant)', UN Doc. E/1991/23, 14 December 1990, para. 9.

retrogressive measures need to be temporary, necessary and proportionate, non-discriminatory, and always respectful of the minimum core obligations of each ESC right.[271] The letter was endorsed by the ESC Committee, which emphasized accessory procedural duties such as the investigation of available alternatives and the possibility of review, in addition to the substantive requirements set out in the letter.[272] The approach has found acclaim and further refinement in the literature.[273] Under this position, retrogression is possible as long as it is proportionate and unless it infringes the minimum requirements. Depending on what use is made of the proportionality principle in this context, this position could potentially sanction sufficiency. Nevertheless, in 2016, the ESC Committee not only announced that it would hold the IMF and the World Bank accountable for the human rights impact of their programmes, but also demanded the mitigation of inequalities if retrogressive measures were unavoidable.[274]

UNCTAD and the General Assembly chose a comparable approach. The 2012 Principles for Responsible Sovereign Lending and Borrowing effectively seek to specify circumstances under which sovereign debt should be restructured.[275] While the text of the Principles does not mention human rights, it frequently refers to the need of borrowing states to safeguard the public interest and meet their obligation towards their citizens, which is only a way of paraphrasing ESC rights, among others. The 2015 UNCTAD Sovereign Debt Roadmap[276] and GA Resolution 69/319,[277] adopted without or against the votes of certain capital-exporting countries, make this relationship explicit by factoring human rights into the notion of debt sustainability. This shift contests the purely financial terms in which the IMF has defined debt sustainability, namely the capacity of a state to roll over its debt without major policy changes.[278] If debt sustainability by definition requires an adequate level of ESC rights enjoyment, the equation changes significantly. Debt sustainability might require policy changes which reduce the

[271] CESCR, Letter by the Chairperson of the ESC Committee, UN Doc. CESCR/48th/SP/MAB/SW, 16 May 2012.

[272] CESCR, Public Debt, Austerity Measures and the International Covenant on Economic, Social and Cultural Rights', UN Doc. E/C.12/2016/1, 22 July 2016, para. 4.

[273] Warwick, 'Socio-Economic Rights During Economic Crises: A Changed Approach to Non-Retrogression', 65 *International and Comparative Law Quarterly* (2016) 249; Krajewski (n. 234) 490; Goldmann (n. 157). On the relationship between debt and taxes, see International Bar Association, 'The Obligation to Mobilise Resources: Bridging Human Rights, Sustainable Development Goals, and Economic and Fiscal Policies' (2017) 50ff.

[274] CESCR 'Public Debt' (n. 272) paras 4 and 8.

[275] UNCTAD, 'Principles on Promoting Responsible Sovereign Lending and Borrowing', 10 January 2012, http://unctad.org/en/PublicationsLibrary/gdsddf2012miscl_en.pdf (last visited 18 November 2023).

[276] UNCTAD, 'Sovereign Debt Workouts: Going Forward. Roadmap and Guide' (2015), http://unctad.org/en/PublicationsLibrary/gdsddf2015miscl_en.pdf (last visited 18 November 2023).

[277] UN General Assembly, Basic Principles on Sovereign Debt Restructuring Processes, UN Doc A/RES/69/319, 29 September 2015.

[278] IMF, 'Assessing Sustainability', IMF Policy Paper (2002); see Bohoslavsky and Goldmann (n. 135).

resources available for debt repayment. Of course, the question how much ESC rights enjoyment is adequate in a debt crisis can hardly be measured objectively. In this respect, it is important to stress that ESC rights go beyond minimum requirements and that proportionality does not mean that the ends of fighting an emergency justify any means.

More recently, the Guiding Principles on Human Rights Impact Assessments of Economic Reforms drafted by the Independent Expert on the effects of foreign debt on the full enjoyment of human rights provide guidance on how to square human rights with austerity.[279] This document applies comprehensively to economic reforms of all kinds, whether adopted in response to acute crises or with a longer-term horizon in mind (Principle 1). Given the frequency of economic crises and the widespread character of austerity, minimizing the difference between crisis measures and a hypothetical 'normality' appears to be an important step to counter the rhetoric of emergencies and the associated tendency to justify highly intrusive means by reference to the urgency of the situation. Moreover, the Guiding Principles place the burden of justifying economic reforms on the debtor state (Principle 3), thereby creating a presumption against the admissibility of austerity measures. Moreover, the principles work against asymmetric structural adjustment policies by requiring the mobilization of all resources, including taxation (Principle 9), and coherence across all economic policies (Principle 11).

It is not an overstatement to say that the entirety of these efforts fostered the conviction among key stakeholders that human rights should have a role to play in the design of adjustment policies. An example of this are the diverging responses of the IMF to the debt crisis following the financial crisis. On the one hand, with respect to debt restructurings, the pre-crisis approach of the IMF remained by and large intact. While the IMF did explore new ways to facilitate debt restructurings to prevent the aggravation and the spread of impending crises,[280] progress has been rather limited. Even at the height of the crisis, a statutory bankruptcy procedure for states seemed further away than ever. Member States showed no desire for institutional reform, and the IMF, possibly still traumatized by the failure of its 2003 attempt to establish a Sovereign Debt Restructuring Mechanism, made no attempt to push states in that direction. Instead, it advocated contractual innovations, an exercise in the coding of capital with doubtful benefit.[281] This approach has given

[279] Human Rights Council, Guiding Principles on Human Rights Impact Assessments of Economic Reforms. Report of the Independent Expert on the Effects of Foreign Debt and Other Related International Financial Obligations of States on the Full enjoyment of Human Rights, Particularly Economic, Social and Cultural Rights, UN Doc. A/HRC/40/57, 19 December 2018.

[280] International Monetary Fund, 'Sovereign Debt Restructuring—Recent Developments and Implications for the Fund's Legal and Policy Framework', IMF Policy Paper (2013); International Monetary Fund, 'Strengthening the Contractual Framework to Address Collective Action Problems in Sovereign Debt Restructuring', IMF Policy Paper (2014).

[281] K. Pistor, *The Code of Capital: How the Law Creates Wealth and Inequality* (2019) does not include a chapter on sovereign debt, but the pattern she reveals applies *mutatis mutandis*.

rise to a myriad of practical difficulties. Generations of collective action clauses in sovereign bonds follow one another, with the new generation revealing its loopholes even before it can effectively replace the previous one. Those loopholes result from the impossibility of preserving essential public interests, like the enjoyment of human rights, while depending on the consent of a majority of creditors. Such an approach puts public interests up for sale. It exposes human rights to a cat-and-mouse game between the debtor state seeking a restructuring, and rent-seeking risk investors aspiring to reach a blocking minority, in which the much-coveted coding skills of a highly specialized elite group of lawyers are the decisive weapon. Policymakers and many courts around the world followed their call, ignoring the key difference between private corporations, which can go into liquidation, and states, which cannot, as they need to ensure the human rights of their citizens.[282]

On the other hand, the IMF did profoundly rethink its adjustment policies. Early into the sovereign debt crisis, the IMF in an important staff paper came to the conclusion that adjustment programmes needed to pay greater heeds to the human condition. While the paper avoids human rights language, it goes significantly beyond minimum requirements when considering the impact of recessions on social cohesion and employment, arguing that recovery in jobs (instead of growth) should have the highest priority in a crisis.[283] Subsequently, the IMF admitted in a sobering assessment of its track record that the pick-and-rush strategy of past adjustment programmes had often relied on overblown growth expectations.[284] Further statements along similar lines followed suit,[285] and they seemed to have had an impact in the form of the 2015 Revised Operational Guidance on Conditionality, which took up human rights language by calling for mitigating programme effects on the 'most vulnerable'.[286] A 2017 report on the IMF approach to social protection by the Independent Evaluation Office followed suit by suggesting in a footnote that the 'targeted approach' pursued by the IMF aligned with a human rights-based approach.[287]

While these developments indicate a noticeable shift towards human rights on 'axis 1', sufficiency still seemed to prevail over cautious attempts to revisit structural

[282] Courts ignoring this difference and violating their duty under international human rights law to avoid obstructing ESC rights enjoyment in debtor states include Germany's Federal Court of Justice (BGH), docket no. XI ZR 193/14, Judgment of 24 February 2015; and the SDNY District Court, *NML Capital, Ltd v Republic of Argentina*, docket no. 08 Civ. 6978(TPG) *et al.*, order of 23 February 2012 (note that the United States is bound only by customary ESC rights). Sadly, once Argentina had paid its debts, it took surprisingly little time for human rights violations to materialize.

[283] M. Dao and P. Loungani, 'The Human Cost of Recessions: Assessing It, Reducing It', IMF Staff Position Note No. SPN/10/17 (2010).

[284] O. Blanchard and D. Leigh, 'Growth Forecast Errors and Fiscal Multipliers', IMF Working Paper No. 1 (2013).

[285] Van Genugten (n. 204) 6ff.

[286] IMF, 'Revised Operational Guidance to IMF Staff on the 2002 Conditionality Guidelines', IMF Policy Paper (2014) para. 2.

[287] Independent Evaluation Office, 'The IMF and Social Protection' (2017) 13 fn. 40.

inequality in the post-crisis era on 'axis 2'. This may have changed somewhat with the 2019 IMF strategy on social spending. Considering the obvious, namely the detrimental effects of IMF adjustment programmes on social spending, and the impact of such spending on economic development and political stability, the new strategy frames social spending as 'macro-critical'. This means nothing but that the IMF is competent to prescribe social spending deemed crucial for internal or external stability, including inclusive growth.[288] The contrast with approaches to previous crises could hardly be stronger, and the difference in practice was notable. While the IMF-supported initial programmes for Greece requested severe cuts to essential social services and near-punitive privatizations of public property,[289] the 2018 programme for Barbados struck a chord with those concerned about human rights in an economic crisis. It emphasizes the importance of social spending, especially expenditure that will directly benefit vulnerable groups, such as cash support or programmes to enhance labour. Cuts to expenditure focus on state-owned enterprises. Strategies to increase revenue include a rebalancing of the tax burden between the population and offshore companies.[290] Similarly, in 2019, the IMF welcomed Argentina's social spending, such as a new universal child allowance as an efficient tool to help families in need, expanded health services and nutrition support for vulnerable groups, and active labour market policies.[291]

Even in Europe, a change of course has set in. Protracted austerity and other trends towards social disintegration like the *Dano* judgment stripping unemployed migrant workers of social benefits ultimately became a risk to European integration.[292] This triggered new calls for strengthening the social aspects of the Union in civil society and in the literature.[293] Multiple reactions by the Commission ensued, each aiming at mitigating the effects of austerity. Initially, the Commission inaugurated the Juncker plan for infrastructure investment in 2014, meant to boost growth and employment. The Commission's reaction took a decisive turn with Juncker's State of the Union Address of September 2015, in which he announced

[288] IMF, 'A Strategy for IMF Engagement on Social Spending—Background Papers', IMF Policy Paper (2019) para. 17. On the concept of macro-criticality, see IMF, 'Guidance Note for Surveillance under Article IV Consultation', IMF Policy Paper (2015) 8, 34.

[289] See e.g. Human Rights Council, Report of the Independent Expert on the Effects of Foreign Debt and Other Related International Financial Obligations of States on the Full Enjoyment of All Human Rights, Particularly Economic, Social and Cultural Rights, Cephas Lumina, Mission to Greece, 22–27 April 2013, UN Doc. A/HRC/25/50/Add. 1, 27 March 2014.

[290] See comprehensively IMF, 'Barbados. Request for an Extended Arrangement under the Extended Fund Facility—Press Release; Staff Report; Staff Supplement; and Statement by the Executive Director for Barbados', IMF Country Report 18/290 (2018). The programme also included rigorous debt restructuring, see M. Anthony, G. Impavido, and B. van Selm, '"Barbados" 2018–19 Sovereign Debt Restructuring—a Sea Change?', IMF Working Paper No. 34 (2020).

[291] IMF, 'Argentina: Third Review under the Stand-by Arrangement, Request for Waivers of Applicability of Performance Criteria, Financing Assurances Review, and Request for Modification of Performance Criteria', 26 March 2019.

[292] CJEU, Case C-333/13, *Dano v Jobcenter Leipzig* (ECLI:EU:C:2014:2358).

[293] E.g. F. Vandenbroucke, C. Barnard, and G. De Baere (eds), *European Social Union: A Political Necessity and an Urgent Research Programme* (2013).

a rights-based strategy centred around a pillar of social rights. It was followed up by a concrete proposal of the Commission and a Council proclamation in 2017.[294] While the document as such is non-binding, it draws on the Union *acquis*, including the Charter of Fundamental Rights and the entire array of documents emphasizing social purposes.[295] The practical impact of the latter, however, has always been mixed at best. Much depends therefore on the implementation of the social rights pillar. This is supposed to happen through the European Semester, a key component for entrenching fiscal consolidation and austerity Union-wide in good or bad times.[296] In principle, this appears to be the right place to push back against austerity. A scoreboard is to measure implementation;[297] its effects remain to be seen.

### 3. Explaining the new paradigm

What emerges from these developments is that a new political paradigm of human rights has been slowly gaining ground in the decade following the global financial crisis. Unlike the liberal paradigm and, to a lesser extent, the transformative paradigm post-1990, it breaks with the idea of the political neutrality of human rights. Instead, human rights, including ESC rights, become an integral part of economic policymaking. This is not inimical to human rights litigation; rather, it assigns to litigation a political function. Courts might review the reasons given and the procedures followed by the political process, and they might set frameworks that political actors have to take into account in the design of structural reforms. In this sense, human rights become a means of political dialogue. In contrast to the early beginnings of the transformative paradigm in the interwar years, the new political paradigm relies to an important extent on human rights impact assessments, expertise, performance criteria, and scoreboards—measures that stem from the shift to governance, but now play a new role in facilitating political dialogue about human rights.

How to explain this shift? For one, the increase in human rights litigation stands on the shoulders of the success of the liberal paradigm, which broke new ground for human rights litigation. To use it against austerity was to some extent conditioned by the prior constitutionalization and internationalization of austerity, which required a legal 'antidote' of at least equivalent constitutional or international rank. The formal status of constitutional and international rights guarantees therefore does indeed matter to the extent that austerity derives from similar sources.

[294] See n. 233.

[295] Z. Rasnača, 'Bridging the Gaps or Falling Short? The European Pillar of Social Rights and What It Can Bring to Eu-Level Policymaking', ETUI Research Paper No. 5 (2017) 15.

[296] Communication from the Commission to the European Parliament, the Council, the European Economic and Social Committee and the Committee of the Regions on Establishing a European Pillar of Social Rights, COM(2017) 250 final, 26 April 2017, 7.

[297] European Commission, *Joint Employment Report 2018* (2017) 16ff.

Moreover, I believe that the development of the *political* paradigm has a lot to do with the legitimacy of international and supranational organizations. As an (unintended) consequence of the liberal paradigm, human rights have become a relevant standard for the legitimacy of international organizations. While one might be tempted to attribute this shift to the constant concerns of civil society and scholarship about the human rights records of international institutions ever since the beginning of the anti-globalization protests in the 1990s, I believe that two different trajectories have been at least as relevant.[298]

For one, international organizations played a key role in the 'war on terror' in the aftermath of 11 September 2001. Observance of human rights standards was initially not among their or their Member States' priorities. This ultimately triggered resistance among domestic courts. Famously, the Security Council's sanctions against suspected individuals without due process prompted the CJEU and the ECtHR to make implementation conditional upon respect for fundamental rights.[299] Threatened with non-compliance, the Security Council had to back down and improve its human rights protections.[300] This development occurred in close proximity to a more general reassessment of the role of international organizations and the conditions for their legitimate operation, which came to be specified by an emerging body of global administrative law (or international public law).[301] Once established as standards for international organizations, it became difficult to ignore them.

Second, the wave of authoritarian nationalism following in the wake of the global financial crisis constitutes in many respects a direct threat to the operation and integrity of international organizations. This explains in particular the reaction of the EU and its belated shift to social rights, which is impressive only if seen against the background of the EU's historical neglect for the issue. Of course, the causes of authoritarian nationalism are manifold, and one should not reduce them to economic issues alone. But the blatant ignorance for the social presented such an open flank that organizations like the IMF and the EU had to do something after all. In addition, arguing with the *acquis* is a smart strategy by the Commission

[298] E.g. Akande, 'The International Court of Justice and the Security Council: Is There Room for Judicial Control of Decisions of the Political Organs of the United Nations?', 46 *International and Comparative Law Quarterly* (1997) 309, at 323. For austerity-related critique, see n. 157.

[299] CJEU, Joined Cases C-402/05 P and C-415/05, *Kadi & Al Barakaat International Foundation v Council and Commission* (ECLI:EU:C:2008:461), paras 283–326; ECtHR, *Al-Jedda v UK*, Appl. no. 27021/08, Judgment of 7 July 2011; ECtHR, *Nada v Switzerland*, Appl. no. 10593/08, Judgment of 12 September 2012.

[300] Feinäugle, 'The UN Security Council Al-Qaida and Taliban Sanctions Committee: Emerging Principles of International Institutional Law for the Protection of Individuals?', in A. von Bogdandy *et al.* (eds), *The Exercise of Public Authority by International Institutions Advancing International Institutional Law* (2010) 101, at 101.

[301] Kingsbury, Krisch, and Stewart, 'The Emergence of Global Administrative Law', 68 *Law and Contemporary Problems* (2005) 15; von Bogdandy, Dann, and Goldmann, 'Developing the Publicness of Public International Law: Towards a Legal Framework for Global Governance Activities', 9 *German Law Journal* (2008) 1375.

to move the Council, certainly the main culprit behind Europe's post-crisis austerity binge.

One further factor may have contributed to the shifting approach of the IMF. While the IMF is still largely under the control of the traditional capital-exporting countries, the seating at its table has changed. Adding to this, that the great financial crisis had discredited the Washington Consensus—the ideological project of the traditional capital-exporting countries—the time seemed ripe for major policy shifts. In this context, putting the emphasis on 'social spending' appears like a shift that takes into account important new political realities in respect of membership and policy preferences.

## 6. Conclusion: A Transformative Role for Human Rights?

This review of the changing human rights paradigms prevalent in discourses about austerity, of their role in the struggle between the economic and the social, yields a number of insights. At a first level, the study reveals how varying human rights paradigms prevailed in sovereign debt discourse. While human rights in the 1970s formed part of a broader conceptual framework aimed at strengthening the effective economic self-determination of countries in the Global South (the structural paradigm of human rights), the connection between human rights and austerity largely disappeared in the 1980s at the time when austerity increased for many countries. A truncated notion of human rights reigned supreme, gaining the status of a global constitutional principle (the liberal paradigm of human rights). Only the aftermath of the 'war on terror' instilled the understanding that international organizations might be subject to human rights law, including when imposing austerity (the transformative paradigm of human rights). The limitations of human rights litigation in the aftermath of the great financial crisis have shifted the focus on policy changes (the political paradigm).

It is difficult to predict whether the future is bright for challenging austerity with human rights. The Covid-19 pandemic reshuffled the cards again and initially made generous moratoriums possible; in the EU, it unleashed an unprecedented wave of fiscal solidarity. One may understand this as the prolongation of the political paradigm. Whether such an approach will continue now that the pandemic is over remains to be seen. The looming debt crisis in the Global South as a result of rising interest rates in the developed world warrants profound scepticism. In Europe, the move away from constitutionalized austerity remains half-hearted. On the other hand, in view of global tensions and massively increased geopolitical competition, there can hardly be any interest in continuing the austerity practised since the Second World War. At least in its previous form, it is closely linked to the hegemony of the Western hemisphere. It seems difficult to imagine that the opportunity to frame alternatives to Western hegemony-cum-austerity in terms of human rights will pass unused.

At a more abstract level, this study shows, first, that human rights discourse is contingent and heavily context-dependent. The history of human rights discourse is characterized by struggles between vastly different paradigms expressing highly diverging views about the role of human rights for the balance between the economic and the social (axis 1), and for material redistribution and equality (axis 2). The relation between the economic and the social can be articulated by vastly different concepts. Depending on the concrete context, human rights were often not necessarily the first choice for those interested in corroborating the social against the economic. Much depends on the one hand on the human rights paradigm prevailing in the specific context, which has seen enormous shifts over the last decades as different actors have pushed human rights discourse to vastly different ends. On the other hand, the availability of ideological and discursive alternatives also matters to a considerable degree. For the understanding of human rights, this means that the narrative about the constant, progressive development of human rights discourse is misplaced.[302] At best, it conceals the fact that human rights are open to very different uses, in accordance with what I have called their paradigms. Hence, a human rights perspective on austerity is per se no guarantee for more than mere minimum guarantees. Austerity may be more or less intrusive with or without explicit reference to human rights. Human rights litigation after the great financial crisis in many cases only implied sufficiency, not equality. Conversely, employing human rights to criticize austerity has allowed the Third World to become a site of epistemic production.[303] Again, context matters.

Second, the preceding prompts the question whether the rise of human rights stands in a causal relationship to the observed focus on minimal requirements and sufficiency, or in different terms, whether there is more than a coincidence behind the parallel rise of neoliberalism and human rights discourse—a fiercely debated issue. From the point of view of the austerity debate, it is safe to rule out human rights' complicity in the rise of neoliberalism, as human rights discourse was consistently entertained to criticize austerity. Nevertheless, there is some plausibility that more egalitarian visions were dropped when human rights, supposedly a more consensual, unifying conceptual framework, replaced heterodox economic approaches as the primary discursive field for challenging austerity. As Samuel Moyn holds, '... a better way to frame the relationship between neoliberalism and human rights, at least based on current research, is in terms of parallel trajectories,

[302] On human rights as a progress narrative, see Altwicker and Diggelmann, 'How Is Progress Constructed in International Legal Scholarship?', 25 *European Journal of International Law* (2014) 425, at 434–435.

[303] Cf. Gathii, 'The Promise of International Law: A Third World View (Including a Twail Bibliography 1996–2019 as an Appendix)', 114 *Proceedings of the ASIL Annual Meeting* (2020) 165.

with the tragic consequence that ... structural insight into the root causes of social suffering went missing at the time that it was badly needed'.[304]

One might even go as far as to speculate that the very idea of the universality of human rights, which is intrinsically related to their supposedly non-political character in accordance with the liberal paradigm,[305] made it difficult to pursue more ambitious agendas and extend the focus of human rights discourse beyond sufficiency and towards more egalitarian solutions. After all, apart from the minimum requirements, very few ESC rights claims will find near-universal acceptance. To preserve the idea of universality inscribed into the liberal paradigm, and to defeat the allegedly political character of ESC rights, one might be inclined to remain on the safe side and stick to sufficiency, avoiding the potential minefield of tough redistributive decisions that more egalitarian visions would have to confront. For human rights to remain the *last utopia*, they had to be framed as being not as utopian as some might have hoped.[306] John Tasioulas endorsed precisely this rationale in a 2017 paper for the World Bank.[307]

Third, the insights into the contingency of human rights discourse begs the question whether it may incline adjustment policies more towards the social at all, i.e. whether it is good for anything in the context of austerity. Unsurprisingly, the answer is that it depends on the particular human rights paradigm employed. Under the current political paradigm, human rights allow consensus-building among a disparate field of austerity sceptics comprising intergovernmental organizations, transnational NGOs of vastly different ideological organizations, local actors, governments, and even international organizations. Given the deep cultural entrenchment of austerity,[308] such a function might not be the least of victories.

Related to this is the capacity of human rights discourse to increase complexity in decision-making which may challenge economic discourse with non-economic arguments. This hits a weak point of the institutions potentially promoting austerity. As the field of economic expertise is the natural habitat of institutions promoting austerity, like the IMF or the European 'troika', confronting them with (heterodox) economic approaches instead of human rights arguments allows them to carry on unabated. They can simply ignore them, claiming to know better, and sweeping the underlying normative disagreement under the carpet. This was the fate of NIEO and of the related interventionist brand of development economics proposed by Prebisch and hedged by UNCTAD. Even the towering authority of Joseph Stiglitz, who had decried the flaws of the orthodox creed for decades,

304 Moyn (n. 10) 159.

305 On the non-political aspirations of human rights discourse: Brown, '"The Most We Can Hope For ...": Human Rights and the Politics of Fatalism', 103 *The South Atlantic Quarterly* (2004) 451, at 456.

306 Moyn (n. 2) 171–172.

307 Tasioulas (n. 214).

308 Blyth (n. 24).

eventually left his position as World Bank Chief Economist over a disagreement about the World Bank's approach to tackling the Asian and Russian crises.[309] Unwelcome expertise can simply be dismissed.

Not so human rights. They shift the discussion from one about growth and efficiency to one in which the primacy of growth is no longer a natural given. Even if the Bretton Woods institutions managed to reinterpret social challenges as questions of growth and effective programme implementation, particularly so with the shift to human capital, human rights defy their expertise to some extent. Ironically, the alleged neutrality of the Bretton Woods institutions and particularly the IMF gives human rights their strength as it silences them on the issue. At the same time, the IMF cannot simply dismiss the debate and consign the toxic impact of austerity on human rights to silence, as in the current state of international law, as that would risk undermining its own legitimacy. Let us not forget that human rights have, for some, acquired the status of constitutional norms.[310] Human rights discourse therefore exposes institutions like the IMF to a kind of scrutiny the terms of which they cannot control as much as they may control the debates about the economic merits of austerity. It is therefore precisely the fact that the IMF considers itself unbound by human rights which makes it vulnerable to human rights discourse. From this angle, much of the doctrinal debate on the human rights obligations of the IMF seems to be beside the point. As a discursive strategy for contesting austerity, its success is premised on the fallacy that there is only one single, universally shared understanding of human rights, which the critics of the IMF can control.

A very important amplifier for human rights discourse in this respect are inter-institutional relations. Sovereign debt crises touch upon many issues, hence many international organizations may chime in on the subject. The staff of these organizations often have considerable leeway, and not all states are always willing to intervene.[311] This enabled UNCTAD in the 1970s and UNICEF in the 1980s to become centres of 'counter-expertise'. In principle, courts could play a similar role.

One major question remains, though. Is it possible to instil egalitarianism into austerity via human rights discourse and to question sufficiency effectively? In the literature, there seems to be disagreement about this point. Samuel Moyn argues that an egalitarian theory of socio-economic distribution would be more

[309] Richard W. Stephenson, 'Outspoken Chief Economist Leaving World Bank', *New York Times*, 25 November 1999, https://www.nytimes.com/1999/11/25/business/outspoken-chief-economist-leaving-world-bank.html (last visited 18 November 2023).

[310] E.g. Kumm, 'The Cosmopolitan Turn in Constitutionalism: An Integrated Conception of Public Law', 20 *Indiana Journal of Global Legal Studies* (2013) 605.

[311] Even the United States dominates the policies of the IFIs in only a few exceptional cases, i.e. when the debtor state is sufficiently important. See Stone, 'The Scope of IMF Conditionality', 62 *International Organization* (2008) 589.

demanding than human rights,[312] while Paul O'Connell, among others, has called for invigorating human rights in the face of austerity.[313]

I believe it is not only possible but also worth trying to entrench more equality. For this to succeed, it is in a first step necessary to take the political paradigm seriously and to debunk the myth of the non-political character of human rights and of the allegedly political character of social rights.[314] This framing of human rights discourse bequeathed from the liberal paradigm only covers up the contingency implicit in the choice for sufficiency and conceals alternative, more egalitarian approaches which fully honour the promise of the progressive realization of socio-economic rights.

Second, it is necessary to question the widespread rhetoric of the state of exception surrounding austerity.[315] The best way of doing so is probably to keep in mind and emphasize that states of crisis are an essential feature of modernity.[316] In line with this insight, austerity has been the normal state of affairs rather than the exception in many heavily and not-so-heavily indebted states over the past decades. Consequently, any retrogressive measures face a high bar—probably a higher one than they do currently.

After preparing the ground in this way, true egalitarian adjustment policies may only come from institutions and procedures for open deliberation. This follows from their political character. Such institutions and deliberation can take different forms, as Amartya Sen has shown.[317] They are not necessarily tied to Western-style liberal democracy, or what is left of it, as long as they allow a reasoned exchange of views about the impact of proposed measures and the goals of society. Of course, deliberative democracy is as much culpable of being a 'powerless companion' to neoliberalism as human rights. Much therefore depends on the paradigmatic understanding of human rights in sovereign debt crises, and more generally on the role of law in the economy.[318] One needs to understand law as a transformative instrument, a receptacle for progressive ideas catalysing political processes of social development and integration, rather than a means of encoding capital, entrenching morality, or stifling over-reliance on courts. As third-wave transformative constitutionalism comes with a heavy focus on courts,[319] such a proposal would require going back to the original idea of transformative constitutionalism

[312] Moyn (n. 10) 168.

[313] O'Connell, 'On Reconciling Irreconcilables: Neo-Liberal Globalisation and Human Rights,' 7 *Human Rights Law Review* (2007) 483.

[314] On this myth, see also Marks, 'Four Human Rights Myths,' in D. Kinley, W. Sadurski, and K. Walton (eds), *Human Rights Old Problems, New Possibilities* (2013) 217, at 217, 229.

[315] On the unwarranted and dangerous use of crisis narratives, see Fischer-Lescano (n. 234) 3ff.

[316] J. Habermas, *Der Philosophische Diskurs der Moderne* (1985) 27.

[317] Sen (n. 215).

[318] On different possible approaches to the function of law in respect to the financial order, see M. Goldmann and S. Steininger (eds), *Democracy and Financial Order: Legal Perspectives* (2018).

[319] See n. 165.

built into constitutions from the interwar and postwar eras that saw politics and social movements at the helm of social transformation,[320] and to advance such an approach to human rights in the context of contemporary institutional frameworks for human rights protection and expertise.

Finally, does the deployment of human rights discourse for more egalitarian ends risk replacing other political utopias? I would go as far as to argue that this would even be desirable, for the most likely alternative to human rights-based equality at present is not some high-flying utopia of emancipatory solidarity, but the brute dystopia of authoritarian liberalist equality in oppression. To expose the role of austerity in the rise of authoritarian liberalism and for human rights violations might be one of the most meaningful ways to combat both.

[320] Goldmann and Menéndez (n. 12).

# 3

# From Corporate Personality to Corporate Governance

## The Transformation of International Human Rights Through Corporate Practice

*Anna Beckers**

## 1. Introduction: The Academy's Heritage on Corporations and Human Rights

The year 2017 was not the first in which the Academy of European Law had hosted a summer school that provoked the participants to think of human rights from a non-state-centric perspective. In 2002, the specialized courses were already concerned with non-state actors and human rights[1] and the faculty's topics were compiled in a widely noted collection edited by Philip Alston.[2] Two years later, in 2004, Andrew Clapham gave the general course, entitled 'Human Rights Obligations of Non-State Actors: Time for a Radical Rethink',[3] the core ideas of which he laid out in the now classic book of the same title.[4] Both the 2002 and the 2004 courses prominently featured the role of companies within the international human rights regime.

As a starting point, looking more closely into the positions of these previous academies is particularly interesting. This is because the publications resulting from the 2002 and 2004 courses have become representative of two diverging perspectives in the academic debate as to whether and how corporations can be conceived of in relation to international human rights law. Clapham and Alston

* I thank Nehal Bhuta, Antoine Duval, Matthias Goldmann, Eliav Lieblich, Maddalena Neglia, Kinanya Pijl, Guy Fiti Sinclair, and Rodrigo Vallejo for their detailed and most helpful comments on the manuscript and I am immensely grateful to Rebecca Kavanagh for her meticulous research and editing assistance. It goes without saying that the responsibility for any remaining errors is mine.

[1] Academy of European Law, Session on Human Rights Law, 17–28 June 2002, https://www.eui.eu/Documents/DepartmentsCentres/AcademyofEuropeanLaw/SummerSchoolProgrammes/HRpro2002.pdf (last visited 20 November 2023).

[2] P. Alston (ed.), *Non-State Actors and Human Rights* (2005).

[3] Academy of European Law, Session on Human Rights Law, 21 June–2 July 2004, https://www.eui.eu/Documents/DepartmentsCentres/AcademyofEuropeanLaw/SummerSchoolProgrammes/ProgrammeHR2004.pdf (last visited 20 November 2023).

[4] A. Clapham, *Human Rights Obligations of Non-State Actors* (2006).

Anna Beckers, *From Corporate Personality to Corporate Governance.* In: *Global Rights?* First Edition. Edited by: Nehal Bhuta and Rodrigo Vallejo, Oxford University Press. © Anna Beckers 2024. DOI: 10.1093/oso/9780198940166.003.0003

shared the normative stance as to a desirability of including companies in the international human rights regime,[5] but their views were quite different, if not opposite, regarding whether such a desirable development was possible within the existing international legal human rights framework. Alston, deriving from a state-centric 'mainstream' conception of international law, concluded rather sceptically that the notions of sovereignty and the related prerogatives in positive international law ultimately prevented the necessary development of opening up international human rights law to private actors.[6] In contrast, Clapham took a pluralist, 'beyond the traditional, narrow, state-focused'[7] approach. On this basis, he concluded with a view to international soft law and corporate and state practice that 'the paradigm shift is coming as business are treated, not only as partners, but as having responsibilities under the international law of human rights' and that 'this point is nearer than is usually imagined. In fact, many of us imagine that it is already there'.[8]

After more than a decade since those discussions took place and given the attention of the 2017 course on human rights in (non-state) global governance, it was a suitable moment to ask: whose prediction proved to be closer to reality? This question not only arises because much has happened in international human rights law since 2004 that has brought companies and human rights closer together, prominently by means of the UN Guiding Principles on Business and Human Rights (UNGP) endorsed by the UN Human Rights Council in 2011[9] and the more recent developments towards a 'legally binding instrument' on business and human rights.[10] Asking this question is also interesting because the recent developments seem at first sight to prove the predictions of both Alston and Clapham correct, but

[5] P. Alston, 'The "Not-a-Cat Syndrome": Can the International Human Rights Regime Accommodate Non-State Actors?', in Alston (n. 2) 3, at 19: '[a]n international human rights regime which is not capable of effectively addressing situations in which powerful corporate actors are involved in major human rights violations, or of ensuring that private actors are held responsible, will not only lose credibility in the years ahead but will render itself unnecessarily irrelevant in relation to important issues'; Clapham (n. 4) 28: 'the existing general rules of international human rights law, created and acknowledged by states, now fix on non-state actors so that they may be held accountable for violations of this law'.

[6] Alston (n. 2) 36. In his contribution, Alston emphasizes the following constraints: the state-centric definition of international personality in international law ('Any entity can aspire to international personality, but it will need to look an awful lot like a traditional state in order to meet the requirements' (20), the limitation of 'mainstream' international lawyers to change this understanding intellectually (21), and the unlikeliness of states to change the status quo through international treaty-making (22–24)).

[7] Clapham (n. 4) 20.

[8] Ibid. 270.

[9] Guiding Principles on Business and Human Rights: Implementing the United Nations 'Protect, Respect and Remedy' Framework, Human Rights Council, 17th session, A/HRC/17/31, 21 March 2011.

[10] Updated draft legally binding instrument (clean version) to regulate, in international human rights law, the activities of transnational corporations and other enterprises. Text submitted in accordance with para. 25(g) of A/HRC/52/41, and in line with para. 25(i) will form the basis for state-led intergovernmental negotiations during the 9th Session of the open-ended intergovernmental working group on transnational corporations and other business enterprises with respect to human rights, July 2023, https://www.ohchr.org/sites/default/files/documents/hrbodies/hrcouncil/igwg-transcorp/session9/igwg-9th-updated-draft-lbi-clean.pdf (last visited 20 November 2023).

with consequences that were probably neither expected nor intended by them. By means of integrating companies into international human rights documents that states have endorsed, Clapham's vision of a stronger responsibility for companies under international human rights law appears to have become reality, yet in a different form than he envisaged. Instead of a gradual evolution of international corporate personality or international human rights obligations through state practice and soft law, corporations are now included in international human rights documents as governance actors. In this sense, as predicted by Alston, the idea of including non-state actors in international law with a formal role and responsibility has not succeeded, but there is a formal, ambiguous, role that focuses on codified responsibilities of corporations to make use of private governance structures.

How can this new governance role that corporations are expected to fulfil be described? And what is the consequence for human rights and human rights law when corporations fulfil this role and integrate human rights within their corporate governance structures? This chapter seeks to answer these questions. To that end, it will develop two interrelated arguments: it first considers how the recent developments in the global governance of business and human rights, notably the UNGP, have led to corporate governance structures becoming instrumentalized as the core and central means for corporate human rights protection at the expense of state-based human rights protection. In fact, in the global governance system for business and human rights, corporations dominate as actors that should use corporate governance to respect human rights with a background role for states that is understood as a role not going beyond developing laws that encourage or oblige companies to make use of their corporate governance systems (Section 2). Second, it considers how this use of corporate governance for international human rights protection is likely to change the very nature of the international human rights that are supposed to be protected. By means of reviewing the empirical studies conducted so far on how corporations incorporate human rights within their governance structure and comparing this to the related understanding in international human rights law, it is revealed how the origin, justification, and content of human rights as well as the required processes and remedies to ensure their protection change in the translation from a state-centric to a corporate understanding (Section 3). This leads to new questions, most importantly whether such a development is to be welcomed or criticized, i.e. whether this 'corporate understanding' of human rights should be accepted or whether it is necessary to 'go back to the starting point' of a state-centric understanding. The chapter tentatively concludes in a twofold direction. It argues for an inevitably stronger role for private law in this 'new reality' of human rights protection, as private law is ultimately the law that may regulate corporations as private actors and may tackle their contracting practices in global supply chains. Simultaneously, the final section outlines and highlights the tensions that lawyers—both human rights lawyers as well as private and corporate lawyers—will face when attempting to realize this goal (Section 4).

## 2. Corporate Governance in International Human Rights Law

In the field of business and human rights and the specific debate of the human rights obligations of corporations, the international human rights document that has had the most significant impact is certainly the UNGP. It is specifically in this document that one can observe the shift from corporate personality to corporate governance. Consequently, the following analysis will predominantly focus on that document and its follow-up policy processes. It is certainly acknowledged that there are also developments beyond the UNGP that may take the debate in a slightly different direction. In particular, in 2014 the international governmental working group explored the options of a binding Treaty on Business and Human Rights.[11] The project received wide academic support[12] and resulted, first, in the publication of the 'zero draft treaty elements' and, most recently, the updated Third Revised Draft of 2023 with textual proposals by states.[13] However, the treaty can be seen as a (complementary[14]) reaction to the previously initiated shift that occurred through the UNGP. While the initial proposal also included a revival of the idea of directly obliging companies under international law and fostering international corporate personality, the more recent development suggests a stronger interlinking of the legally binding instrument with the UNGP. In particular, the most recent draft and resulting political discussions address the question of state obligations. These state obligations are directed towards strengthening and revising the concept of mandatory due diligence and access to remedy as laid down

[11] Proposal by Ecuador and South Africa Regarding the Elaboration of an International Legally Binding Instrument on Transnational Corporations and Other Business Enterprises with Respect to Human Rights, HRC 26th Session, A/HRC/26/L.22/Rev.1, 25 June 2014. At the same session, a proposal was put forward by Norway to establish an open-ended working group on human rights and transnational corporations that should inter alia explore the options of a legally binding instrument, HRC 26th Session, A/HRC/26/L.1, 23 June 2014.

[12] See e.g. for the academic proponents of the treaty De Schutter, 'Towards A Treaty on Business and Human Rights', 1 *Business and Human Rights Journal* (2016) 41; Cassell and Ramasastry, 'White Paper: Options for a Treaty on Business and Human Rights', 6 *Notre Dame Journal of International and Comparative Law* (2016) 1; McConnell, 'Assessing the Feasibility of a Business and Human Rights Treaty', 66 *International & Comparative Law Quarterly* (2017) 143; S. Deva and D. Bilchitz (eds), *Building a Treaty on Business and Human Rights: Context and Contours* (2017). For critical positions: Backer, 'Moving Forward the UN Guiding Principles for Business and Human Rights: Between Enterprise Social Norm, State Domestic Legal Orders, and the Treaty Law That Might Bind Them All', 38 *Fordham International Law Journal* (2015) 457; Ruggie, 'Get Real or We'll Get Nothing: Reflections on the First Session of the Intergovernmental Working Group on a Business & Human Rights Treaty', Harvard Kennedy School (2015), https://www.hks.harvard.edu/sites/default/files/centers/mrcbg/programs/cri/files/Ruggie_Get_Real.pdf (last visited 20 November 2023). Cf. for the debate on the treaty, the different contributions on the 'Debate the Treaty Blog', hosted by the Business and Human Rights Resource Centre, https://www.business-humanrights.org/en/about-us/blog/debate-the-treaty (last visited 20 November 2023).

[13] See n. 10.

[14] It is discussed to what extent the Treaty Project is a complementary or competing agenda to the UNGP. However, as the first draft of the Legally Binding Instrument (the Zero Draft) already takes note of the UNGP and relies on many of its concepts (e.g. due diligence), it seems that the description of it as a complementary initiative is more accurate.

in the UNGP. Therefore, the legally binding instrument can be read as a continuation of the core ideas of corporate human rights respect, as already laid down in the UNGP. The chapter will, therefore, focus on the origin of the concepts in the UNGP but indicate, wherever necessary, how the draft binding instrument may change the situation.

## A. Polycentric Governance: Theoretical Conception and Practical Realization in the UNGP

The shift from establishing international corporate personality towards centring corporate governance had already been initiated with the inception of the mandate that led to the UNGP. Mandating John Ruggie as the Special Representative of the Secretary-General (SRSG) on Business and Human Rights and assigning the task of restating the status quo on business and human rights in 2005 paved the way for a specific understanding of global governance and the related role of corporations. Ruggie, in his earlier academic career as well as in previous policy mandates,[15] strongly advocated the idea of global governance as polycentric governance in the tradition of 'embedded liberalism'.[16] In this sense, taking up the first mandate of the SRSG in 2005 marked the end of decades-long policy discussions at the UN and related international legal academic writings that were directed towards the formal inclusion of corporations as non-state actors in international law as obligated parties. Ruggie explicitly broke with the Draft Norms on Transnational Corporations, an ambitious and equally controversial project to develop an internationally binding document with direct human rights obligations for multinational corporations.[17] Instead, he focused his mandate on restating the status quo in the field of business and human rights, but with a direct and strong influence of his own conceptual ideas as to how global governance does and can function. It therefore comes as no surprise that some commentators and observers of the process leading to the UNGP deliberately describe the UNGP as 'the Ruggie principles', i.e.

[15] Ruggie was the initiator of the UN Global, a controversially debated forum for companies to participate by committing to its ten principles and communicating on the processes to realize them. See https://www.unglobalcompact.org/ (last visited 20 November 2023).

[16] Ruggie, 'International Regimes, Transactions, and Change: Embedded Liberalism in the Postwar Economic Order', 36 *International Organization* (1982) 379.; Ruggie, 'Taking Embedded Liberalism Global: The Corporate Connection', in D. Held and M. Koenig-Archibugi (eds), *Taming Globalization: Frontiers of Governance* (2003) 93.

[17] Draft Norms on the Responsibilities of Transnational Corporations and Other Business Enterprises with Regard to Human Rights, E/CN.4/Sub.2/2003/12 (2003). See on Ruggie's rejection of the norms: J. G. Ruggie, *Just Business. Multinational Corporations and Human Rights* (2013) 54: 'In my first report to the Human Rights Commission, I concluded ... that the Norms suffered from "exaggerated legal claims and conceptual ambiguities" and that they were "engulfed by [their] own doctrinal excesses".'

as principles that echoed the convictions of its author more than the official line of the Human Rights Council.[18]

With the idea of 'embedded liberalism', Ruggie relied on the embeddedness concept of Polanyi[19] and applied it to global capitalism. He did so to argue for the embedding of global capitalism within a social community of values. The means to achieve this is to rely on the interaction between civil society (civil governance), business (corporate governance), and the public sector (public governance) as contributions to an effectively functioning global governance framework. The Protect, Respect and Remedy Framework and, ultimately, the UNGP rest heavily on this idea of an interaction between these three actors and their governance regimes as the basis for global polycentric governance. Translated into the governance of human rights, this means that states, corporations, and civil society each serve as actors that are expected to invoke their governance systems for the benefit of human rights. In the understanding and repeated description by Ruggie himself, the polycentric governance model for business and human rights is supposed to rest on the 'traditional' system of public law and governance (national and international) with its instruments of law and policy, the civil governance system in the form of societal pressure by NGOs and certification systems and various other compliance systems, and the system of corporate governance with its internal rules.[20] Ruggie continuously emphasized that the polycentric governance that he envisaged should be about the equal participation of all three systems of governance.[21] This description might suggest that while Ruggie deliberately introduced private, corporate, and civil governance structures into the debate on business and human rights, and helped them become formally introduced as new governance actors, there has not been a direct intention to *centre* corporate governance structures, as this chapter argues. On the contrary, in the interaction between the three governance systems, corporate governance was defined as the one 'which internalizes elements of the other two [i.e. civil and public governance]'.[22] The autonomy of corporations for how they participate in the polycentric governance of human

[18] See for this terminological choice between the Ruggie Framework, UN Framework, and SRSG Framework, as partly conscious choices by the commentators to reveal the specific normative underpinning, the preface by Mares in R. Mares (ed.), *The UN Guiding Principles on Business and Human Rights: Foundations and Implementation* (2012) xiii: 'Other writers refer to the Ruggie Framework for simplicity while still others use it to impress the idea that the normative choices reflected in the Framework and Guiding Principles reflect the world view of their author, an outlook which is not necessarily the best way forward for business and human rights.'

[19] K. Polanyi, *The Great Transformation. The Political and Economic Origins of Our Time* (2001 [1944]).

[20] Ruggie, 'Global Governance and "New Governance Theory": Lessons from Business and Human Rights', 20 *Global Governance* (2014) 5, at 8–10.

[21] Ruggie (n. 17) 78: 'A new regulatory dynamic was required under which public and private governance systems—corporate and civil—each come to add a distinct value, compensate for one another's weaknesses, and play mutually reinforcing roles—out of which a more comprehensive and effective global regime might evolve, including specific legal measures.'

[22] Ruggie (n. 20) 9.

rights should thus be restricted. Civil society should pressurize companies to integrate human rights concerns into their own governance structures and collaborate with companies to improve corporate governance structures for the benefit of human rights, and the system of public law and governance should ideally regulate and, through policies, reduce constraints for companies engaging in human rights protection. Hence, polycentric governance according to Ruggie shares a lot with theories of responsive regulation[23] and post-regulatory law.[24]

However, looking more closely at the UNGP's conceptual framing, historical development, and subsequent implementation, as I will do in the following section, one can see that corporate governance is much more prominently featured in the UNGP with a strong background role for the system of public governance and the system of civil governance. The pillar that specifies corporate responsibilities is comparably strong in terms of not only alignment to existing corporate governance practices, but even elevating them to some form of authority in international human rights law by including them in an international human rights document (Section B). This does not equally apply to the pillar that focuses on states and the provisions that indirectly touch upon the role of civil society (Section C). This suggests that the UNGP can also be described as a document that, while recognizing the three interlinked governance systems, places emphasis and thus centres corporate governance structures for international human rights protection with an open, but less ambitious, role for states and their public law governance system to contribute to the public domain (and an only indirectly specified role for the civil society system of governance in the third pillar[25]).

Before developing this argument, a few words are necessary to provide a tentative explanation and possible justification for this focus on corporate governance. As much as the development of the UNGP was conceptually influenced by the ideal of polycentric governance, the policy process and the ultimate drafting of the principles were also guided by the constraints that characterizes every policy process. In this regard, the policy process was strongly influenced by another approach that Ruggie advocated: his so-called 'principled pragmatism'. Constantly throughout the process, Ruggie emphasized his desire to achieve 'the maximum reduction in corporate-related human rights harm in the shortest possible period of time'[26] and to adopt 'whatever measures work best, in creating change where it

[23] I. Ayres and J. Braithwaite, *Responsive Regulation. Transcending the Deregulation Debate* (1992).

[24] Teubner, 'After Legal Instrumentalisation? Strategic Models of Post-Regulatory Law', in G. Teubner (ed.), *Dilemmas of Law in the Welfare State* (1986) 299.

[25] The fact that civil society has given only an indirect role with only an occasional explicit mention in the UNGP has also been criticized. For a particularly pointed critique: Melish and Meidinger, 'Protect, Respect, Remedy and Participate: "New Governance" Lessons for the Ruggie Framework' in Mares (n. 18) 303.

[26] Ruggie, 'Speech, Sir Geoffrey Chandler Annual Lecture', Sir Geoffrey Chandler Speaker Series, The Royal Society for the Encouragement of Arts, Manufacturers and Commerce (2011) 13.

matters the most'.[27] Hence, the project was strongly influenced by a tendency to get a quick result rather than fighting ideological battles and to pay due respect to the possibilities and constraints of practice in the realization of an academic concept. Against this background, it comes as no surprise that the adoption of the framework needed to build consensus among the many actors involved and, as a result, required moving away from contested positions in the debate, in particular the idea of a stronger role for public law and governance as a means of regulating companies.

## B. The UNGP's Second Pillar: Corporate Governance for Human Rights Respect

The second pillar of the UNGP is the one providing for the conceptual basis and operationalization of how corporations should act in order to respect human rights. The provisions relating to this pillar provide for the elements that constitute a corporate responsibility for human rights respect and specify its meaning in terms of the scope and obligatory nature. They further provide guidance for companies on the tools necessary to put into practice this responsibility within corporate governance structures.

### 1. Conceptual basis

The second pillar of the UNGP lays down a responsibility (not a legal duty) of companies to respect human rights. This responsibility is, as the commentary of Principle 11 states, independent of any obligation of states to protect human rights and it is a responsibility that exists in addition to the obligation of businesses to comply with national laws. Hence, the UNGP specify that companies are independent from states in being responsible for human rights protection and thus have their own separate responsibility. The most notable aspects of this corporate responsibility to respect human rights (CR2R) are its specification as a responsibility rather than a legal duty and the embedding of that concept of responsibility within the idea of a 'social standard of expected conduct'.

This terminological move from duty to responsibility and it being related to a 'social expectation' is not only the clearest move away from any development of international legal corporate personality, but also an interesting development in terms of describing international responsibilities of companies in line with concepts that are familiar to companies.

[27] Letter from John G. Ruggie to Olivier De Schutter, Secretary General and Antoine Bernard, Executive Director, FIDH, 20 March 2006, https://www.fidh.org/en/issues/globalisation-human-rights/business-and-human-rights/Comment-on-FIDH-Position-Paper-by (last visited 20 November 2023).

This idea of a social expectation of businesses acting responsibly and avoiding harm for other societal actors is conceptually closely related to the understanding of corporate social responsibility (CSR) and thus allows companies to link their human rights responsibility to existing corporate CSR and social performance practices.[28] Traditionally, CSR denotes the responsibility of companies for their impact on societal values and actors in a way that exists beyond and next to legal responsibilities.[29] It is a concept that has evolved from business ethics (as a moral obligation) and business management (as a strategic, profit-enhancing management tool). Integrating human rights respect as a 'potential societal impact' may certainly have advantages. First, it allows companies to link the concept of human rights respect to familiar notions. Second, it enriches the concept of CSR with an explicit human rights dimension which has so far largely been absent.[30] However, it comes at the expense of conceptualizing human rights very differently in terms of what type of human rights ought to be protected and the content of their obligatory character. Wettstein argues precisely this point when he demonstrates that the predominant political and legal conception of human rights in the international human rights debate and their related obligatory character conflicts with the debate on CSR in which social responsibilities were conceptualized as legally voluntarily, but at the same time as morally and socially significant.[31] In the course of relating the concept of CSR to the concept of international human rights protection, the UNGP aim to bridge this divide by two moves: first, by means of relating the concept of corporate responsibility to social expectations—in the words of the UNGP as a 'global standard of expected conduct'[32]—and, second, by enumerating the International Bill of Rights and the International Labour Organization's (ILO's)

[28] See, for a similar observation, Lagoutte, 'The UN Guiding Principles on Business and Human Rights', in S. Lagoutte, T. Gammeltoft-Hansen, and J. Cerone (eds), *Tracing the Roles of Soft Law in Human Rights* (2016) 235, at 247: 'Ruggie's work is successful in connecting the language of public international law with the practical discourse of CSR.'

[29] See e.g. on this conception from the perspective of business ethics: Carroll, 'A Three-Dimensional Conceptual Model of Corporate Social Performance', 4 *Academy of Management Review* (1979) 497; from the perspective of business administration and the idea of the 'bottom-line': J. Elkington, *Cannibals with Forks* (1997); and the legal perspective: McBarnet, 'Corporate Social Responsibility beyond Law, through Law, for Law: The New Corporate Accountability', in D. McBarnet, A. Voiculescu, and T. Campbell (eds), *The New Corporate Accountability. Corporate Social Responsibility and the Law* (2007) 9. For evidence of this concept of CSR in the policy debate, see European Commission, A Renewed EU Strategy 2011–14 for Corporate Social Responsibility, COM(2011) 681 final, 6: 'The Commission puts forward a new definition of CSR as "the responsibility of enterprises for their impacts on society".'

[30] On the previous absence of human rights in the CSR debate, see e.g. Robinson, 'Foreword', in R. Sullivan (ed.), *Business and Human Rights: Dilemmas and Solutions* (2003) 9, at 9; Campbell, 'A Human Rights Approach to Developing Voluntary Codes of Conduct for Multinational Corporations', 16 *Business Ethics Quarterly* (2006) 255, at 256.

[31] Wettstein, 'CSR and the Debate on Business and Human Rights: Bridging the Great Divide', 22 *Business Ethics Quarterly* (2012) 739, at 748–751 calls this the problems of voluntariness and of non-political responsibility. Cf. in a similar direction Lagoutte (n. 28) 247.

[32] See UN Guiding Principles (n. 9) Principle 11, Commentary: 'The responsibility to respect human rights is a global standard of expected conduct for all businesses wherever they operate.'

core labour convention as what should be perceived by companies as the accepted international human rights frameworks.[33] While this is a notable endeavour to align CSR with the rights-based character of the international human rights regime, it remains questionable as to what extent this can be successful from a human rights perspective. From the legal perspective of international human rights law, the understanding of 'social expectations' as a basis for human rights respect remains much closer to the concept of corporate social responsibilities as a voluntary activity than to the legal rights-based conception. This is due to the fact that, despite referring to international legal human rights frameworks, the CR2R does not consider human rights responsibilities to be of—legal or moral—authority, but rather is vaguely defined by what society—however defined—expects.[34] As a result, it is left to the societal actors, in particular companies in their interaction with stakeholders, to define how to make sense of human rights and 'live' them within their governance structures. The normative force of human rights becomes subject to changing expectations.

Of course, there is a possibility to restrict this autonomous choice by companies of how they define human rights by means of a strong state duty to regulate corporations. However, as will be shown later,[35] the specification of the duties of states in relation to furthering corporate human rights respect through law and policies relies on a background role for the state that is directed towards facilitating and encouraging corporations with the instruments of market incentives and market regulation. As a result, the foundational principles in the UNGP on the CR2R align with companies by means of relying conceptually on familiar categories of CSR, the social licence to operate, and the need to autonomously invoke corporate governance and elevates the principles to a formal status in an international human rights document.

## 2. Operationalization

This perspective of relying on the system of corporate governance and its conceptual techniques to relate them to international human rights continues in the

[33] Ibid. Principle 12.

[34] It comes as no surprise that the strongest criticism towards the conceptual embedding of the CR2R within global social expectations comes, on the one hand, from legal theory scholars who conceptualize corporations as global legal orders (e.g. Lindahl, 'One Pillar: Legal Authority and a Social License to Operate in a Global Context', 23 *Indiana Journal of Global Legal Studies* (2016) 201) and, on the other hand, human rights treaty advocates (e.g. Deva, 'Treating Human Rights Lightly: A Critique of the Consensus Rhetoric and the Language Employed by the Guiding Principles', in D. Bilchitz and S. Deva (eds), *Human Rights Obligations of Business: Beyond the Corporate Responsibility to Respect?* (2013) 78; cf. also Nolan, 'The Corporate Responsibility to Respect Human Rights: Soft Law or Not Law?', in Bilchitz and Deva ibid. 138, at 155–156). In contrast, it is unsurprisingly viewed favourably by those who take a sociological and business perspective on global business regulation. See with manifold references to the literature: Buhmann, 'Public Regulators and CSR: The "Social Licence to Operate" in Recent United Nations Instruments on Business and Human Rights and the Juridification of CSR', 136 *Journal of Business Ethics* (2016) 699.

[35] See Section 2C.

operationalization of the CR2R. The principles in the UNGP concerned with the operationalization of the CR2R focus on two central requirements to ensure human rights respect: the requirements for companies to have in place a policy commitment and to establish due diligence processes.

As to the need for a policy commitment, Principle 16 UNGP specifies that companies are expected to express their commitment to meet their responsibility to respect 'through a statement of policy'. This policy has to be approved by the senior management, it has to stipulate the expectations for individual employees and business partners, and it is required to be externally communicated to the public and internally integrated through operational policies. This idea of requiring a policy commitment again strongly connects to the practice of companies to integrate social responsibilities into operational practice and to demonstrate that to the public. It specifically links to a tendency among large companies since the 1990s to develop codes of conduct on public interest issues, specifically workplace standards, environmental protection, and ethical business, and integrate them into their internal operations.[36]

The socio-legal literature on such codes of conduct has, subject to much controversy, framed these codes of conduct theoretically in constitutional terms: for corporations, these codes function in an equivalent manner to public law constitutions for states. They are a quasi-constitutional codification of human rights within private governance. As part of the corporate constitution, these policy commitments form the basis for the corporate governance structure and global corporate practice.[37] Using this established corporate practice, the UNGP embrace this idea of the policy commitment as a quasi-constitutional basis to achieve the operational integration of human rights in corporate governance. The policy commitment forms 'the basis for embedding' the responsibility to respect internally across all functions and procedures and serves as the externally communicated commitment by companies to respect human rights.[38]

However, these policy commitments differ significantly from established notions of international or national constitutions, as predominantly understood by public law scholars. As foundational principles for the corporate entity, such policy

[36] See for the practice of companies to develop corporate codes of conduct, Kolk and van Tulder, 'Setting New Global Rules? TNCs and Codes of Conduct', 14 *Transnational Corporations* (2005) 1. For studies that locate these business commitments even earlier, specifically among American companies, cf. Benson, 'Codes of Ethics', 8 *Journal of Business Ethics* (1989) 305, at 306.

[37] Backer, 'Transnational Corporations' Outward Expression of Inward Self-Constitution: The Enforcement of Human Rights by Apple, Inc', 20 *Indiana Journal of Global Legal Studies* (2013) 805; Teubner, 'Self-Constitutionalizing Transnational Corporations? On the Linkage of "Private" and "Public" Corporate Codes of Conduct', 18 *Indiana Journal of Global Legal Studies* (2011) 17; G. Teubner, *Constitutional Fragments. Societal Constitutionalism in the Globalization* (2012) 56; J. Eijsbouts, *Corporate Responsibility, Beyond Voluntarism. Regulatory Options to Reinforce the License to Operate* (2011) 49–54; Lambooy, 'Corporate Law and CSR: Will There be a Constitution for Multinational Companies in 2030?', in S. Muller *et al.* (eds), *The Law of the Future and the Future of the Law* (2011) 273.

[38] UN Guiding Principles (n. 9) Principle 16, Commentary, 17.

commitments rely on the insight and specification of the respective company and its 'constitutional moment'. The external grounding of these commitments is merely through the requirement for them to be informed by 'external expertise' and be based on the previously identified social expectations on compliance with a minimum set of codified international human rights. In particular, two aspects place emphasis on the autonomy of companies and only indirect influence by other social and public actors to shape human rights responsibilities: policy commitments need only be 'informed' by external expertise and they need to rely on acceptance and approval within the business organization. The determination of corporate human rights responsibilities through accepted international human rights thus remains indirect; the way in which and the type of human rights to be emphasized in the policy commitment are subject to the autonomy of corporations and their decision-making.

The second core operational concept by which the CR2R is specified is the requirement for companies to conduct due diligence. Principles 17–19 lay down that companies, in order to meet their responsibility, have to make a human rights impact assessment, integrate its findings, track the responses, and communicate how they address such responses. The introduction of human rights due diligence can be seen as a good example of how Ruggie intended to overcome the different and partly incompatible understandings between the different parties involved in the process and how he intended to combine insights from both the corporate and the human rights side. Due diligence, so the underlying reasoning went, is a concept that all affected parties—business representatives and corporate lawyers, human rights advocates and public international lawyers, as well as states—are familiar with and thus will buy into.[39] However, in the reality of specifying how to conduct due diligence, the concept appears to be in much closer proximity to its use by business as opposed to its use by states.[40] To be more precise on this point, due diligence, from the perspective of corporate lawyers, is mainly understood as a *process* within a company to manage risks (partly based on legal obligations[41]), among them the legal risks involved for the company. It is commonly understood 'as a

[39] Lambooy, 'Corporate Due Diligence as a Tool to Respect Human Rights', 28 *Netherlands Quarterly of Human Rights* (2010) 404, at 446: 'Ruggie has established a link between two areas of law, that is human rights law and corporate law, which were long considered to be unrelated'; Bonnitcha and McCorquodale, 'The Concept of "Due Diligence" in the UN Guiding Principles on Business and Human Rights', 28 *European Journal of International Law* (2017) 899, at 900: 'a clever and deliberate tactic, as it is familiar to business people, human rights lawyers and states, among whom Ruggie sought to build consensus on his approach'.

[40] See for a similar observation: Buhmann, 'Navigating From "Train Wreck" to being "Welcomed": Negotiation Strategies and Argumentative Patterns in the Development of the UN Framework', in Bilchitz and Deva, *Human Rights Obligations of Business* (n. 34) 29, at 25: '... the SRSG shifted focus from states to companies, supporting the legal system practice with economic system arguments (such as risk management)'.

[41] See, in particular, the origin of due diligence in corporate law in s. 11(b)(3) US Securities Act 1933, which treated due diligence as a potential defence for a false securities registration statement.

process of discovery that is relevant in key business transactions as well as operational activities'.[42] As such, due diligence is a tool for corporations in the process of decision-making as regards joint ventures, mergers and acquisition, selection of partners, choice of jurisdiction or location, and the buying and selling of assets to identify the risks for a company.[43] This corporate risk-based understanding can be identified on several occasions within the UNGP, most prominently in the description of human rights due diligence as a *process* to be initiated by businesses.[44] In that sense, the UNGP embrace established corporate practice and interpret it from the perspective of human rights law. Human rights due diligence means that companies should use established operational processes, but with a view to preventing and mitigating the risks for human rights. It also includes reparation for those who have been harmed by human rights violations.

By means of relating human rights element to due diligence, it is assumed that links are equally established to the concept of due diligence as it is understood in international law and by human rights lawyers. However, despite the terminological overlap, the UNGP do not rely in a similarly strong manner on the public international law due diligence concept, at least not in the second pillar, i.e. when companies are addressed.[45] In international law, due diligence specifies the standard of conduct that states are required to apply in order to meet their duty to prevent negative human rights impacts by third parties.[46] Hence, it is a concept that flows directly from the international *duty* to protect human rights in the event that they are infringed by others. In this context, to exercise due diligence means for states a requirement to prevent a violation by means of the use of considerable state resources without any clear specification as to what processes states are expected to initiate.[47] From the perspective of corporate and private lawyers, such

[42] L. Spedding, *The Due Diligence Handbook: Corporate Governance, Risk Management and Business Planning* (2009) 3.

[43] Ibid. 3–5.

[44] See UN Guiding Principles (n. 9) Principle 15 (b): 'business enterprises should have in place policies and *processes* ... including, (b) A human rights due diligence *process* to identify, prevent, mitigate and account for how they address their impacts on human rights'; Principle 17: '... business should carry out human rights due diligence. *This process* should include assessing actual and potential human rights impact, integrating and acting upon the findings, and communicating how impacts are addressed' (emphasis added). Critically on this process-related understanding in the UNGP, Landau, 'Human Rights Due Diligence and the Risk of Cosmetic Compliance', 20 *Melbourne Journal of International Law* (2019) 221.

[45] As will be shown, the first pillar on the state duty embraces the concept of due diligence for states; see Section C1.

[46] See on this international legal concept of due diligence and its limited consideration in the second pillar of the UN Guiding Principles, Bonnitcha and McCorquodale (n. 39) 909–910.

[47] See e.g. Basic Principles and Guidelines on the Right to a Remedy and Reparation for Victims of Gross Human Rights Violations of International Human Rights Law and Serious Violations of International Humanitarian Law, GA Res. A/RES/60/147, 16 December 2005, Annex, paras 3, 4: 'The obligation to respect, ensure respect for and implement international human rights law ... includes, inter alia, the duty to (a) take appropriate legislative and administrative and other appropriate measures to prevent violations.' Cf. also on this point with reference to the relevant case law, McCorquodale, 'Non-State Actors and International Human Rights Law', in S. Joseph and A. McBeth (eds), *Research Handbook on International Human Rights Law* (2010) 97, at 104–105.

an understanding of due diligence is much better mirrored with the concepts of the duty of care and the standard of a reasonable person in company and tort law. The difference is that the state duty to conduct due diligence is stricter than the 'reasonable person test' applicable to individuals under tort and corporate law.[48] If the international legal understanding of due diligence had been influential in the current context, a much stronger emphasis would need to have been placed on the concept of due diligence as a standard of conduct for companies towards those threatened by human rights harms, including actors for which a company is said to be responsible. Due diligence would have needed to be related to the concept of the duty of care and the reasonable person standard without specifying it as a concrete process with specified steps that companies would be required to take. However, this link between due diligence and the duty of care is absent, although it is possible that such a link may still be initiated through legislative actions by states (as part of their duty to protect in the first pillar)[49] or a related interpretation by courts under corporate and tort law (as part of the third pillar).[50] The stronger rights-based and result-oriented character also permeates the discussions surrounding the Legally Binding Instrument aim on the concept of due diligence.[51]

The first national legislative attempts to rely on the due diligence approach, notably the so-called '*devoir de vigilance*' in France[52] and the German Act on Corporate Due Diligence Obligations in Supply Chains,[53] suggest, however, that the idea incepted in the UNGP is in fact being followed. The current national legislative frameworks as well as the adopted EU directive[54] view due diligence as a corporate duty to implement a certain process. These national sustainability laws contain obligations to conduct adequate governance within the group and the

[48] McCorquodale Smit, 'Human Rights, Responsibilities and Due Diligence: Key Issues for a Treaty', in Deva and Bilchitz, *Building a Treaty on Business and Human Rights* (n. 12) 216, at 219.

[49] See for related proposals: Ortega-Martin, 'Human Rights Due Diligence for Corporations: From Voluntary Standards to Hard Law at Last?', 32 *Netherlands Quarterly of Human Rights* (2014) 44, at 72 who argues that it is the surrounding process by states and international organizations to integrate due diligence into regulation and policy processes (with a specific view to the minerals conflict in the DRC) that could, however, lead to a transformation of due diligence into a standard of care and see van Dam and Gregor, 'Corporate Responsibility to Respect Human Rights Vis-à-Vis Legal Duty of Care', in J. J. Álvarez Rubio and K. Yiannibas (eds), *Human Rights in Business: Removal of Barriers to Access to Justice in the European Union* (2017) 119, at 130–138.

[50] See on the potential of translating due diligence into a standard of care under the duty of care in tort law through transnational tort litigation: Cassel, 'Outlining the Case for a Common Law Duty of Care of Business to Exercise Human Rights Due Diligence', 1 *Business and Human Rights Journal* (2016) 179; Muchlinski, 'Implementing the New UN Corporate Human Rights Framework: Implications for Corporate Law, Governance, and Regulation', 22 *Business Ethics Quarterly* (2012) 145, at 157–161.

[51] Third Revised Draft of the Legally Binding Instrument (n. 10), Arts 6.2 and 6.3 emphasize state obligations to ensure corporate human rights respect and, for that purpose, require corporations to undertake due diligence.

[52] Loi No. 2017-399 relative au devoir de vigilance des sociétés mères et des enterprises donneuses d'ordre, 27 March 2017.

[53] Lieferkettensorgfaltspflichtengesetz, 16 July 2021.

[54] Directive (EU) 2024/1760 of the European Parliament and of the Council of 13 June 2024 on corporate sustainability due diligence and amending Directive (EU) 2019/1937 and Regulation (EU) 2023/2859, OJ 5 July 2024, L2024/1760.

value chain through implementation of certain processes.[55] Compliance with this obligation is currently done through the requirement for corporations to set up a plan to tackle its human rights impact, implement the plan effectively through establishing processes, and report on the steps that they have decided to implement.[56] In particular, the French *devoir de vigilance* can be considered a paradigmatic example in this regard. The law specifies the obligation for large companies to conduct human rights due diligence understood as the requirement to 'establish and implement an effective vigilance plan', which shall include 'reasonable vigilance measures to allow for risk identification and for the prevention of severe violations of human rights and fundamental freedoms ...'[57] Hence, the obligation of the law is the development of a plan with a specific focus on implementing measures for identifying risks; whether failure to comply with such a requirement will result in civil liability as a breach of the duty of care is highly uncertain; currently, the only strong measure indicated by the law after the constitutional review is the possibility for a court to order a company to publish and implement in an effective manner its vigilance plan.[58] In this regard, the *devoir de vigilance* has been understood by the government as creating an obligation of means rather than an obligation of results, which leads to considerable uncertainties as to how cases of liability will be interpreted.[59] Current litigation surrounding the implementation of the law indicates that the core controversies over compliance by companies are not the liability consequences for violations of human rights; instead, they concern the formal aspects of the competence of the courts in relation to reviewing the vigilance plans, about authorship in large corporate groups, and identification of the correct annual plan in the court proceedings. As a result, civil society organizations have already indicated that the implementation of the law by companies has led merely to a transformation of the former reporting practices into a vigilance

[55] Salminen and Rajavuori, 'Transnational Sustainability Laws and the Regulation of Global Value Chains: Comparison and Framework for Analysis', 26 *Maastricht Journal of European and Comparative Law* (2019) 602.

[56] Unsurprisingly, therefore, international lawyers in particular urge the further development of the concept of human rights due diligence towards a standard of conduct in the further implementation of the UNGP and in the current discussions on a Treaty on Business and Human Rights, see specifically on this point McCorquodale and Smit, 'Human Rights, Responsibilities and Due Diligence: Key Issues for a Treaty', in Deva and Bilchitz, *Building a Treaty on Business and Human Rights* (n. 12) 216.

[57] See French Corporate Duty of Vigilance Law, art. L. 225-102-4-I., unofficial translation of the law at http://www.respect.international/french-corporate-duty-of-vigilance-law-english-translation/ (last visited 21 November 2023).

[58] Rühmkorf, 'Global Supply Chain Governance: The Search for "What Works"', 23 *Deakin Law Review* (2018) 63, at 77–78; Brabant and Savourey, 'French Law on the Corporate Duty of Vigilance', 50 *Revue Internationale de la compliance et de l'éthique des affaires* (2017); Section 'A Closer Look at the Penalties Faced by Companies' in https://media.business-humanrights.org/media/documents/d32b6e38d5c199f8912367a5a0a6137f49d21d91.pdf (last visited 5 March 2024).

[59] Triponel and Sherman, 'Legislating Human Rights Due Diligence: Opportunities and Pitfalls to the French Duty of Vigilance Law', International Bar Association, Corporate and M&A Law Committee Publications, 17 May 2017, https://respect.international/wp-content/uploads/2018/08/Legislating-human-rights-due-diligence-opportunities-and-potential-pitfalls-to-the-French-duty-of-vigilance-law.pdf (last visited 5 March 2024); Brabant and Savourey (n. 58) 2–3.

plan.[60] The focus of the law thus remains on creating obligations for companies to leverage their own governance systems for human rights protection rather than making human rights binding upon companies. It is thus a law that contributes to rather than countervails the centring of corporate governance rather than corporate personality in the context of human rights.

Again, it is the basic principles of the CR2R (that informed the due diligence laws) that is a likely reason for this focus on corporate due diligence rather than international law due diligence. As due diligence aims to operationalize corporate responsibility as a social expectation and not an international legal duty, it is difficult to conceive how it could have been envisaged as a standard of conduct for companies that is directed towards specifying the expectations to fulfil an international legal duty.[61] This insight underlines once more how, in conceptualizing and operationalizing the responsibility of companies as part of international human rights law, a significant move can be observed to repeat and codify elements established in corporate governance to specify the relation between companies and human rights and elevate it to gain a formal meaning in an international human rights document and related national legislation that builds upon it.

## C. The UNGP's First Pillar: The Soft (and Limited Hard) Role of Public Governance

This strong emphasis on corporate governance structures and concepts familiar to companies within the UNGP could, of course, be constrained if the duty of states is understood in a complementarily broad manner, namely as one that explicitly requires states to regulate companies in relation to their global operations and hold corporations accountable through appropriate redress procedures in the event of corporate human rights violations. If this were to be achieved, one could argue that while companies may be encouraged to use their governance systems, states also have the duty to comprehensively regulate companies in order to fulfil their own duty to respect human rights. This, as a result, would mean that corporate governance structures to respect human rights would exist *in addition* to strong legal obligations for companies under national law. Yet, the following section will show that, in relation to both the basis and the operationalization, the duties of states in the first pillar (SD2P) is specified as one that is primarily directed towards

[60] ActionAid, Les Amis de la Terre France, Amnesty International, Terre Solidaire, Collectif ethique sur l'etiquette, Sherpa, 'The Law on Duty of Vigilance of Parent and Outsourcing Companies, Year 1: Companies Must Do Better', February 2019, 15, https://respect.international/the-law-on-duty-of-vigilance-of-parent-and-outsourcing-companies-year-1-companies-must-do-better/ (last visited 5 March 2024).

[61] Ruggie and Sherman, 'The Concept of "Due Diligence" in the UN Guiding Principles on Business and Human Rights: A Reply to Jonathan Bonnitcha and Robert McCorquodale', 28 *European Journal of International Law* (2017) 921, at 925–926.

supporting human rights protection through corporate governance structures rather than regulating companies in a way that human rights obligations are imposed on them. The regulatory component is strongly limited in its territorial and substantive scope.

### 1. Conceptual basis

The state duty to protect is built on the established international law duty of states to respect, protect, and fulfil human rights; it specifies—in contrast to the concept of due diligence in the second pillar—a standard of conduct that obliges states to take appropriate measures to prevent, investigate, punish, and redress abuse by companies.[62] In this sense, the foundational principle restates the existing obligations under international law that require states to enforce their laws effectively to ensure that human rights are not violated, but also review their laws as to their potential human rights impact. In addition to this obligation to enforce the law, the first pillar contains a second component, namely that states should adopt a 'smart mix of measures—national and international, mandatory and voluntary—to foster business respect for human rights'.[63] The duty of states for human rights protection according to the UNGP is thus composed of the international legal obligation to regulate within their territory and of recommendations to adopt soft law measures, without, however, always distinguishing clearly between them.[64] In any case, both elements codify the state duty in a limited and traditional manner and thus do not open up many routes for the adoption of stronger legal obligations for companies.

First, the specification of the international legal duty of states to respect, protect, and fulfil is explicitly defined as a territorially confined duty that restricts the requirements for states to regulate companies to their territory and/or jurisdiction. In this respect, a clear (and rather traditional) stance is taken on the question whether states may or should regulate extraterritorially to prevent a negative human rights impact. It is also mentioned in the commentary that states *are allowed* to take measures with extraterritorial effect (e.g. requiring companies within their territory to report on their global operations).[65] This understanding of the state duty to protect has been subject to resilient controversy. It has been emphasized that a restatement on the international legal obligations of states could have embraced a more progressive understanding.[66] Some commentators on the

62 UN Guiding Principles (n. 9) Principle 1, Commentary.

63 Ibid. Principle 3, Commentary.

64 See Lagoutte (n. 28) 248–249.

65 UN Guiding Principles (n. 9) Principle 2, Commentary: 'At present States are generally not required under international human rights law to regulate the extraterritorial activities of businesses domiciled in their territory and/or jurisdiction. Nor are they generally prohibited from doing so, provided there is a recognized jurisdictional basis. Within these parameters some human rights treaty bodies recommend that home States take steps to prevent abuse abroad by business enterprises within their jurisdiction.'

66 Knox, 'The Ruggie Rules: Applying Human Rights Law to Corporations', in R. Mares (ed.), *The UN Guiding Principles on Business and Human Rights: Foundations and Implementation* (2012) 51, at 81,

UNGP even state that international human rights law already today not only provides for extraterritorial regulation, but even obliges states to do so in some situations.[67] Arguments in favour of such an understanding are the specification of the commentaries of the covenants that indicate the possibilities of extraterritorial regulation for companies that fall within the jurisdiction of a state[68] and the international due diligence obligation for states.[69] In addition, critics emphasize processes initiated on academic and policy levels that are directed towards specifying the law as it stands on the content and scope of extraterritorial state obligations[70] and the gradual tendency of regional human rights courts to such accept extraterritorial obligations.[71] These, so the argument goes, should have at least been taken

who is also critical that despite this being an accepted traditional perception, the UNGP 'could have done more to acknowledge the movement towards greater recognition of such [extraterritorial] duties'.

[67] See Augenstein and Kinley, 'When Human Rights "Responsibilities" Become "Duties": The Extra-Territorial Obligations of States that Bind Corporations', in Bilchitz and Deva, *Human Rights Obligations of Business* (n. 34) 271.

[68] Committee on Economic, Social and Cultural Rights Statement, Statement on the obligations of State parties regarding the corporate sector and economic, social and cultural rights, E/C.12/2011/1, 12 July 2011, para 5: 'States parties should also take steps to prevent human rights contraventions abroad by corporations which have their main offices under their jurisdiction, without infringing the sovereignty or diminishing the obligations of the host States under the Covenant'; General Comment No. 24 on State Obligations under the International Covenant on Economic, Social and Cultural Rights in the Context of Business Activities, E/C.12/GC/24, 23 June 2017, para 27: 'Such extraterritorial obligations of States under the Covenant follow from the fact that the obligations of the Covenant are expressed without any restriction linked to territory or jurisdiction' and para 28: 'Extraterritorial obligations arise when a State Party may influence situations located outside its territory, consistent with the limits imposed by international law, by controlling the activities of corporations domiciled in its territory and/or jurisdiction, and thus may contribute to the effective enjoyment of economic, social and cultural rights outside its national territory.' On this basis, some critical voices of the UNGP even argue that the commentary is incorrect, see e.g. De Schutter, 'Regulating Transnational Corporations: A Duty under International Human Rights Law', Contribution of the Special Rapporteur on the Right to Food, Mr Olivier de Schutter, to the workshop 'Human Rights and Transnational Corporations: Paving the way for a legally binding instrument' convened by Ecuador (2014) 5; De Schutter (n. 12) 45–46; Simons, 'The Value-Added of a Treaty to Regulate Transnational Corporations and Other Business Enterprises', in Deva and Bilchitz, *Building a Treaty on Business and Human Rights* (n. 12) 48, at 59.

[69] Narula, 'International Financial Institutions, Transnational Corporations and Duties of States', in M. Langford *et al.* (eds), *Global Justice, State Duties: The Extraterritorial Scope of Economic, Social, and Cultural Rights in International Law* (2013) 114, at 144–147.

[70] The most notable endeavour that is frequently referred to in the debate is the Maastricht Principles on the Extraterritorial Obligations of States in the Area of Economic, Social and Cultural Rights, adopted in Maastricht on 28 September 2011. But for a detailed and critical analysis of the process behind the Maastricht Principles and their potential to change the negative side effects of economic globalization and global business activities, see Wilde, 'Dilemmas in Promoting Global Economic Justice through Human Rights Law', in N. Bhuta (ed.), *The Frontiers of Human Rights: Extraterritoriality and its Challenges* (2016) 127.

[71] However, in this context, it needs to be emphasized that the case law on extraterritorial obligations has largely developed in relation to constellations of the military occupation of states or the custodial control of individuals (and not in relation to regulating the conduct of private globally operating companies) and are therefore narrowly confined. See for an analysis of the case law and the resulting difficulty of applying the existing case law to other situations including the regulation of private companies, Cuinn and Skogly, 'Understanding Human Rights Obligations of States Engaged in Public Activity Overseas: The Case of Transnational Education', 20 *The International Journal of Human Rights* (2016) 761, at 761–766.

up in the specification of the first pillar, as, after all, these developments towards extraterritoriality can be considered to be evolving positive international law. By ignoring these developments, the UNGP not only take a conservative stance, they also codify—hereby attempting to roll-back—this development. The way in which the duty of states in the UNGP is stated presupposes the existence of states that are powerful and willing enough to develop related duties for corporations. The UNGP assume that states as human rights duty bearers are neither in the position nor under the obligation to act as global regulators to establish corporate human rights obligations for their own corporations when they act overseas in order to compensate for the lack of willingness or capacity of other states (mostly host states of multinationals subsidiaries).

Second, even when looking into the specification in the UNGP on how they define the territorially confined duty of states to protect in relation to transnationally operating companies, the actual duties are relatively limited. For this purpose, it is necessary to look into the underlying theoretical concepts that informed Ruggie on how corporate human rights violations can be mitigated through state action. Principle 2 UNGP provides that states should '*set out clearly the expectation* that all business enterprises domiciled in their territory and/or jurisdiction respect human rights throughout their operation'.[72] This phrasing is inspired by the idea of 'orchestration' as employed by Abbott and Snidal.[73] The core idea of orchestration, as these authors suggest, is to rely on private governance, by corporations and civil society, with the support of directive and facilitative state action. Directive orchestration is mostly intended for the national context through which states incorporate private governance schemes into governmental programmes, mandate substantive principles that private governance schemes have to meet, and provide a background threat of mandatory regulation.[74] Facilitative orchestration is the main form to be employed in a transnational context and should rely on 'convening, facilitating, legitimating, negotiating, publicizing, ratifying, supervising, partnering and otherwise interacting' with private governance schemes.[75] In both forms, the role of the state is not primarily to regulate corporations and intervene in their operations through laws, but rather to support and indirectly regulate the measures that private actors employ within their own governance schemes. This already suggests that the underlying idea of *how* and *when* states are supposed to act to ensure that corporations fulfil their responsibility to respect relies on a form of public governance that is placed in the background by setting expectations that corporate governance structures are used for the benefit of human rights.

[72] Emphasis added.
[73] Ruggie (n. 20) 10.
[74] Abbott and Snidal, 'Strengthening International Regulation Through Transnational New Governance: Overcoming the Orchestration Deficit', 42 *Vanderbilt Journal of Transnational Law* (2009) 501, at 555–573.
[75] Ibid. 573.

The proximity of this understanding to other related concepts of international regulation is apparent. Ruggie's inspiration for his work on the UNGP and the first pillar was based on two theories of how states can regulate globally. First, he embraced the new governance theory in international relations that postulates the presence of international regime complexes without a (public) actor that is hierarchically superior and in the position to regulate.[76] Second, Ruggie favours legal theory approaches that draw on the idea of regime complexes and, on this basis, postulates that international regulation is characterized by collisions between different regimes and the lack of an overarching ordering and regulating body.[77] In the same vein as orchestration, such theories do not see the state as the central ordering unit in international law; instead, law produced by states is just one of the competing regulatory orders on an international level. In this context, the most relevant requirements for states to realize their human rights obligations are to develop policy coherence with the aim to urge companies to consider and mitigate their negative human rights impact and, for this purpose, to provide market incentives that make companies institutionalize a human rights culture and provide for remedies in the event of violations.[78] Through this technique, states may achieve change in corporate behaviour through indirect so-called social acculturation dynamics. By this, it is meant that changing the institutional environment in which companies act changes the social expectations with which companies ultimately want to align.[79] In specifying the duty of states as one that is directed towards institutionalizing new expectations for businesses within their territory with a high degree of autonomy for states, the UNGP, rather than pushing the legal boundaries of international human rights law further to bring states under a stronger duty, engage in what two observers call 'framing tactics' that 'are designed to facilitate a familiarity and comfort with the framework that will promote voluntary buy-in and elite management with the new international regime, whilst allowing a large degree of creative ambiguity about what such engagement must in fact entail'.[80]

As a result, this presents states in the UNGP as the primary guardians for international human rights protection as territorially confined entities. To this end,

[76] Keohane and Victor, 'The Regime Complex for Climate Change', 9 *Perspectives on Politics* (2011) 7, at 8: 'Regime complexes are marked by connections between the specific and relatively narrow regimes but an absence of an overall architecture or hierarchy that structures the whole set' (explicitly referenced by Ruggie in his elaborations on the governance architecture underlying the UNGP, in Ruggie (n. 20) fn. 27).

[77] Fischer-Lescano and Teubner, 'Regime-Collisions: The Vain Search for Legal Unity in the Fragmentation of Global Law', 25 *Michigan Journal of International Law* (2004) 999 (see Ruggie (n. 20) text referenced in fn. 26).

[78] Melish and Meidinger (n. 25) 308.

[79] See on the idea of social acculturation dynamics in international human rights law (with a view to the conduct of states as international actors), Goodman and Jinks, 'How to Influence States: Socialization and International Human Rights Law', 54 *Duke Law Journal* (2004) 621.

[80] Melish and Meidinger (n. 25) 308.

they may only carefully and within limits cross their territorial borders even in relation to transnationally operating companies. States further remain background facilitators with the responsibility to change the environment in which companies operate on a national level with the hope that this will lead to incremental changes within the corporate culture.

## 2. Operationalization

This background understanding of the state is repeated in the principles that operationalize the state duty to protect and the way that these principles have been taken up by states in subsequent policy and regulatory processes. The main principle for this purpose is Principle 3, which specifies the links between the first and the second pillars. Apart from enforcing (existing) laws that aim at ensuring business respect for human rights, states should specifically ensure that a good legal and policy climate exists for businesses to meet their responsibility to respect. More precisely, states should ensure that their corporate laws *enable* respect for human rights by businesses, provide *effective guidance* to business enterprises on how they can ensure human rights respect, and *encourage, and where appropriate require,* business enterprises to *communicate* how they address human rights impacts. The use of the language of enabling, guiding, and encouraging underlines the role of the state in influencing and vitalizing systems of corporate governance. The only stronger phrasing—i.e. 'require'—appears in relation to corporate reporting and, even there, it is linked with the limitation 'where appropriate'. This does not mean that states may not use laws and policies to regulate how corporations have to meet the responsibility to respect, but equally it does not place the emphasis on such regulatory components. The only stronger regulatory requirements are set out in relation to businesses which are controlled or owned by the state and thus could qualify as agents of the state[81] or when states privatize state services.[82]

At first sight, these operational principles may not weigh too strongly, as one may argue that they still allow states to go beyond such an indirect background role. However, in the theory of the 'social acculturation dynamics' discussed earlier, such phrasing may have a strong influence on states in how they perceive their duties. A closer look at the policy processes that were initiated by states in the aftermath of the UNGP confirms that this authoritative framing through the UNGP has been successful in shaping how states perceive their role as regulators. This is visible in, on the one hand, the National Action Plans (NAPs) that states have initiated as a reaction to the UNGP and that contain their intended policy and legislative measures to implement the UNGP and, on the other hand, in the analysis of the type of core legislative developments to which the UNGP have led.

[81] UN Guiding Principles (n. 9) Principle 4, which specifies obligations for states for business enterprises that are owned or controlled by the state.

[82] Ibid. Principle 5.

Following the endorsement of the UNGP, states started to implement the SD2P with NAPs which aimed to specify what type of policies and legislative initiatives would be developed in order to meet the state duty to protect. Today, several countries have developed such action plans (although there is still criticism that too few countries have done so). In 2014, a first study was conducted on the content of NAPs, which was followed up by two updates, the latest in 2017 after a number of additional countries had adopted NAPs.[83] One of the major findings that this study revealed was the core emphasis in the NAPs on soft law and other facilitative policy measures as the primary mechanisms to push companies into socially responsible behaviour. In contrast, the exploration of legal–regulatory measures that aim to create legal obligations for companies, even within their territory, was mostly absent. As the 2017 report states: '[o]ne of the most significant weaknesses of the content of the assessed NAPs thus far is their failure to sufficiently explore regulatory options to ensure adequate human rights protection and access to remedy. The majority of action points included in the assessed NAPs are primarily focused on actions that involve awareness-raising, training, research, and other voluntary measures, with very little focus on supporting the development of regulatory actions.'[84] Furthermore, a study by the European Parliament on the implementation of the UNGP in the European Union adds that a reason for the backward-looking and soft law-oriented nature of existing NAPs can be found in the fact that the implementation of the first pillar is linked to the narrative on CSR, i.e. the second pillar.[85]

[83] See International Corporate Accountability Roundtable (ICAR) and European Coalition for Corporate Justice (ECCJ), 'Assessment of Existing National Action Plans on Business and Human Rights', November 2014, https://static1.squarespace.com/static/583f3fca725e25fcd45aa446/t/59998094cd39c36f1e0d1726/1503232152737/ICAR-ECCJ+Assessments+of+Existing+NAPs.pdf (last visited 21 November 2023); November 2015 update https://static1.squarespace.com/static/583f3fca725e25fcd45aa446/t/58da9ec3e3df280b4c4d95cd/1490722506902/ICAR-ECCJ-Assessments-of-Existing-NAPs-2015-Update.pdf (last visited 21 November 2023); ICAR, ECCJ, and Dejusticia, 'Assessment of Existing National Action Plans on Business and Human Rights—2017 Update', August 2017, https://static1.squarespace.com/static/583f3fca725e25fcd45aa446/t/599c543ae9bfdf40b5b6f055/1503417406364/NAP+Assessment+Aug+2017+FINAL.pdf (last visited 21 November 2023).

[84] See ICAR, ECCJ, and Dejusticia, 2017 update (n. 83) 5. Cf. for a similar critique of the lack of emphasis on regulation in the NAP, Augenstein, Dawson, and Thielbörger, 'Implementing the UNGPs in the European Union: Towards an Open Method of Coordination for Business and Human Rights', EUI Working Papers No. 2017/01, Department of Law (2017) 1, at 6–12; O'Brien *et al.*, 'National Action Plans: Current Status and Future Prospects for a New Business and Human Rights Governance Tool', 1 *Business and Human Rights Journal* (2015) 117, at 118.

[85] European Parliament, Directorate General, Implementation of the UN Guiding Principles on Business and Human Rights, EP/EXPO/B/COMMITTEE/FWC/2013-08/Lot8/09, 23–24:

> Given that in some (including EU) states discussions about NAPs are conducted in the shadow of the debate on CSR, with there being little understanding of the differences between the two approaches, this automatically comes up against a major obstacle—an unwillingness of states to regulate due to fears of the impact it might have on their investment attractiveness. ... It is also part of the reason why many of the NAPs developed so far are rather declaratory and stock-taking in nature, rather than focused on future-oriented actions.

Despite the emphasis on voluntary and soft policy measures, one can identify two exceptions in which several NAPs do specify regulatory action and which have led to the adoption of laws: disclosure and reporting laws and laws that require corporations to conduct due diligence.[86] In the following section, the focus will be on the reporting requirements with a view to the type of regulation that they embrace. This is, first, due to the fact that this is certainly the area 'where the Principles have triggered widespread convergence'[87] and, second, because the due diligence laws have already been discussed earlier as a national specification of the corporate due diligence concept and characterized as an indirect form of 'reflexive regulation'.[88] In this regard, the initiated laws on non-financial reporting in general and reporting on due diligence in particular[89] can be considered as an almost perfect example of how states have realized their duty in Principle 3 (d), namely to require business enterprises to communicate how they address their human rights impacts. Reliance on the regulation of corporate human rights communication through advertisement laws is another example that—notably already prior to the UNGP[90]—has been discussed as a potentially effective measure to regulate corporate human rights impacts and that has also led to updates on the related laws.[91]

But how precisely are reporting requirements envisaged to work in relation to regulating companies? What type of obligations do they impose on companies?

[86] See on this classification on the basis of reviewing NAPs, Neglia, 'The UNGPs—Five Years on: From Consensus to Divergence in Public Regulation on Business and Human Rights', 34 *Netherlands Quarterly of Human Rights* (2016) 289, at 292: '… the original consensus [on which the UNGP are based] has split up into two divergent approaches to the regulation of business and human rights. The first is based on a 'comply or explain' principle and only imposes transparency obligations on companies. The latter, on the contrary, imposes a human rights due diligence obligation for large corporations together with pervasive *ex ante* and *ex post* judicial control.'

[87] Ibid. 304.

[88] Text accompanying Loi No. 2017-399 (n. 52).

[89] For the EU: Directive 2014/95/EU of the European Parliament and of the Council amending Directive 2013/34/EU as regards disclosure on non-financial and diversity information by certain large undertakings and groups, OJ 2014 L 330/1: as of 2023, the Directive will be gradually replaced by Directive 2022/2464/EU of the European Parliament and of the Council of 14 December 2022 amending Regulation (EU) No. 537/2014, Directive 2004/109/EC, Directive 2006/43/EC and Directive 2013/34/EC, as regards corporate sustainability reporting, OJ 2022 L 322; in the United States: Dodd-Franck Wall Street Reform and Consumer Protection Act 2010, s. 1502, see for the UK: Modern Slavery Act 2015, s. 54.

[90] See S. Joseph, *Corporations and Transnational Human Rights Litigation* (2004) ch. 5; Wouters and Chanet, 'Corporate Human Rights Responsibility: A European Perspective', 6 *Northwestern Journal of International Law and Business* (2008) 262, at 285ff; De Schutter, 'Corporate Social Responsibility European Style', 14 *European Law Journal* (2008) 203, at 232–234. See for case law related to advertisement and human rights, *Kasky v Nike*, 45 P 3d 243; *Verbraucherzentrale Hamburg v Lidl*, Statement of Complaint filed 6 April 2010, Judgment of 14 April 2010. Cf. also the lawsuit initiated by Sherpa and ActionAid France against Samsung, 11 January 2018, https://business-humanrights.org/en/france-rights-groups-file-misleading-advertising-lawsuit-against-samsung-in-relation-to-labor-rights-violations-in-factories (last visited 23 November 2023).

[91] See European Commission (n. 29) 9. On the application of CSR and human rights communication to the European Unfair Commercial Practices Directive, see Beckers, 'The Regulation of Market Communication and Market Behaviour: Corporate Social Responsibility and the Directives on Unfair Commercial Practices and Unfair Contract Terms', 54 *Common Market Law Review* (2017) 475.

And what is their desired effect? To rely on communication requirements for companies remains an indirect form of regulation that is directed towards invoking the potential of companies to engage in organizational learning and thereby change their behaviour towards human rights protection. Two core assumptions are behind the use of reporting requirements as regulatory means in terms of gearing corporations towards meeting their corporate responsibility to respect. First, public communication by companies on their human rights impact is viewed as a means to empower the addressees of such communication, i.e. shareholders, consumers, and eventually the wider public, to themselves regulate corporations. It is this active pressure by external stakeholders and the attitude of companies to try to pre-empt negative publicity that would push corporations into greater human rights compliance.[92] Hence, reporting laws work because there is an effectively functioning system of civil society governance that uses reporting actions and the omission thereof to pressure companies into human rights compliance. Second, reporting requirements rely on theories of organizational learning that envisage the company as a social actor that may change its behaviour and its corporate culture because of the need to communicate. The logic behind this is to impose a communication requirement on companies as a norm and hereby force them to institutionalize processes, management systems, and related techniques because that would be the only way for them to report appropriately.[93] However, while this approach of reflexive regulation through reporting may very well be conceivable in theory, it is also subject to several practical obstacles that may prevent the regulatory goal being fulfilled.

As to the component of inducing organizational learning, studies on organizational learning in companies suggest that the regulatory link between requiring disclosure and changing corporate behaviour does not paint an accurate picture. It ignores, for instance, that communication requirements mostly focus on *ex post* behaviour, such as the EU non-financial reporting framework, adopted in the aftermath of the UNGP (i.e. to report what the company has done, so that others can hold it to account). This does not necessarily lead to change within the company to effectively address its human rights impacts if it is not combined with *ex ante* organizational learning.[94] Choosing an *ex-post* approach, is, however, a crucial component to fulfil the first regulation strategy, namely to use communication as a

[92] See Buhmann (n. 34) 710: 'These initiatives seek to induce business self-regulation on human rights through the modalities of CSR transparency and reporting. Facing business with potential civil society critique and reputational accountability, these measures draw on business interest in preserving its SLO [social licence to operate]'; Neglia (n. 86) 309.

[93] On this mechanism of regulation, its limits, and its potential to be influenced by corporate practice, Backer, 'Transparency and Business in International Law: Governance Between Norm and Technique', in A. Bianchi and A. Peters (eds), *Transparency in International Law* (2013) 477.

[94] Buhmann, 'Neglecting the Proactive Aspect of Human Rights Due Diligence? A Critical Appraisal of the EU's Non-Financial Reporting Directive as Pillar One Avenue for Promoting Pillar Two Action', 3 *Business and Human Rights Journal* (2017) 23, at 26.

means to empower addressees to hold companies accountable. If companies were only obliged to report what they intend to change and how they would do it, civil society actors would have limited means to hold companies to account for their irresponsible behaviour. Moreover, as far as this component of regulation through civil society pressure is concerned, there are also questions as to whether communication, in reality, allows societal actors to increase accountability. At least in relation to consumers and investors, the behavioural literature controversially debates whether the mere provision of information (in the light of information overload and the complexity of the information) actually helps market actors, in particular consumers, to make decisions.[95] In addition, it is disputed whether consumers actually orient their decisions on aspects such as the human rights performance of companies.[96] Consequently, reliance on reporting requirements as a regulatory technique must assume a mediating function of civil society actors, such as NGOs, that would condense and, through scandal and media attention, publicize information or institutional investors that pressurize companies into meeting their responsibility to respect by means of threatening to withdraw their investments. Hence, in the implementation of regulatory measures to address corporate human rights impacts, the main hope with requiring states to adopt reporting laws rests on civil society and its capability to regulate. Yet, civil society remains ironically the governance system that the UNGP does not address directly with obligations and capacities.

Similar arguments can be made in relation to the more recent move towards due diligence. While moving towards a mandatory character by obliging companies to conduct due diligence, these laws equally place a strong emphasis on the autonomy of corporations in translating human rights into their governance practice and a related supervisory role for civil society and industry initiatives.[97]

As a result of the analysis, one can conclude that the UNGP have integrated core elements of corporate governance systems (CSR, policy commitments, and due diligence) within the international human rights regime. At the same time, the

[95] See from the consumer law literature: Ben-Shahar, 'The Myth of the Opportunity to Read', 5 *European Review of Contract Law* (2009) 1; Ben-Shahar and Schneider, 'The Failure of Mandated Disclosure', 159 *University of Pennsylvania Law Review* (2011) 647; Busch, 'The Future of Pre-Contractual Information Duties: From Behavioural Insights to Big Data', in C. Twigg-Flesner (ed.), *Research Handbook on EU Consumer and Contract Law* (2016) 221.

[96] See conceptually on the potential and limits of consumers as actors who help to mitigate the impact of human rights, Micheletti and Follesdal, 'Shopping for Human Rights', 30 *Journal of Consumer Policy* (2007) 167. For evidence of the limits, see Salcito, Wielga, and Singer, 'Corporate Human Rights Commitments and the Psychology of Business Acceptance of Human Rights Duties: A Multi-Industry Analysis', 19 *The International Journal of Human Rights* (2015) 673, at 688–689.

[97] Wiater 'Unternehmerische Menschenrechtsbindung nach Maßgabe des Lieferkettengesetzes, 77 *Juristenzeitung* (2022), 859, at 862–863 conceptualizes this—with a view specifically to the German Due Diligence in Supply Chains Act—as a new form of contractual human rights obligations. See also, for a strong critique in this direction of mandatory due diligence legislation, Deva 'Mandatory Human Rights Due Diligence Laws in Europe: A Mirage for Rightsholders?', 36 *Leiden Journal of International Law* (2023), 389, at 398–399.

UNGP rest on the idea (and have been realized in this way by states in mandatory due diligence laws) of a background facilitative role of the territorially confined state to assist companies with the autonomous integration of human rights within their corporate governance structures. It remains to be seen to what extent the developments towards the Legally Binding Instrument are capable of changing this. Its strong focus on states as human rights duty bearers with obligations to regulate and provide access to remedy their promising, but the still ambiguous navigation between the concepts of the UNGP and an autonomous rights-centric direction, blur the view on what change the treaty may actually bring. The recent attempts towards forging political consensus by changing the treaty into a framework convention[98] could be politically successful, but they may come at the expense of leaving the conceptual apparatus taken so far in due diligence intact rather than changing its direction.

## 3. Transformations: Human Rights in the 'Business' of Corporate Governance

Given the prominent role of the system of corporate governance to enhance corporate respect for human rights, the inevitable questions are: what does it lead to when human rights obligations are conceptualized as responsibilities that need to be realized in corporate governance? What consequences does this have for the character of human rights and the way in which they are protected?

There are empirical studies that have been conducted to shed light on whether and with what tools and techniques corporations seek to meet their CR2R against the background of the specifications in the UNGP. These provide insights into how human rights respect is practised by companies and consequently can serve as a good basis to discuss on a conceptual level what the character of human rights within corporate governance structures is, in terms of the type of rights protected, the organizational processes to prevent violations *ex ante*, and the related institutions that are available *ex post* for victims to seek redress. To that end, the following empirical–theoretical analysis will show that the new social expectation to 'live' human rights respect within corporate governance structures may indeed help, at least in some cases, to further a corporate culture for human rights respect. It may lead to greater sensitivity in corporate practice towards the issue of human rights and thus help to institutionalize the previously indicated 'social acculturation'[99] dynamics.

[98] See on this rather recent attempt, Deva *et al.*, 'A Framework Agreement in Business and Human Rights', *Völkerrechtsblog*, 24 June 2022, https://voelkerrechtsblog.org/de/a-framework-agreement-in-business-and-human-rights/ (last visited 23 November 2023).

[99] See n. 79.

Yet, in this process of integrating human rights into the private governance system, a notable, quite fundamental, transformation can be observed regarding how human rights are understood and practised. One study on corporate reporting of human rights observed this astutely: 'Corporations do not put rights to work neutrally ... Business and human rights is ... not just a matter of rights: It is a matter of business.'[100] Empirically, this transformation of human rights into business practices reveals itself in new narratives on the origin and justification of human rights respect and the related prioritization by companies in their codes and management tactics, the processes that are installed to ensure human rights respect, and the character and type of redress procedures that are put in place (Section A). Theoretically, this can be conceptualized as a new form of institutionalizing human rights in the private sphere that is based on social persuasion and autonomous decision-making within corporations which is separate from state-centric human rights conceptions (Section B).

## A. Corporate Practices to Respect Human Rights

In order to structure the findings from the various studies and to be able to compare them with the established notions of human rights in international human rights law, this review classifies them along the different elements of corporate human rights practice. The following sections will analyse the substance of human rights that companies deem relevant as part of their corporate responsibility, more specifically, the content and the authoritative justification as perceived by corporate managers and related documents (Section 1), the organization of compliance processes and other practices within the company to ensure human rights respect (Section 2), and, finally, the redress structure that is established (Section 3). This distinction reflects the threefold structure through which the UNGP operationalize the corporate responsibility to respect, i.e. the policy commitment to internationally recognized human rights as the 'quasi-constitutional codification' of human rights, the process of due diligence as the core process of how companies should ensure human rights respect, and the provision of remediation in the form of own-grievance mechanisms. Moreover, such a structure facilitates identifying analogies to the standard of human rights protection that is derived from international human rights law in its application to states.

[100] O'Kelly, 'Human Rights and the Grammar of Corporate Social Responsibility', 28 *Social & Legal Studies* (2019) 625, at 642.

### 1. Selection, content, and justification: corporate perceptions of human rights respect

The first notable observation of corporate practices for human rights respect relates to the type of human rights that corporations integrate within their corporate governance structures. The UNGP require companies generally to respect 'internationally recognized human rights' that are specified at a minimum as those expressed in the International Bill of Rights and the International Labour Organization (ILO) core labour rights.[101] This, indeed, broadly specifies the international human rights which are legally codified, with a slight emphasis on employment-related rights. The practice of corporations in naming and selecting applicable rights confirms this slight employment focus. Scholars who have analysed the intersection between corporate social responsibility practices and the business and human rights discourse have frequently emphasized that the origin of human rights awareness in relation to companies departs from a central focus on employment-related rights.[102] The reason is, first, the focus of scandalization by civil society on companies' disrespect for fundamental labour standards. This was particularly obvious in the early 1990s where the use of child and forced labour in supply chains in 'sweatshops' was a prominent topic for debate and initiated lively discussions on how to address corporate human rights violations.[103] Moreover, employment-related rights are the most familiar type of rights to companies. Companies act as employers within employment relationships and are, in this capacity, in many countries legally required to respect the specific rights of their employees.[104] Finally, there may also have been a good deal of successful lobbying involved on the side of the ILO to expand the reach of international labour rights by means of framing them in human rights terms. It, therefore, comes as no surprise that studies on corporate policies on human rights respect identify as the most common denominator a continuous reference to the ILO core labour conventions.[105] As an early study put it: 'companies recognize labour rights with

[101] UN Guiding Principles (n. 9) Principle 12.

[102] Wettstein (n. 31) 746–747. See for an early study that highlights the predominance of labour rights as mentioned in codes of conduct, Organization for Economic Co-operation and Development, 'Codes of Conduct: Expanded Review of their Contents', OECD Working Paper Series on International Investment No. 6 (2001) 1, at 8. For a more recent study, see Preuss and Brown, 'Business Policies on Human Rights: An Analysis of Their Content and Prevalence Among FTSE 100 Firms', 109 *Journal of Business Ethics* (2012) 289, at 295.

[103] See e.g. N. Klein, *No Logo: Taking Aim at the Brand Bullies* (2000); A. Fung, D. O'Rourke, and C. Sabel, *Can We Put an End to Sweatshops?* (2001).

[104] Obara, 'What Does This Mean? How UK Companies Make Sense of Human Rights', 2 *Business and Human Rights Journal* (2017) 249, at 262–263.

[105] Kocher, 'Codes of Conduct and Framework Agreements on Social Minimum Standards—Private Regulation?', in O. Dilling, M. Herberg, and G. Winter (eds), *Responsible Business. Self-Governance and Law in Transnational Economic Transactions* (2008) 67, at 70; European Commission, 'An Analysis of Policy References made by Large EU Companies to Internationally Recognised CSR Guidelines and Principles' (2013) 6–7; Global Reporting Initiative, 'Reporting on Human Rights 2008', https://www.globalreporting.org/resourcelibrary/Reporting-On-Human-Rights.pdf, 10 (last visited 23 November 2023).

greater frequency than any other human rights'.[106] A recent study on how companies conduct human rights due diligence further notes that there are a considerable number of companies that understand human rights respect 'as part of other processes, predominantly workplace health and safety, labour rights, equality and non-discrimination, and community, indigenous or land rights'.[107]

It is notable that the endorsement of the UNGP and the greater awareness of companies have led to a greater sensitivity by companies to consider other types of rights, although a recent study suggests that this trend is limited to a handful of frontrunner companies and, thus, has not reached 'average' companies.[108] However, the evolution of the type of rights that companies ought to and do respect shows a significant deviation from the evolution of the original set of international human rights. As a separate body of legal rights, human rights evolved through the covenants from the initial issue of civil and political liberties towards a focus on realizing economic and social rights. Hence, from their inception, human rights had a civil and humanitarian origin with an inherent claim for universal recognition that had its legal–political origin in the Universal Declaration of Human Rights and the philosophical basis grounded in the idea of equal human dignity.[109] In corporate practice, this civil and humanitarian origin as rights for all human beings differs. Human rights respect becomes subject to prioritization by companies on the ground of the notion of proximity of rights with the corporate organization. Rights are accepted more easily when they relate to those who are directly affected by the corporate organization, i.e. rights of employees and, very broadly speaking, rights of 'stakeholders'. Theoretically, it is possible to describe this transformation of individual rights into stakeholder relations as a somewhat 'obscure' or 'specific' form of functional equivalence by which elements developed for a political infrastructure are translated into those non-state systems that take over political functions.[110] But can one really speak here about equivalents? The first studies on corporate practices in relation to corporate human rights respect suggest that

[106] Wright and Lehr, 'Business Recognition of Human Rights', Corporate Social Responsibility Initiative Working Paper No. 31/2006 (2006) 1, at 3.

[107] McCorquodale *et al.*, 'Human Rights Due Diligence in Law and Practice: Good Practices and Challenges for Business Enterprises', 2 *Business and Human Rights Journal* (2017) 195, at 205.

[108] Ibid. 204. On the basis of public corporate communications and interviews, they conclude that almost half of the responding companies had not conducted any human rights due diligence processes.

[109] See e.g. with further references to the debate, McCorquodale (n. 47) 109–111. On the intersection of the Universal Declaration of Human Rights and the concept and function of human dignity, see Carozza, 'Human Dignity', in D. Shelton (ed.), *The Oxford Handbook of International Human Rights Law* (2013) 345.

[110] E.g. Kjaer, 'The Concept of the Political in the Concept of Transnational Constitutionalism', in C. Joerges and R. Tommi (eds), *After Globalization— New Patterns of Conflict and their Sociological and Legal Reconstruction* (2011) 285, at 316. Cf. also MacDonald and MacDonald, 'Non-Electoral Accountability in Global Politics: Strengthening Democratic Control within the Global Garment Industry', 17 *European Journal of International Law* (2006) 89; Backer, 'Multinational Corporations as Objects and Sources of Transnational Regulation', 14 *ILSA Journal of International & Comparative Law* (2008) 499.

the lack of employing established human rights terminology bears the realistic risk of overlooking essential aspects of potential corporate human rights violations. Conversely, companies interviewed for one study have indicated that precisely the use of human rights terminology and related expertise from international human rights lawyers assisted the responsible staff in those companies to better understand and work with human rights.[111] If such external expertise is used, companies tend to identify more human rights impacts and have greater sensitivity towards the complexity of the issue. Hence, the prioritization and autonomous perception of what human rights entail appears by no means equivalent to the way international human rights are viewed and do not necessarily lead to similar results. On the contrary, the prioritization of human rights according to economic needs and the related prioritization of specific types of rights shapes the way in which companies identify rights-affectedness.

The second aspect in which companies appear to change their concepts of human rights relates to the meaning that they attach to the selected rights. Already in a study from 2005, McBeth and Joseph had identified considerable differences between the corporate perception of the content of human rights and the content of the rights that human rights lawyers would attach to them. Relying on interviews with corporate managers, it was found that they were relatively unacquainted with established notions of human rights and, as a result, interpreted the meaning from their own perspectives. The most striking examples are managers who did not consider the 'right to life' relevant for corporate operations on the ground that it was seen as being mainly about the abortion debate and a lack of linking specific corporate practices, such as bribery or marketing of health products, to threats to human rights.[112] This even applied to employment-related rights that companies are perceived to be the most familiar with. The right to education was chosen by some companies as a relevant human right for a company because job training was provided for their staff and the right to social security was chosen because of the company's offer of a pension.[113] In a 2017 study on corporate human rights perception, Obara appears to have confirmed these findings even in the aftermath of the adoption of the UNGP. Through interviews with corporate officials, she revealed that there is a mismatch between the official and external use of human rights terminology, primarily in their official corporate material and the internal practices and language. In establishing internal means for human rights respect, companies translated the official human rights documents internally into everyday practices and communicative materials that used the terminology of corporate responsibility, corporate social responsibility, and sustainability.[114] The reasons for

[111] McCorquodale *et al.* (n. 107) 99, 222.

[112] McBeth and Joseph, 'Same Words, Different Language: Corporate Perceptions of Human Rights Responsibilities', 11 *Australian Journal of Human Rights* (2005) 95, at 101.

[113] Ibid. 100.

[114] Obara (n. 104) 267. See also J. Morrison and D. Vermijs, 'The "State of Play" of Human Rights Due Diligence: Anticipating the Next Five Years', Institute for Human Rights and Business London (2011)

this translation of human rights language into the familiar language of CSR are twofold: first, terms such as CSR have an established meaning within the corporate culture and are thus more relatable to employees and managers. Second, corporate managers perceive the term human rights to be too vague, abstract, and broad to have any meaningful sense in day-to-day corporate practices. Moreover, the link between human rights and companies has had a bad public reputation.[115] As the study summarizes: '[m]any respondents spoke at length about the need to translate and adapt the human rights concept and label into language that is meaningful, well-known and grounded in the everyday experiences of stakeholders'.[116] This observation is indeed very much in line with Ruggie's objective that in order for companies to mitigate human rights impact rules and processes, they have to be designed in a way that they 'make sense inside the company',[117] i.e. that companies are able to relate to them. However, it differs significantly from the established perceptions in international human rights law where human rights are considered to have a meaning that is independent from the actors that are obliged to respect and protect them and where specific authoritative bodies and courts add meaning to what is meant by international human rights protection.

The third element in which corporate perceptions towards human rights respect in their governance structures differ from the international human rights discourse relates to the origin and justification for requiring corporate human rights respect. Several studies have underlined that corporate justifications for practising human rights respect can be split into three aspects: philanthropy, economic motives, and risk management. First, human rights respect is treated as a matter of giving something back to society in exchange for the social approval to operate as a business (the so-called social licence to operate). In this regard, human rights perceptions overlap and in a complex manner interact with the understanding of CSR within companies, either as building upon CSR strategies or as 'pushing the boundaries'.[118] This philanthropic understanding has shaped human rights understanding for many years. In the previously cited 2005 interview study, corporate managers identified as human rights respect donations to schools and charities as well as fundraising schemes.[119] The also mentioned 2017 interview study emphasized that a frequent response by managers is to frame respect for human rights as

1, at 36–37 who suggest that companies should—in order to be able to make sense of human rights—adopt an explicit human rights approach as an input, but then translate it internally into the context of business management with a 'self-conscious' rights-aware approach that may or may not use human rights terminology.

[115] Obara (n. 104) 267–268.

[116] Ibid. 267.

[117] Ruggie, 'Business and Human Rights: Together at Last? A Conversation with John Ruggie', 35 *Fletcher Forum of World Affairs* (2016) 117, at 119.

[118] Obara and Peattie, 'Bridging the Great Divide? Making Sense of the Human Rights-CSR Relationship in UK Multinational Enterprises', 53 *Journal of World Business* (2018) 781, at 786.

[119] McBeth and Joseph (n. 112) 102.

'the right thing to do' and established a link between human rights and 'the importance of giving back to society and/or the local community, and the personal values of employees'.[120] This suggests that, within companies, human rights have become grounded in a, however broadly defined, social expectation that businesses perceive as relevant for running their business. Hence, human rights are not treated as an obligation that is based on moral persuasiveness or legal authority, but as a matter of reciprocally (and voluntarily) returning to society 'something' for being accepted as a member of that society. Second, corporations also treat human rights respect, more or less openly, as being relevant for their economic performance. Human rights become a matter of risk management by which companies mitigate risks for their own sustainable performance.[121] Again, it is interesting that some managers even deemed economic considerations to be the most important reason for engaging in human rights respect because 'an economic narrative was more believable than a morally based argument within a corporate setting'.[122] Third, to the extent that human rights respect is increasingly made a legal binding obligation, in the form of due diligence laws and reporting laws, and due to public exposure and scandal, corporations treat human rights respect as a prerequisite for conducting effective risk management. As O'Kelly emphasized in a study on the terms used in corporate human rights accounts: 'corporate approaches to human rights issues would draw on narratives of risk and so rights clarify the idea of what might be amenable to risk management (alongside environmental, social, financial risk, etc.). Risk management lends a sense of proactive engagement and procedural attention to the firm's invocation of human rights.'[123]

This threefold justification narrative of philanthropy, profit, and risk mirrors how the UNGP foresaw the corporate responsibility to respect and its work in practice. Being grounded in a sense of pragmatism and leveraging as many governance sources as possible, the UNGP took seriously corporate governance as a system that strongly relies on economic incentives and a sense of societal acceptance of business activities. Accordingly, notions of the 'social licence to operate' and the 'business case for respecting human rights' appear to have been necessary to achieve the buy-in of the business side in the UNGP and increase the chances for their realization.[124] At the same time, invoking such justification changes the answer to the question of why corporations have to respect human rights. From a critical perspective, it has already been emphasized that such a pragmatic grounding of

[120] Obara (n. 104) 265.

[121] Ibid. 264–265. See for a critical analysis of this narrative as a foundation of UNGP's second pillar and the resulting problems for corporate practice: Cragg, 'Ethics, Enlightened Self-Interest, and the Corporate Responsibility to Respect Human Rights: A Critical Outlook at the Justificatory Foundations of the UN Framework', 22 *Business Ethics Quarterly* (2012) 9.

[122] Obara (n. 104) 264.

[123] O'Kelly (n. 100) 640.

[124] Cragg (n. 121) 10. On the notion of the 'business case for respecting human rights' generally, C. van Dam, *Enhancing Human Rights Protection: A Company Lawyer's Business* (2015).

political concepts may result in 'market capture'.[125] It has further been emphasized that such justification may reach practical limits, as it does not work in all types of sectors and equally not for all types of corporations. Developing a clear 'business case' for human rights respect and aligning economic motives towards financial prosperity with an 'investment' in human rights is limited to sectors in which social reputation may have direct effects on financial performance.[126] However, leaving aside such questions as the effectiveness of such a justificatory rationale as well as the fundamental critique that is often brought forward against aligning public values (e.g. human rights) with markets, such a change in the rationale from legal and moral to an instrumental reputational and financial grounding does have implications for how human rights are practised. Social and economic narratives are much more strongly context-dependent on the functioning of a particular market and current societal perceptions and are much more fluid in comparison to legal or moral norms that have evolved over a long historical period. This allows the actor being bound to respect human rights to use and interpret this justification in a much more flexible way. To be more concrete, whereas states, in shaping their duty to respect human rights, may have to rely on established historically grown notions in international legal frameworks with related commentaries and moral justifications, companies, in recurring to social expectation and economic incentives, may prioritize and interpret human rights in the light of how they perceive such expectations to be under current economic conditions.

### 2. Behaviour and organization: corporate compliance processes

Following on from the discussion of *why* corporations perceive human rights respect as crucial and *what* type of human rights that may entail and how this differs from how human rights obligations for states are perceived, this section will continue with an analysis of *how* corporations practise human rights respect, i.e. how far they perceive their responsibility to reach and what type of processes they develop for that purpose. Two aspects deserve special attention in this respect: first, the specification of the expected behaviour, i.e. what does it mean to respect human rights, and, second, the character of related processes within the company to ensure that this is met.

As to the specification of the required behaviour, one finding in empirical studies is the focus of companies on their passive responsibility, i.e. the focus on 'do no harm' and the related terminology.[127] This is particularly apparent in relation to human rights practices in supply chains. For this constellation, scholars

[125] Christodoulidis, 'On the Politics of Societal Constitutionalism', 20 *Indiana Journal of Global Legal Studies* (2013) 629; Shamir, 'Capitalism, Governance and Authority: The Case of Corporate Social Responsibility', 6 *Annual Review of Law and Social Science* (2010) 531.

[126] See for this famous critique on the business case with this argument, D. Vogel, *The Market for Virtue* (2005) 45.

[127] Obara (n. 104) 264.

who have investigated the contracting and enforcement practice of companies towards suppliers have identified a strong tendency by companies to impose human rights standards on their supply chains and install related auditing procedures without necessarily simultaneously embracing a fully collaborative and integrated approach that is directed towards tackling the root causes of the violation.[128] This understanding of human rights respect as a negative responsibility resembles again the approach taken by the UNGP. The UNGP frame the core responsibility of business as being to 'avoid causing or contributing' and 'seek[ing] to prevent or mitigate' negative human rights impact[129] and throughout the document contrast the corporate responsibility to respect with the state's duty to respect, protect, and fulfil human rights. Moreover, the UNGP distinguish between the responsibility of companies to avoid causing harm or contributing to it through their own activities and preventing and seeking to mitigate it whenever there is a human rights threat that is directly linked to them. Hence, there is a layered responsibility that is oriented on the question of how closely their own behaviour is linked to a potential human rights violation.

This establishes a different narrative for corporate human rights respect than that which international human rights law requires from states. The focal point of corporate human rights respect is negative (avoid 'causing trouble') and the degree of responsibility is specified with the proximity of the behaviour to the human rights violation. In contrast, in relation to states, the threshold is not primarily the capability of the state to interfere and the degree to which it actively contributed to the violation, but the desired result of achieving greater human rights protection. A practical comparison between the expected behaviour of states and corporations may clarify this: whereas the human rights duty of states goes as far as to prevent human rights violations by third parties and requires appropriate and effective measures to that end (at least if harm occurs within their territory), including putting pressure on the perpetrator to prevent the human rights abuse from (re) occurring, corporations may comply with their human rights responsibilities by means of ultimately cutting ties with the perpetrator regardless of whether that may end the human rights violation.[130] Hence, in the corporate practice of human rights, there seems to be a shift from the recognition of an international standard that specifies the conduct expected to protect human rights, towards a stronger differentiation as to the type of behaviour that is required by different actors. Although not necessarily intended, human rights protection, when integrated into

[128] LeBaron, Lister, and Dauvergne, 'The New Gatekeeper: Ethical Audits as a Mechanism of Global Value Chain Governance', in A. C. Cutler and T. Dietz (eds), *The Politics of Transnational Governance by Contract* (2017) 97; R. Locke, *The Promise and Limits of Private Power: Promoting Labour Standards in a Global Economy* (2013) ch. 3.

[129] UN Guiding Principles (n. 9) Principle 13.

[130] Wettstein, 'Silence as Complicity: Elements of a Corporate Duty to Speak Out Against the Violation of Human Rights', 22 *Business Ethics Quarterly* (2012) 63.

private governance, evolves in a twofold direction. Corporate governance is perceived as a system on which 'secondary', or critically framed 'incomplete', human rights responsibilities are placed in contrast to states as the 'primary' bearers.[131]

This leads to the second aspect, namely the type of processes that companies install to ensure that 'no harm is done'. For states, there is no comprehensive list of the type of measures that they have to adopt in order to meet their international human rights obligations. On the contrary, states have to do their utmost to ensure that human rights are protected and install appropriate and effective measures for that purpose.[132] For companies, the UNGP prescribe companies to take a specific type of action, namely to conduct the process of due diligence. With regard to this process, there are empirical studies that analyse the set-up of due diligence within companies more closely in light of the requirements set forth in the UNGP. Based on the framing in the UNGP, the concept of due diligence is mainly understood as a management process. In this sense, the UNGP's due diligence requirement can be classified primarily as a 'management, governance and communication process' that aims at 'making human rights manageable' for companies[133] and that works as a risk management tool.[134] It has already been noted earlier that this conception differs from how the due diligence obligations of states are defined under international human rights law.[135] It is notable that this expected process-oriented form of due diligence and its understanding as a management tool is reflected in corporate practice. Companies interpret the requirement to respect human rights as a responsibility to incorporate concrete processes in their business operations that allow them to identify and remedy their human rights impact and assess existing policies and practices. Rather than taking a holistic approach to human rights respect that is informed by external expertise on what it means to respect human rights, companies have—as a response to the UNGP—started to engage in reviewing their own internal processes to make them 'Ruggie-proof'.[136]

This focus on human rights due diligence as a process to comply with risks may result in human rights respect ending up in a merely box-ticking exercise by which companies develop checklists and internal compliance processes as proxies for meeting their human rights responsibilities.[137] In a 2017 study on how due

[131] In this regard, it seems that there is a move towards a conceptualization that had already been discussed in relation to the UN Draft Norms (n. 17), which differentiate in their preamble between states and companies by means of the recognition that states have the '*primary* responsibility' for human rights and corporations that 'as organs of society are *also* responsible for promoting and securing human rights' (emphasis added).

[132] See, for elaboration, the text accompanying n. 47.

[133] Fasterling and Demuijnck, 'Human Rights in the Void? Due Diligence in the UN Guiding Principles on Business and Human Rights', 116 *Journal of Business Ethics* (2013) 799, at 801.

[134] McCorquodale, 'Corporate Social Responsibility and International Human Rights Law', 87 *Journal of Business Ethics* (2009) 385, at 392.

[135] See Section 2B2.

[136] Ruggie (n. 26) 14. On the notion of making human rights practices 'Ruggie-proof', see Fasterling and Demuijnck (n. 133) 805.

[137] Fasterling and Demuijnck (n. 133) 806. Cf. also Muchlinski (n. 50) 156.

diligence is practised within companies, McCorquodale and others identified that there are huge differences in terms of how companies practise human rights due diligence. While some companies have developed specific human rights due diligence, others have integrated concern for human rights into other already existing due diligence processes.[138] Interestingly, there is a significant difference between these two approaches in terms of the result, namely whether a potential corporate human rights impact was identified. Companies that developed specific human rights due diligence mechanisms through the lenses of human rights language, external human rights expertise, and by means of taking a holistic approach that focused appropriate mechanisms with a view to the outcome are much more likely to identify any adverse human rights impact of their activities than those companies that equalize human rights responsibility with the setting up or integration of human rights concerns into an already existing corporate process.[139] This difference between companies conducting dedicated human rights due diligence and those integrating it into other processes is also linked to which departments were involved in the development of internal processes. While most companies seem to place human rights protection and human rights due diligence under the competence of corporate social responsibility, labour/human resources, and compliance departments,[140] those viewing due diligence through the lens of human rights protection gave the main task of identifying negative human rights impact to the CSR department and the legal department with considerable use of external human rights expertise.[141] Not surprisingly, the authors of the study therefore suggest that the process of taking human rights seriously as an end within a corporate compliance process requires setting up multifunctional teams that operate across different departments and make use of external human rights expertise.[142] Similar findings on the transformation of human respect as a manageable risk-oriented practice can be observed when analysing corporate reporting on human rights.[143] In this regard, it is also notable that inevitably tools evolve and become best practice to make human rights-compliance measurable, in particular benchmarking[144] and the development and practice of indicators.[145] Human rights-compliance becomes intrinsically linked to strategies of knowing and processing

[138] McCorquodale *et al.* (n. 107) 205.

[139] Ibid. 206, 214, 221.

[140] See on this finding, also Morrison and Vermijs (n. 114) 13.

[141] McCorquodale *et al.* (n. 107) 209–210.

[142] Ibid. 222.

[143] O'Kelly (n. 100).

[144] See the Corporate Human Rights Benchmark, https://www.corporatebenchmark.org/ (last visited 23 November 2023). See for a pointed critical analysis on the Corporate Human Rights Benchmark, Maher, 'De-Contextualized Corporate Human Rights Benchmarks: Whose Perspective Counts? See Disclaimer', *Business and Human Rights Journal* (2019) 1.

[145] Shamir and Weiss, 'Semiotics of Indicators: The Case of Corporate Human Rights Responsibility', in K. Davis *et al.* (eds), *Governance by Indicators: Global Power Through Quantification and Rankings* (2012) 110.

through measuring. This trend is amplified by the trend to measure human rights-compliance through software tools throughout the corporate organization and global supply chains. As a response to the UNGP and national mandatory due diligence laws, companies have started to rely on IT software to measure human rights performance. Such development has led to another change in human rights that will become the next frontier of the relationship between business and human rights: the algorithmization of human rights[146] and the translation of human rights into quantitative data[147] that is viewed by managers only through a computer interface that breaks down the data into colourings and warnings. The magnitude of this transformation of human rights into business software will deserve its own analysis; in the context of this analysis, it is mentioned as the preliminary end of a description of human rights transformation through business management.

To conclude, the focus on providing manageable guidance for companies on how to achieve greater human rights respect risks changing the way in which human rights respect is interpreted from a holistic result-orientation towards a measurable process-orientation. It is then not the result of not violating human rights that is the threshold to determine what is considered appropriate action; instead, a particular process is specified and related to measurable indicators that are put in place and, even if only implemented consistently, establish a presumption that the corporation has acted in a way such that human rights are respected.

### 3. Remedies: informal redress and its relation to remedies

The concept of access to remedy is an indispensable element of human rights protection in international law.[148] Accordingly, the requirement to guarantee access to remedy for victims of corporate human rights violations also forms a core part of the UNGP. For companies, the expectations are to establish grievance mechanisms and to cooperate in existing remediation processes (judicial and non-judicial). In the most general terms, access to remedy under international human rights law is understood as the duty to engage in prompt, fair, and thorough investigations, to provide prompt, effective, and independent remedial mechanisms, to impose appropriate sanctions on the perpetrators, and to provide for appropriate forms of reparation.[149] It is obvious that it is not possible for companies to set up remedies

[146] Backer and McQuilla, 'The Algorithmic Law of Business and Human Rights: Constructing Private Transnational Law of Ratings, Social Credit and Accountability Measures', 19/1 *International Journal of Law in Context* (2023) 32.

[147] Sarfaty, 'Translating Modern Slavery into Management Practice', 45 *Law & Social Inquiry* (2020) 1027.

[148] O. De Schutter, *International Human Rights Law: Cases, Materials, Commentary* (2010) 365.

[149] Human Rights Council, 'Promotion of all human rights, civil, political, economic, social and cultural rights, including the right to development', Report of the Special Representative of the Secretary-General on the issue of human rights and transnational corporations and other business enterprises, John Ruggie. Addendum: State obligations to provide access to remedy for human rights abuses by third parties, including business: an overview of international and regional provisions, commentary and decisions, A/HRC/11/13/Add.1, 15 May 2009, 2–3.

themselves in a way that all these requirements are fulfilled. Therefore, the expectation set forth in the UNGP has been to rely on the interaction between states and their obligation to provide access to remedy and the additional responsibility of companies to autonomously develop grievance mechanisms that allow for early intervention and potential informal remediation before a situation escalates.

However, as far as this duty of states to provide access to remedy is concerned, early studies suggest that significant legal and practical obstacles still exist for victims to access remedies and that states have not taken sufficient steps in relation to providing remedies for corporate human rights violations. A 2017 study on the removal of barriers to access to justice in the EU underlined that, legally, it is the rules on jurisdiction as laid down in the Brussels (recast) Regulation that considerably restrict bringing claims against corporations in EU Member States.[150] While the recast Brussels Regulation allows companies to be sued in the country of their incorporation or main place of business and has further prohibited the application of the controversial doctrine of *forum non conveniens*,[151] the complex structure of corporate groups in which violations may also have occurred by a subsidiary is not adequately addressed. Regularly, the rules provide for jurisdiction against the parent company, but these claims may easily fail at the level of substance due to the difficulty for victims to understand internal corporate decision-making structures and thus their inability to prove sufficient involvement of the parent company in the operations of the subsidiary. As far as related claims against a foreign subsidiary are concerned, it is, on the other hand, difficult to establish jurisdiction, as the subsidiaries are legally separate entities with their place of incorporation in another country. As the observers of the study note: 'the Brussels I regime is expressly designed with a presumption against claimants, and centralizes the defendant's domicile as its main ground for jurisdiction'.[152] Furthermore, the national rules on jurisdiction that consequently determine jurisdiction for human rights cases where a subsidiary or a supplier is involved, appear to be very divided on the issue of whether granting jurisdiction against such affiliated companies is possible. Some national courts in EU Member States have provided for extended possibilities for courts to hear connected claims against the parent company and the subsidiary.[153] They have based their verdict on the ruling of the Court of Justice of the EU that suing two related defendants together in one Member State is possible under the Brussels regime when the two claims are related and it is foreseeable

[150] Augenstein and Jägers, 'Judicial Remedies: The Issue of Jurisdiction', in Álvarez Rubio and Yiannibas (n. 49) 7.

[151] Case C-281/02, *Andrew Owusu v N. B. Jackson* (ECLI:EU:C:2005:120).

[152] Augenstein and Jägers (n. 150) 27.

[153] Cf, in particular the cases of Nigerian Farmers against Shell: *Fildelis Ayoro Oguru and others v Royal Dutch Shell and others* (ECLI:NL:GHDHA:2021:132), *Eric Barizaa Doo and others v Royal Dutch Shell and others* (ECLI:NL:GHDHA:2021:133), *Royal Dutch Shell and others v Friday Alfred Akpan* (ECLI:NL:GHDHA:2021:134), all Court of Appeal in The Hague, 29 January 2021 (ECLI:NL:RBDHA:2013:BY9845).

for the defendants that they might be sued together in the Member State of domicile of either one of them.[154] However, the fact that the claimant has to prove the foreseeability of the defendant and the connection between the claims on the ground of involvement of the parent within the subsidiary's operations places a high threshold for victims to surpass in order to access justice. In addition, under some national laws, victims need to prove that a claim against the parent company has, in substance, a reasonable chance of success. This puts a heavy burden on victims to develop legal arguments on the parent company's liability in tort law, in particular because no established doctrine has yet evolved and conflicting judgments exist.[155] Given the decision in *Kiobel*[156] and related later rulings[157] which imposed significant restrictions on bringing claims in the United States under the Alien Torts Statute and the strong influence of the *forum non conveniens* doctrine in corporate group liability cases, similar problems relating to access to justice have also been discussed in jurisdictions outside the EU.[158] In addition to the problem of jurisdiction, the rules on the applicable law may prove to be significant obstacles. These regularly lead to the application of the law of the country where the effects of the violations occurred (normally the place where the damage occurred).[159] This is, as such, not a problem, but studies on existing cases against corporate groups and supply chains have underlined that the selection of the applicable law may lead to obstacles when the procedural and substantive rules on limitations and the burden of proof restrict the possibilities for victims to bring their claims within an appropriate time period.[160] Other than the legal barriers, studies have also underlined the significant practical barriers that may impede access to remedy, such as the financial burden related to initiating legal proceedings in the home countries of companies and to the complexity of the issues that require legal expertise. The restriction for collective redress procedures and the lack of third-party standing have equally been highlighted as aspects that impede access to justice. Against this background, the authors of studies on access to justice urge states to develop legislation

[154] For the EU, this criterion was specified in Case C-145/10 *Eva-Maria Painer v Standard VerlagsGmbH and others* (ECLI:EU:C:2011:798), para. 81.

[155] See for cases that have assumed jurisdiction, *Lungowe and others v Vedanta Resources Plc and Konkola Copper Mines Plc* [2019] UKSC 20 (UK); *Okpabi v Shell* [2021] UKSC 3 (UK); and *Choc v Hudbay Minerals Inc.* 2013 ONSC 1414 (Canada); and for cases having dismissed jurisdiction *AAA & Others v Unilever Plc & Another* [2017] EWHC 371 (QB), upheld by the Court of Appeal [2018] EWCA Civ 1532 (UK).

[156] *Kiobel v Royal Dutch Petroleum Co.*, 133 S. Ct 1659.

[157] In particular *Jesner v Arab Bank plc*, 138 S. Ct 1386; *Nestlé USA, Inc v Doe*, 141 S. Ct 1931.

[158] G. Skinner, R. McCorquodale, and O. De Schutter, *Access to Judicial Remedies for Human Rights Violations by Transnational Business* (2013) 18–29. See also on the relevance of *forum non conveniens* for the successful UK cases (n. 155) post-Brexit, Aristova, 'The Future of Tort Litigation Against Transnational Corporations in the English Courts: Is *Forum [Non] Conveniens* Back?', 6 *Business and Human Rights Journal* (2021) 399.

[159] See e.g. for the EU: Art. 4(1) Regulation (EC) 864/2007 on the law applicable to non-contractual relations (Rome II), OJ 2007 L 199/40.

[160] See Skinner, McCorquodale, and De Schutter (n. 158) 41–43; Enneking, 'Judicial Remedies: The Issue of the Applicable Law', in Álvarez Rubio and Yiannibas (n. 49) 38.

that reduces these obstacles and have specifically urged courts to interpret their rules on jurisdiction and procedural rules in the light of the requirements in international human rights law and the need for access to remedy;[161] so far, significant steps by states remain underdeveloped.[162]

In the light of these obstacles that currently impede access to state-based remedies, it has been observed that non-judicial remedies, as also prescribed by the UNGP, have in practice become a substitute for guaranteeing access to remedy. As the observers of a study on the role and impact of non-judicial grievance mechanisms emphasize: '[t]he tendency that can be observed is that non-judicial grievance mechanisms try to fill the governance gap that ineffective judicial governance structures opened'.[163] There are instances where severe violations amounting in part to international crimes have been brought before non-judicial grievance bodies for the simple fact that these appear to be more easily accessible.[164]

This, as such, would not necessarily pose a problem if those non-judicial, private-based grievance mechanisms functioned equivalently to how the right of access to remedy is supposed to be realized. However, looking at studies of non-judicial grievance mechanisms, suggests that such mechanisms work quite differently to formal judicial remedies. In the context of this chapter with its focus on the integration of human rights into corporate governance structures, the examination of the character of non-judicial grievance mechanisms will be limited to corporate practices for internal grievances, although it is acknowledged that other types of grievance mechanisms exist which have been set up by public actors or international organizations[165] and also civil society mechanisms that operate with monitoring and certification.[166]

As far as company-based grievance mechanisms are concerned, studies underline a tendency on the side of companies to establish remedies in an autonomous

[161] Skinner, McCorquodale, and De Schutter (n. 158) 12; Álvarez Rubio and Yiannibas, 'Conclusions', in Álvarez Rubio and Yiannibas (n. 49) 139.

[162] This has been pointed out particularly by the studies that have investigated the NAP and the role that the implementation of the third pillar plays, see n. 83, specifically the ICAR, ECCJ, Dejusticia 2017 report, at 5; Augenstein, 'Negotiating the Hard/Soft Law Divide in Business and Human Rights: The Implementation of the UNGPs in the European Union', 9 *Global Policy* (2018) 254, at 257. It is also telling that the Business and Human Rights Forum (a forum established through UN Human Rights Council Res. A/HRC/Res/17/4, para. 12 that endorses the UNGP) has taken as its central theme 'Realizing Access to Effective Remedy' on the ground that (as the UN Working Group on Business and Human Rights describes it in a background note) the third pillar 'has been regularly described as the "forgotten pillar"'.

[163] K. Lukas *et al.*, *Corporate Accountability: The Role and Impact of Non-Judicial Grievance Mechanisms* (2017) 325.

[164] Ibid. 326.

[165] For these types of grievances, the most notable are the National Contact Points under the OECD Guidelines for Multinational Enterprises, the Inspection Panel, and the Compliance Advisor Ombudsman of the World Bank.

[166] E.g. sector-specific multi-stakeholder mechanisms (such as the Fair Labor Association, the Ethical Trading Initiative, or the Voluntary Principles for Security and Human Rights) and industry-based initiatives (such as the International Council of Toy Industries or the Electronic Industry Code of Conduct).

fashion with a high degree of informality and limitations as to who may file a claim. An analysis of published company practices on the implementation of the UNGP demonstrates that the remedy pillar is so far the one that is the least focused on by companies. Rather than developing internal processes that allow victims to claim human rights violations and receive redress, companies tend to focus on their policy commitments and on developing due diligence mechanisms.[167] As to the extent that operational grievance mechanisms are developed by companies, they focus predominantly on grievances and complaints for internal stakeholders only.[168] Hence, it is mostly internal employees who may express complaints and act as whistle-blowers for human rights violations; rights-based mechanisms for those external to the company remain scarce. Such internal complaints mechanisms mostly take the form of complaint hotlines; for certain types of external stakeholders (e.g. workers in supply chains or local communities), auditing procedures and third-party complaint processes exist.[169] In relation to responsibility within supply chains, ample research exists on remediation procedures. What can be taken from these studies is that the remedial focus within the company–supplier relationship is set on auditing procedures, capacity-building among suppliers, and contractual remedies in the case of severe violations.[170] While such mechanisms can certainly be useful to track supplier performance in relation to human rights respect, they lack the essential characteristics that are necessary for them to qualify as an independent remedy. First, such contract-based remedies are only indirectly available to victims of human rights violations; instead, it is the company itself that may have remedies available against suppliers for non-compliance with contractually agreed human rights. In this light, an empirical study in 2017 on audit design and enforcement within global value chains has suggested that audits need to be understood as a mechanism that primarily benefits large corporations at the expense of the supplier and the intended beneficiaries of the audit (i.e. employees, local communities).[171] Those suffering from human rights violations, the workers in the factory, and local communities are only indirectly heard within the remedy processes either as part of the internal complaints by employees or as part of the contractual remedies carried out by companies against their suppliers. As one author had already argued in 2008: 'but what of the objects of all of this activity—the businesspeople operating supplier factories, or their subcontractors, the children

[167] Salcito, Wielga, and Singer (n. 96) 681.

[168] McCorquodale *et al.* (n. 107) 211, at 220–221.

[169] See for this purpose, the company case studies on grievance mechanisms by Lukas *et al.* (n. 163) ch. 4.

[170] See on this point, the empirical studies on contracting practice in relation to sustainability, CSR, and human rights clauses: Cafaggi, 'The Regulatory Functions of Transnational Commercial Contracts: New Architectures', 36 *Fordham International Law Journal* (2013) 1557; Mitkidis, 'Sustainability Clauses in International Supply Chain Contracts: Regulation, Enforceability and Effects of Ethical Requirements', 1 *Nordic Journal of Commercial Law* (2014) 1.

[171] LeBaron, Lister, and Dauvergne (n. 128). See also P. Paiement, *Transnational Sustainability Laws* (2017) 215.

and their families, and the local communities in which all these activities occur? Those are the groups that seem to be cut out of the process. Things are done on their behalf.'[172] Sociologist Tim Bartley has further conducted empirical studies on the organization of private supply chains and multi-stakeholder initiatives in various countries around the world and how they ultimately benefit those who ought to be protected. He observed that privately-organized regulation systems, in respect to specifically the establishment of rights of workers and villagers, 'have proven especially challenging terrain for private regulation, generating fragile agreements, weak committees, and monetary respect at best—and endorsing the *denial* of rights at worst'.[173] In this respect, he also criticizes the focus of the UNGP as being the establishment of governance architectures for business networks rather than on improving enforcement structures.[174] Similar conclusions on the lack of a rights-based approach have been drawn with respect to company case studies on their internal grievance mechanisms. An in-depth study on the established human rights grievance mechanisms of two companies concluded that, to the extent that grievance mechanisms were identified, they were 'rooted in rather more general corporate social responsibility or compliance standards, emphasizing, for example, anti-corruption policies within companies or community relations' with little transparency about accessibility, competence of the deciding department in the company, and implementation.[175] The authors of the studies also underlined that the expectations for non-judicial mechanisms including towards companies 'have become exponentially high' given the lack of accessible judicial remedies, but that 'their structure, mandate and capacity to deliver on all of these expectations' was not sufficient and thus could not account for such expectations.[176] Company-based mechanisms are simply not equipped to conduct thorough fact-finding: they may not impose meaningful sanctions on the perpetrator, they lack clear rules on the appropriate remedial action in a given case, and they lack the means to provide for systemic improvements that go beyond the internal change of management and procurement practices.

Given this lack of non-judicial, company-based grievance mechanisms as a functional equivalent to access to remedy, it can be concluded that the understanding of the right to remedy as part of international human rights obligations also significantly changes when practised within corporate governance structures. Access to remedy, in international human rights law viewed as the reverse side to the obligation to protect human rights, becomes detached from its obligatory

[172] Backer (n. 110) 522.

[173] T. Bartley, *Rules without Rights: Land, Labor, and Private Authority in the Global Economy* (2018) 258.

[174] Ibid. 278.

[175] Häusler, Lukas, and Planitzer, 'Non-Judicial Remedies: Company-Based Grievance Mechanisms and International Arbitration', in Álvarez Rubio and Yiannibas (n. 49) 78, at 114–115.

[176] Lukas *et al.* (n. 163) 327.

component in corporate practice. Companies are expected to, and do, provide some form of remedy without being obliged and, even from the outset, without perceiving themselves to be obliged to protect human rights.[177] Hence, human rights grievance mechanisms in corporate governance structures are remedies without rights. Moreover, in establishing grievance mechanisms as a substitute for remedies, a high degree of informality and links to existing corporate compliance processes can be observed. As opposed to being rights-based and oriented on what is necessary to remedy the violation for the victims, grievance mechanisms focus on improving management processes on behalf of those affected. Ultimately, this seems to transform the concept of remedy into an objective process-based mechanism for improvement that is detached from those who have suffered a violation of their rights. Moreover, because of the low-level of accessibility to these grievance mechanisms and the lack of progress in improving access to judicial remedies, operational grievance mechanisms seem in practice to be a substitute for providing some form of remedial measure in cases of corporate human rights violations.

## B. Making Sense? Conceptualizing Human Rights for Corporate Governance

The presented empirical material on the character, processes, and remedial consequences of human rights practices within corporate governance systems certainly leaves one puzzled, conceptually and normatively. It leaves human rights lawyers, understandably, with a sense of discomfort and alienation. How is it possible, if at all, to make sense of this new form of human rights protection within the concept of international human rights protection? Is this a new type of human rights protection or does this differ too strongly from established human rights understandings?

Further, normative questions arise as to how such a development should be assessed. Is such a transformation a necessary development in order to address corporate human rights violations, i.e. an unavoidable trade-off in order to achieve 'the maximum reduction in corporate-related human rights harm in the shortest possible period of time',[178] as Ruggie has framed it? Can it even be understood as a desirable development that opens up new pathways to 'think' about human rights in relation to non-state actors? Or is this a step towards stripping human rights of their core content and meaning, denying their very characteristics and replacing them with a purported 'functionally equivalent' private meaning? Certainly, an exhaustive answer to these questions would deserve a monograph that cannot be

[177] See for a similar point, Bilchitz, 'Introduction: Putting Flesh to the Bone', in Deva and Bilchitz, *Building a Treaty on Business and Human Rights* (n. 12) 1, at 9.

[178] See n. 26.

provided here. However, what the following sections can do is to set out a perspective that provide directions for addressing these questions with the help of the most radical theories on human rights in non-state orders.

Following the theory of human rights in the Arendtian tradition, which has a strong influence as a legal theory of human rights, human rights are famously based on the so-called 'right to have rights'.[179] It has been argued that such an understanding is based on a presupposition of the concrete order, be that the order of the state, i.e. the Westphalian origin of the international legal order,[180] or at least some form of concrete 'proto-political community'.[181] Thus, pursuant to this understanding, the existence of a legal conception of human rights depends on the existence of an authoritative (legal or ethical) origin of human rights that is recognizable and realizable within some form of political community.

For this purpose, one can invoke Lindahl's understanding of human rights in non-state orders, as he convincingly argues that human rights claims can be addressed to companies precisely because companies are concrete legal orders in their own right.[182] In explaining how human rights can be conceived in relation to companies, he departs slightly from the human rights understanding in the Arendtian tradition. To him, human rights are moral or political claims that address a collective, but they are not the 'rights of others' within a political community that claim reciprocity; instead, human rights are the rights of strangers who are outside the political community and who claim normatively a right against the political community.[183] In this regard, they are the rights that 'do not fit' the specifics of a political community, or—as Lindahl defines it: '[c]laims to human rights indirectly evoke the normative blind spot of a collective's legal order'.[184] It is precisely in this capacity that human rights are able to trigger the political self-restraint of the addressed collective and can ultimately be realized. Citing Lindahl again: 'normatively speaking, human rights summon us, the collective, to political self-restraint because much of what is human is strange to us'.[185] This understanding fits precisely how human rights claims can and cannot work in relation to companies. Primarily, claims to human rights obligations are an artificial concept

[179] H. Arendt, *The Origins of Totaliarianism* (1966) 296–298.

[180] See Bhuta, 'The Frontiers of Extraterritoriality—Human Rights Law as Global Law', in N. Bhuta (ed.), *The Frontiers of Human Rights: Extraterritoriality and its Challenges* (2016) 1, at 2: 'At their inception, human rights treaties took for granted, rather than broke from, the so-called "Westphalian frame". Human rights did not purport to create, but rather *presupposed*, the Arendtian right to have rights: the legal framework for the realization of human rights depended upon and was expected to act through functioning political communities organized as sovereign states.'

[181] Lindahl, 'In Between: Immigration, Distributive Justice, and Political Dialogue', 8 *Contemporary Political Theory* (2009) 425.

[182] For an extensive analysis on companies as concrete legal orders, Lindahl, 'A-Legality: Postnationalism and the Question of Legal Boundaries', 73 *Modern Law Review* (2010) 30.

[183] H. Lindahl, *Fault Lines of Globalization: Legal Order and the Politics of A-Legality* (2014) 239–248.

[184] Ibid. 248 (emphasis in original).

[185] Ibid.

that do not easily fit within the governance structure of corporations. They address corporations as private actors that, by their nature, do not function according to the concept of a political community. As such, human rights claims in regard to companies are always a 'matter of strangeness'. However, by means of addressing companies with human rights claims, it might be possible to trigger self-restraint by companies precisely by integrating such claims within the corporate organization.

The main question then is whether human rights as conceptualized in the UNGP and as accordingly practised by companies fulfil this requirement as a self-restraint for the 'strange' concept of human rights. Two aspects are important: first, is the global standard of expected conduct, the concept of social expectations as the origin of human rights responsibilities for companies in the UNGP, sufficient as a blind spot of the collective order that may lead to self-restraint? Second, has this specific form of human rights practices led to sufficient self-restraint in practice within the concrete order of companies as a political community? Lindahl himself would not buy into the first aspect. Although he accepts the comparability of states and corporations as sufficiently concrete legal orders that—in principle—can be the addressees of human rights claims, the framing of human rights claims in terms of social expectations is, according to Lindahl, insufficient. In an article on the UNGP specifically, he criticized the differentiation in the UNGP between 'obligations' and 'responsibilities'—i.e. into an international legal standard and a social licence respectively—as obscuring the conception of human rights as global public goods of a common legal order of world society that claim universality in relation to any concrete legal order.[186] But what precisely is conceptually problematic with equalizing social expectations with an authoritative legal or moral origin of human rights? Such a sociological understanding of human rights is based on social theory approaches that rely on the work of Émile Durkheim. In this understanding, the origin of human rights is identified in the *colère publique*, i.e. in the normative practices of social actors that may then be taken up by the courts of public opinion and legal courts.[187] According to this perspective, human rights are not limits to political power, but serve as structurally limiting institutions to the various social systems that may affect the rights of others.[188] One can certainly criticize this account for the inherent inability of clearly delineating the content and origin of such *colère publique* in global protest movements or in world society,[189] but this seems unfair, as legal or moral conception of human rights are also inherently unspecific. However, sociological conceptions of

[186] Lindahl (n. 34) 217.

[187] The theoretical basis for this understanding is A. Fischer-Lescano, *Globalverfassung. Die Geltungsbegründung der Menschenrechte* (2005); Teubner (n. 37) 127–128.

[188] Teubner, 'The Anonymous Matrix: Human Rights Violations by "Private" Transnational Actors', 69 *Modern Law Review* (2006) 327, at 338–342.

[189] This is precisely one of the points made by Lindahl (n. 183) 219. See on this point, also Bilchitz, 'A Chasm between "Is" and "Ought"? A Critique on the Normative Foundations of the SRSG's Framework and the Guiding Principles', in Bilchitz and Deva, *Human Rights Obligations of Business* (n. 34) 107, at 120–123.

human rights do not equalize the validity of human rights with the mere existence or normative claims of social movements. Rather, they link the validity of human rights claims to their integration and realization within the concrete legal order. Teubner speaks here of the 'concrete decisions which establish validity in regime-specific institutions',[190] i.e. the practice of the regime affected. Hence, in order for human rights claims to be valid, not only the concrete (legal) order of corporations is presupposed, but also their validity decisions in the form of establishing human rights mechanisms. In short, human rights claims (normatively) exist only in a vague form prior to being recognized within the concrete order of companies and thus lose their credibility as normative rights claims against concrete orders.

This linking of the origin of human rights outside the concrete order and the realization of political self-restraint within leads to the main point of concern: can corporations and their practices for showing respect for human rights be conceptually equal to how states as political communities are addressed by claim for respect for human rights and how they practice this? Recent political and social theory research has indeed argued that the role of corporations in global governance, including the governance of international human rights, has shifted from a merely economic to a political role. This shift makes it possible to assert that they are bound by human rights.[191] Arguably, however, the observed practice of realizing human rights within corporate governance structures suggests that there are significant differences between the political character of states and the purported political element in corporations that take over public functions. First of all, despite potentially being legal orders in themselves, corporations do not provide a similar conception of a political community for the realization of rights. The way in which they practise human rights, i.e. as processes with 'grievance mechanisms' that originate from economic and social pressures and a sense of philanthropy, does not rely on any delineated political community that works with an inclusion/exclusion dichotomy that is characteristic of the political system. Instead, the boundaries that are set by corporate organizations are defined by the vague category of who is a stakeholder, i.e. has an interest in the corporate organization.[192] Second, putting

[190] Teubner (n. 37) 128.

[191] Such a perspective on corporations can be found in the political-economic literature that is based on the idea of 'corporate citizenship', e.g. Scherer and Palazzo, 'The New Political Role of Business in a Globalized World: A Review of a New Perspective on CSR and its Implications for the Firm, Governance, and Democracy', 48 *Journal of Management Studies* (2011) 899; in business ethics, e.g. F. Wettstein, *Multinational Corporations and Global Justice: Human Rights Obligations of a Quasi-Governmental Institution* (2009) ch. 6; and in legal and political theory that identifies corporate constitutions, see n. 37.

[192] Of course, it is possible to define who belongs to the category of a 'stakeholder' and it is increasingly expected that companies are transparent as to who they consider to be their stakeholders. See e.g. for arguments in this direction, Kjaer (n. 110) 316ff, and MacDonald and MacDonald (n. 110) 94. This, however, does not resolve the inside/outside dichotomy, as there is no *common* understanding among companies on what the stakeholder concept implies. Instead, political communities—with their concepts of citizenship and territory—operate with generalizable criteria for the inside/outside dichotomy. See on the critique of equalizing stakeholders with political communities, Sand, 'A Comment on Kjaer',

companies on a par with states encounters some problems because this equalizes aspects in which states and companies differ quite significantly, namely the rationality that they both invoke (and which makes a difference as to how human rights are practised), and institutional processes that they both possess. The rationality of states is one that invokes a political and legal narrative for the operation: it is in this interactive process, in reference to the rule of law and the political community, in which boundaries are set. Yet, there is a long history of treating corporations as core actors in the private sphere and depoliticizing them in the interest of allowing them to act as autonomous organizational elements in society.[193] As a result, corporations function, from the moment of their incorporation, as actors that operate according to economic and organizational rationalities. This leads to the previously observed tendency of transforming human rights claims into a matter of economic pressure and corporate philanthropy and into rights that are related to the private sphere, such as the rights of employees, consumers, and neighbouring communities. The rationality that companies employ does not account for a similar reference to human rights as universal rights.[194] Moreover, there are manifold structural institutions, both administrative and judicial, in the infrastructure of the state that are necessary for the realization of human rights upon which corporations as private organizations cannot build. There is, amongst others, a lack of competence within companies in initiating investigations, their lack of separating powers within the corporate organizations and formally enforcing their 'rulings'. Hence, in order to realize human rights protection in relation to corporations, there is a need to rely on the institutional infrastructure of the state.[195]

Thus, in relying on human rights against companies, the tendency to instrumentalize companies and their governance structures might add some practical value to those suffering violations: it may give them an additional forum to express a claim, and it may result in some form of remedial consequence that may help them in their suffering. At the same time, there is a price to pay for this possible practical improvement of the situation. Expressing concern for human rights in the context of corporate governance structures may result in discussions that are less guided by predictable procedures and rules and more by a corporate sense of 'what is the right thing to do' and the prioritization within the company. In short, the standard for human rights protection shifts from what is normatively required to what works in practice.

in C. Joerges and T. Ralli (eds), *After Globalization—New Patterns of Conflict and their Sociological and Legal Reconstruction* (2011) 323, at 326.

[193] Willke and Willke, 'Corporate Moral Legitimacy and the Legitimacy of Morals: A Critique of Palazzo/Scherer's Communicative Framework', 81 *Journal of Business Ethics* (2008) 27, at 32–35.

[194] In this regard, it is notable that this tendency towards questioning the universality of human rights is not only driven by corporations, but also by some (powerful) states themselves.

[195] See for a strong argument in this direction, Schrempf-Stirling, 'State Power: Rethinking the Role of the State in Political Corporate Social Responsibility', 150 *Journal of Business Ethics* (2018) 1, at 4–6.

To conclude, human rights claims can in principle be made against companies. However, the way in which this has been done in the UNGP suffers from a distinction between states and companies as global legal orders. Moreover, even if claims are addressed to companies properly—as alternative approaches such as the discussions surrounding the proposed Treaty on Business and Human Rights have done—such claims face the difficulty of being realized as political rights within the inherently non-political order of companies.

## 4. (Re-)vitalizing the Law? A Tentative Conclusion

This chapter has, at its core, developed two interrelated arguments. Taking stock of previous influential discussions among international human rights lawyers on the human rights obligations of corporate actors, it has argued that recently—notably through the UNGP—a shift from binding corporations to human rights towards centring corporate governance as a structural prerequisite for enhancing corporate respect for human rights can be observed. This comes at the expense of a background role for the state as a regulator. On this basis, it was asked what the consequences of this shift are for the understanding of human rights, both as empirically observable and, building on this, conceptually for the theory of human rights. This second question was answered by emphasizing a transformation of human rights as regards their origin, practical realization, and their enforcement structure. Inevitably, such observations lead to a follow-up question as to the desirability of such a development: is it better to free companies from human rights claims and focus on states as addressees of human rights (including their obligation to regulate corporations)? Or should one accept the 'incompleteness' of human rights within corporate governance structures, namely their significant transformation under the current conditions of non-state orders?

Proponents of a non-state understanding of human rights appear to have a clear stance on this. Internal self-restraint, according to the specifics of the non-state order in question, is the only way in which human rights protection can be effectively translated into the private sphere under the conditions of a differentiated global society. Prescribing companies to respect human rights may only be a second-best option but it is the only real, possible way to proceed. The fragmentation of international law in the collision of different normative rationalities, in our case between the corporate spheres and the sphere of international human rights law, cannot be overcome. As Fischer-Lescano and Teubner prominently put it: '[i]n the place of an illusionary integration of a differentiated global society, law can only, at the very best, offer a kind of damage limitation', it can 'achieve weak compatibility between the fragments'.[196] In this context, hope is put on ongoing

[196] Fischer-Lescano and Teubner (n. 77) 1045.

social pressure—including legal pressure through litigation and legislation—to push corporate human rights practice in a political direction. In relation to our constellation of human rights in corporate governance, this effectively means that the observed transformation is inevitable, and it must be other social actors—in Ruggie's understanding of polycentric governance, the system of civil society—who push companies towards improving their governance structures to ensure 'weak compatibility' with the core of international human rights.

On the other side of the spectrum, there are also those who insist that such an understanding undermines the very foundation and heritage of international human rights and the fact that they historically, conceptually, and normatively are not made to account for such a non-state expansion. The evolution of international human rights is simply too strongly linked to political power (some would even argue to states) to qualify reasoning that is used within private relations to protect one party against the excesses of another as genuine human rights protection.[197] More precisely, human rights require in their language a universal reference to the rights of human beings, not a partial emphasis on specific groups or interests that are constitutive for the corporate and market system; remedies presuppose a functioning judicial and administrative legal system, nationally or internationally, and may therefore structurally not be able to expand to spontaneous, informal mechanisms. Duties to protect human rights have evolved to denote a holistic approach that requires from obligated parties action towards achieving a result (with an assumption that such parties are in the position to do so), not the installation of processes that should provide safeguards against negative 'impacts' on human rights.

And in between these two poles, one can find those from the fields of both public and private international law who insist that, even if corporate governance becomes a new structure that is directed towards respecting human rights, the law has some means to provide related rules that bind companies to human rights protection. These attempts thus rest on the hope that the state, with its formal legal system and the related international obligations imposed on it, is and must be capable of taming how corporations practise respect for human rights. In public international law, an early proponent of linking public and private concepts was Craig Scott who criticized the tendency 'to organize the normative world of human rights in terms of (unduly) dichotomous ways of thinking'[198] and suggested

[197] Among private lawyers, this point is strongly emphasized: Collins, 'On the (In)compatibility of Human Rights Discourse and Private Law', in H. Micklitz (ed.), *Constitutionalization of Private Law* (2014) 26, at 26–27; Collins, 'The Challenges Presented by Fundamental Rights to Private Law', in K. Barker, K. Fairweather, and R. Grantham (eds), *Private Law in the 21st Century* (2017) 213.

[198] Scott, 'Translating Torture into Transnational Tort: Conceptual Divides in the Debate on Corporate Accountability for Human Rights Harms', in C. Scott (ed.), *Torture as Tort: Comparative Perspectives on the Development of Transnational Human Rights Litigation* (2001) 45, at 45. Critically on this translation of international human rights into national torts, however Bhuta, 'The Ninth Life of the Alien Torts Statute—Kiobel and After', 12 *Journal of International Criminal Justice* (2014) 539, at 459: 'Recourse to domestic law torts of negligence, assault and breach of statutory duty, might prove

that—particularly in relation to corporate human rights violations—public and private law norms have to engage in a 'two-way-traffic' by which the core understanding of human rights (torture) has to be translated into private law (tort).[199] Building upon this thinking, lawyers have recently engaged in discussions on the different options of how public and private international law concepts should be used to regulate corporate governance structures with a view to ensuring that human rights are duly considered. From the public law perspective, the analysis focuses on human rights in international conventions that arguably prescribe states to develop substantive and procedural mechanisms to ensure that not only corporate human rights violations can be taken to court (i.e. improvement of access to remedy), but also that corporations that do not or only incompletely implement human rights into their governance structures in a way which complies with international human rights standards can be challenged legally.[200] From the private law perspective, it has been Muir Watt in particular who has continuously criticized the historically evolved 'public law taboo'[201] of private international law and who argues for an 'overhaul' of private international law to accommodate human rights and other public interests when assigning jurisdiction and regulating the applicable law in relation to transnational corporate activity.[202] Others have made similar claims in relation to substantive private law concepts, corporate governance laws and regulation, civil liability, consumer law, and contract law as areas that may integrate human rights.[203] In the German debate following the mandatory due diligence legislation, this idea has recently found its way into the debate as the concept of contractual corporate human rights obligations.[204] Here, the approach of Shamir to translate human rights claims and policies (in relation to anti-trafficking) into private law concepts (labour law and rights) can be pointed out as a particularly prominent and promising approach.[205] These attempts link to recent

unwieldy and inapposite legal frameworks for capturing the harms allegedly suffered by the plaintiffs, and may impose significant hurdles to finding liability ...'.

[199] Scott (n. 198) 61.

[200] See, in particular, Augenstein, 'Torture as Tort? Transnational Tort Litigation for Corporate-Related Human Rights Violations and the Human Right to Remedy', 18 *Human Rights Law Review* (2018) 593; D. Palombo, *Business and Human Rights: The Obligation of the European Home State* (2017).

[201] Muir Watt, 'Private International Law Beyond the Schism', 2 *Transnational Legal Theory* (2011) 347, at 362.

[202] Ibid; Muir Watt, 'Conflicts of Laws Unbounded: The Case for a Legal-Pluralist Revival', 7 *Transnational Legal Theory* (2016) 313. See also Wai, 'Transnational Liftoff and Juridical Touchdown: The Regulatory Function of Private International Law in an Era of Globalization', 40 *Columbia Journal of Transnational Law* (2002) 209.

[203] On corporate and tort law, see e.g. Muchlinski (n. 50) 157–162; on civil liability, see e.g. van Dam and Gregor (n. 49).

[204] Wiater, 'Unternehmerische Menschenrechtsbindung nach Maßgabe des Lieferkettengesetzes', 77 *Juristenzeitung* (2022) 859, at 862–863.

[205] Shamir, 'A Labor Paradigm for Human Trafficking', 60 *UCLA Law Review* (2012) 76.

theoretical studies that look into the conceptual possibilities of treating human rights as an inherent aspect in private law thinking and argue that specific types of human rights obligations, constituted through the idea of interpersonal independence and violability, do exist in private law although they cannot be conceived in the same way as for states.[206]

These latter avenues appear to be the most promising as they do provide for a compromise in the face of reality and a utopian vision. Instead of bemoaning the decline of a state-based understanding of human rights combined with efforts to restore it by erasing corporate actors from the international human rights landscape, the intersection between human rights law and corporate law is taken seriously as part of the 'new reality' in the evolution of global non-state governance orders that human rights and corporate lawyers are faced with. Yet, by means of attempting to bring them back within the authority of the state through private law, a corrective measure is proposed that allows contestation and resistance.[207] If this option is relied upon, the future of transforming human rights in corporate governance structures may still be found in the state and its judicial system. In this sense, it may, ironically, connect well to the state-centric heritage of international human rights protection that understands human rights as being predicated upon and presupposing an existing state apparatus, this time only in the need to turn to the rules that constitute and regulate horizontal relations between corporations and those suffering from corporate human rights violations in an attempt to reform them.

However, the question remains of whether a project of turning these private law rules for the regulation of private relations upside-down from a facilitative to a regulatory attitude to corporate governance structures and including human rights is possible at all. It is the turn of private lawyers to discuss whether the facilitative liberal heritage of private law is ripe for this human rights revolution. It further remains to be seen how far existing legal fields, such as human rights law and private law, may depart from their own distinct heritage and enter into new legal fields. Can international human rights standards become part of private law without compromising its very heritage? The fact that there is a list of past legal fields in which such two-way traffic has proved to be successful—ranging from the protection of consumers between contract law and competition and economic law

206 Dagan and Dorfman, 'Interpersonal Human Rights', 51 *Cornell International Law Journal* (2018) conceptualize these as interpersonal human rights within the privity of private relations as private law's *ius gentium*; J. Thomas, *Public Rights, Private Relations* (2015) uses the concepts of interpersonal dependency and violability within private relations constituted through power asymmetries in a relation as a basis for extrapolating new types of private law obligations from 'the set of fundamental public law standards' (18).

207 Wai, 'Private v Private: Transnational Private Law and Contestation in Global Economic Governance', in H. Muir Watt and D. P. Fernández Arroyo (eds), *Private International Law and Global Governance* (2014) 34, at 45–47.

to the evolution of environmental law between tort law and administrative law—provides ground for hope, but is no panacea.[208]

This brings us back to the beginning of this chapter with the predictions made in previous Academy summer courses and their anticipation of the uneasiness of international lawyers (and, I would also add, corporate lawyers) to come to terms with the new reality of relating human rights and corporate governance and the difficulty of aligning the two in the light of a strong state-centred heritage of (international) human rights law. However, it also emphasizes the current attempts to choose new directions that—even if conceptually artificial at first sight and alienated from existing practices—may suggest a new direction for the evolution of international human rights law.

[208] Zumbansen, 'The Invisible College of Transnational Lawyers: Observations regarding Private Regulatory Governance and the Law(yer)'s Role in Global Markets', Working Paper for the Conference Transnational Governance Business Interactions, Toronto, 16–17 May 2016, 25.

# 4

# Beyond Accountability?

## Human Rights, Global Governance, and the World Bank Inspection Panel

*Guy Fiti Sinclair**

### 1. Introduction

One day in late June 1999, two protestors climbed the outside of the World Bank's headquarters in Washington DC, and unfurled a banner that proclaimed, 'World Bank Approves China's Genocide in Tibet'.[1] The protest related to the World Bank-financed China: Western Poverty Reduction Project (CWPRP or Project), which aimed at reducing absolute poverty in remote rural areas in three provinces in the west of China.[2] Among other interventions, Part C of the CWPRP involved the voluntary resettlement of almost 60,000 farmers from the eastern part of Qinghai province to a sparsely populated Mongol and Tibetan Autonomous Prefecture in the west of the same province. Tibetan rights activists, who viewed such population-transfer programmes in China as a grave threat to Tibetan cultural identity, launched the largest campaign against the World Bank to that point, placing the Project under intense media scrutiny.

The campaign culminated in a complaint filed to the World Bank Inspection Panel (WBIP or Panel), a mechanism available to groups who believe they are, or will be, adversely affected by a Bank-funded project. Among other things, the complaint alleged that aspects of the CWPRP's design and implementation had breached the Bank's policies on indigenous peoples, involuntary resettlement, and

* Versions of this chapter were presented at workshops at the European University Institute and the University of Edinburgh. Thanks to the participants in those workshops for their very helpful comments and suggestions, in particular Nehal Bhuta, Dimitri Van den Meerssche, Rodrigo Vallejo, Andrew Lang, and Morten Jerven. Thanks also to Georgia Whelan, Steven Reinhold, and Nopera Dennis-McCarthy for excellent research assistance. I remain individually accountable for all errors and deficiencies.

[1] Sewell, 'High-Wire Protest at World Bank', *The Washington Post*, 26 June 1999, B02.

[2] The World Bank comprises the International Bank for Reconstruction and Development (IBRD) and the International Development Association (IDA). Though formally separate international organizations, the IBRD and IDA effectively operate as one institution offering distinct programmes. This chapter uses 'the Bank' and 'the World Bank' interchangeably.

Guy Fiti Sinclair, *Beyond Accountability?* In: *Global Rights?* First Edition. Edited by: Nehal Bhuta and Rodrigo Vallejo, Oxford University Press. © Guy Fiti Sinclair 2024. DOI: 10.1093/oso/9780198940166.003.0004

environmental assessment.[3] The WBIP's final report, issued in April 2000, found significant violations of those policies. Notwithstanding proposals from the Bank's management to bring the Project into compliance, in July 2000 a majority of the Bank's board of executive directors voted against proceeding with the Project. China then withdrew the Project from the Bank, stating it would proceed to implement the Project with its own financing.

In most tellings, this is a story about the human rights accountability of an important institution of global governance.[4] Hailed by the World Bank's president, James Wolfensohn, as 'a bold experiment in transparency and accountability that has worked to the benefit of all concerned',[5] the WBIP has been described even by critics as a 'precedent-setting public accountability mechanism',[6] supplying a template for similar mechanisms in other multilateral development banks.[7] From the point of view of human rights and environmental activists, the CWPRP case was a landmark success for civil society organizations calling attention to, and holding the World Bank accountable for, the human rights violations associated with its activities.[8] For those more sympathetic to the Bank's institutional mandate, on the other hand, it was a case of 'accountability gone wrong': a campaign led by NGOs based in the Global North, in collaboration with elements of the US government, to selectively apply a 'notion of punishment-based accountability' through the WBIP, thereby to frustrate a project aimed at the worthy development goal of reducing absolute poverty.[9] International lawyers, too,

[3] The complaint also alleged violations of World Bank policies on disclosure of operational information, pest management, safety of dams, retroactive financing, and investment lending. However, this chapter will focus on the three policies central to the claim.

[4] For an official account, see World Bank, *Accountability at the World Bank: The Inspection Panel 10 Years On* (2003) 69–79.

[5] Wolfensohn, 'Foreword', in A. Umaña (ed.), *The World Bank Inspection Panel: The First Four Years (1994–1998)* (1998) vii, vii.

[6] Fox, 'The World Bank Inspection Panel: Lessons from the First Five Years', 6 *Global Governance* (2000) 279, at 279.

[7] See generally Suzuki and Nanwani, 'Responsibility of International Organizations: The Accountability Mechanisms of Multilateral Development Banks', 27 *Michigan Journal of International Law* (2005) 177; Bradlow, 'Private Complainants and International Organizations: A Comparative Study of the Independent Inspection Mechanisms in International Financial Institutions', 36 *Georgetown Journal of International Law* (2005) 403. Wong and Mayer argue that 'while not providing affected persons a legal avenue for redress, the Inspection Panel, if used strategically as part of larger advocacy strategies, particularly by increasing media coverage on problematic projects, can nevertheless serve as a useful tool in helping redress wrongs committed as a result of the Bank's failure to comply with its own policies'. Wong and Mayer, 'The World Bank's Inspection Panel: A Tool for Accountability?', in J. Wouters *et al.* (eds), *The World Bank Legal Review*, vol. 6: *Improving Delivery in Development: The Role of Voice, Social Contract, and Accountability* (2015) 495, at 496.

[8] Fox, 'Transnational Civil Society Campaigns and the World Bank Inspection Panel', in A. Brysk (ed.), *Globalization and Human Rights* (2002) 171, at 173. For a detailed account of the case from the perspective of human rights and environmental advocates, see Clark and Treakle, 'The China Western Poverty Reduction Project', in D. Clark, J. Fox, and K. Treakle (eds), *Demanding Accountability: Civil Society Claims and the World Bank Inspection Panel* (2003) ch. 10.

[9] Wade, 'Accountability Gone Wrong: The World Bank, Non-Governmental Organisations and the US Government in a Fight over China', 14 *New Political Economy* (2009) 25, at 26.

have analysed the case as a paradigmatic example of the WBIP's accountability function.[10]

The accountability of international organizations for failures to observe or adequately integrate human rights norms in their operations is a topic of rising importance in international law.[11] Traditionally, international lawyers have tended to view international organizations as champions and instruments of human rights. It is only within the past few decades that the potential responsibility of international organizations for breaches of such rights has been seriously contemplated.[12] Likewise, human rights textbooks typically contain long passages outlining the international institutional mechanisms for developing, monitoring, and enforcing human rights norms; only lately have they started to include (brief) discussions of the human rights obligations of international organizations.[13] Increasing attention to this question has been prompted by the expanding powers of governance exercised by international organizations generally,[14] and by a series of high-profile cases involving the United Nations in particular.[15]

[10] For a lengthy legal analysis of the CWPRP case, see Roos, 'The World Bank Inspection Panel in its Seventh Year: An Analysis of its Process, Mandate, and Desirability with Special Reference to the China (Tibet) Case', 5 *Max Planck Yearbook of United Nations Law* (2001) 473. For other legal analyses of the WBIP as an accountability mechanism, see generally Orakhelashvili, 'The World Bank Inspection Panel in Context: Institutional Aspects of the Accountability of International Organizations', 2 *International Organizations Law Review* (2005) 57; Suzuki and Nanwani, 'Responsibility of International Organizations: The Accountability Mechanisms of Multilateral Development Banks', 27 *Michigan Journal of International Law* (2005) 177; Bradlow (n. 7); Wong and Mayer (n. 7). The most authoritative account of the establishment and (early) procedures of the WBIP remains I. F. I. Shihata, *The World Bank Inspection Panel: In Practice* (2nd ed., 2000).

[11] As in most texts in international organizations law, 'international organizations' here refers to public (or intergovernmental) organizations, established between states on the basis of a treaty or other instrument governed by international law, and possessing international legal personality or organs capable of expressing their will.

[12] See e.g. M. Hirsch, *The Responsibility of International Organizations toward Third Parties* (1995); A. Reinisch, *International Organizations before National Courts* (2000); Reinisch, 'Securing the Accountability of International Organisations', 7 *Global Governance* (2001) 131; Hoffman and Mégret, 'Fostering Human Rights Accountability: An Ombudsperson for the United Nations?', 11 *Global Governance* (2005) 43; G. Verdirame, *The UN and Human Rights: Who Guards the Guardians?* (2011).

[13] See e.g. O. De Schutter *International Human Rights Law: Cases, Materials, Commentary* (2010); S. Joseph and A. McBeth (eds), *Research Handbook on International Human Rights Law* (2010); and R. Smith, *Textbook on International Human Rights* (6th ed., 2016) (which do not contain any significant discussion of the human rights obligations of international organizations). But compare with D. L. Shelton, *Advanced Introduction to International Human Rights Law* (2014) 215–217; H. J. Steiner, P. Aston, and R. Goodman, *International Human Rights in Context* (3rd ed., 2008) 670, 680–686, 1385–1387 (though previous editions of this textbook did not include this discussion); and P. Alston (ed.), *Non-State Actors and Human Rights* (2005).

[14] See generally G. F. Sinclair, *To Reform the World: International Organizations and the Making of Modern States* (2017); J. E. Alvarez, *International Organizations as Law-Makers* (2005).

[15] These cases have involved, among other things, sexual exploitation and abuse by peacekeepers; failure to prevent mass killings in Rwanda, the former Yugoslavia, and elsewhere; targeted sanctions imposed on individuals by the Security Council; and the role of peacekeepers in causing a cholera outbreak in Haiti in 2010 that killed thousands. See e.g. P. Schmitt, *Access to Justice and International Organizations: The Case of Individual Victims of Human Rights Violations* (2017); M. Heupel and M. Zürn (eds), *Protecting the Individual from International Authority: Human Rights in International Organizations* (2017); Verdirame (n. 12); Daugirdas, 'Reputation and the Responsibility of International Organizations', 25 *European Journal of International Law* (*EJIL*) (2015) 991.

As is well recognized, serious obstacles stand in the way of holding international organizations responsible for human rights violations. Difficult questions arise as to whether (and which) international human rights norms are binding on international organizations; what the sources of those obligations are; the distribution of responsibility between organizations and their members; the lack of an international court or tribunal with general jurisdiction over such matters; and the consistent interpretation of international organizations' immunities as near-absolute by domestic courts.[16] The International Law Commission's draft articles on the responsibility of international organizations did little to resolve these questions.[17] A parallel project by the International Law Association explored broader concepts of accountability, including political, administrative, and financial, as well as legal modalities.[18] Yet suspicions remain that international organizations remain largely beyond the reach of accountability for their part in the violation of human rights norms.

The World Bank presents an especially hard case for international legal accountability, above and beyond the problems and difficulties already noted.[19] Successive general counsel of the Bank have understood the 'political prohibition' in the Bank's Articles of Agreement (the Articles) as excluding consideration of human rights from its decision-making processes,[20] a view that has been persuasive to

[16] See generally Wouters *et al.*, 'Accountability for Human Rights Violations by International Organisations: Introductory Remarks', in J. Wouters *et al.* (eds), *Accountability for Human Rights Violations by International Organisations* (2010) 1, and references therein.

[17] Indeed they added new difficulties, such as only making provision for the invocation of responsibility of an international organization for a breach of international law by a state or another international organization. See generally International Law Commission, Draft Articles on the Responsibility of International Organizations, with Commentaries, in Report on the Work of Its Sixty-third Session (2011), UN Doc. A/66/10, Arts 43–49; but see Art. 50.

[18] International Law Association, Final Report of the Committee on the Accountability of International Organizations, Berlin Conference, 2004.

[19] See generally McInerney-Lankford, 'International Financial Institutions and Human Rights: Select Perspectives on Legal Obligations', in D. D. Bradlow and D. B. Hunter (eds), *International Financial Institutions and International Law* (2010) 239, at 240 (arguing that 'the World Bank epitomizes the challenges of accountability and the limits of the law as it stands').

[20] See IBRD Articles of Agreement, Art. III, section 5(b) ('The Bank shall make arrangements to ensure that the proceeds of any loan are used only for the purposes for which the loan was granted, with due attention to considerations of economy and efficiency and without regard to political or other non-economic influences or considerations'); and Art. IV, section 10 ('The Bank and its officers shall not interfere in the political affairs of any member; nor shall they be influenced in their decisions by the political character of the member or members concerned. Only economic considerations shall be relevant to their decisions, and these considerations shall be weighed impartially in order to achieve the purposes stated in Article I'). The Articles of Agreement of the International Development Association contain parallel provisions: see Art. V, Section 1(g), and Art. V, section 6. For analyses by the World Bank's General Counsel from 1983 to 1998, see Shihata, 'The World Bank and Human Rights: An Analysis of the Legal Issues and the Record of Achievements', 17 *Denver Journal of International Law & Policy* (1988) 39; and I. F. I. Shihata, *The World Bank Legal Papers* (2000) ch. 9 ('Political Activity Prohibited'). Subsequent General Counsel have followed Shihata's reasoning to a greater or lesser extent. For a somewhat more open view towards human rights, see Dañino, 'The Legal Aspects of the World Bank's Work on Human Rights: Some Preliminary Thoughts', in P. Alston and M. Robinson (eds), *Human Rights and Development: Towards Mutual Reinforcement* (2005) ch. 20.

the Bank's management, executive directors, and board of governors. The latter two organs have exclusive authority to decide on questions concerning the interpretation of the Articles;[21] accordingly, there is vanishingly little chance that an international court or tribunal could directly review any complaint implicating the international legal responsibility of the Bank. Furthermore, any such complaint would raise extremely complicated questions of causation and the allocation of responsibility between the Bank and borrower members, given the nature of the loan agreements entered into between them and the notion of 'country ownership' that has been increasingly adopted by the Bank.[22]

This chapter seeks to move beyond the accountability framework within which the WBIP is usually analysed, instead using the CWPRP case to consider other aspects of the relationship between human rights and the governance of international organizations. This is not to deny that the WBIP is an important mechanism of accountability, or that there is value in evaluating the WBIP as such, including in relation to human rights norms. However, it is equally important to acknowledge the limits of such a mode of analysis. The deeply state-centred and hierarchical normative assumptions of the human rights project, when applied to international organizations, can lead international lawyers, consciously or unconsciously, to treat these organizations as if they were states and to measure the 'success' or 'failure' of the WBIP against an imagined archetype of judicial review.[23] Moreover, an accountability framework can tend to obscure other significant dimensions of the effectivity of human rights in the WBIP, and in global governance more broadly.

In contrast to the statist and hierarchical assumptions of the accountability framework, this chapter conceptualizes global governance in relatively horizontal, relational, and dynamic terms, involving the interaction of multiple actors and sources of authority.[24] Others have explored how human rights take effect through iterative processes of interaction that mobilize and empower a wide range of transnational actors.[25] I aim to complement these accounts, deploying a different

[21] IBRD Articles (n. 20) Art. IX.

[22] See e.g. IBRD/World Bank, *Toward Country-Led Development: A Multi-Partner Evaluation of the Comprehensive Development Framework* (2003).

[23] On the difficulty of fitting the WBIP into an accountability framework centred on the international legal concept of responsibility, see Baimu and Panou, 'Responsibility of International Organizations and the World Bank Inspection Panel: Parallel Tracks Unlikely to Converge?', in H. Cissé, D. D. Bradlow, and B. Kingsbury (eds), *The World Bank Legal Review*, vol. 3: *International Financial Institutions and Global Legal Governance* (2012) 147. More generally, see Bhuta, 'The Frontiers of Extraterritoriality—Human Rights Law as Global Law', in N. Bhuta (ed.), *The Frontiers of Human Rights* (2016) 4 (arguing that '[t]he determinate content of rights, and their interpretation and application ... are predicated on the legal order of the state in all its social, historical and political particularity').

[24] See generally Avant, Finnemore, and Sell, 'Who Governs the Globe?', in D. D. Avant, M. Finnemore, and S. K. Sell (eds), *Who Governs the Globe?* (2010) 1.

[25] See e.g. de Búrca, 'Human Rights Experimentalism', 111 *American Journal of International Law* (2017) 277; Daugirdas, 'Reputation and the Responsibility of International Organizations', 25 *EJIL* (2015) 991; Koh, 'Why Do Nations Obey International Law?', 106 *Yale Law Journal* (1997) 2599.

conceptual framework which could also illuminate cases that might not end in 'success' from a human rights advocacy perspective—that is to say, which do not necessarily result in any net improvement in human rights outcomes—but where there is, nevertheless, a series of observable effects on global governance.

In particular, the chapter makes two key analytical moves. First, it conceptualizes international institutions such as the World Bank and the WBIP as complex assemblages of diverse elements, with an appearance of solidity and 'thingness'. This move draws attention to the manifold practices that connect the innumerable actors involved in constructing, processing, and contesting a WBIP complaint. Second, the chapter widens the frame from accountability to examine the dynamics of authority at play between the various actors in a WBIP case. In this perspective, human rights appear not so much as a fixed set of standards against which the WBIP seeks to hold the Bank accountable for its actions, but rather as one among a number of vocabularies of authority deployed by sundry entities engaged in a variety of complex interactions. As such, human rights are continually constructed, defined, and distinguished from other modes of discourse and practice in the making (and unmaking) of global governance.

Rather than remain at a purely conceptual level, the chapter proceeds through an examination of the WBIP's processes, illuminated by the empirical details of the CWPRP complaint. As a case which attracted an especially high degree of controversy, CWPRP usefully illustrates the ways in which each Panel investigation involves a delicate series of interconnections among heterogeneous elements. Section 2 of the chapter introduces the WBIP through a brief account of its establishment and procedures, before outlining the main phases in the CWPRP case. Section 3 then shows how the World Bank and the WBIP can be viewed as constituted through the assemblage or networking of a vast series of associations through practices of strategic, physical, and linguistic translation. This section of the chapter draws on a set of loosely-related analytical categories and tools associated with assemblage theory and actor-network theory (ANT).[26] While a full application of the kind of ethnomethodology and storytelling associated with certain genres of ANT scholarship is not possible in this limited space,[27] the chapter aims to indicate, in a preliminary and experimental way, the potential usefulness of these approaches for further studies exploring the varied places of human rights in global governance.

[26] For present purposes, I set aside the question of whether 'actor-network theory' is the best name for the varied studies usually designated by that name. An alternative, 'sociology of translation', centres the concept of 'translation' and avoids the complications associated with the term 'theory', but for convenience I have opted to use the more commonly recognized name here. See generally Latour, 'On Recalling ANT', 47/1 *Sociological Review* (1999) 15; Mol, 'Actor-Network Theory: Sensitive Terms and Enduring Tensions', 50 *Kölner Zeitschrift für Soziologie und Sozialpsychologie* (2010) 253.

[27] See e.g. B. Latour, *Reassembling the Social: An Introduction to Actor-Network-Theory* (2007).

Finally, Section 4 examines how human rights claims and norms connect with, transform, and in turn are transformed by other modes of authority through the successive translations involved in the ongoing processes of (re)assemblage undertaken in a WBIP case. What emerges is an image of human rights as multivalent, fluid, and contested, far from the static and hierarchical vision associated with most accountability framings.

## 2. A Case for Accountability? The WBIP and the CWPRP

Since its creation near the end of the Second World War, the World Bank has become a key institution of global governance writ large, and of the global development enterprise in particular. Over the past three-quarters of a century, the Bank has proven astonishingly adaptive, expanding the range of its activities from providing loans and guarantees for reconstruction and development projects to embrace programmes addressing poverty and overpopulation, structural adjustment, good governance, environmental sustainability, and much more.[28] Although its lending volume has recently been overtaken by other sources of development finance, such as foreign direct investment, remittances, and newer institutions like the Asian Infrastructure Investment Bank (AIIB), the World Bank remains an important international lender for development purposes.[29] Even more significant, however, is the Bank's enduring influence on development thinking, through the massive number of reports it publishes each year—especially the annual *World Development Report*—and other devices such as statistical tools and indicators.[30]

Indeed, as a flagship institution of economic globalization, the World Bank is frequently condemned as a leading source of neoliberal policy prescriptions, giving rise to a variety of negative outcomes.[31] This section of the chapter introduces the WBIP as a key mechanism established in response to calls for greater accountability at the Bank, and then provides an outline of the CWPRP case as a way of illustrating the Panel's processes.

[28] See generally Sinclair (n. 14) chs 5–6; Einhorn, 'The World Bank's Mission Creep', 80 *Foreign Affairs* (2001) 22; M. Goldman, *Imperial Nature: The World Bank and Struggles for Social Justice in the Age of Globalization* (2005).

[29] On the AIIB, see Ong, 'The Asian Infrastructure Investment Bank: Bringing "Asian Values" to Global Economic Governance?', 20 *Journal of International Economic Law* (2017) 535.

[30] Stern and Ferreira, 'The World Bank as "Intellectual Actor"', in D. Kapur, J. P. Lewis, and R. C. Webb (eds), *The World Bank: Its First Half Century*, vol. 2 (1997) ch. 12; S. E. Merry, K. E. Davis, and B. Kingsbury (eds), *The Quiet Power of Indicators* (2015).

[31] See e.g. R. Peet, *Unholy Trinity: The IMF, World Bank and WTO* (2003); N. Woods, *The Globalizers: The IMF, the World Bank, and their Borrowers* (2006).

## A. The Inspection Panel: Establishment and Procedures

The background to the creation of the WBIP is quite well known among international lawyers, and is sketched only briefly here.[32] Already by the early 1980s, the World Bank was receiving negative coverage for the adverse impacts of its large-scale development projects, impacting on both indigenous communities and the natural environment.[33] This prompted the Bank to incorporate into its operational manual a series of policies and procedures—later collectively designated the 'environmental and social safeguard policies'—such as those addressing 'Social Issues Associated with Involuntary Resettlement in Bank-Financed Projects' (1980), 'Tribal People in Bank-Financed-Projects' (1982), and 'Environmental Aspects of Bank Work' (1984).[34] Despite these initiatives, criticism of the World Bank continued throughout the 1980s and heightened at the start of the following decade, as repeated failures by the Bank to comply with its own policies came to light.[35] Around the same time, concerns with the performance of the World Bank's lending operations led to an internal evaluation of its portfolio management, which found a 'culture of loan approval' in the Bank that did not give enough attention to whether loans were properly implemented or even worthwhile.[36]

Against this background, the most direct impetus for establishing the WBIP came from the controversy surrounding the World Bank's financing of projects on the Narmada River in India.[37] Local and international NGO activism centring on the Narmada projects' environmental and social impacts, including the anticipated resettlement of over 200,000 people, prompted the Bank's president to commission an independent review.[38] Dissatisfaction with the World Bank management's response to the review's findings led to further negative reactions and raised the possibility that US funding of the IDA might be blocked until the

[32] See generally Shihata (n. 10) ch. 1.

[33] For an articulation of these criticisms, see C. Payer, *The World Bank: A Critical Analysis* (1982).

[34] World Bank Management, Background Paper on the Management Report and Recommendation in Response to the WBIP Investigation Report, 12 June 2000, 7–8. The Bank's new Environmental and Social Framework (ESF), replacing the previous environmental and social safeguard policies, was approved in 2016. See generally World Bank, Environmental and Social Framework, https://worldbank.org/en/projects-operations/environmental-and-social-framework (last visited 24 November 2023). Also see generally Van Den Meerssche, 'Accountability in International Organisations: Reviewing the World Bank's Environmental and Social Framework', in E. Sciso (ed.), *Accountability, Transparency and Democracy in the Functioning of Bretton Woods Institutions* (2017) 157; C. Passoni, A. Rosenbaum, and E. Vermunt (eds), 'Empowering the Inspection Panel: the Impact of the World Bank's Safeguards Review', NYU Law School Clinic on International Organizations (2016), http://www.iilj.org/wp-content/uploads/2016/08/Empowering_the_Inspection_Panel_Web.pdf (last visited 24 November 2023).

[35] See generally K. Danaher (ed.), *50 Years Is Enough* (1994); J. A. Fox and L. D. Brown (eds), *The Struggle for Accountability* (1998); Wade, 'Greening the Bank: The Struggle over the Environment, 1970–1995', in Kapur, Lewis, and Webb (n. 30) ch. 13.

[36] W. A. Wapenhans, Portfolio Management Task Force, World Bank, Effective Implementation: Key to Development Impact, 1 September 1992, Report 11536, R92-195.

[37] See generally Shihata (n. 10) 5–16; Udall, 'The World Bank and Public Accountability: Has Anything Changed?', in J. A. Fox and L. D. Brown (eds), *The Struggle for Accountability* (1998) ch. 11.

[38] B. Morse and T. R. Berger, *Sardar Sarovar: Report of the Independent Review* (1992).

Bank had established more adequate mechanisms to increase access to information, public participation, and accountability in Bank-funded projects.[39] Designs for an ad hoc inspection capacity, an ombudsman, and an 'Independent Appeals Commission' were all considered and rejected by the Bank's management, before settling on a proposal for an independent Inspection Panel, adopted by a resolution of the executive directors on 22 September 1993.[40]

As mandated by its founding resolution, the WBIP consisted of three members of different nationalities from World Bank member countries.[41] Panel members were nominated by the Bank's president, and appointed by the Bank's executive directors, based on 'their ability to deal thoroughly and fairly with the requests brought to them, their integrity and their independence from the Bank's management, and their exposure to developmental issues and to living conditions in developing countries'.[42] The WBIP started working in August 1994 and adopted operating procedures the same month.[43] A review was carried out two years after the appointment of the first Panel members, resulting in the issuance of a number of 'clarifications' by the executive directors.[44] Another review resulted in further clarifications in 1999.[45]

The WBIP provided the first institutional mechanism by which individuals outside an international organization could bring a complaint against that organization. According to the Panel's founding resolution, any 'affected party' consisting of a group of two or more individuals who are in the borrower's territory (the 'requesters'), and who believe their rights or interests have been or are likely to be directly affected by a World Bank-supported project, may submit a request in writing for an inspection by the WBIP (a 'request'),[46] setting out certain facts relating to the project, the alleged harm, and steps already taken to deal with the issue.[47] Importantly, the reference to affected parties' 'rights' in the WBIP's procedures does not empower requesters to base their complaints on alleged violations of human rights norms. Rather, requests must be based on a claim that the Bank has

[39] For an account of the WBIP's establishment which focuses on the role of the US Congress, see Heupel, 'Human Rights Protection in World Bank Lending: Following the Lead of the US Congress', in M. Heupel and M. Zürn (eds), *Protecting the Individual from International Authority: Human Rights in International Organizations* (2017) ch. 11.

[40] Board of Directors of the IBRD and IDA, Resolution Establishing the World Bank Inspection Panel, IBRD Res. 93-10, IDA Res. 93-6, 22 September 1993.

[41] The initial members had different terms of appointment to allow subsequent appointments to be staggered. Ibid. paras 2–3.

[42] Ibid. para. 4.

[43] Operating Procedures of the World Bank Inspection Panel 1994, in Shihata (n. 10). Updated WBIP Operating Procedures were subsequently adopted in April 2014 and December 2022.

[44] Board of Directors of the IBRD and IDA, Review of the Resolution Establishing the Inspection Panel: 1996 Clarification of Certain Aspects of the Resolution (1996).

[45] Board of Directors of the IBRD and IDA, Clarification of the Board's Second Review of the Inspection Panel (1999).

[46] Board of Directors (n. 40), para. 12; Board of Directors (n. 45), para. 9a.

[47] Board of Directors (n. 40), para. 12.

failed to follow its own operational policies and procedures with respect to the design, appraisal, and/or implementation of the relevant project.[48]

In most cases, requests must be submitted by the affected persons themselves, or by a 'local representative'. However, in 'exceptional cases' where the requesters believe (and the executive directors agree) that 'appropriate representation is not locally available', another (non-local) representative may submit the request. Alternatively, an investigation may be initiated by any individual executive director, or by the executive directors acting as a board.[49] Requests must also meet certain minimum requirements, including that the alleged violation of World Bank policies and procedures is 'of a serious character',[50] and that there is a plausible link between the alleged harm and a project or programme which is being supported (or considered for support) by the Bank.[51] Requests filed after the closing date of a project, or after 95 per cent or more of the Bank's financing has been disbursed, will be ineligible.[52] Requests that concern issues of procurement, or which relate to matters on which the WBIP has already made a recommendation, are also ineligible.[53]

Once a request has been registered, the next phase centres on the decision whether to conduct an investigation into the matters presented in the request.[54] Within 21 working days after receiving the notice of registration, management must submit a response providing 'evidence that it has complied, or intends to comply with the Bank's relevant policies and procedures'.[55] Within 21 working days after receiving management's response, the WBIP must submit a report and recommendation to the board of executive directors, stating whether it recommends an investigation.[56] At this stage, the WBIP confirms that certain technical eligibility criteria are met, including some of the basic requirements verified in the previous phase. Importantly, the WBIP seeks to confirm that the request alleging violation of the Bank's policies is of a serious character, likely to have a material adverse effect on the requester;[57] that the subject matter of the request has been brought to management's attention; and that management has 'failed to demonstrate that it has followed, or is taking steps to follow the Bank's policies and

48 Ibid. para. 12.

49 Ibid. para. 12.

50 Ibid. para. 13. See also Board of Directors (n. 43), para. 25(a), which requires verification that the request 'is not frivolous, absurd or anonymous'.

51 Board of Directors (n. 40), para. 12; Board of Directors (n. 43), para. 25(b) and (c).

52 Board of Directors (n. 40), para. 14(c); Board of Directors (n. 43), para. 25(d) and (e).

53 Board of Directors (n. 40), para. 14(b) and (d). Some of the technical eligibility criteria may be confirmed in the next phase of the process.

54 The 2022 WBIP Operating Procedures identify six phases in an investigation: see Section 3.

55 Board of Directors (n. 40) para. 18.

56 Ibid. para. 19; 2022 WBIP Operating Procedures, para. 41. The WBIP may decide to visit the project country if it considers this necessary to determine the eligibility of the request. 1999 WBIP Clarification (n. 45) para. 7.

57 Resolution Establishing the WBIP (n. 40) para. 13; 2022 WBIP Operating Procedures, para. 44.

procedures'.[58] If the WBIP so recommends, the board will then authorize an investigation 'without making a judgment on the merits' of the request, and without discussion except with respect to technical eligibility criteria.[59]

Once the board has authorized an investigation, the WBIP chair designates one or more Panel members with primary responsibility to conduct the investigation.[60] The length of an investigation is normally in the range of four to six weeks but may vary depending on the nature of the request. Provisions are made for members of the WBIP to have access to all relevant World Bank staff, and documents and investigations are carried out in consultation with the borrowing country, and with its consent for any inspections conducted on its territory.[61] The WBIP's final investigation report, stating its findings on whether the Bank has complied with all relevant Bank policies and procedures, is submitted to the board of executive directors and conveyed to management via the Bank's president.[62] Within six weeks after receiving the investigation report, management must submit to the board a 'Management Report and Recommendation in Response to the Inspection Panel Investigation Report', including proposed actions in response to the WBIP's findings.[63]

Since it began operations in 1994, the WBIP has received 166 requests. Of these, 122 requests have been registered, 50 investigations recommended, and 41 investigations undertaken.[64] To illustrate these processes, the next section outlines the main documents filed and steps taken at each stage of the CWPRP case—the first in which a full Panel process was undertaken, culminating in an investigation report and a final management report and recommendation.

## B. The CWPRP Case: An Outline

The proceedings in the CWPRP case began with a request—the sixteenth registered by the WBIP—on 18 June 1999. Submitted by the International Campaign for Tibet (ICT), this was the first request made by a non-local representative under the 'exceptional cases' provision of the WBIP's founding resolution.[65] The request

[58] Resolution Establishing the WBIP (n. 40) para. 13. See also '1999 WBIP Clarification' (n. 45) para. 9(b) and (c); and 2022 WBIP Operating Procedures, para. 44. See also World Bank Inspection Panel, Report and Recommendation on Request for Inspection China: Western Poverty Reduction Project, 18 August 1999, Annex C 'Attempts to raise Concerns with Bank Staff'.

[59] 1999 WBIP Clarification (n. 45) para. 9.

[60] Resolution Establishing the WBIP (n. 40) para. 20.

[61] Ibid. para. 21. For details of WBIP actions during the investigation, see 2022 WBIP Operating Procedures, paras 61–75.

[62] Resolution Establishing the WBIP (n. 40) para. 22.

[63] Ibid. para. 23.

[64] As at 6 December 2023. See World Bank Inspection Panel, Cases Processing History, https://www.inspectionpanel.org/panel-cases/data (last visited 6 December 2023).

[65] Resolution Establishing the WBIP (n. 40) para. 12.

thus described the ICT as 'a US-based non-governmental organization, acting in representational capacity for people who are living in the project area',[66] and Annexes A and B to the request presented arguments in support of the ICT's authority to act in this capacity, supported by affidavits and statements by human rights activists.[67] In addition, Annex C provided details of prior attempts to raise concerns with Bank staff, fulfilling the requirement that the requesters must demonstrate the steps already taken to deal with the issue and that management has failed to take steps to follow its own policies and procedures.[68]

The main body of the request set out the substantive allegations of breaches of World Bank policies and procedures. Of these, the alleged violations of the Bank's operational directive (OD) 4.20 (Indigenous Peoples) were clearly central, occupying a full ten pages out of 24 in the request—much more than any other issue.[69] Among other things, the request stated that Bank staff had erred in interpreting OD 4.20 as not requiring an indigenous peoples development plan (IPDP) for the Project;[70] that the 'project area' for the purposes of determining the Project's impact on indigenous peoples had been incorrectly defined;[71] and that the population transfers effected under the Project, in significantly reducing the percentages of Tibetan and Mongolian peoples within the relevant area, 'would create further strains on Tibetan and Mongol culture, religion and way of life',[72] increase the likelihood of ethnic conflict,[73] and result in a transfer of resources 'away from ethnic minorities in favour of the dominant national groups'.[74] All these features of the Project were 'in direct contrast with the terms and objectives' of OD 4.20.[75] Moreover, the request alleged that the CWPRP had been mistakenly screened under OD 4.01 (Environmental Assessment) as a Category B project, rather than as Category A, with the result that Bank staff had failed to assess adequately the 'significant risks and potentially devastating environmental and social impacts' of the Project.[76]

The chair of the WBIP, Jim MacNeill, registered the CWPRP request in the Inspection Panel register on the same date it was submitted. The notice of

[66] Request for Inspection to the World Bank Inspection Panel: China Poverty Reduction Project, 18 June 1999, 1

[67] Ibid. Annex B.

[68] Ibid. Annex C.

[69] In contrast, the request raised concerns relating to the World Bank's Environmental Assessment (OD 4.01) and other environmental policies over less than five pages, ibid. 14–19); the pest management policies (OP 4.09 and BP 4.01) over four pages (ibid. 19–22); and the policies on Resettlement (OD 4.30), Retroactive Financing (OD 12.10), and Investment Lending: Identification to Board Presentation (OD 10.00) over less than a page each (ibid. 22–24).

[70] Ibid. 4, 10–14.

[71] Ibid. 5.

[72] Ibid. 5.

[73] Ibid. 6.

[74] Ibid. 7.

[75] Ibid. 7.

[76] Ibid. 4.

registration informed the World Bank's president that Bank management had until 20 July 1999 to provide the Panel with 'written evidence that it has complied, or intends to comply with the relevant policies and procedures in the design and implementation' of the Project, after which the Panel would determine whether the request had met the eligibility criteria.[77] The Bank's board of executive directors had already been scheduled to meet a few days later to decide on whether to approve financing for the Project. At that meeting, the board decided to finance the equivalent of US$160 million out of the $311 million needed for the Project, provided that the $40 million for the Qinghai component of the Project would not be disbursed until after the board had reviewed the results of any WBIP investigation.[78]

Management submitted its response to the request on 19 July 1999. Over a span of 29 pages, the main body of the response addressed each of the claims made in the request. Overall, management concluded that World Bank staff had taken the steps required by the relevant policies and procedures, including building into the Project significant 'indigenous culture bolstering activities', such as '[b]ilingual education and training for Mongols and Tibetans, culturally appropriate health care and pharmacologies, and full respect for religious activities and religious sites' for affected indigenous minorities.[79] Management acknowledged, however, that certain qualitative aspects of the Project could be improved,[80] and provided assurances that these aspects would be 'further addressed with added resources and attention within the mandate of the Bank' as the Project moved forward.[81] Certain other claims made in the request were outside the scope of Bank policy, the response asserted, whether because they related to 'concerns about issues of political economy'[82] or because they addressed matters, such as *voluntary* population movements, on which no Bank policy existed.[83] Eighteen separate annexes, over 90 pages, provided more in-depth detail and analysis of the planning, consultation, and implementation processes carried out in connection with the Project.[84]

On 18 August 1999, the Panel sent its report and recommendation to the World Bank's board of executive directors, authorizing an investigation into the matters alleged in the CWPRP request. A relatively sparse document at only six pages (though attaching all the previous documents filed in the case), the report and recommendation set out basic details of the Project; summarized the allegations

[77] World Bank Inspection Panel, Notice of Registration Re Request for Inspection: China Poverty Reduction Project, 18 June 1999, 2.

[78] WBIP Report and Recommendation on Request for Inspection (n. 58) 3–4.

[79] World Bank Management, Management Response to WBIP Request for Inspection: China Poverty Reduction Project, 19 July 1999, 7.

[80] Ibid. 2.

[81] Ibid. 2.

[82] Ibid. 2.

[83] Ibid. 6.

[84] Ibid. 30–122, Annexes 1–18.

set out in the request, the current state of Bank financing for the Project, and management's response to the allegations; and confirmed that the Panel was satisfied that the request met the technical eligibility criteria, subject to the board's decision regarding non-local representation.[85] On 9 September 1999, the board approved an investigation of the Qinghai component of the Project, and the WBIP assigned two of its members to the task.[86]

The investigation took over six months, including two field visits to Qinghai province, and resulted in an enormous investigation report—more than 200 pages, including six annexes and two maps—which was submitted on 28 April 2000. Following an executive summary,[87] the main body of the report was divided into four parts. Part One, the introduction, reprised the basic details of the Project and the WBIP process undertaken up to that point.[88] Part Two then addressed matters of general compliance, including interpretation of the Bank's policies and procedures, the definition of the project area, the consultation and survey methods used, and consideration of alternatives.[89] Part Three dealt with environmental compliance, centring on the question of environmental screening and assessment of the Project.[90] Finally, Part Four addressed social compliance, most importantly the issues relating to indigenous peoples and involuntary resettlement. Overall, the investigation report found extensive violations of Bank policies, including OD 4.01 (Environmental Assessment), OD 4.20 (Indigenous Peoples), and OD 4.30 (Involuntary Resettlement).

Most analyses of the CWPRP case end with the investigation report, noting the board's subsequent decision not to fund the Qinghai component and China's withdrawal of the Project from the World Bank. However, it is important also to consider management's final report and recommendation before the board reached that decision. Once again, this was a substantial document, comprising some 80 pages. Notably, in addition to recommending particular actions in response to the Panel's findings, management's report and recommendation in response to the investigation report included a lengthy 'Background Paper' addressing the Project and country context, and the environmental and social safeguards.[91] The next part of this chapter builds on the outline of key documents and actions in this section to reframe the WBIP and all phases of its procedures—up to and including management's final report and recommendation—as contributing to an ongoing process of assemblage.

[85] Report and Recommendation on Request for Inspection: China Western Poverty Reduction Project (n. 58) 1–6.

[86] World Bank Inspection Panel, Investigation Report on the Qinghai Project: A Component of the China Western Poverty Reduction Project, 28 April 2000, iv.

[87] Ibid. xii–xxx.

[88] Ibid. 2–15.

[89] Ibid. 16–58.

[90] Ibid. 60–99.

[91] Management Report and Recommendation Background Paper (n. 34).

## 3. From Institutions to Assemblage

This section of the chapter argues that the WBIP should be understood as an assemblage or network of heterogeneous elements which is cobbled together in an ongoing and improvisational way. To develop this argument, I begin by introducing a toolbox of conceptual and analytical categories, drawn from a range of kindred sociological approaches, which have rarely been brought into conversation with international legal scholarship, whether on human rights or international organizations.[92] Applying this toolbox to international institutions such as the WBIP highlights the repeated practices through which they are assembled in more-or-less stable and 'solid' forms, and without which they are susceptible to disintegration and failure. In particular, I argue that the concept of 'translation' helps to draw attention to the many transformations in meaning, strategic moves, and material mobilizations that make assemblages possible. Finally, I show how these analytical insights enable us to see the formation of the WBIP and each case considered by the WBIP—taking the CWPRP case as an example—as an opportunity for network formation, assemblage, and reassemblage.

### A. Practices of Assemblage

As noted previously, existing approaches to the WBIP tend to emphasize the accountability aspects of its operations. Sophisticated observers have noted the complex, indirect, and often attenuated means by which the WBIP's processes offer accountability. For example, Jonathan Fox has analysed the way reformist elements within the World Bank and donor and borrowing governments bolster the efforts of North–South NGO coalitions, drawing on advocacy groups from both donor and borrowing countries, in bringing a request to the WBIP.[93] Moreover, as the

[92] For other examples of the application of these approaches in international law and related fields, see D. Van Den Meerssche, *The World Bank's Lawyers: The Life of International Law as Institutional Practice* (2022); Brandenburg, 'EU Mediation as an Assemblage of Practices: Introducing a New Approach to the Study of EU Conflict Resolution', 55 *Journal of Common Market Studies* (2017) 993; N. M. Rajkovic *et al.* (eds), *The Power of Legality: Practices of International Law and their Politics* (2016); Bueger, 'Making Things Known: Epistemic Practices, the United Nations, and the Translation of Piracy', 9 *International Political Sociology* (2015) 1; Srivastava, 'Assembling International Organizations', *Journal of International Organization Studies* (2013) 72; J. Best and W. Walters (eds), 'Forum on "Actor-Network Theory" and International Relationality: Lost (and Found) in Translation', 7 *International Political Sociology* (2013) 332–349; Murphy and Ó Cuinn, 'Taking Technology Seriously: STS as a Human Rights Method', in M. L. Flear *et al.* (eds), *European Law and New Health Technologies* (2013) ch. 13; Shamir and Weiss, 'Semiotics of Indicators: The Case of Corporate Human Rights Responsibility', in K. Davis *et al.* (eds), *Governance by Indicators: Global Power through Quantification and Rankings* (2012); E. Adler and V. Pouliot (eds), *International Practices* (2011).

[93] Fox, 'Transnational Civil Society Campaigns and the World Bank Inspection Panel', in A. Brysk (ed.), *Globalization and Human Rights* (2002) 171 (ch. 9), at 192–195. Along similar lines, Wong and Mayer argue that 'while not providing affected persons a legal avenue for redress, the Inspection Panel, if used strategically as part of larger advocacy strategies, particularly by increasing media coverage on

possible outcomes of an investigation include termination of Bank financing for a project, non-state actors often bring claims against the Bank through the WBIP with the ultimate aim of influencing the conduct of the borrowing country. As Robert Wade has put it, the WBIP process can serve as 'a mechanism for project-affected people, or NGOs acting in their name, to launch a boomerang—to pitch complaints against the borrowing government into an international venue and then to generate pressure from the rich countries on the borrowing government'.[94] Yet even these analyses, as illuminating as they are, tend to measure the WBIP's effects in terms of its 'success' as a mechanism of accountability, conceived in necessarily adversarial or oppositional terms.

In contrast, I propose viewing the WBIP as an ongoing process of assemblage, or 'the continuous work of pulling disparate elements together'.[95] Assemblage theorists view organizations—indeed, each action by an organization—as being made possible only by an extensive network of heterogeneous and often ill-fitting elements, such as existing bureaucratic systems and procedures, different kinds of expertise and know-how, pragmatic instruments of observation and measurement, methods of notation and calculation, architectural plans and arrangements of space, physical mechanisms and devices, and actors who may have their own, quite distinct goals.[96] As a particular variant of assemblage theory, actor-network theory begins from the premise that 'relations are primary to entities'.[97] Accordingly, organizations are not understood as 'real' or 'solid' things in and of themselves; rather, they exist only as assemblages-in-action, or actor-networks. Furthermore, new actors, objects, concepts, and forms of knowledge and power are simultaneously and continually constituted as effects of the assemblage or network.[98]

The aim of analysis, then, is to understand how assemblages come to have the appearance of solidity; how they are put together, incorporate resistances, take effect, succeed, and fail. Recognition of the heterogeneous make-up of assemblages requires analysing not only their networked elements—human and non-human, material and non-material—but also the practices that interlink

problematic projects, can nevertheless serve as a useful tool in helping redress wrongs committed as a result of the Bank's failure to comply with its own policies'. Wong and Mayer (n. 7) 496.

94 Wade (n. 9) 29 (adapting the 'boomerang' metaphor from M. E. Keck and K. Sikkink, *Activists beyond Borders: Advocacy Networks in International Politics* (1998) 12–13).

95 Murray Li, 'Practices of Assemblage and Community Forest Management', 36 *Economy and Society* (2007) 264. In this chapter, I aim to highlight commonalities among a number of different theoretical and methodological approaches, not all of whose proponents would describe them as 'assemblage theories'. E.g. I treat actor-network theory as a particular kind of assemblage theory, and use the terms 'assemblage' and 'actor-network' accordingly.

96 On assemblages in government, see generally Rose and Miller, 'Political Power Beyond the State: Problematics of Government', 43 *British Journal of Sociology* (1992) 173; Dean, 'Putting the Technological into Government', 9 *History of the Human Sciences* (1996) 47; Murray Li (n. 95).

97 Brandenburg (n. 92) 996.

98 Bueger and Bethke, 'Actor-Networking the "Failed State"—an Enquiry into the Life of Concepts', 17 *Journal of International Relations and Development* (2014) 38, at 38.

them.[99] Assemblages are inherently fragile and require continuous efforts to maintain. As Tania Murray Li has noted, the term 'assemblage' draws attention to the practices involved in *assembling*, as well as their outcome: 'Assemblage flags agency, the hard work required to draw heterogeneous elements together, forge connections between them and sustain these connections in the face of tension.'[100] Moreover, assemblages are sites of struggle, particularly as they undergo strategic elaborations over time:[101]

> Thus, the analysis of ordering struggle is central to actor-network theory. The object is to explore and describe local processes of patterning, social orchestration, ordering, and resistance. ... This ... is the core of the actor-network approach: a concern with how actors and organizations mobilize, juxtapose, and hold together the bits and pieces out of which they are composed; how they are sometimes able to prevent those bits and pieces from following their own inclinations and making off...

Studies in the ANT tradition provide useful examples of the kinds of practices involved in assemblage. In a classic case study, Michel Callon distinguished four 'moments', which may in fact overlap in time, in the construction of a network of relationships among a diverse set of actors, which included fishermen, scallops, researchers, and their scientific colleagues.[102] First, a group of actors (here, the researchers) identify a problem ('problematization'), in the course of which they attempt to define the identities of other actors and position themselves as an 'obligatory passage point' for the resolution of the problem.[103] Second, they use a variety of '*interessement* devices' to induce the interest of the other targeted actors, with the aim of stabilizing the identities and goals of the latter as tentatively defined and locking them into a system of alliances.[104] Third, if successful, these efforts result in the provisional 'enrolment' of the targeted actors into the alliance.[105] Finally, the assemblage is stabilized through the designation of official representatives or 'spokespeople' to speak on behalf of the enrolled actors.[106]

At any point, a network may fail or a counter-enrolment effort, undertaken by a different set of actors possessing different goals and interests, may succeed.[107]

99 On practices in international relations, see generally Adler and Pouliot (n. 92).

100 Murray Li (n. 95) 264.

101 Law, 'Notes on the Theory of the Actor-Network: Ordering, Strategy, and Heterogeneity', 5 *Systems Practice* (1992) 379, at 386.

102 Callon, 'Some Elements of a Sociology of Translation: Domestication of the Scallops and the Fishermen of St. Brieuc Bay', in B. Biagioli (ed.), *The Science Studies Reader* (1999 [1986]) 67 (ch. 5).

103 Ibid. 69–70.

104 Ibid. 71–74.

105 Ibid. 74.

106 Ibid. 74–76.

107 Also see generally Callon and Law, 'On Interests and their Transformation: Enrolment and Counter-Enrolment', 12 *Social Studies of Science* (1982) 615; B. Latour, *Science in Action* (1987).

As Callon put it, the processes of *interessement* and enrolment are accompanied by a 'group of multilateral negotiations, trials of strength, and tricks'.[108] Bruno Latour has detailed a similar series of strategies and tactics whereby scientists enlist others to their endeavours, such as by persuading them that their interests are identical, or should change, or can be achieved by another route; or by presenting them with a problem that displaces their initial goals, devising new goals for them, even inventing new groups that could then be oriented towards the new goals.[109] After groups are enrolled into a network, more work is necessary to control them and 'make their behaviour predictable', recruit new allies to replace those that have fallen away, and bind the whole assemblage together.[110] Along the way, resistances, compromises, and counter-enrolments may result in 'more fragile textures and less orderly webs'.[111]

While initially formulated to follow the work of scientists, the concepts and categories devised by actor-network theorists are equally apt for analysing other processes of social ordering. Problem-definition and formation of identities, interests, goals, alliances, and representation are all crucial moments in any effort of governance. When certain actors attempt to enrol others by mapping and transforming their interests, they can be understood as 'trying to impose order on a part of the social world':[112]

> They are trying to build a version of social structure. On this view interests (and other categories such as desires, motives and wishes) ... are attempts to define (and, most importantly, to enforce) the institutions, groups or organizations that exist from time to time in the social world.

In the works of Callon, Law, and Latour, the term 'translation' is used to denote the full range of moves and transformations—strategic, physical, and linguistic—required to establish and maintain a network of associations.[113] In all cases, translation involves treating things that are unlike as if they are identical:[114] 'To translate is to create convergences and homologies out of particularities.'[115] In its strategic sense, as already noted, translation involves transforming interests so that they align and match up. In its physical or geometric sense, translation involves the logistical exercise of mobilizing an array of human and non-human

[108] Callon (n. 102) 74.
[109] See generally Latour (n. 107) 108–116.
[110] Ibid. 121–129.
[111] Bueger and Bethke (n. 98) 40.
[112] Callon and Law (n. 107) 622.
[113] Wæraas and Nielsen, 'Translation Theory Translated: Three Perspectives on Translation in Organizational Research', 18 *International Journal of Management Reviews* (2016) 236, at 237. See e.g. Callon (n. 102); Callon and Law (n. 107); Latour (n. 107).
[114] Callon and Law (n. 107) 619.
[115] Callon (n. 102) 197.

actors, or 'actants'—defined as anything which 'acts or to which activity is granted by others'.[116] Problematization, *interessement*, and enrolment are made possible through simplified, durable representations of knowledge, or 'inscription devices', whether in the form of words, numbers, graphs, diagrams, or other visual displays.[117] Once captured in a relatively stable form, inscriptions can be moved around, accumulated in paper or computer files, and compared at 'centres of calculation', such as laboratories, statistical bureaus, and legal registries.[118]

These material conditions of knowledge production—inscription, mobilization, and calculation in particular artefacts and sites—are central to the construction of networks, and so to all manner of governance activities that create the appearance of institutional 'solidity'.[119] Much of the work of experts in international organizations thus involves translating the messiness of the world into useful abstractions (reports, tables, matrices, scores, indexes) that can then be deployed to govern their unruly objects. To grasp the dynamics of global governance, we therefore need to understand the production of expert knowledge as a kind of concrete practice.[120]

In its linguistic sense, translation denotes the many transformations in meaning that occur as knowledge, goals, and interests are reframed and rephrased in the process of drawing potential allies into an assemblage.[121] As is well recognized, translation is never perfect: the 'effect of sameness-in-difference'[122] sought by translation always leads to a loss of meaning, and an element of betrayal.[123] But translation adds as well as subtracts, resulting in new meanings, generating 'new objects, practices, person-types, and knowledge'.[124] In both injecting and removing meaning, translation can be 'an asymmetrical, power-drenched practice that forms subaltern subjectivities' and produces 'incommensurabilities, disjunctures, and power differentials'.[125] However, certain kinds of translation, such as what Sally Engle Merry has termed 'vernacularization', involve the transformation of meaning 'from below', such that 'the global becomes localized, no longer simply

[116] Latour, 'On Actor-Network Theory: A Few Clarifications', 47 *Soziale Welt* (1996) 369, at 373. Latour goes on to explain that the term 'actant' 'implies *no* special motivation of *human individual* actors, nor of humans in general. An actant can literally be anything provided it is granted to be the source of an action.' Ibid. (emphasis in original).

[117] Ibid. 64–69. See also Best and Walters (n. 92) 332; Walters, 'The Power of Inscription: Beyond Social Construction and Deconstruction in European Integration Studies', 31 *Millennium: Journal of International Studies* (2002) 83, at 91.

[118] Latour (n. 107) ch. 6.

[119] Joyce and Mukerji, 'The State of Things: State History and Theory Reconfigured', 46 *Theory and Society* (2017) 1, at 10; also see generally Rose and Miller (n. 96) 185–186.

[120] Best and Walters (n. 92) 348. For illustrations of such work, see generally K. Davis *et al.* (eds), *Governance by Indicators: Global Power through Quantification and Rankings* (2012).

[121] Gal, 'Politics of Translation', 44 *Annual Review of Anthropology* (2015) 225, at 227.

[122] Ibid. 226.

[123] '*Traduttore, traditore*'; Best and Walters (n. 92) 333.

[124] Gal (n. 121) 236.

[125] Ibid. 228, 226.

a global imposition but something which is infused with the meanings, signs, and practices of local places'.[126]

While appearing to produce commensurability, translation also creates boundaries. Languages are marked as distinctive and different in the process of translation. Intralingually, 'registers' are associated with particular social perspectives, positions, 'person-types', and sets of practices. Yet translation from one register to another—whether scientific, literary, religious, or legal—does not simply create a bridge between the two, but also simultaneously reinforces the borders between them and helps to construct them as different.[127] In complex settings involving multiple registers, therefore, actors may have to 'double voice their knowledge' so as to make their claims legible to others and enrol allies into their networks.[128] In doing so, they may need to speak a different conceptual and metaphorical vocabulary, add or remove emotional affect, change the pacing of their speech, even adopt different bodily postures.[129]

## B. The Inspection Panel in Assemblage

These various practices of translation can be seen in the assemblage of international organizations. Though apparently stable and 'solid', each organization is in fact sustained only through a whole host of mundane, mostly unremarked practices of (re)assemblage—problematization, *interessement*, enrolment, representation, and so on—carried out in an endlessly recursive fashion. International organizations can thus be understood as 'perpetual works in progress', marking a theoretical shift in focus 'from the effects *of* [international organizations] to [international organizations] *as* effects'.[130] Close attention to the practices of assemblage that constitute international organizations promises to reveal greater insights into *how* they come to appear 'real' and assert authority in the world, or fail to do so.[131]

Viewed from this perspective, the World Bank itself can be understood as the effect of an intensive, contested process of assemblage linking together many different actants, each of which can in turn be analysed as an assemblage or actor-network. Though often imagined as a single, coherent 'thing', the Bank comprises thousands of individuals assembled in a vast network across continents, linked together by multiple devices including continuous flows of correspondence, emails, and reports, meetings, shared computer databases, websites, and more. Bank

[126] Merry, 'Legal Vernacularization and Ka Ho'okolokolonui Kanaka Maoli, The People's International Tribunal, Hawai'i', 19 *PoLAR: Political and Legal Anthropology Review* (1996) 67, at 80.

[127] Gal (n. 121) 230, 232.

[128] Ibid. 233.

[129] See e.g. B. Latour, *The Making of Law: An Ethnography of the Conseil d'Etat* (2010) 68.

[130] Srivastava (n. 92) 73 (emphasis added).

[131] See generally M. Barnett and M. Finnemore, *Rules for the World: International Organizations in Global Politics* (2004); M. Barnett and R. Duvall (eds), *Power in Global Governance* (2005).

management is a further network or assemblage within the Bank-as-network. The executive directors, as another network-within-a-network, link to yet more actor-networks of more or less cohesiveness 'outside' the Bank: the executive and legislative branches of the governments of the countries they represent, including 'Part II' (borrower) members and powerful 'Part I' (lender) members, such as the United States. NGOs, activists, and academics—scientists, development experts, lawyers, and others—form more or less stable advocacy networks that engaged directly and indirectly with the Bank and established relationships with project-affected local populations and international media organizations.

For the WBIP to come into existence and appear as a 'solid' institution, then, a complex series of strategic manoeuvres had to be carried out to link up among these various actor-networks. If we choose for a moment to follow World Bank management as our primary actant, we can see how management sought to problematize the concerns arising from the Narmada and other projects, as well as those relating to the Bank's 'culture of loan approval', as both arising from failures to correctly follow Bank policies and procedures.[132] To marshal the interest of other relevant actants, management deployed a number of identifiable tactics, for example signalling to 'external' human rights and environmental activists and 'internal' stakeholders (such as the US government and Congress) that they shared a common goal, by appointing a retired Administrator of the UN Development Programme and former US Congressman, Bradford Morse, to head the review of the Narmada projects.[133]

Of course, the same analysis could just as well be undertaken from the point of view of any of the other actants initially identified, each of which sought to enrol the others into *its* network, according to *its* problematization and conception of its own interests. Nor should the agency of non-human actants be overlooked. Consider, for example, the environmental conditions that prompted the building of a dam on the Narmada, the gradient and force of the river that determined the costs of building the dam, and so on, ad infinitum.[134]

The sequence of events that led to the initial assemblage of the WBIP placed the World Bank in a network of relationships with other actants, transforming each of their interests and identities while binding them together to a greater or lesser extent. The processes of producing, receiving, and debating different proposals for control and accountability mechanisms are examples of the kinds of 'multilateral negotiations, trials of strength and tricks that accompany *interessements* and enable them to succeed'.[135] Other, related *interessement* devices included a series of steps taken to enhance the Bank's 'transparency' and 'participation': the issuance

[132] Shihata (n. 10) 1–2, 8–16.

[133] Morse was appointed by the President of the World Bank, at the request of some executive directors. Ibid. 11.

[134] Cf. T. Mitchell, *The Rule of Experts* (2002) ch. 1.

[135] Callon (n. 102) 74.

of a revised disclosure policy; the establishment of a Public Information Centre; a three-year study that documented the Bank's growing efforts in participatory development; and the involvement of NGOs in the design, implementation, and appraisal of Bank-funded projects to an unprecedented level.[136] All these moves constructed the WBIP as one more link within a network of policies and procedures, together working to attract and consolidate the interest of actors 'outside' the Bank. From this perspective, the appointment of the first Panel members as representatives or spokespersons achieved a temporary stability in the construction of a new network of relationships.

Each request for investigation made to the WBIP can be analysed along similar lines—as involving the provisional enrolment of requesters, through their spokespersons, into the WBIP's network. That enrolment is formalized via a series of distinct steps, by which a request is submitted, registered, and assessed by the Panel as meeting certain technical eligibility criteria.[137] Yet, even before this, the requesters must themselves have been formed as an actor-network. Among the WBIP's technical eligibility criteria is the requirement that '[t]he affected party consists of any two or more persons with common interests or concerns who are in the borrower's territory'.[138] Though not detailed in the filed documents, and therefore difficult to access and analyse, each request must therefore be preceded by a lengthy process of problematization, *interessement*, and enrolment, establishing the 'common interests or concerns' on which the request is based, and leading to the appointment of representatives to speak on behalf of the (potentially) affected parties. Once the eligibility criteria have been satisfied, the requesters are then treated as an incontrovertible 'black box', with any distinctions between their interests ignored for the purposes of the WBIP process.[139]

The CWPRP case provides an interesting example of the practices associated with the 'spokesperson' or 'representation' moment in actor-network formation. As noted, the case involved the first request submitted to the WBIP by a non-local representative—the ICT.[140] Even here, however, it is apparent that the ICT first had to take certain steps to attract the interest of and enrol individuals affected by the Project. Annex B to the request presented the Panel with written evidence that it was acting as the 'agent of the party on behalf of which the request is made', including signed letters of appointment, affidavits, and statements in support by human rights experts and activists.[141] Additional evidence, in the

136 Sinclair (n. 14) 266–267.

137 See nn. 46–53 and accompanying text.

138 1999 WBIP Clarification (n. 45) para. 9a.

139 See generally Latour (n. 107) 131 ('When many elements are made to act as one, this is what I will now call a black box'), 2–4 and 80–83.

140 See WBIP Request for Inspection: China Poverty Reduction Project (n. 66) and accompanying text.

141 Report and Recommendation on Request for Inspection (n. 58) Annex B1 'International Campaign for Tibet Representational Authority'.

form of letters sent from inside Qinghai province, was disclosed to the Panel in Annex A ('Confidential Documents'), but redacted in the copy of the request to be transmitted to management.[142] Whatever one's view on the merits of the case, then, it is apparent that even the ostensibly 'first step' of bringing the request to the WBIP required a lengthy antecedent process of assemblage, involving the painstaking enrolment of 'a multitude of actors' into a single 'party'.[143]

What followed in the CWPRP case was a further series of alternating efforts at (re)problematization, *interessement*, and enrolment by the requesters, World Bank management, and the WBIP. In order to capture the interest of the WBIP and provisionally enrol its members in the requesters' network, the request had to problematize the case in a language, and present it in a form, acceptable to the Panel—otherwise, the requesters' effort at assemblage would fail and the request would not proceed to an investigation. In its initial response to the request, management attempted to re-enrol WBIP members and the requesters back into the Bank's network by persuading them that they shared with the Bank a set of common interests; that the Bank itself was the 'obligatory passage point' through which any problems associated with the Project could be addressed. This involved a series of tactical manoeuvres on the part of management to reframe the problems identified in the request as either having been resolved, in the course of being resolved, or incapable of being addressed by the Bank.[144]

The WBIP's 130-page investigation report nicely illustrates the practices of assemblage, emphasising how much of the Panel members' work involved attempts to recruit and enlist new allies into its network. In conducting their investigation, the panellists met with and interviewed hundreds of people, including the requesters and individuals in the project area; World Bank staff and consultants; the executive director representing China at the Bank; Chinese central and provincial government officials; representatives and officials of several embassies in Beijing; representatives of other international organizations; and NGOs such as the Ford Foundation.[145] In all of these interactions, they both drew on these individuals' experiences and expertise and sought to bring them into alignment with the WBIP's own institutional mission and interests. The investigation report

[142] Ibid. Annex A.

[143] Wade (n. 9) 32. Wade argues that the protests against the CWPRP project were concocted by the 'Tibet lobby' as a 'campaign vehicle to focus world attention on Chinese abuses in Tibet', and that they presented misleading information about the project and its anticipated outcomes. Wade (n. 9) 31, 32–33. For views more sympathetic to the protestors, see Clark 'The World Bank Inspection Panel', in M. Langford (ed.), *Social Rights Jurisprudence: Emerging Trends in International Law* (2009) 628; Fox 'Transnational Civil Society Campaigns and the World Bank Inspection Panel', in A. Brysk (ed.), *Globalization and Human Rights* (2002) 171 (ch. 9).

[144] Management Response to the Request for Inspection (n. 79) 1–2.

[145] WBIP Investigation Report (n. 86) iv–v. The other international organizations consulted by the Panel included the UN Development Programme, the UN Office for Project Services, the European Commission, and the World Food Programme.

> indicates the difficulty of this assemblage work, describing the various subterfuges and ruses deployed by the Panel members to meet with local residents privately, so that they could express their views freely:[146] Team members often asked to visit sites without prior notification, or changed itinerary without advance notice, in order to interview Project-affected persons in a more open manner. In addition, some Team members often disengaged themselves from the group in the evenings, in order to interview more people about their opinions of the Project. They found disturbing evidence that many people were clearly afraid to talk about the Project ...

Here, too, we can view each document collected and each witness or expert testimony gathered as an inscription device. Power flowed to the WBIP, making it appear more 'solid', to the extent that it became a centre of calculation where such documents could be compiled and sorted, their contents summarized, aggregated, and compared.[147] The investigation report thus involved a restatement (and subtle transformation) of the Bank's, the requesters', and the WBIP's own interests, refining the problematization presented by the requesters while retaining management as an ally in its network.[148] Yet at each stage, failure threatened—if the WBIP was unable to enrol crucial allies, or lost allies from the network, or was unable to draw adequate linkages between the documents and actants in its network-information. Conversely, missing links of information or poor-quality inscriptions gathered by other actants reduced the cohesiveness of their networks, and thereby the persuasiveness of their claims vis-à-vis the Panel. The WBIP's investigation report thus noted that minutes cited by management made no mention of an environmental assessment that should have taken place,[149] and that '[t]he standard of maps, charts and references' produced by management was 'inadequate'.[150]

Management's report and recommendation in response to the investigation report demonstrate how the process of assemblage in global governance must be understood as ongoing, ever-contested, and never final or complete. In that document, management accepted some of the Panel's findings and made recommendations to address them.[151] At the same time, however, management noted its disagreement with the Panel on a number of findings, proposing actions that differed from those proposed by the Panel,[152] and seeking to reframe the whole investigation by attaching a 'Background Paper' which set the entire process in a wider context of changes in Bank policies and approaches over time.[153] While

[146] Ibid. 52.
[147] Cf. Rose and Miller (n. 96) 200.
[148] WBIP Investigation Report (n. 86).
[149] Ibid. 69.
[150] Ibid. xxiv, 78–82.
[151] World Bank Management, Management Report and Recommendation in Response to the WBIP Investigation Report, 13 June 2000, 2–3.
[152] Ibid. 4–5.
[153] Management Report and Recommendation Background Paper (n. 34).

management failed to enrol the WBIP in its view of the case, then, management conversely remained unconvinced of the WBIP's problematization of the case. Moreover, China's eventual withdrawal of the Project from the Bank in July 2000 also suggests a failure to enrol China in the WBIP's network and, at least temporarily and in relation to this specific Project, in the Bank's. The next section of this chapter explores the implications of this view of the WBIP-as-assemblage for our understanding of the role of human rights in its operations.

## 4. Human Rights in Translation

Building on the analytical framework introduced in Section 3, this part of the chapter examines the effects of human rights—and the effects *on* human rights—in the innumerable translations involved in the ongoing assemblage of the WBIP. I argue that human rights play a much more multivalent, fluid role in the operation of the WBIP, and thus in the governance of the World Bank, than is generally recognized. Among other things, focusing on practices of translation promises to help situate human rights as one element among others, shaping and being shaped in the networks of assemblage and reassemblage in which the WBIP is constantly engaged. I begin by proposing a broadening of focus from accountability to authority, and then trace the consequences of that wider focus for our understanding of the role of human rights in the CWPRP case.

### A. From Accountability to Authority

Existing analyses of human rights in the work of the WBIP adopt approaches that assume an accountability framework. For example, activist and policy-oriented scholars have examined the WBIP's casework to identify ways in which the Panel incorporates human rights considerations into its reports, with a view to promoting greater compliance with those standards.[154] One such study argues that the WBIP contributes to protecting and developing human rights by:

> progressively interpreting the Bank's policies and procedures which incorporate human rights-related standards, and applying a high degree of scrutiny to the Bank's due diligence obligations' ... by interpreting the Bank's policies in light of relevant international law standards ... [and] by requiring that the Bank consider

[154] S. Herz and A. Perrault, 'Bringing Human Rights Claims to the World Bank Inspection Panel', October 2009; Vita, Tan, and Panjshiri, 'The World Bank Inspection Panel and International Human Rights Law', NYU Law School Clinic on International Organizations (2016), https://www.iilj.org/wp-content/uploads/2017/08/The-World-Bank-Inspection-Panel-FINAL-REPORT.pdf (last visited 1 December 2023).

> human rights violations which could impede the achievement of the project's sustainable development objectives and the Bank's broader mission.[155]

Another study offers a similar list of lessons drawn from the WBIP's reports, adding that '[t]he Bank must consider human rights protections enshrined in national constitutions or other sources of domestic law'.[156] Others have been more critical, describing the WBIP's practice in taking human rights into consideration as 'inconsistent and piecemeal'.[157] For example, in advocating a more forthright adoption of human rights discourse and language by the Bank, Philip Alston argues that rights are 'inseparable from the notion of accountability. Where rights are ignored or violated, there must be accountability'.[158] A considerable body of scholarship thus argues for and against the desirability—and the possibility—of holding the World Bank accountable for human rights violations, whether through the WBIP or otherwise.[159]

Arguments on both sides of this scholarship share a view of accountability and human rights that assumes a kind of institutional and normative 'solidity'. For the WBIP to hold World Bank operations to account for non-compliance with human rights, the WBIP and the Bank must be distinct entities in a more-or-less hierarchical relationship—in one formulation, the 'accountability holder' and the 'power-wielder', respectively[160]—and human rights must provide a set of standards that are independent of both, which the WBIP can therefore apply to displace other considerations. In this respect, Galit Sarfaty has analysed the clash between the 'distinctive logics' of economics and human rights in the World Bank, arguing that human rights have remained marginal by being 'accommodated within the economic calculus of the Bank as a normative technology of audit'.[161] Along similar lines, Alston argues that human rights provide 'a detailed and balanced framework'

155 Vita et al. (n. 154) 11.

156 Herz and Perrault (n. 154) 2.

157 UNHCR, Report of the Special Rapporteur on Extreme Poverty and Human Rights, 4 August 2015, A/70/274, para. 32.

158 Ibid. para. 65.

159 See e.g. De Feyter, 'The International Financial Institutions and Human Rights: Law and Practice', 6 *Human Rights Review* (2004) 56; Wahi, 'Human Rights Accountability of the IMF and the World Bank: A Critique of Existing Mechanisms and Articulation of a Theory of Horizontal Accountability', 12 *UC Davis Journal of International Law & Policy* (2006) 331; Schlemmer-Schulte, 'The World Bank and Human Rights', 4 *Austrian Review of International and European Law* (1999) 230; McInerney-Lankford (n. 19); Fox (n. 6); Fox (n. 8); Wong and Mayer (n. 7); Clark (n. 143); Suzuki and Nanwani (n. 7); Wade (n. 9); Fujita, 'The Challenges of Mainstreaming Human Rights in the World Bank', 15 *International Journal of Human Rights* (2011) 374.

160 See generally Grant and Keohane, 'Accountability and Abuses of Power in World Politics', 99 *American Political Science Review* (2005) 29.

161 G. Sarfaty, *Values in Translation: Human Rights and the Culture of the World Bank* (2012) 12. Sarfaty distinguishes between the consequentialist and deontological rationalities of mainstream economics and human rights theory, respectively, arguing that the former 'is a discipline based on the value of efficiency, perfect markets, rational actors, and resource constraints', whereas the latter 'is premised on the inherent dignity of persons and a system of universal, inalienable truths from which are derived absolute freedoms and basic duties'. Ibid. 10.

involving 'specific legal obligations' which bring 'a degree of normative certainty', including 'certain values [which] are non-negotiable'.[162]

There are reasons, however, to doubt the suitability of this view of human rights and accountability to the conditions of global governance. As Nico Krisch has argued, existing framings of accountability may be inapt 'when the locus of authority is no longer clearly defined, when it is in flux, informal and relational'.[163] Deborah Avant and her co-authors have likewise analysed global governance as a dynamic, ongoing process that involves the interaction of multiple actors, each of whom draws upon one or more sources of authority.[164] In such circumstances, where no actor has command authority over others, and states and international institutions exist in non-hierarchical relationships of alternating cooperating and competition, it becomes necessary to conceptualize authority as a function of these mutual relations and interplay. Krisch thus defines 'liquid authority' in global governance as possessing four characteristic features:[165]

> ... the use of informal rather than formal and binding means; the reliance on substantive rather than formal resources as grounds of authority; a multiplicity of actors instead of a unitary or focal authority; and a dynamic rather than stable nature of authority constellations.

All of these features are present to a significant extent in the WBIP's operations. While its authority has been formally prescribed and delimited in various documents, it is clear that, unlike a court or other judicial body, the WBIP is not able to make binding decisions. As indicated in Section 3 of this chapter, therefore, the Panel seeks to induce the deference of multiple others—requesters, borrowers, World Bank management, and ultimately the board—to its processes and findings by means of persuasion. Moreover, in WBIP proceedings the language of human rights mingles, intersects, and interacts with legal, moral, and expert claims of all kinds, in innumerable variations.

In contrast to an accountability-focused approach, then, this section of the chapter is concerned with tracing the myriad ways in which human rights discourse connects with, transforms, and in turn is transformed through the WBIP's processes. Despite sharing a common vocabulary of 'translation', I depart from Sarfaty's analysis in refusing to assign an essentialist 'logic' or 'rationality' to

[162] Report of the Special Rapporteur on Extreme Poverty and Human Rights (n. 157) para. 65. See also Alston, 'Rethinking the World Bank's Approach to Human Rights, Keynote address to the Nordic Trust Fund for Human Rights and Development Annual Workshop on "The Way Forward"', The World Bank, Washington DC, 15 October 2014, https://www.law.nyu.edu/news/philip-alston-world-bank-human-rights (last visited 1 December 2023), 7–8.

[163] Krisch, 'Liquid Authority in Global Governance', 9 *International Theory* (2017) 237, at 250.

[164] See generally Avant, Finnemore, and Sell (n. 24).

[165] Krisch, 'Authority, Solid and Liquid, in Postnational Governance', in R. Cotterell and M. Del Mar (eds), *Authority in Transnational Legal Theory* (2016) 39. Also see generally N. Krisch (ed.), 'Symposium on Liquid Authority', 9 *International Theory* (2017) 237.

either human rights or economics, which then 'compete' and 'clash' in a zero-sum manner.[166] Rather, human rights can be seen as a discourse or register of surprising flexibility and transformative power. On the one hand, human rights often appear as a source of ethical principle and morality; on the other hand, they link to expert processes as an expression of due process and a guide to administrative procedure. Between these two, human rights can be positioned at any point along the legal continuum, from a thick idea of the rule of law to a thin principle of legality.[167]

Indeed, the success of efforts by advocates and others to incorporate human rights claims into WBIP requests depends crucially on their ability to move fluidly along this continuum between different registers. If 'law is made through chains of networks and translations',[168] then so too is authority in global governance writ large. The translation of claims from expert, moral, or legal registers into and through the register of human rights itself performs and constructs human rights—as well as those other registers—as distinct and different.[169] Furthermore, the transformation of a human rights claim by its revoicing in another register will always retain a remnant of the original, and vice versa.

These dynamics of translation and transformation can be observed in the very establishment of the WBIP. As we have seen, the motivations for establishing the WBIP comprised a mix of 'managerial' or administrative concerns—the failure of Bank staff to adhere to its internal rules—and external criticisms that problematized the Bank's apparent breach of international human rights and environmental law standards.[170] That combination of concerns had already had an effect over the previous decades, with the adoption of environmental and social safeguard policies and procedures that incorporated international legal norms. For example, the Bank's revised OD 4.20 (Indigenous Peoples) was adopted in 1991 following close collaboration with the International Labour Organization, using ILO Convention 169 on Indigenous and Tribal Peoples (1989) as a framework,[171] with the express purpose of ensuring 'that the development process fosters full respect for [indigenous peoples'] dignity, human rights, and cultural uniqueness'.[172]

[166] See Sarfaty (n. 161). It is noteworthy that Sarfaty's analysis largely ignores the WBIP and is confined to the 'clash of expertise' within the Bank itself.

[167] Thanks to Jutta Brunnée for discussions on this point.

[168] Levi and Valverde, 'Studying Law by Association: Bruno Latour Goes to the *Conseil d'État*', 33 *Law & Social Inquiry* (2008) 805, at 813.

[169] Cf. Gal (n. 121) 229.

[170] Shihata (n. 10) 2.

[171] Kingsbury, 'Operational Policies of International Institutions as Part of the Law-Making Process: The World Bank and Indigenous Peoples', in G. S. Goodwin-Gill and S. Talmon (eds), *The Reality of International Law* (1999) 323, at 341, 340–341. See generally OPCS Working Paper, Implementation of the World Bank's Indigenous Peoples Policy: A Learning Review, August 2011, 1, para. 2, https://documents.worldbank.org/en/publication/documents-reports/documentdetail/427941468163488772/implementation-of-the-world-banks-indigenous-peoples-policy-a-learning-review-fy2006-2008 (last visited 1 December 2023).

[172] World Bank, Operational Directive on Indigenous Peoples, September 1991, OD 4.20, para. 6. This remains the only express reference to human rights in World Bank policies and procedures.

In contrast, the Bank's policy on involuntary resettlement made no express mention of human rights or dignity; instead, it used the managerial language of 'safeguards to address and mitigate ... impoverishment risks'.[173] Yet with this combination of moral, legal, and administrative registers, the World Bank's policies appear to have served as sufficiently effective *interessement* devices—especially when linked procedurally to the WBIP—to attract the (provisional) enrolment of human rights activists and NGOs.

At the point when a complaint against the World Bank is framed as a request to the WBIP, a further series of translations are necessary. These translations lead eventually to the appointment of representatives who will voice that complaint primarily as a matter of faulty administration or poor governance, in a register appropriate to the kind of administrative review process undertaken by the Panel. In making their grievances legible to and actionable by the WBIP, people affected by a Bank-financed project must therefore devote time and resources to the request, narrow the scope of their claims, divert energy away from other initiatives, possibly abandon broader grievances about social inequality and injustice, and even come to think of themselves as belonging to a new category—'requesters'. Without access to the negotiations and manoeuvres that preceded each request to the WBIP, it is not possible to know whether the original complaint in any particular case was initially framed in human rights terms—that is, prior to the request being formulated—or whether that framing came about through an antecedent series of translations and transformations of interests among actors in the relevant project-affected area.

In this context, one might reasonably worry that framing claims in human rights terms has the effect of crowding out and delegitimizing other strategies for emancipation.[174] Of course, the possibility remains that other actors may at any time refuse the translation of their interests into the administrative register of WBIP procedure. One request expressed this possibility in especially dramatic terms:[175]

> In the absence of any favourable response we have no other way than resorting to appropriate means of struggle against the implementation of the project. And this will be a 'struggle unto death', for we prefer to die with dignity fighting to retain our 'home lands' and identity, rather than allowing others to 'kill' us.

It is worth noting that even this request framed the harms being alleged as both 'blatant Human Rights violations and rampant negligence of World Bank Policies and directives'—combining multiple registers in a single statement.[176] Other

[173] World Bank, Operational Directive on Involuntary Resettlement, December 2001, revised April 2013, para. 1.

[174] Kennedy, 'The International Human Rights Movement: Part of the Problem?', 15 *Harvard Human Rights Journal* (2002) 101, at 108.

[175] WBIP Request for Inspection: India Ecodevelopment Project, 3 April 1998, 5–6.

[176] Ibid. 5–6.

requests have linked 'respect for human rights' with 'proper governance', recalling the managerial language of 'good governance';[177] or reached explicitly beyond the Bank's policies and procedures to claim breaches of international human rights instruments, such as ILO Convention 169.[178] In all these cases, the multivalence and fluidity of human rights is demonstrated in their ability to connect with both moral and expert claims, and to translate seamlessly between them.

## B. Lost (and Found) in Translation: Human Rights in the CWPRP Case

The CWPRP case again provides a useful window into the multiple translations and transformations involving human rights in WBIP proceedings. Given the intensity of the protests against the Project, it is remarkable that the explosive human rights language of the NGO campaign had already largely been transposed into an administrative register in the request. The main body of the request, 24 pages long, made very few direct mentions of human rights.[179] It cited the human rights language in the stated objectives of OD 4.20;[180] it noted that Chinese state and law 'will not tolerate challenges ... on the basis of violation of human rights, nationality's issues [sic], or other issues which the Chinese government will view as offenses against ethnic unity';[181] and at the very end it quoted from a statement made at an earlier meeting between Tibetans and Bank staff 'that by approving this project, "the Bank is contributing to the ethnic annihilation of Tibetans"'.[182] However, it made no reference to the Universal Declaration of Human Rights, ILO Convention 169, or other human rights instruments and interpretations that might be relevant. Rather, for the most part its claims were advanced in comparatively flat, unemotional terms, alleging miscategorization of the Project as a 'Category B' environmental assessment, and various violations of the Bank's policies.

In contrast, the most detailed references to human rights appeared in annexes to the request, ostensibly in support of a mere administrative requirement—establishing the ICT's representational authority.[183] Here, we find allegations regarding the 'Communist Chinese policy' of 'ethnic cleansing of the Tibetan people', carried out in part by stoking resource conflicts and ethnic tensions between Tibetans and Muslims, and the human rights abuses that would be inflicted

[177] WBIP Request for Inspection: Chad Petroleum Development Project, 15 December 2000, para. 2.

[178] See e.g. WBIP Request for Inspection: Honduras Land Administration Project, 3 January 2006, para. 2.

[179] WBIP Request for Inspection: China Poverty Reduction Project (n. 66) 7, 8, 12, 18.

[180] Ibid. 7.

[181] Ibid. 7.

[182] Ibid. 24.

[183] Ibid. Annex A: Confidential Documents and Annex B: Justification of the Non-Local Representational Authority.

on ethnic minorities were they to make their complaints openly,[184] as well as detailed analysis of Chinese law and judicial processes.[185] This information would certainly have been considered by the WBIP members as part of the technical eligibility screening process;[186] it also would have been read by management and, by way of the Bank's relatively open disclosure policies, the wider public. However, its presentation as being in support of non-local representation made it possible to address the concerns raised as violations of Bank policy, without falling foul of the Bank's self-understanding of the 'political prohibition' in its Articles.[187]

The documents subsequently filed in the registration stage largely remained in an administrative mode. The bulk of management's initial response set out, under bureaucratic form-like headings, summary statements of the concerns and claims that had been raised in the request, followed by management's responses with reference to policy objectives, policy requirements, good practice guidance, and evidence of compliance.[188] The same document addressed human rights only in terms of the OD 4.20 policy objective, expressing management's belief that measures had been included in the project design to meet that objective. In this connection, it made a rather oblique and restrained reference to the larger human rights campaign being waged against the Bank in connection with the Project:[189]

> Some of those who take exception to the type of political system in China could take the view that these objectives cannot be met in the framework of this system. This is an issue that goes beyond any single project, or compliance with Bank policies.

In other words, complaints about human rights abuses that were not voiced as allegations of project-specific violations of Bank policy had no place in a WBIP process. More than 90 pages annexed to the response underscored the administrative nature of the process, setting out technical details of the Project, tables of data, and steps taken to consult with affected persons, conveying an impression of managerial proficiency. Elsewhere in its response, management reasserted what it saw as the correct frame of problematization. Noting that '[t]he Bank does not have a policy governing voluntary population movements and issues associated with ethnic demographic shifts', the implication was that any complaint addressing

[184] Ibid. Annex B: Justification of the Non-Local Representational Authority, Annex B1, 36–7; Annex B2, 3–4. These passages quote selectively from confidential documents in Annex 1, which are not publicly accessible.

[185] Ibid. Annex B: Justification of the Non-Local Representational Authority, Annex B3: Memorandum on China's Constitutional and Judicial Process.

[186] Ibid. Annex B: Justification of the Non-Local Representational Authority, Annex B3: Memorandum on China's Constitutional and Judicial Process.

[187] Ibid. Annex B: Justification of the Non-Local Representational Authority, Annex B3: Memorandum on China's Constitutional and Judicial Process.

[188] Ibid. 6–28.

[189] Ibid. 12.

that subject matter could not be made through the WBIP.[190] Moreover, it initially seemed that the WBIP might have accepted this framing: its eligibility report summarized the request in terms of alleged violations of eight Bank policies, and recommended that the board authorize an investigation of the matters alleged, without making a single mention of human rights.[191]

It is arguable, then, that the translation of human rights norms into an administrative register had the effect of diluting and attenuating the moral force of the requesters' complaint against the World Bank. Certainly, the malleable compatibility of human rights with an administrative register facilitated the enrolment of actants with widely disparate interests into a single network or assemblage, however provisionally. Yet it is too facile to conclude that the 'original' human rights impulse of the CWPRP claim was simply lost in the successive translations from request to registration, and thereafter had no influence on the investigation. Most obviously, a trace of that impulse can be found in the text of the WBIP's investigation report, in the form of repeated references to the policy objective of OD 4.20 'to ensure that the development process fosters full respect for [indigenous peoples'] dignity, human rights, and cultural uniqueness'.[192] More subtly, but perhaps even more tellingly, the investigation report described the implicit rationale for the poverty alleviation plan for the 'move-out area' in terms that, consciously or unconsciously, invoked the protestors' claims that the Bank was enabling cultural cleansing or genocide:[193]

> The assumption is made that the reduction in population numbers will almost automatically *generate greater lebensraum* and a better quality of life for villages remaining in the Move-out villages.

Furthermore, close examination of the WBIP's reasoning reveals a series of subtle translations and transformations that implicate human rights in the interplay between expert, moral, and legal grounds of authority. Central to the WBIP's analysis of the CWPRP case was the 'legal' question of how best to interpret and apply the World Bank's operational policies and procedures. At no point, however, did the Panel articulate a positive theory of interpretation. Instead, what we find is the Panel disassembling the network of arguments and evidence put forward by the World Bank's management and staff, and then assembling another documentary network in which legal reasoning linked up with and connected expert and moral grounds of authority in a particular, acceptable arrangement. As the following analysis shows, the interplay of arguments between the WBIP and management can

190 Ibid. 6.

191 Report and Recommendation on Request for Inspection (n. 58).

192 Investigation Report on the Qinghai Project: A Component of the China Western Poverty Reduction Project (n. 86) xxvii, 101, 110.

193 Ibid. 86, para. 220 (emphasis added).

be seen as competing efforts to assert authority and induce deference in the other party, carried out in terms of a contest over interpretive control.[194]

On the interpretation of World Bank policies, the Panel reported that its interviews with Bank staff had revealed 'an unusually and disturbingly wide range of divergent and, often, opposing views'.[195] As the investigation report described them, the various approaches taken by Bank staff could be distributed along a continuum from those who viewed Bank policies as 'simply idealized policy statements, ... a set of goals to be striven after', to those who saw them as more concrete, to be 'employed as benchmarks against which to measure compliance'.[196] At the first end of the continuum, the Bank's operational directives articulated aspirational, even moral, principles, which could however be interpreted with some flexibility and even overridden at management's discretion.[197] But the second view—of policies as mere 'checklists' or processes to be followed mechanically—was not satisfactory either, despite its contrary appeal to expertise.[198] The Panel further expressed disagreement with the claim that 'past practice', 'experience', or (using the legal term) 'precedent' could 'determine what is required by the policies'.[199]

In evaluating the project design, the investigation report scrutinized each piece of the expert evidence provided by management in support of the Project. While a 'checklist' approach to compliance was insufficient, the report implied that some higher, 'professionally acceptable standards of quality' could be identified and should be attained.[200] In assessing the environmental screening of the Project as faulty, therefore, the Panel invoked the expert witness of a 'senior official ... with strong credentials in the field'.[201] Seeking to define the scope of the Project 'in space and time', the Panel found the quality of the inscription devices adduced by management, such as maps, to be poor, resulting in 'a high level of ambiguity, uncertainty and inconsistency in the use of the term "project area" '.[202] A detailed analysis of social scientific methodologies, including the sampling procedures and survey methods employed by the Bank, likewise left the Panel unconvinced;[203] the Bank made reference to expert practices outside the Bank, including other international organizations such as the Food & Agriculture Organization, as meeting the appropriate standard.[204] In sum, each evidentiary link in the network of files assembled

[194] Cf. Black, '"Says Who?" Liquid Authority and Interpretive Control in Transnational Regulatory Regimes', 9 *International Theory* (2017) 286.

[195] Investigation Report on the Qinghai Project: A Component of the China Western Poverty Reduction Project (n. 86) iv.

[196] Ibid. xiv, para. 10.

[197] Ibid. xiv–xv, para. 1.1

[198] Ibid. xv, para. 12.

[199] Ibid. xv, para. 13.

[200] Ibid. xv, para. 12.

[201] Ibid. xxii, para. 45.

[202] Ibid. xvi.

[203] Ibid. 39.

[204] Ibid. 51, para. 118.

by management—comprising dossiers of scientific methodologies, facts, and expert testimony—was put to the test, and much of it found wanting.

Yet the Panel did not dispute the hermeneutic approaches invoked by World Bank staff—whether purposive, textual, or practice-based—so much as the particular network or sequence into which they had been arranged. The relative weight to be given to each link of scientific evidence required a process of (legal) textual analysis. For example, whereas management had argued that China had demonstrated its capacity to complete the Project in compliance with Bank policies, based on its success in undertaking similar and larger projects in the past, the Panel rejected this invocation of expertise and 'precedent', and instead reverted to the text of the 'law':[205]

> The Panel has carefully examined the policies and has failed to find any grounds for the view that precedents in a country, or a country's 'social and political systems,' can in any way determine what is required by the policies. ... There is indeed room for some flexibility and interpretation but, as provided in the Resolution that established the Panel, the Operational Directives (and updated OPs, BPs, GPs, etc.) are the primary source of Bank policy for purposes of assessing compliance.

Legal hermeneutics—particularly contextual and purposive approaches to interpreting Bank policies—also provided a keyhole through which moral considerations, including human rights standards, could re-enter the WBIP's evaluation of the Project. In criticizing management's interpretation of 'environment' in OD 4.01 as excluding 'socio-cultural elements', for example, the Panel instead adopted a more contextual reading of the policy, making reference to criteria set out in an annex to the policy.[206] Elsewhere, the Panel adopted a teleological hermeneutic commonly used in interpreting the founding treaties of international organizations, such as the Bank's Articles.[207] For example, management claimed to have designed the Project in its entirety to fulfil the policy requirement to produce an 'Indigenous Peoples Development Plan' (IDPD), as one sentence in OD 4.20 indicated was possible when the bulk of the project beneficiaries were indigenous people.[208] However, the Panel argued, that sentence had to be read in light of the policy's objective, with its standards of 'dignity, human rights, and cultural uniqueness', which forced the conclusion that 'separate, free-standing IPDPs' were

[205] Ibid. xv.

[206] Ibid. 77, paras 191–192 ('Although not as clearly stated in the main text of OD 4.01, it is clear from Annex A to OD 4.01 "Checklist of Potential issues for an EA" that a limited definition of the term "environment" is neither intended nor possible').

[207] See e.g. Shihata, 'The Dynamic Evolution of International Organizations: The Case of the World Bank', 2 *Journal of the History of International Law* (2000) 217, at 225–31.

[208] Investigation Report on the Qinghai Project: A Component of the China Western Poverty Reduction Project' (n. 86) 106, para. 271.

required for each ethnic minority in the Move-in area.[209] As if to underscore the moral quality of that objective, the Panel described it as 'clear in letter and spirit',[210] requiring management to define the boundaries of the project area and ethnic composition of impacted populations broadly.[211]

In its final report and recommendation in response to the investigation report, World Bank management resisted the WBIP's attempted integration of human rights claims into its analysis. Here, also, legal hermeneutics played a key role, albeit in the direction of an expert register. Acknowledging a 'disconnect' between its own understanding of the relevant policies and that of the Panel, management attributed that disconnect to 'the interpretation of key words and phrases', such as 'meaningful consultation' (in OD 4.20), 'significant, irreversible and sector-wide impacts' (OD 4.01), and 'illustrative only' (OD 4.01). These phrases were 'fundamental to choices made in the implementation of the safeguard policies', but were nevertheless 'obviously open to interpretation'.[212] In interpreting them, Bank staff and management had taken into consideration their two decades of experience in China,[213] their knowledge of the quality of the Project, including its environmental and social safeguards, and China's 'strong record on project preparation and implementation, poverty reduction and resettlement'—all matters of expertise.[214] Moreover, management bolstered its expert credentials by referring to other international organizations with which it had worked closely on poverty-reduction programmes in China,[215] and affirming that Bank staff had consulted 'a large number of expert analyses' produced by non-governmental organizations.[216]

It is notable that, contrary to Sarfaty's account of a 'clash' between the logics of human rights and economics, the dominant register adopted by management in its final report and recommendation was that of administrative and scientific expertise. Accordingly, significant passages in the report adopted the technical vocabulary of 'risk management' and 'due diligence'.[217] Pushing back against the WBIP finding that the Project had been wrongly categorized, management argued that 'potential direct impacts would be limited in their scope and could be addressed through mitigation measures that had previously been used successfully

[209] Ibid. xxvi–xxvii, paras 63–65.

[210] Ibid. 101. Compare 2 Corinthians 3:6 (New International Version): 'He has made us competent as ministers of a new covenant—not of the letter but of the Spirit; for the letter kills, but the Spirit gives life.'

[211] Ibid. 38.

[212] Management Report and Recommendation in Response to the WBIP Investigation Report (n. 151) 7.

[213] Ibid. 18.

[214] Ibid. 7.

[215] See generally ibid. 8–12. The Response referred specifically to the International Fund for Agricultural Development, the Food & Agriculture Organization, the United Nations Development Programme, the World Food Programme, and 'various bilateral organizations'. Ibid. 9.

[216] The Response referred to reports produced by the World Wide Fund for Nature International, the International Union for Conservation of Nature, the International Council for Bird Preservation, and International Waterfowl and Wetlands Research Bureau. Ibid. 19.

[217] Ibid. 12, 16.

in other projects'.[218] Moreover, management suggested that certain WBIP findings had raised larger questions of Bank policy, exceeding the WBIP's mandate to review the execution of particular projects:[219]

> [T]he Panel's finding that it is inappropriate to consider the Project as a whole as a proper IPDP substitute is more a comment on the OD rather than a critique of this particular Project. The OD is clear that treating the entire Project as an IPDP is warranted in the case where the bulk of those who benefit from the Project are indigenous peoples.

Yet, even though management's report and recommendation made no mention of human rights, it was far from the last word on the matter. As the attached 'Background Paper' made clear, the policies and procedures comprising the Bank's operational manual had already undergone a series of revisions.[220] In particular, the conversion to a new format distinguishing operational policies, bank procedures, and good practice statements—ongoing at the time of the CWPRP's approval and the WBIP's investigation—had created unanticipated complications for interpretation, requiring a new level of 'legal exactitude' and raising difficult questions of inter-temporality.[221] Additional complexity arose from the Bank's simultaneous reorganization according to a matrix management structure, with impacts on the accountabilities of different units,[222] and an increasing country focus.[223]

Moreover, the interests and identities of all actors remained in a constant state of flux: an alliance is always threatened with disintegration. It was imperative, therefore, for the WBIP to undergo continuous reforms, clarifying the terms of its mandate,[224] piloting new approaches,[225] and updating its operating procedures.[226] Finally, the consultations surrounding the review and update of the World Bank's 'safeguard' policies, leading to the adoption of a new 'Environmental and Social Framework' in 2018, again disturbed and forced a reassemblage of the networks of which the WBIP forms a part.[227] All of these may be seen as (partial) flow-on effects of the CWPRP case, which in turn effected further translations and

[218] Ibid. 16.
[219] See e.g. ibid. 22.
[220] Management Report and Recommendation Background Paper (n. 34) 7–11.
[221] Ibid. 8.
[222] Ibid. 16–17.
[223] Ibid. 18–23.
[224] World Bank Inspection Panel, Joint Statement on the Use of Country Systems, 8 June 2004.
[225] World Bank Inspection Panel, Piloting a New Approach to Support Early Solutions in the Inspection Panel Process, 6 November 2013.
[226] See e.g. Operating Procedures of the World Bank Inspection Panel 2014, Annex 2 (Enhancing Consultation with Requesters and Tracking Action Plans) added February 2016.
[227] World Bank, Review and Update of the World Bank Safeguard Policies, https://consultations.worldbank.org/en/consultations/detail/review-and-update-world-bank-safeguard-policies (last visited 6 December 2023). Also see generally Van Den Meerssche (n. 34); Passoni, Rosenbaum, and Vermunt (n. 34).

transformations in the World Bank, the WBIP, and their interactions with each other. In all these moments, the protean, shape-shifting intertranslatability of human rights can be seen as strengthening its ability to serve in various ways as an instrument of *interessement* and enrolment.

## 5. Conclusion

This chapter has proposed a mode of analysing human rights in global governance that looks beyond the usual accountability framework. Most scholarship on the World Bank and the WBIP assumes, implicitly or explicitly, that human rights represent particular, fixed standards, however attenuated in their articulation in Bank policies; and that the WBIP will be more or (likelier) less successful in holding the Bank accountable against standards. In this view, a case such as CWPRP demonstrates how human rights clash with other, more central values in the Bank—economic efficiency foremost amongst them—and fail to gain purchase. In contrast, I have suggested that we might obtain better purchase on the multivalent roles of human rights in global governance if we instead conceptualize international institutions as assemblages comprising complex networks of innumerable, interacting actants, and investigate what part human rights play in the translations that hold these assemblages together and make them appear 'solid' and 'real'.

Viewed in this way, the WBIP is neither simply an accountability mechanism nor an instrument or mask for the World Bank's managerial ends. Instead, the kind of detailed analytics proposed and tentatively sketched out in this chapter show how WBIP processes have definite effects in global governance, even when a request is not 'successful' from the requesters' point of view. We can thus see how the WBIP acts to enrol a range of different actors into a particular network of relationships, and to hold them within that network through never-ending series of negotiations and mutual adjustments. We can observe how those same processes of assemblage can create new actors, with new identities and solidarities; and how, even where 'accountability' fails, those ongoing enrolments, negotiations, and adjustments can nevertheless effect a subtle transformation in all actants, including the Bank itself. And, finally, we can bear witness to the multiplicity of ways that the language and normativity of human rights can be channelled, absorbed, and translated into the life of global governance.

# 5

# The International Political Economy of the Right to Food, 1960–2019

*Michael Fakhri**

## 1. Introduction

Although it falls within the purview of the human rights enterprise, the right to food is better understood as part of the global politics of food and the socio-economy of growing, gathering, hunting, and herding. Relatively recently, food sovereignty movements have activated the right to food in novel ways. Since 1993, people have taken up and wielded the right to food as a tool intended to fundamentally uproot the authority of international institutions such as the World Trade Organization (WTO). People have also used it to engage with and infiltrate other institutions like the Food & Agriculture Organization (FAO).

A key element within food sovereignty movements has been La Vía Campesina, one of the most dynamic and influential transnational peasant movements in its own right. La Vía Campesina comprises peasants, small and medium-sized farmers, landless people, rural women and youth, Indigenous peoples, migrants, and agricultural workers from around the world. Its members include 182 organizations spanning 81 countries and, by their own count, represent over 200 million people.[1]

Generally, there are two different platforms that provide food sovereignty movements with the ability to organize internationally and transnationally: the International Planning Committee for Food Sovereignty (IPC) and the People's Coalition for Food Sovereignty. The IPC tends to be more willing to directly engage with institutions than the People's Coalition for Food Sovereignty (though both are tactically careful when deciding when and how to engage), which is why

* This chapter was completed in spring 2019. Since then, I have been selected to be the UN Special Rapporteur on the Right to Food, a new Director General was elected to lead the FAO, and the world has been pushed into a prolonged food crisis triggered by the Covid-19 pandemic. I think this chapter remains more relevant than ever and I have heavily relied on this research during my work as Special Rapporteur. I do not address the contemporary issues and let the chapter stand as it was originally written since it remains pertinent as it is.

[1] La Vía Campesina, 'Who Are We?', https://viacampesina.org/en/who-are-we/ (last visited 17 January 2024).

Michael Fakhri, *The International Political Economy of the Right to Food, 1960–2019*. In: *Global Rights?* First Edition.
Edited by: Nehal Bhuta and Rodrigo Vallejo, Oxford University Press. © Michael Fakhri 2024.
DOI: 10.1093/oso/9780198940166.003.0005

I focus on the IPC. The IPC 'facilitates dialogue and debate' and creates a space for discussion that is autonomous from 'political parties, institutions, governments and private sector'.[2] Its members include transnational social movements (e.g. La Vía Campesina, World Forum of Fishers People, and the World Alliance of Mobile Indigenous Peoples); regional organizations (e.g. ROPPA, PROPAC, and Movimento Agro Ecologico Latino Americano); and NGOs that provide support (e.g. FIAN and Friends of the Earth International).[3] So while La Vía Campesina took to the streets to protest against the WTO, IPC provided support to its members who wanted to work with the FAO and other international institutions to develop new programmes and policies.[4]

Food sovereignty movements want the WTO out of international agriculture. Some people in the movement think that the FAO is instead the most appropriate international institution to address trade.[5]

My argument is that this institutional strategy has a particular history. I begin by explaining, in Section 2, how I rely on and critically engage with the food regime literature. In doing so, I identify who I am learning from and writing with. Then, in Section 3, I provide a historical account of the FAO as a trade and development institution. I additionally highlight how the FAO has always been the principal international institution providing legal meaning and political power to the right to food. My corollary argument is that one cannot understand the right to food today without understanding the history of the FAO. This historical account is what leads me to think that the right-to-food narrative does not fit within any study of human rights as a general concept or movement. This is a story about an economic/social/cultural right that is not defined by human rights institutions ultimately accountable to the UN General Assembly in Geneva. It is instead under the auspices of the food institutions and food diplomats based in Rome.

After explaining what the political and legal implications of being an autonomous or semi-autonomous UN institution in Rome mean, I return to the present in Section 4 and outline how food sovereignty movements have used the right to food to both strengthen the FAO's legitimacy and enact their own agenda. I conclude, in Section 5, with thoughts on future legal work that might serve the movements' ambitions.

[2] International Planning Committee for Food Sovereignty, 'About Us', https://www.foodsovereignty.org/about/ (last visited 14 March 2024).

[3] Ibid.

[4] P. Claeys, *Human Rights and the Food Sovereignty Movement: Reclaiming Control* (2015) 5. The food sovereignty movement also includes other small, transnational agrarian movements and is supported by academics and NGOs.

[5] McKeon, 'Who Speaks for Peasants? Civil Society, Social Movements and the Global Governance of Food and Agriculture', 1 *Interface* (2009) 48, at 69.

## 2. Method and Perspective

### A. Political Economy

Some new histories of international human rights are too narrow and do not capture the dynamics of the right to food;[6] whereas the recent sustained burst of work on social, economic, and cultural rights has been inspiring.[7] But the right to food does not neatly fit that context either. To understand the right to food, you have to focus on the political economy of food procurement and making.

By focusing on the political economy of the right to food, what I mean is that I look at the distribution of power and wealth generated by the institutions, practices, legal rules, and social organizations surrounding (or laying claim to) the right to food. In this particular instance, I focus on the relationship between social movements and international institutions (namely the FAO), as well as some degree of inter-institutional jockeying for jurisdiction over food.

This is different to the work in human rights literature and practice which focuses on working abstract human rights into institutions of implementation and operational rules. This is not to say that the network of people and organizations centred around the right to food have not been active.[8] But I find that, until 2019, food sovereignty movements—despite their ambivalent relationship to rights discourse—and the FAO drove the right-to-food agenda in novel ways. Their emphasis is more on how the right to food can serve a larger programme. I therefore study how the right to food is embedded within existing international institutional practices—it is here where some meaning and power is given to the right.

I watch for how the right to food has been wielded by institutional actors in order to assert authority over certain issues; this authority justifies the institution's existence and, if successful, lends credence to arguments to donors in favour of increasing (or maintaining) the institution's budget. Meanwhile, academics and NGO professionals use the right to food to extract value and wealth from the 'economy of implementation of knowledge practices'.[9] So when they deploy the

[6] S. Moyn, *Not Enough: Human Rights in an Unequal World* (2018).

[7] Parmar, 'Revisiting the Human Right to Water', 28 *Australian Feminist Law Journal* (2008) 77; L. E. White and J. Perelman (eds), *Stones of Hope: How African Activists Reclaim Human Rights to Challenge Global Poverty* (2010); A. Nolan (ed.), *Economic and Social Rights After the Global Financial Crises* (2014); A. Nolan, 'Not Fit for Purpose? Human Rights in Times of Financial and Economic Crisis', 4 *European Human Rights Law Review* (2015) 358; D. A. Desierto, *Public Policy in International Economic Law: The ICESCR in Trade, Finance, and Investment* (2015); H. Alviar García, K. E. Klare, and L. A. Williams (eds), *Social and Economic Rights in Theory and Practice: A Critical Inquiries* (2015); J. Whyte, 'Human Rights and the Collateral Damage of Neoliberalism', 20 *Theory & Event* (2017) 137; J. Wills, *Contesting World Order?: Socioeconomic Rights and Global Justice Movements* (2017); G. MacNaughton and D. F. Frey, *Economic and Social Rights in a Neoliberal World* (2018).

[8] Claeys (n. 4) 6.

[9] D. Desai and M. Schomerus, '"There Was A Third Man . . .": Tales from a Global Policy Consultation on Indicators for the Sustainable Development Goals', 49 *Development and Change* (2017) 89, at 92.

right to food, I take it that these experts are staking out 'a position so that at some point in the future they might get money to develop statistical capacity, build research budgets and so on'.[10]

The other advantage that experts seek is not only from commissioned projects but also the power to dictate what counts as a legitimate right-to-food law and policy and thus influence where and how institutional resources will be directed.[11] In sum, the right to food allows certain actors to raise and organize capital and allows others access to that capital, resulting in a particular pattern of circulation.

I take this power to access and direct institutional resources to be the most attractive aspect of the right to food for participants within institutions and for social movements.[12] I imagine the person in the social movement as a 'cunning citizen' who is looking to determine what transnational alliances and networks they need to make with other agrarians and food producers, experts, NGOs, international institutions, and state actors if they want to articulate their particular interest as a global claim.[13] Their call to reconstrue the existing mechanisms of wealth and power on more equitable terms is a matter of survival and not simply principle.

I then imagine this study as tracking and learning from the tactical manoeuvrings of this cunning citizen who wants to start with understanding what mechanisms of power and wealth are already at play because that will determine what they understand their interest to be, conditions what goals they want to achieve, and determines what tactics are available. What makes such a citizen cunning is that they have to deftly negotiate with the same institution or individual as both ally and adversary, while also developing ever-shifting coalitions.

In institutional terms, part of the political economy of the right to food involves the FAO Director-General navigating the demands from donors while seeking authority and legitimacy from the FAO Council (made up of national government delegates), the right-to-food NGOs, and transnational food movements. The right-to-food academics and NGOs look to the FAO for access to resources but also work in alliance with social movements to influence FAO budget decisions. Food sovereignty movements comprise people who have the most to lose if they

[10] Ibid.

[11] Ibid.

[12] NGOs like FIAN provide support to the IPC, but they are not the food sovereignty organization's principal driving force. International Planning Committee for Food Sovereignty (n. 2).

[13] I take, and slightly modify, the term 'cunning citizen' from Randeria, 'Legal Pluralism, Social Movements and the Post-Colonial State in India: Fractured Sovereignty and Differential Citizenship Rights', in B. de S. Santos (ed.), *Another Knowledge Is Possible: Beyond Northern Epistemologies* (2007) 41, at 69. I also build on Hannah Wittman's notion of the 'agrarian citizen', see H. Wittman, 'Reworking the Metabolic Rift: La Vía Campesina, Agrarian Citizenship, and Food Sovereignty', 36 *Journal of Peasant Studies* (2009) 805, at 807–808, 'Agrarian citizens, in theory, would expect state protection for local rights to produce and protect the environment, but would also depend on local and global social networks and traditional ecological knowledge of agrarian conditions to enact those rights.' I use citizen as a way of imagining oneself as part of a particular community, not as a strict legal category that distributes state entitlements to a select group of people.

do not effectively ensure that national governments and international institutions implement the right to food in a way that best serves members of the movement; the current food system is not just a threat to the economic livelihood of people in food sovereignty movements, but also to their sense of who they are and where they are from.

## B. International Law and Food Regimes

Many studies of food sovereignty significantly rely on the work done on food regimes as developed by Harriett Friedmann and Philip McMichael. A food regime is the set of explicit and implicit rules governing the production and consumption of food on a world scale.[14] Determining what the rules are is part of the hard work of food regime (or food regime complex)[15] studies since implicit rules, or rationalities, play a significant part in constituting the regime. These implicit rules arise in part of by the web of practices and interactions among different people in response to questions of food production and distribution; how all these groups interact creates a certain 'stable pattern of production and power' that in effect governs food over several decades.[16] The emphasis is on describing the 'implicitly shared ideological or discursive aspects' of a stable, operational regime.[17]

What remains underexamined in food regime literature is how legal concepts and doctrines operate in ways that form, stabilize, and transform the food regime as a whole.[18] More specifically, food regime studies often treat international institutions either as epiphenomena of global power or expressions of a singular rationality. A legal analysis opens up international institutions as sites of struggle within themselves where power and meaning are negotiated and mediated; international institutions can be understood as places which may not always provide a coherent

[14] Friedmann, 'The Political Economy of Food: A Global Crisis', 197 *New Left Review* (1993) 29, at 30–31.

[15] Margulis, 'The Regime Complex for Food Security: Implications for the Global Hunger Challenge', 19 *Global Governance* (2013) 53.

[16] Friedmann (n. 14) 30–31.

[17] Friedmann, 'Discussion: Moving Food Regimes Forward: Reflections on Symposium Essays', 26 *Agriculture and Human Values* (2009) 335, at 335.

[18] For work in this vein, see Chadwick, 'World Hunger, the "Global" Food Crisis and (International) Law', 14 *Manchester Journal of International Economic Law* (2017) 92; Cohen, 'The Law and Political Economy of Contemporary Food: Some Reflections on the Local and the Small', 78 *Law and Contemporary Problems* (2015) 101; M. Fakhri, *Sugar and the Making of International Trade Law* (2014); Fakhri, 'Globalizations of Law From the Perspective of International Trade Law (and Agricultural Commodities)', 1 *Jindal Law Review* (2018) 18; Saab, 'An International Law Approach to Food Regime Theory', 31 *Leiden Journal of International Law* (2018) 251. See also Clapp, 'Food Security and Contested Agricultural Trade Norms', 11 *Journal of International Law and International Relations* (2015) 104; Margulis (n. 15).

rule as such but rather a place where actors and networks coalesce around different ideas and interests.[19]

By centring on international law, it becomes easier to see how different institutions that govern food and agriculture interact, irritate, overlap, and interlock—all despite being driven by different and at times antonymous values and rationalities. Law provides insight into how particular rationalities emerge and change; law also allows us to see how value and meaning are created from the tensions within and between institutions. Studying law and food is about looking at how law encodes particular assumptions about the market, the state, law, technology, and sociocultural relations that structure the food regime; at the same time, the food movement has articulated its own understanding of law as it navigates the existing institutional landscape in effect revealing the possibilities and limits of contemporary law.[20] To be sure, this account of law is not the only way to tell the story of the right to food, as demonstrated by the rich literature that draws from accounts by participant-observers and activist-academics.[21]

## C. A Different Historiography of Today's Food Regime

As commonly done in food regime literature, I take the second food regime to span from 1947 to the 1970s. As a moment of institutional and normative stability, this means that this was a time when diplomats and international civil servants shared a certain set of beliefs; these assumptions operated as rules that were taken for granted and treated as natural. The period of 1974 to 1986 was a transition period of intense debate and negotiation in which not just the rules were made explicit, but debates over how to characterize the same phenomenon ensued. The central argument at the time was whether the sale of subsidized wheat from the United States to Third World countries was a matter of aid or dumping.

In my characterization of the period after the mid-1980s until today, I differ from a common narrative. According to Friedmann, '[o]ne of the goals of the trade negotiations that began in 1986 was to reframe agriculture as trade. [The United States and EU] succeeded in 1995, when an Agreement on Agriculture became part of the World Trade Organization (WTO).'[22]

I diverge on three points, which also act as the premise of this chapter. First, food and agriculture have always been central to multilateral trade institutions.

[19] Fakhri, *Sugar* (n. 18); G. F. Sinclair, *To Reform the World: International Organizations and the Making of Modern States* (2017).

[20] Cohen (n. 18).

[21] This comprises most of the secondary literature I rely on in Section 4.

[22] Friedmann, 'From Colonialism to Green Capitalism: Social Movements and Emergence of Food Regimes', in F. H. Buttel and P. McMichael (eds), *New Directions in the Sociology of Global Development*, vol. 11 (2005) 227, at 233.

What changes is the meaning of trade. This leads me to my second point, that international trade is not only defined by the doctrine of freer trade, but also by the doctrines of market stabilization and food security. In studying how these three doctrines constituted trade institutions, in previous work I tracked how they were defined at particular moments and how their definitions changed. Third, my institutional purview for trade extends beyond just the General Agreement on Tariffs and Trade (GATT)/WTO. I look at the multiple institutions that have been key sites where people have argued over these doctrines' meanings and configurations: the GATT/WTO, International Commodity Agreements (ICAs), the UN Conference on Trade and Development (UNCTAD), and the FAO.[23]

The pay-off of situating the right to food within the context of these three doctrines across different institutions is that we can now see how the power and meaning of the right to food have changed over time. Scholars and activists today often posit 'food sovereignty' in opposition to 'food security'.[24] For those who want to sharpen the distinction, food security is taken to focus on people's *access* to food without a primary regard to the socio-ecological source or implications of the food. Food security is also a perspective that tends to assume a clear difference between food producers and consumers; whereas food sovereignty emphasizes people's *control* over how they get and eat food. Here the assumption is that if people have more control over their own food, the less likely they will be hungry. While food sovereignty movements are by and large a producer's movement, the line between producer and consumer is blurred, especially in light of the fact that 70 per cent of the nearly one billion people who chronically suffer from starvation are small-hold farmers and agricultural workers.[25]

But the meaning of these terms is relational, not strictly oppositional, and has changed over time. Early food security discourses in the 1970s were very similar to early food sovereignty discourses in the 1990s since both referenced the right to food, and both emphasized 'state responsibility to provide food for their citizens to strategies of self-reliance and food reserves'.[26] In the 1980s and 1990s, food security continued its tacit acceptance of whatever the dominant development discourse was (or at times heterodox development theories). That meant for the time,

[23] Fakhri, 'A History of Food Security and Agriculture in International Trade Law, 1945–2015', in A. Rasulov and J. Haskell (eds), *International Economic Law: New Voices, New Perspectives* (2020) 55.

[24] Holt Giménez and Shattuck, 'Food Crises, Food Regimes and Food Movements: Rumblings of Reform or Tides of Transformation?', 38 *Journal of Peasant Studies* (2011) 109; W. D. Schanbacher, *The Politics of Food: The Global Conflict between Food Security and Food Sovereignty* (2010); M. Windfuhr and J. Jonsén, *Food Sovereignty: Towards Democracy in Localized Food Systems* (2005); Wittman, 'Food Sovereignty: A New Rights Framework for Food and Nature?', 2 *Environment and Society: Advances in Research* (2011) 87.

[25] United Nations Conference on Trade and Development, *Trade and Environment Review 2013: Wake Up Before It Is Too Late* (2013) 11.

[26] Jarosz, 'Comparing Food Security and Food Sovereignty Discourses', 4 *Dialogues in Human Geography* (2014) 168, at 179.

that when most people evoked food security in the 1980s–1990s, they defined their goals in terms of market access.

This was when the food sovereignty movements started to emerge and at times participate in the broader alter-globalization social movements. Food sovereignty movements would later succeed in creating new ideas that provided people and international institutions a viable alternative for the future and break with development discourse in its entirety and move 'beyond colonialism, development, and globalization'.[27] I would also add, they also moved beyond narrow calculations of nutrition and static measurements of scarcity. They did this by creating the notion of food sovereignty and used this broad idea and agenda to appropriate and redefine the right to food.

With all this in mind, I differ from the common way of telling the story of food sovereignty. Instead of positing food sovereignty movements' use of the right to food as an external alternative to the existing food regime as commonly done, I shift the emphasis and situate it within the food regime itself as an agitating force.[28] The right to food is a tool that opponents can use against each other, and La Vía Campesina managed to wield it best. To food sovereignty movements, the right to food has been a relatively successful way to define and access sites of global governance. Until 2019, they successfully disrupted business as usual at the FAO and have been constantly innovative in how they manoeuvre.

Food security first emerged in the 1970s as a way for the FAO, national leaders, and experts to address the political aspects of hunger; since its inception and evolution, the idea of food security has always made significant room for the right to food. By successfully claiming authority over the right to food, food sovereignty movements have been able to limit food security's purview, while also diminishing some of its legitimacy.

But as members of the movements knew, this tool comes with its own costs: the right to food would require the movements to significantly invest time and resources into the politics of international law and institutions, which could otherwise be spent on local or regional politics. That is to say, members of the movements

[27] Caouette and Kapoor, 'Beyond Colonialism, Development and Globalization: Social Movements and Critical Perspectives', in D. Kapoor and D. Caouette (eds), *Beyond Colonialism, Development and Globalization: Social Movements and Critical Perspectives* (2016) 1. See also Al Attar, 'The Transnational Peasant Movement—Legalising Freedom from Want', 8 *New Zealand Yearbook of International Law* (2011) 107; Chimni, 'Anti-Imperialism: Then and Now', in L. Eslava, M. Fakhri, and V. Nesiah (eds), *Bandung, Global History, and International Law* (2017) 35; Gathii, 'Food Sovereignty for Poor Countries in the Global Trading System', 57 *Loyola Law Review* (2011) 509; Gonzalez, 'The Global Food Crisis: Law, Policy, and the Elusive Quest for Justice', 13 *Yale Human Rights and Development Journal* (2010) 4; S. Marks and A. Clapham, *International Human Rights Lexicon* (2005) 163–178 ('Food').

[28] See also Fairbairn, 'Framing Resistance: International Food Regimes & the Roots of Food Sovereignty', in H. K. Wittman, A. A. Desmarais, and N. Wiebe (eds), *Food Sovereignty: Reconnecting Food, Nature and Community* (2010) 15; Schiavoni, 'The Contested Terrain of Food Sovereignty Construction: Toward a Historical, Relational and Interactive Approach', 44 *Journal of Peasant Studies* (2017) 1.

knew that the right to food could be wielded in a way to serve their more ambitious agenda, but that tool would always be enmeshed within the existing global structures of power and patterns of wealth. This meant that, as had been done in the past,[29] at any point the movements could lose the right to food to their opponents who would transform it in a way that could be used against the world's most vulnerable food producers.

My purpose is to understand, as La Vía Campesina and its allies already do, what conditions have allowed the right to food to become a powerful tool to start changing the existing regime. The calculation that people in the movements made was that, as detailed in the next section, from the 1960s until 2019, the FAO asserted its own authority through the right to food. Thus, by redefining the right to food, food sovereignty movements had a shot at redefining the FAO's mandate. Also, with the right to food in hand, they can make a hard distinction against food producers that only focus on economic growth with little regard for the social, cultural, and spiritual aspect of eating. The industrial agriculture producers' countermove has been to justify their industrial agricultural practices in food security terms, arguing that they can always produce more food to meet all the world's caloric need—an argument that correctly falls within recent understandings of food security.

## 3. The FAO at the Centre of the Right to Food

### A. Initial Activation of the Right to Food

#### 1. B. R. Sen and the 'Freedom From Hunger' Campaign (1960–1967)

While you can find a reference to the right to food in Article 25 of the Universal Declaration of Human Rights, this right derives much of its legal power and meaning from Article 11 of the International Covenant on Economic, Social and Cultural Rights (ICESCR). The early legal history of the right to food, however, starts with the FAO and Third World politics.

From its inception and still today, the FAO can be understood as a development institution.[30] This is reflected in FAO practice and is exemplified in the preamble to the FAO Constitution, which states that the organization was founded with a view to promoting common welfare by raising levels of nutrition and standards of living, securing improvements in the efficiency of the production and distribution of all food and agricultural products, and bettering the condition of rural populations.

[29] Whyte, 'Powerless Companions or Fellow Travellers? Human Rights and the Neoliberal Assault on Post-Colonial Economic Justice', 2 *Radical Philosophy* (2018) 13.

[30] Fakhri (n. 23); A. L. S. Staples, *The Birth of Development: How the World Bank, Food and Agriculture Organization, and World Health Organization Changed the World, 1945–1965* (2006).

A particular tension, however, always lay at the core of the FAO: should food be framed as a matter of nutrition and scarcity, or is hunger best addressed as an item on an economic development agenda that emphasizes the improvement of living conditions? And, as a matter of policy, should food surplus be used to feed the hungry or improve the economic lives of the poor?[31] The first Director-General of the FAO, James Boyd Orr, navigated these tensions and pushed food to the forefront of international law and politics when he published his famous tract in 1946, *Proposals for a World Food Board*.[32] The World Food Board's purpose was intended to rationally organize world food production and distribution in order to meet people's nutritional needs and eliminate hunger. According to this perspective, people first had to be adequately fed in order to be healthy and markets had to be stabilized so that people were fully employed with good wages, before trade was liberalized.

This proposal called for the creation of agricultural ICAs under the FAO's purview, which would stabilize prices. These prices would allow the FAO to fund agricultural surpluses, which would then be redirected to countries with food needs. This in effect competed with the proposal to grant the International Trade Organization (ITO) such power. US and British diplomats felt that this conflicted with their trade agenda, insisted that these discussions be held under the ITO, and asked Orr to withdraw his proposal.[33]

Orr refused to comply and argued that the World Food Board would actually increase world trade. The World Food Board, however, never took off. Meanwhile, the ITO collapsed to leave the GATT in its wake. The FAO attempted other international food schemes, such as the International Commodity Clearing House (1949) and the World Food Reserve (1954) but to no avail.[34]

The FAO, under the leadership of B. R. Sen (1956–1967), decisively made food a development issue. From 1963 to 1965, Sen, an eminent Indian diplomat, turned to the right to food to change the FAO from an institution that gathered and published statistics to an institution that created and implemented specific programmes. On 14 March 1963, Sen assembled 28 world-renowned personalities in Rome with the objective of 'bringing their moral authority to bear on the aims and purposes' of a 'Freedom From Hunger' campaign. This 'Special Assembly on Man's Right to Freedom from Hunger', as it was known, released a manifesto that stated: 'Freedom from hunger is man's first fundamental right.'[35] This was the

[31] Rietkerk, '"The Constructive Use of Abundance": The UN World Food Programme and the Evolution of the International Food-Aid System during the Post-War Decades', 38 *International History Review* (2016) 788; Trentmann, 'Coping with Shortage: The Problem of Food Security and Global Visions of Coordination, *c.* 1890s–1950', in F. Trentmann and F. Just (eds), *Food and Conflict in Europe in the Age of the Two World Wars* (2006) 13, at 32.

[32] Food and Agricultural Organization of the United Nations, *Proposals for a World Food Board* (1946).

[33] J. B. Orr, *As I Recall* (1966) 172–173; C. Wilcox, *A Charter for World Trade* (1949) 42.

[34] D. J. Shaw, *World Food Security: A History Since 1945* (2007) 15–57.

[35] Ibid. 82.

prelude to the World Food Congress in June 1963, which brought in more than 1,300 private citizens, academics, national diplomats, and NGOs.[36]

This empowered Sen to argue during ICESCR treaty-drafting negotiations that hunger is such an important issue that it warrants specific enumeration within the covenant itself.[37] While this proposition was controversial in how it singled out the right to food and granted legal obligations to *how* the right was to be realized (rather than leaving it to each state), two different proposals took up Sen's ideas (one from Saudi Arabia and the other from Chile, Colombia, Ecuador, and Uganda).[38] Sen's proposition provided the basic language for Article 11 as we have it today.

The result is that the right to food is unique in the ICESCR in that it is more detailed and specific than the other enumerated rights: Article 11 first introduces the right to adequate food in paragraph 1 as part of the series of rights necessary to achieve the broader right of an adequate standard of living (clothing, housing, and continuous improvement of living conditions); then paragraph 2 focuses on the specific ways to achieve this right (framing the right as a 'freedom from hunger'), namely through programmes that do the following: improve methods of production, conservation, and distribution of food by making full use of technical and scientific knowledge; disseminate knowledge of the principles of nutrition and by developing or reforming agrarian systems in such a way as to achieve the most efficient development and utilization of natural resources; and take into account the problems of both food-importing and food-exporting countries, to ensure an equitable distribution of world food supplies in relation to need. The terms 'right to adequate food' and 'freedom from hunger' are essentially similar in meaning. The discrepancy in language is a historical and not a normative matter since Sen put forward the language of 'freedom from hunger' to reflect the name of the FAO 1963 campaign.[39]

Sen was clear that he wanted to include language detailing how the right to food would be implemented in the ICESCR in order to provide his campaign with legal force.[40] Indeed, the enumerated means reflect the FAO's mandate. This boosted the FAO's prominence since Sen could now argue, with the treaty in hand, that national governments had a national obligation under human rights law to develop and implement FAO-led programmes combating hunger, thereby enhancing the FAO's prominence. By 1965, Sen was able to state in his introduction to the FAO's annual flagship publication:

[36] Staples (n. 30) 118.

[37] UN General Assembly, Report of the Economic and Social Council, UN Doc. A/C.3/SR.1232, 15 October 1963.

[38] UN General Assembly, Draft International Covenants on Human Rights, UN Doc. A/C.3/SR.1264, 15 November 1963.

[39] Alston, 'International Law and the Human Right to Food', in P. Alston and K. Tomaševski (eds), *The Right to Food* (1984) 9, at 33.

[40] UN General Assembly (n. 38) para. 56.

> Man's right to food has come to be universally recognized as one of his fundamental rights. Agriculture has gained in status in the economy of developing countries. Food surpluses have become available for the relief of malnutrition and for assisting the economic growth of food-deficient nations. ... I earnestly hope that in this next phase of FAO's history more and more attention will be given to the human factor in economic and social progress ...[41]

Sen's institutional aspirations were quite successful. When Sen arrived at the FAO, member governments gave the international institution little credence. When he left, the FAO was a more powerful institution that had gained the confidence of member governments.[42] After Sen successfully activated the right to food at the ICESCR, the FAO Council and Conference, in turn, responded to the human rights treaty (not wanting the human rights treaty to be more detailed than the FAO Constitution) by amending the FAO Constitution in 1965 to include amongst its purposes 'ensuring humanity's freedom from hunger'.[43] The right to food allowed the FAO to argue that rich countries and international institutions should invest more in the FAO in order for it to achieve the ambitions outlined in the 'Freedom From Hunger' campaign.

After the World Food Congress, and with the right to food in tow, Sen had a strong argument that the world would need 'extensive and continuing FAO action' to address world hunger.[44] It was as if Sen was designing the right to food to be the FAO's perpetual motion machine. Under Sen, the capital accumulated through the FAO was used to amass agricultural experts from around the world; these experts then created a particular kind of technical knowledge with the intention of serving the world's poorest farmers in the hungriest communities. In those terms, Sen's campaign was a success because it expanded the creation, dissemination, and implementation of new agricultural knowledge directly to farmers in the Third World. Moreover, he increased the FAO's budget from less than US$7 million in 1958 to US$83.5 million by the end of his tenure in 1967.[45] In other words, he succeeded in organizing global capital in a particular way that redistributed wealth from rich countries to poor countries, while also increasing the FAO's control over that capital through the right to food.

[41] Food and Agriculture Organization, *The State of Food and Agriculture 1965* (1965) 4.

[42] Staples (n. 30) 104.

[43] Mechlem, 'Food Security and the Right to Food in the Discourse of the United Nations', 10 *European Law Journal* (2004) 631, at 647. See FAO, *Report of the Forty-Fourth Session of the Council of the FAO* (1965) 26; Report of the Thirteenth Session of the FAO Conference (1965); FAO Res. No. 12/65, 1 December 1965.

[44] Staples (n. 30) 180.

[45] Ibid. 120.

## 2. Trade and Development

Neither Sen nor the ICESR, however, were able to shift national discourses and international debates about trade and development towards a rights-based language. The US federal government did not support Sen's ideas because it thought it threatened its programme of sending subsidized, surplus grain directly to poor countries; by providing cheap grain to Third World countries the United States provided a guaranteed market for US farmers, and ensured that people in Third World countries would depend more on cheap US imports and less on local production.[46] The United States called this aid, while others called it dumping. In international agricultural diplomacy, however, the US government perspective was the minority. To B. R. Sen and Third World governments, rich countries were obliged to share their surplus with poorer countries and were not allowed to use their surplus to destabilize local markets and consolidate geopolitical power.

During Sen's tenure, the FAO represented a left critique of international agricultural law and policy, while the US Department of State represented a right critique—all within a developmentalist mindset. To understand where the political centre at the time was, it is then worth discussing in some detail the agricultural trade policies that formed the background to the right to food from 1945 to 1972.

From the 1930s until the 1980s, ICAs were the principal form of international agricultural trade law.[47] ICAs aimed to stabilize the world price of particular commodities using different supply-management mechanisms. The question had always been how these autonomous treaty-based institutions should relate to other trade institutions. As mentioned earlier, right after the war, the FAO, under Orr's leadership, tried to be that umbrella institution but lost out to the ITO.

Under the ITO, international trade in agriculture was never intended to be governed by the GATT. Chapter VI of the ITO Charter addressed agriculture trade by regulating Inter-Governmental Commodity Agreements. The ITO delegates' assumption was that Chapter IV (which became the GATT) would principally be geared towards manufactured products. Thus, Article XX(h) GATT exempts ICAs from GATT rules.

The end of the ITO, however, was not the end of trying to cover ICAs under a multilateral umbrella. The end of the ITO is well documented. But what is often forgotten or ignored is that with the end of the ITO two trade institutions emerged with 'a kind of independent existence'[48]—the GATT *and* the Interim Co-coordinating Committee for International Commodity Agreements (ICCICA). In 1947, the UN Economic and Social Council (ECOSOC) was granted provisional

[46] Jarosz, 'The Political Economy of Global Governance and the World Food Crisis: The Case of the FAO', *Review (Fernand Braudel Center)* (2009) 37, at 45; Staples (n. 30) 109.

[47] Fakhri, *Sugar* (n. 18).

[48] W. Diebold, *The End of ITO* (1952) 26–27.

status with regard to regulating the international trade in commodities much like the GATT was originally granted provisional status with regard to international tariffs. This was actually at the behest of Western industrialized countries since it allowed them to maintain the principles and concessions they received from the ITO Charter negotiations regarding commodity trade.[49]

ECOSOC continued to apply the principles established by the ITO Charter: ICAs would be adopted only to deal with severe market disruption; their aim would be price stabilization and not price increases; and importing and exporting countries would have equal voting power.[50] ECOSOC also set up the ICCICA in order to implement and coordinate efforts to conclude commodity agreements according to these principles. A number of ICAs for commodities such as sugar, coffee, tin, and wheat were concluded under the direction of the ICCICA.[51]

By the mid-1960s, Third World countries were working together to try and renegotiate the terms of international trade in agriculture. Again, the question arose over the appropriate institutional and doctrinal path. The General Assembly declared the 1960s to be the 'development decade' and trade was considered to be the primary instrument for development.[52] In this spirit, the UN Conference on Trade and Development (UNCTAD) was created and came into effect in 1964.[53]

UNCTAD inherited the functions performed by the ICCICA and occupied the centre of international agricultural trade law and policy.[54] This meant that UNCTAD was the primary international institution responsible for negotiating and coordinating international commodity policy. Raúl Prebisch, UNCTAD's first and most famous Secretary-General (1964–1969), took this mandate very seriously, especially in the context of the development decade. To Prebisch, UNCTAD would clarify ideas that were still vague and confusing at the Havana ITO Conference. UNCTAD looked to Chapter VI of the ITO Charter and the ICAs of the 1930s (which included sugar, wheat, rubber, tin, and tea) and used these historical moments to provide legitimacy to the idea of ICAs.[55] It was an institutional ambition that led Thomas Franck to call Prebisch the Grotius of the late twentieth century.[56]

[49] Finlayson and Zacher, 'International Trade Institutions and North/South Dialogue', 36 *International Journal* (1981) 732, at 739.

[50] ECOSOC Res. 30 (IV), 28 March 1947, at 3.

[51] A. Maizels, *Commodities in Crisis: The Commodity Crisis of the 1980s and the Political Economy of International Commodity Policies* (1992) 104; J. Rowe, *Primary Commodities in International Trade* (1965) 155–163.

[52] GA Res. 1710 (XVI), 19 December 1961; GA Res. 1707 (XVI), 19 December 1961.

[53] GA Res. 1897 (XVIII), 11 November 1963.

[54] GA Res. 1995 (XIX), 30 December 1964, para. 23(a).

[55] J. Toye and R. Toye, *The UN and Global Political Economy: Trade, Finance, and Development* (2004) 41–42, 214.

[56] Franck, 'Book Review of *The Changing Structures of International Law* by Wolfgang Friedmann', 40 *NYU Law Review* (1965) 98, at 101.

At the inception of the FAO, the central dilemma was whether the FAO would be an 'activist organization' that made bold moves to stimulate agriculture production and to stabilize prices or whether it would focus more on data collection and act as a diplomatic forum.[57] When the FAO was shut out by the ITO and UNCTAD took over the role of stabilizing prices through international commodity agreements, this left the FAO to focus on using technical knowledge to serve Third World national agricultural production programmes.[58]

During Sen's tenure at the FAO, there was some popular hope and broad international political will at the time to institutionally connect questions of food production, economic development, and trade to the problem of hunger. The GATT Kennedy Round provided the foundations for the only trade agreement that explicitly encoded this ambition. The 1967 GATT Memorandum of Agreement provided the basic elements of a world grains arrangement amongst the United States, Canada, Australia, Argentina, and the EEC. Later that year, at the International Wheat Conference in Rome, this became the 1967 International Wheat Arrangement (aka International Grains Arrangement).[59] What is remarkable about this treaty was that it was made up of a Wheat Trade Convention and (the first ever) Food Aid Convention. Because of the latter, it was understood at the time to be a clear benefit for developing countries since it created a scheme to distinguish food aid from dumping.[60]

As such, the 1967 International Wheat Arrangement was a rare configuration of liberal trade institutions, market stabilization schemes, and food security policies. Even though Orr's call for interlacing food security and trade was initially excluded from GATT, it still resonated (and resonates) within the trade regime. In 1954, the FAO developed a set of principles to address situations where surplus disposal in the form of aid could act as an export subsidy and displace commercial imports and discourage local production in recipient countries.[61] The FAO principles were incorporated into the 1967 International Wheat Arrangement and 1994 Agreement on Agriculture (Art. 10(4)(b)).

[57] Staples (n. 30) 77.

[58] Not to say that there was no agricultural activity within GATT. There was a lot. But UNCTAD proposed new types of powers for international institutions; whereas GATT was more about managing different types of domestic market economies. UNCTAD and the FAO were in more direct competition because they were each articulating a vision of a global market.

[59] O'Connor, 'Going Against the Grain: The Regulation of the International Wheat Trade from 1933 to the 1980 Soviet Grain Embargo', 5 *Boston College International & Comparative Law Review* (1982) 225.

[60] M. Davies and R. Woodward, *International Organizations: A Companion* (2014) 376.

[61] Food and Agriculture Organization, *Disposal of Agricultural Surpluses: Principles Recommended by FAO* (1954). This was after an unsuccessful attempt by Australia to pass a new provision within GATT to address the non-commercial disposal of agricultural surplus (BISD 5S/87).

## B. The First Articulation of Food Security (1971–1977)

In the early 1970s, a large number of people, predominantly in the Third World, faced hunger or famine. All the while, very few international institutional resources were being devoted to responding to people's demands for food, which had risen to a near-global scale by around 1971.

The FAO under Addeke Hendrik Boerma (1968–1975) was under fire for not responding to the crisis. Boerma, in turn, framed the problem as a matter of national interest taking priority over the global crisis and the lack of political will.[62] What was challenged was not only the FAO's response but its ideological agenda at the time. Boerma was originally devoted to the Green Revolution. This was a programme committed to investing in technology and systems of governance that prioritized an every-increasing amount of production at almost any cost. Thus, it privileged industrial agriculture that took the language of factories—input, output, efficiency—and applied it to farming.

The Green Revolution was providing an answer but did not have a clear question—it demanded a permanent and exponential increase of agricultural production as the universal answer. It did not matter whether the problem was framed in terms of hunger, famine, nutrition, or poverty. According to the precepts of the Green Revolution, any question of scarcity was always to be addressed by making and selling more.

Global governance in trade and agriculture was rattled by the World Food Crisis of 1972–1975. World grain prices skyrocketed, devastating the lives of millions of people. The global era of a food and trade politics based on surplus management was over. Many have looked to the 1970s to compare and contrast with the aftermath of the 2007–2008 and 2010–2012 food crises.[63]

Ecologically, El Niño and a significant global temperature drop made the weather so unstable that some experts wondered whether the climate itself was changing. Anchovy catches, a significant source of animal feed, off the coast of Peru were decimated due to changes in ocean currents and overfishing. In Southeast Asia and parts of Africa, the peanut crop yield was low enough to threaten sources of animal feed and cooking oil. The world's food output dropped for the first time in 20 years, down 33 million tons, from 1,200 million tons.[64] Later in 1974, flooding in Bangladesh and drought in India, Ethiopia, and the Sahel region brought famine to the lives of millions.

[62] A. H. Boerma, *Political Will and the World Food Problem* (1975), cited in Jarosz (n. 46) 48.

[63] Díaz-Bonilla, 'Globalisation of Agriculture and Food Crises: Then and Now', in B. Karapinar and C. Haberli (eds), *Food Crises and the WTO* (2010) 49; D. Headey and S. Fan, *Reflections on the Global Food Crisis: How Did It Happen? How Has It Hurt? And How Can We Prevent the Next One?* (2010); Horton, 'The 1974 and 2008 Food Price Crises: Déjà Vu?', in J. Clapp and M. J. Cohen (eds), *The Global Food Crisis: Governance Challenges and Opportunities* (2009) 29.

[64] *TIME*, 'The World Food Crisis', 11 November 1974, https://content.time.com/time/subscriber/article/0,33009,911503,00.html (last visited 17 January 2024).

Despite these declining yields, the problem was not that there was too little food and too many people. Amartya Sen famously recast the issue of famine as a matter of political economy, distribution, and government decision-making.[65] For example, the Bangladesh famine was caused by the Bangladeshi reliance on food imports, the global rise in grain prices, and—most crucially—the US decision to cease food aid and trade to Bangladesh because of Bangladesh's jute trade with Cuba.[66]

The crisis was triggered when the Soviet Union purchased 30 million metric tons of grain to compensate for production shortfalls and feed its people. This amounted to three-quarters of all grain on the world market.[67] As part of détente politics of the time, the United States agreed to sell a significant amount of its wheat (known as the 1972–1973 Soviet–US grain deals). The United States had little to export thereafter since the government had just incentivized farmers to cut wheat production. All this caused prices to quickly rise. By that point, the economic provisions under the 1967 Wheat Trade Convention were suspended and the successor 1971 Wheat Trade Convention included none, leaving global leaders no international mechanism to at least attempt to stabilize the price of wheat.

While the climate and agricultural yields improved in 1973, that same year the price of oil rocketed, making all transport more expensive, thereby raising fertilizer and food costs.[68] All this was going on while international understandings and institutions unravelled.[69] For example, to many people's surprise, Nixon ended dollar convertibility to gold in 1971 and essentially ended the Bretton Woods system. By 1973, most major world economies had allowed their currencies to float freely against the dollar. It was a 'rocky transition' characterized by plummeting stock prices, bank failures, and inflation.[70] It was during this era of unstable market conditions that food security and freer trade were at the forefront of international negotiations. A World Food Conference was convened in 1974 and held in Rome, where 'food security' was officially defined for the first time and promulgated on the international agenda.[71]

[65] A. Sen, *Poverty and Famines: An Essay on Entitlement and Deprivation* (1981).

[66] Ibid. 135–136.

[67] Friedmann (n. 14) 40.

[68] The common account of the 1973 oil shock is that Arab oil-producing countries imposed an embargo through OPEC in order to punish countries like the United States and the Netherlands for their support of Israel in the Yom Kippur/October war against Egypt. But recent scholarship suggests that the price of oil may have been more affected by other factors such as: the financial instability created by the end of the Bretton Woods system, the global rise of primary commodity prices, nationalizations and spreading fear of natural resource exhaustion, US oil production peaks, and the rise of environmental concerns. See Garavini, 'Completing Decolonization: The 1973 "Oil Shock" and the Struggle for Economic Rights', 33 *International History Review* (2011) 473.

[69] Ruggie, 'International Regimes, Transactions, and Change: Embedded Liberalism in the Postwar Economic Order', 36 *International Organizations* (1982) 379.

[70] M. J. Stephey, 'Brief History of Bretton Woods System', *TIME*, 21 October 2008 http://content.time.com/time/business/article/0,8599,1852254,00.html (last visited 17 January 2024).

[71] UN, Report of the World Food Conference Rome, 5–16 November 1974 (1975); S. Aziz, *Hunger, Politics, and Markets: The Real Issues in the Food Crisis* (1975).

Many of the proposals emanating from this first call for food security as defined in this declaration were not new.[72] The proposal to increase food production in developing countries, which included integrating approximately 100 million subsistence farmers into the world economy, was in line with orthodox development policies of the time. There was a call for nutrition programmes to improve consumption and nutrition patterns while ensuring adequate food availability to people in developing countries; this supported FAO policies in place since Orr's tenure. Promoting international trade and strengthening the sharing of technical information was already within the mandate of several international institutions.

## C. The Institutional Landscape of Food Security

Delegates to the World Food Conference enacted the Universal Declaration on the Eradication of Hunger and Malnutrition and introduced the doctrine of 'food security' to international legal and diplomatic discourse.[73] What made 'food security' unique for its time, and the reason why delegates may have thought they needed to put forward a new term, was that this was an attempt to connect all the factors—development, trade, and nutrition—together as a singular obligation for national governments and international law. Using the term 'security' also meant that what was at stake was hunger on a scale that challenged the foundations of society and world order. With the states under pressure from the demands of their people, they turned to international institutions for help.

By including human rights within the concept of food security, this ensured that food would always be understood as a matter of hunger and not strictly as a commodity (as was done in ICAs). The Declaration preamble includes the desire to ensure that '[t]he well-being of the peoples of the world largely depends on . . . a world food security system which would ensure adequate availability of, and reasonable prices for, food at all times'. The point being that states had to do so, 'irrespective of periodic fluctuations and vagaries of weather and free of political and economic pressures'. This imperative, driven by the right to food, meant that national governments had to change the way they governed in order to eradicate hunger and famine. Food security was defined in a way that inherently linked it to a call for the establishment of stable and fair markets.

The remaining resolutions focus on state responsibilities. While the Declaration emphasized that each state was sovereign in deciding how it would implement its obligations, the Declaration provided a plan. According to the Declaration, the

[72] Gerlach, 'Famine Responses in the World Food Crisis 1972–5 and the World Food Conference of 1974', 22 *European Review of History: Revue Européenne d'histoire* (2015) 929; D. E. Hathaway, *The World Food Crisis: Periodic or Perpetual?* (1975); Shaw (n. 34) 115–154.

[73] Adopted on 16 November 1974 by the World Food Conference convened under GA Res. 3180 (XXVIII), 17 December 1973; endorsed by GA Res. 3348 (XXIX), 17 December 1974.

right to food was understood as a problem created by global inequality, not production capacity. It therefore took the position that while the eradication of hunger was a common objective of all the countries of the international community, the developed countries and others were in the best position to help.[74]

You should keep in mind that international human rights law always requires a degree of domestic implementation. This was the 1960s and 1970s and not yet a time when human rights included the politics of naming and shaming. It was not until 1986 that the Committee on Economic, Social and Cultural Rights was created to monitor states parties' compliance with their obligations to the ICESCR.

This meant that at that time a human rights approach in relation to international institutions was predominantly about using international institutions to support or act as domestic institutions. From the perspective of the Third World, the line between the domestic and international was rarely a clear one. This was one reason that international law and the institutions acted both as support against and the source of vulnerability. If your country depends on international institutions for governance support, it remains vulnerable to the geopolitics of how international institutions collect and redistribute funds and resources.

At the heart of the idea of food security, though not in the Declaration on the Eradication of Hunger, was the idea of self-reliance or self-sufficiency—which complicated the relationship between trade and food security.[75] The final consensus at the World Food Conference over stock-holding policies and international trade did not put forward any new policies and reflected the existing trade policies of UNCTAD and GATT.[76] Some of the First World delegates at the World Food Conference preferred to leave trade discussions to the ongoing GATT negotiations at the Tokyo Round.[77] Six months after the World Food Conference in May, negotiators at the Tokyo Round took up the call to address the world grain problem that had generated the food crisis. Talks at the International Wheat Council (later renamed the International Grains Council) had gone nowhere in February.[78]

On the market stabilization front, the Tokyo Round was not very successful since the two ICAs that were finalized—on bovine meat and dairy products—only had nominal stabilizing mechanisms.[79] To many commentators today, the bigger failure was that no progress was made on liberalizing trade in agriculture. But the real failure of the Tokyo Round, measured in the political terms of the time, was the inability to conclude a grain agreement that employed principles of market stabilization and trade liberalization to serve food security needs.

[74] Ibid. para. 1.
[75] FAO, 'The Struggle for Food Security' (1979).
[76] Universal Declaration on the Eradication of Hunger and Malnutrition (n. 73) para. 11.
[77] Report of the World Food Conference Rome (n. 71) 36.
[78] Shaw (n. 34) 155–158.
[79] BISD 26S/84; BISD 26/91 (1980).

UNCTAD was invited to the Tokyo Round Sub-Group negotiations on grain. In fact, Third World countries during the World Food Conference were not keen on talking about trade in Rome and preferred to leave it to UNCTAD.[80] By now, the Third World was mobilizing through UNCTAD and passed a General Assembly resolution calling for the establishment of a New International Economic Order (NIEO).[81] The regulation of primary commodities was the first thing on the list of the NIEO Programme of Action.[82]

The Third World, through things such as NIEO, used the term 'self-reliance' to mean not having to depend on resources that were controlled by more powerful, richer states. Set in the context of the Third World, self-reliance was not isolationist and included an understanding of solidarity, since the NIEO Programme of Action called for 'collective self-reliance'.

This notion of self-reliance had at least two, unresolved, meanings at the time held by different people within the Third World: it could mean that citizens had access to enough food at all times to meet nutritional requirements or it meant that domestic production adequately met domestic demand.[83] The former came from countries that relied on food imports and therefore demanded a more equitable trading system, the latter came from places where farmers and peasants served the domestic market and had enough political power to argue that the international trade regime should not govern food. Thus, the doctrine of food security was deployed with this duality built into its definition to reflect the different understandings of hunger.

The right to food gave World Food Conference delegates, especially Third World governments, the ability to connect all these matters in terms of global equity and fairness, not just economic or political terms. To some degree, this was a continuation of B. R. Sen's vision. The key (and now ironic) difference was that food security as a right-to-food concept was being developed as a more powerful crystallization of new policies to counteract the FAO's Green Revolution under Boerma. By 1974, Boerma had adopted the language of the right to food as a way to stave off criticism and re-establish the FAO's authority.

Nonetheless, the World Food Conference acted upon national governments' lack of confidence in the FAO and eroded much of the international institution's power. The resulting innovations then were not just discursive but also institutional. First, the UN World Food Programme (created in 1961) took more of a lead in emergency aid delivery from surplus countries to those in need, a role previously driven by the FAO. Second, Resolution XIII established the World Food Council (WFC) and the International Fund for Agricultural Development (IFAD). The

[80] Shaw (n. 34) 125.
[81] UN GA Res. 3201 (S-VII), 1 May 1974.
[82] UN GA Res. 3202 (S-VI), 1 May 1974.
[83] Pinstrup-Andersen, 'Food Security: Definition and Measurement', 1 *Food Security* (2009) 5.

WFC was a compromise between the Third World's desire to create a World Food Security Council (akin to the UN Security Council) and the First World countries who did not want any new UN machinery to address the problems. In the end, the WFC reported directly to the UN General Assembly, derived its budget from the UN's regular budget, and was the only UN body to be specifically set up at the ministerial or plenipotentiary level.[84]

This tension suggests that 'security' was maybe chosen to indicate that food is an overarching concern connected to the avoidance of war—the Bandung Final Communiqué, for example, stated that 'peace is correlative with the problem of international security'.[85] Whereas Bandung articulated security as a response to the rise of nuclear weapons, 'food security' may have been a response to political threats of hunger and starvation. The Third World may have also used the term 'security' to respond to direct threats from people like US Secretary of Agriculture Earl Butz who, in the mid-1970s, admitted to using food and hunger for geopolitical gains when he famously stated, 'Food is a weapon. It is now one of the principal tools in our negotiating kit.'[86]

The G77, a coalition of Third World states, successfully ensured that WFC procedural rules provided a geographical and political balance between developing and developed countries and would not become a tool of the powerful developed nations. The thinking was that if hunger was a political problem, then the world needed a new political institution directing technical institutions like the FAO to resolve the problem.[87] The WFC at its most ambitious was intended to be 'a political overview body' and 'to serve as the eyes, ears and conscience of the UN system regarding world food security issues'.[88] The intention was that it was to 'act as advocate, catalyst and coordinator, stimulating governments and the international community as a whole to adopt mutually beneficial policies and programmes to alleviate hunger and malnutrition in the world'.[89] In practice, its policy achievements were modest and its coordination efforts ineffective and redundant.[90] The WFC was discontinued in 1996 and its functions were absorbed by the FAO and the WFP.[91]

The second institutional innovation of the time was the creation of IFAD, which remains active today. It also came out of the complex aspects of Third World politics. Building from the 1973 Non-Aligned Movement Summit in Algiers and the

[84] Mechlem, 'Food, Right to, International Protection', in *Max Planck Encyclopaedia of Public International Law* (2008); Shaw (n. 34) 168.

[85] Ministry of Foreign Affairs, Republic of Indonesia (ed.), *Asia-Africa speak from Bandung* (1955) 161.

[86] *TIME*, 'What To Do: Costly Choices', 11 November 1974, https://content.time.com/time/subscriber/article/0,33009,911505,00.html (last visited 17 January 2024).

[87] Shaw (n. 34) 168–169.

[88] Ibid. 170.

[89] Mechlem (n. 84).

[90] Ibid.

[91] UN GA Res. 50/227, 24 May 1996.

NIEO, IFAD was designed to accumulate resources for the purpose of lending money on concessional terms to developing countries for agricultural projects. Its governance design was a unique tripartite structure reflecting the politics of the time. Member States are individual members but also members of a formal group. The three groups are developed countries (mostly OECD countries), Organization of the Petroleum Exporting Countries (OPEC), and beneficiary countries.

Just as the WFC council eroded some of the FAO's existing power, IFAD challenged the FAO's sole authority in rural development programmes and food aid. But IFAD also took some power away from UNCTAD. Representatives from Third World countries all agreed through the NIEO that global market agricultural prices were too volatile and needed to be stabilized. They disagreed over how best to implement these doctrines of market stabilization. They were divided over whether power should be delegated to national governments and ICAs or more centralized to UNCTAD.

In 1976, under the leadership of Gamani Corea, an economist and high-ranking civil servant from Sri Lanka, UNCTAD led the effort to operationalize the NIEO call especially in the area of commodity regulation.[92] This included creating the Integrated Programme for Commodities and, later in 1980, the Common Fund for Commodities. Until this point, ICAs were negotiated on a commodity-by-commodity basis by essentially independent bodies, with no clear common objective.[93] The Integrated Programme for Commodities was the first time that one international organization, since the ITO, had attempted to bring all ICAs within a single institution, directed by a single fund.

This reflected the dominant thinking at the time that assumed that international agriculture should be rationally organized for the purpose of price regulation. This was also a plan designed to benefit countries of the Third World.[94] UNCTAD's working premise was that the global commodity market was primarily embedded in a global social context, and thus only a global institution would be able to regulate commodities—thereby moving away from the pre-existing emphasis on coordinating and buttressing domestic institutions.

The Integrated Programme for Commodities was intended to cover a wide range of commodities in order to permit and encourage simultaneous negotiations, which would allow for an overall balancing of interests. The Common Fund

92 UN GA Res. 3202 (S-VI), 1 May 1974, para. 3(a)(iv).

93 R. Presbisch, 'Towards a Global Strategy of Development: Report by the Secretary-General of the United Nations Conference on Trade and Development to the Second Session of the Conference' (1968) 16–18; UNCTAD, *Proceedings of the United Nations Conference on Trade and Development*, 2nd Session, vol. 1 (1968) 34–38.

94 See G. Corea, *Taming Commodity Markets: The Integrated Programme and the Common Fund in UNCTAD* (1992); Cuddy, 'Theory and Practice in NIEO Negotiations on Commodities', in G. K. Helleiner, *For Good or Evil: Economic Theory and North-South Negotiations* (1982) 33.

was to be partially funded by OPEC and was intended to promote the timely conclusion of ICAs since the question of financing would be prearranged.[95]

Western countries preferred to negotiate ICAs in a piecemeal fashion and had regularly opposed Prebisch's suggestion of integrating commodity policies.[96] According to some, OPEC's success in raising oil prices in 1973–1974 provided evidence of the potential strength of commodity producers of the South in relation to the North.[97] Thus, the Integrated Programme for Commodities was also thought to be bold in its politics since it allowed developing countries to negotiate as a bloc.

When the Integrated Programme for Commodities was launched in 1976, six ICAs were already in operation—tin, coffee, cocoa, sugar, wheat, and olive oil.[98] Cocoa, tin, sugar, and wheat negotiations were thought by some to be nominally UN undertakings because G77 or NIEO doctrine barely appeared in most commodity negotiations. With the exception of Prebisch's involvement in the 1968 International Sugar Agreement negotiations, the UNCTAD Secretariat's main contribution during the negotiations was thought to be the provision of conference facilities.[99]

Up until that moment, different ICAs employed diverse forms of supply management, all of which included the international regulation of commodity prices through both international and domestic institutions. NIEO only focused on redistribution of wealth on an international scale and did not address or make provision for domestic policies of redistribution. The fact that the Integrated Programme for Commodities was a plan to control international commodities through a stock held, controlled, and financed by UNCTAD did not sit too easily with national governments. Commodity producers, especially Latin American countries, expressed anxiety about the Common Fund because they feared that they would lose decision-making power over certain products, such as setting maximum and minimum prices, to a forum where countries without an interest in those products would participate. What is also telling is that major commodity producers such as Brazil, Malaysia, Ivory Coast, Chile, and Colombia did not lead in creating the Integrated Programme.[100]

National governments' fears of the potential demise of ICAs and losing control of commodity trade to UNCTAD were not unfounded. Members of the UNCTAD Secretariat thought that a single agency, most likely the Common Fund, could regulate commodity price fluctuation;[101] whereas the Latin American countries

[95] Maizels, 'Reforming the World Economy', in M. Zammit Cutajar (ed.), *UNCTAD and The North South Dialogue: The First Twenty Years; Essays in Memory of W. R. Malinowski* (1985) 101, at 106.

[96] Corea (n. 94) 44–45.

[97] T. G. Weiss *et al.* (eds), *UN Voices: The Struggle for Development and Social Justice* (2005) 225–232.

[98] Corea (n. 94) 141.

[99] T. G. Weiss, *Multilateral Development in Diplomacy in UNCTAD: The Lessons of Group Negotiations, 1964–84* (1986) 104–105.

[100] Ibid. 44–45.

[101] Corea (n. 94) 34.

would insist that the Common Fund would regulate commodity markets through individual ICAs.[102]

By now, industrialized countries were, for the most part, responsive to the idea of commodity regulation and ICAs. They reacted most vehemently against the idea of the Common Fund. According to Corea, 'to the developed countries the Common Fund was the most dangerous element of the Integrated Programme and the one to be resisted most fiercely'.[103]

From all this we can detect that national governments from both the North and South accepted ICAs to some degree, yet they were either cautious or opposed outright to the idea of UNCTAD gaining power over the regulation of commodities. The UNCTAD Secretariat positioned the Integrated Programme for Commodities and the Common Fund as an 'all or nothing' component of NIEO,[104] thereby raising the stakes behind ICAs and interlinking the fate of the commodity policy with NIEO doctrines.

Ironically, the fizzling out of the Common Fund did not come from the First World but from within the Third World. OPEC ended up devoting the majority of its resources to IFAD (where it had more power and control) and not the Common Fund for Commodities.[105] The doctrinal result was that a significant number of international resources were directed more towards treating food as a right and as a matter of hunger rather than as a commodity in terms of trade and development.

In sum, each institution of the time had its own concept of trade. The World Food Conference prioritized and enhanced the right to food with a food security plan, leaving doctrines of market stability and trade liberalization unclear; the GATT Tokyo Round split over whether market stabilization or trade liberalization would best serve food security demands; and NIEO prioritized market stabilization, emphasized that food security is linked to development, and treated trade liberalization as a secondary (but necessary) issue.

In terms of international trade policy, UNCTAD and the FAO shared a lot the same premises. They both placed an emphasis on coordinating global surplus and inequality, transforming subsistence agriculture into a market economy, and increasing productivity. B. R. Sen, drawing on the work of Hans Singer and others, endorsed the idea that national food reserves should be regulated through international coordination; these reserves would buffer against supply fluctuations caused by ecological conditions, and stabilize prices to balance between increasing productivity and addressing sharp increases in cost of living.[106] This vision called for stable and coordinated expansion of agricultural trade.[107] Politically, both

[102] Toye and Toye (n. 55) 245.

[103] Corea (n. 94) 45.

[104] UNCTAD, *History of UNCTAD 1964–1984* (1985) 64.

[105] I. Shihata, *The Other Face of OPEC: Financial Assistance and the Third World* (1982) 89–92.

[106] Singer *et al.*, 'Report by the Expert Group to the Director-General of FAO', in FAO (ed.), *Development Through Food: A Strategy for Surplus Utilization* (FFHC Basic Study) (1962) 25.

[107] FAO, ibid. 41

institutions empowered Third World countries and also provided a forum for the Third World to negotiate with richer countries.

One difference lay in how each institution put theory into practice and operationalized trade—UNCTAD developed global supply mechanisms and coordinated ICAs while FAO turned technical knowledge into tools for national governments and FAO agents to boldly use to create and share development-friendly, small-scale knowledge intended to serve poor farmers and empower women.

Another key difference was how agriculture was understood. UNCTAD represented the dominant thinking taken up by Third World governments at the time. From the 1950s on, whether it was through import substitution industrialization or export-oriented policies, Third World governments sought to leverage their dependence on agriculture as a means towards industrialization. For decades, Third World governments, sponsored by international organizations like the World Bank, favoured industry over agriculture, shifting resources from the historical rural communities and agricultural sectors to the burgeoning urbanized and manufacturing sectors; whereas the FAO took on the minority Third Worldist perspective and often focused on agriculture reform as an end in and of itself.

## 4. Food Sovereignty Movements Transform the Right to Food

### A. Crises of the 1970s and 1980s

Just when most people in the world started to recover from the World Food Crisis, they were hit by the global commodity crisis in 1978 when prices collapsed across the board and would not recover until 1986. In the Third World, a large number of people's livelihoods depended on selling what they grew and raised, whether it was through local, regional, or international markets. Those people who worked with or serviced those producers were also hard hit.[108] Moreover, a second oil shock hit the world in 1978–1980, further destabilizing petroleum-dependent societies and economies and quickly raising the cost of living.

The 1970s was also the era of the second development decade during which Third World countries continued pursuing large development projects that emphasized industrialization. But Third World countries had to borrow money to fund their industrialization projects; this was because most of these countries depended on exporting primary commodities that did not bring a lot of capital into local economies. The price spike of the first oil shock generated large amounts of extra money for oil-exporting countries, which they deposited into Western banks. The banks then loaned much of that money to developing countries for

[108] Corea (n. 94) 153–158; Maizels (n. 51).

development projects. However, when commodity prices collapsed dragging everyone into recession in 1979, developing countries were no longer able to repay their debts.

This ushered in a new ideological and financial era that would later be called the Washington Consensus or neoliberalism. The Third World debt crisis was most acutely felt in non-oil-producing Latin American countries. Countries that were unable to pay their debts turned to the International Monetary Fund (IMF) which provided money for loans and unpaid debts. In return, the IMF forced developing countries to make structural-adjustment reforms that undid subsidies, reduced tariffs, and promoted the market as the principal social institution.

During this time, policymakers, politicians, and experts were redefining food security in more market-oriented terms. They were focusing more on household purchasing power, access to global agricultural markets, and narrowing government social policy.[109] This could be interpreted as an attempt to delink food security from its human rights origins by treating food more as a commodity. It was, however, more likely part of the emerging trend in human rights discourse writ large towards a 'trade-related, market friendly' framework.[110]

By 1982, NIEO and the Third World project were dead.[111] The post-colonial world regrouped as the Global South.[112] The institutional corollary was that ICAs and UNCTAD were outdone by the GATT. ICAs were no longer designed to stabilize the prices of commodities and were relegated to administrative functions and knowledge-sharing endeavours. Starting around 1979, UNCTAD started looking for a 'different analytical base'.[113] Soon after, UNCTAD went through a 'crisis, retreat, and reinvention'. By the mid-1980s, as the Uruguay Round began, UNCTAD and many developing-country leaders decided that their countries should direct most of their trade law and policy energy into the GATT.[114]

Despite the ideological shift in the 1980s, the post-colonial world still had some power and influence within certain international institutions. While the FAO under Edouard Saouma (1976–1993) also embraced the language of markets and market-friendly human rights, Saouma adeptly deployed a Third World-friendly

[109] Fairbairn (n. 28) 24–26; McMichael, 'Global Development and The Corporate Food Regime', in F. H. Buttel and P. McMichael (eds), *New Directions in the Sociology of Global Development, Research in Rural Sociology and Development*, vol. 11 (2006) 265.

[110] Baxi, 'Market Fundamentalisms: Business Ethics at the Altar of Human Rights', 5 *Human Rights Law Review* (2005) 1. See also Cohen (n. 18) 116; Whyte (n. 29).

[111] Tomlinson, 'What Was the Third World?', 38 *Journal of Contemporary History* (2003) 307, at 214; Toye and Toye (n. 55) 272–274; T. G. Weiss *et al.*, *UN Voices: The Struggle for Development and Social Justice* (2005) 258.

[112] S. Alam *et al.* (eds), *International Environmental Law and the Global South* (2016); V. Prashad, *The Poorer Nations: A Possible History of the Global South* (2014).

[113] Weiss *et al.* (n. 111) 198.

[114] S. Kasahara and C. Gore (eds), *Beyond Conventional Wisdom in Development Policy: An Intellectual History of UNCTAD 1964–2004* (2004) 5–10; I. Taylor and K. Smith, *United Nations Conference on Trade and Development (UNCTAD)* (2007) 67–90.

institutional strategy. He significantly restructured the FAO so that its operations were decentralized. The result was that the FAO redistributed wealth from rich donor countries to semi-autonomous regional and national offices (staffed by people from the region) in developing countries. This supported Third World national governments because it not only provided local jobs at a premium salary, but it also allowed local actors to control a significant amount of capital dedicated to local projects. While First World countries deplored Saouma and attacked him both personally and professionally, they could not dispute his ability to do more with less; he significantly reduced administrative costs while also increasing the FAO's political legitimacy amongst the governments of most of the world's people.[115]

## B. Rise of Food Sovereignty Movements, 1993–1999

By the 1990s, however, small-holder farmers and other small-scale food producers around the world were fed up with international economic institutions, disappointed with their national governments, and cynical when it came to development discourse. They were hit from multiple directions and on different scales. As mentioned previously, for 50 years most national governments across the Third World were preoccupied with development. Regardless of their particular understanding of development, very few governments and advisors were committed to easing conditions for food producers in a way that allowed them to continue their way of life. The emphasis was on industrialization—generally, the plan was to industrialize agriculture in order to reduce labour costs and then funnel that surplus labour to cities. Once rural people moved to the cities, they could work in the manufacturing and service sectors. With this plan, national governments disinvested from the agricultural sector in order to create a cheap work base for the manufacturing sector.

During this time, food producers in different countries organized protests against their governments and resisted this plan. Small-holder farmers, other small-scale food producers, and Indigenous peoples around the world, especially in South America and Mexico, began to organize themselves into transnational movements committed to opposing international economic institutions like NAFTA and the World Bank. By May 1993, the movement became global when La Vía Campesina was formed in Mons, Belgium.[116] Seven

[115] Jarosz (n. 46) 51–52; Schindler, 'Man Versus State: Contested Agency in the United Nations', 43 *Millennium* (2014) 3; Schindler, 'The Morality of Bureaucratic Politics: Allegations of "Spoiling" in a UN Inter-Agency War', 5 *Journal of International Organization Studies* (2014) 59.

[116] La Vía Campesina, 'Mons Declaration' (1993) https://viacampesina.org/en/mons-declaration (last visited 17 January 2024).

months later, this new movement marched in Geneva against the newly created WTO.[117]

In the past, small-scale producer groups could at least rely on the fact that their perspective was influential in their national governments, ICAs, and UNCTAD—all of which were no longer politically viable paths for them. Recalling the UN's track record as more egalitarian and poor-friendly than the WTO, World Bank, and the IMF, these groups turned their attention to influencing and changing the FAO.[118]

La Vía Campesina's first international political opportunity arose when, in 1996, Jacques Diouf (FAO Secretary-General 1993–2011) called for a high-level World Food Summit, and the FAO Council unanimously agreed.[119] Part of Diouf's plan was to re-establish the FAO as a principal international agricultural institution. Due to recent changes in ECOSOC procedures, civil society organizations were now allowed to formally participate in international summits—the thinking was that this would allow civil society organizations to have greater influence over how international standards were set and more leverage in ensuring that those standards were domestically implemented.[120]

Even with new procedural rules, however, it was not easy for La Vía Campesina to access the FAO. Civil society organizations (CSOs) were a relatively new concept, and there was no clear process to determine how FAO delegates and staff (or any other institution) could decide how to organize CSO participation and who would be allowed to be part of the process. La Vía Campesina's application for their members to attend as official delegates to the 1996 World Food Summit was rejected.[121] In response, they attended the parallel official NGO Forum.

This forum had its own political dynamics.[122] First, Southern organizations confronted Northern NGOs for acting as gatekeepers to international organizations. More specifically, many Northern (urban) NGOs assumed peasant groups were not 'capable and articulate' enough to represent their own interests.[123] Second, the private sector was well represented in the NGO forum through non-profit business associations. That meant that the space itself was a place for social movements, NGOs, and private companies to confront each other, contest claims, and potentially compromise. Third, people went to the forum to sharpen the distinction between people's organizations/social movements established by and

[117] Desmarais, 'The Vía Campesina: Consolidating an International Peasant and Farm Movement', 29 *Journal of Peasant Studies* (2002) 91, at 93.

[118] McKeon (n. 5).

[119] Ibid. 53.

[120] Ibid. 51. ECOSOC Res. 1996/31, 25 July 1996, https://www.un.org/esa/coordination/ngo/Resolution_1996_31/ (last visited 17 January 2024).

[121] Desmarais (n. 117) 104.

[122] McKeon (n. 5).

[123] Desmarais (n. 117) 103.

representing particular groups versus NGOs which did not represent the population they served nor were they accountable to them.

Even though the concept of food sovereignty was still a sketch and not widely understood outside the movement, La Vía Campesina deftly navigated the forum and was able to ensure that its new concept was prominent in the final official NGO Statement.[124] Even with that, however, La Vía Campesina distanced itself from the Statement since it thought it still granted too much power to NGOs who claimed to speak on behalf of peasants and farmers.[125] It instead released a separate document during the World Food Summit, which was, in effect, its first official definition of food sovereignty.[126]

As compared to previous statements, the Rome Declaration on World Food Security was not novel in framing issues in terms of the right to food. The most significant difference was that, unlike in the past, this Declaration did not identify global inequality as a cause of food insecurity,[127] and took a position somewhere between ambivalence towards and support of the newly created WTO.[128] It did, nevertheless, expand the understanding of food security to include a wider political and cultural scope.

La Vía Campesina's initial definition of food sovereignty was also not the most novel concept. La Vía Campesina's official definition of food sovereignty was still state-centric and echoed older doctrines such as Permanent Sovereignty Over Natural Resources and the right to development.[129]

But the politics were new. La Vía Campesina deployed food sovereignty as a way to claim and redefine the right to food, and this changed the meaning of the concepts at play. Its goal was to sharpen the difference between food policies that fed people but without any regard for concentrations of political power versus those policies that empowered the large number of decentralized small-scale food producers. It sharpened the difference by highlighting how food security frames hunger as a problem

[124] NGO Forum Statement, 'For Few or Food For All?—Food Sovereignty and Security to Eliminate the Globalisation of Hunger', 17 November 1996, https://www.ukabc.org/wfs+5_NGO_FORUM96.doc (last visited 17 January 2024). The version that appears in the FAO Final Report does not include the complete title; see also M. Karl (ed.), *Partners for Food Security* (1996) 145, http://www.fao.org/3/a-w3055e.pdf (last visited 17 January 2024).

[125] Desmarais (n. 117) 104.

[126] La Vía Campesina, 'The Right to Produce and Access to Land. Food Sovereignty: A Future without Hunger', 11–17 November 1996, https://viacampesina.org/en/wp-content/uploads/sites/2/2021/11/1996-Rom-en.pdf (last visited 17 January 2024).

[127] Wills (n. 7) 116.

[128] FAO, Rome Declaration of the World Food Security, http://www.fao.org/3/w3613e/w3613e00.htm (last visited 17 January 2024): 'We will strive to ensure that food, agricultural trade and overall trade policies are conducive to fostering food security for all through a fair and market-oriented world trade system.' The reference to a market-oriented world trade system is in effect affirming the WTO. But the WTO has a very unclear mandate when it comes to food security. Thus the reference ensuring trade fosters food security sits in tension with the WTO and leaves it unclear exactly what the relationship is between food security and fair trade.

[129] La Vía Campesina, 'The Right to Produce' (n. 126).

of distribution (with a focus on access and commerce). Food sovereignty instead asks the question: who controls the systems of production and consumption?[130] The tactic was to wrestle the right to food away from food security towards food sovereignty, thereby delegitimizing food security and its beneficiaries (agribusiness).

Romano Prodi, as chairman, provided the World Food Summit's terms of success. The goal was for the Summit to 'serve as a point of reference for future discussions on global [food and agricultural] issues'. The thinking was that the FAO would act as the coordinating institution and national governments would decide for themselves how to implement international obligations through national law. Prodi explicitly identified the fact that this was all to ensure that the FAO and the Summit would remain central to agricultural negotiations despite the activation of the WTO in 1995.[131]

Now that all international trade law and policy in agriculture was at the WTO, the FAO needed to find a way to ensure it maintained some authority over international economic law and agricultural policy. In 1999, with the support of the government of the Netherlands, the FAO tried to gain ground by organizing an International Conference on the Multifunctional Character of Trade; these efforts were shut down by the Cairns Group government representatives in the FAO.[132] While the WTO Agreement of Agriculture made reference to food security, it framed food security as an exception to trade law. Under Pascal Lamy (2005–2013), the WTO Secretariat interpreted this to mean that the WTO governed international agriculture but had no role to play in food security matters,[133] whereas the FAO could rely on the right to food and claim direct authority over food security. Therefore, La Vía Campesina's tactic was to use food sovereignty to control the meaning of the right to food thereby gaining access to the FAO, while at the same time deploying it against the WTO to try to get the WTO out of agriculture entirely.[134]

The Summit's Declaration and Plan of Action reinvigorated institutional commitments to the right to food and generated several important doctrinal and

[130] Patel, 'What Does Food Sovereignty Look Like?', 36 *Journal of Peasant Studies* (2009) 663; Wittman, Desmarais, and Wiebe, 'The Origins & Potential of Food Sovereignty', in H. Wittman, A. A. Desmarais, and N. Wiebe (eds), *Food Sovereignty: Reconnecting Food, Nature and Community* (2010) 1.

[131] 'H. E. Romano Prodi, President of the Council of Ministers of the Italian Republic and Chairman of the World Food Summit, 13 November 1996', in FAO, *Report of the World Food Summit 13–17 November 1996* (1996) Annex I.

[132] N. McKeon, *Food Security Governance: Empowering Communities, Regulating Corporations* (2015) 87. The Cairns Group is an alliance of governments for the purpose of WTO negotiations. The group is led by Australia and sometimes Argentina or Canada. It is a diverse coalition bringing together 20 developed and developing countries from North and South America, Africa, and the Asia-Pacific region. The group accounts for over 25 per cent of the world's agricultural exports. The countries in the group are: Argentina, Australia, Bolivia, Brazil, Canada, Chile, Colombia, Costa Rica, Guatemala, Indonesia, Malaysia, New Zealand, Pakistan, Paraguay, Peru, the Philippines, South Africa, Thailand, Uruguay, and Vietnam.

[133] Fakhri, 'Food as a Matter of Global Governance', 11 *Journal of International Law and International Relations* (2015) 68.

[134] P. Rosset, *Food Is Different: Why We Must Get the WTO Out of Agriculture* (2006).

institutional developments.[135] Over in Geneva, the Committee on Economic, Social and Cultural Rights responded to the call to clarify the meaning of the right to food[136] and published General Comment No. 12.[137] The UN Commission on Human Rights also responded and, in 2000, appointed the first UN Special Rapporteur on the Right to Food. In 2002, this work was further boosted by the World Food Summit + 5, which attracted even more agrarian activists than the first summit. The FAO created an intergovernmental working group and brought in CSOs to draft the Voluntary Right to Food Guidelines, which the FAO adopted in 2004.[138]

In these terms, the World Food Summit was a success. After the Summit, the FAO, La Vía Campesina, and right-to-food NGOs used the right to food to work together and align their interests. This new relationship can be understood in terms of authority and resource distribution. The FAO made room for a debate about food sovereignty and a definition of the right to food that served poor and vulnerable food producers.[139] While food sovereignty as such was not adopted as a defining doctrine within the FAO, La Vía Campesina gained access to the FAO staff and resources.[140] NGOs were provided with contract work to implement the Plan of Action. Right-to-food NGOs worked closely with La Vía Campesina to ensure that NGO work aligned with food producers' needs. And the FAO and NGOs gained the legitimacy they needed by working with La Vía Campesina holding themselves accountable to the people they served.[141]

[135] Edelman, 'Linking the Rights of Peasants to the Right to Food in the United Nations', 10 *Law, Culture and the Humanities* (2014) 196, at 203; Wills (n. 7) 115–137.

[136] World Food Summit Plan of Action, in FAO, Report of the World Food Summit 13–17 November 1996 (1996) Appendix, Objective 7.4.

[137] Committee on Economic, Social and Cultural Rights, General Comment No. 12: The Right to Adequate Food (Art. 11), UN Doc. E/C.12/1999/5, 12 May 1999.

[138] FAO, 'Voluntary Guidelines to support the Progressive Realization of the Right to Adequate Food in the Context of National Food Security' (2005) http://www.fao.org/3/a-y7937e.pdf (last visited 17 January 2024).

[139] For debates about food sovereignty within FAO, see Report of the 32nd Session of the Regional Conference for Latin America and the Caribbean, 26–30 March 2012, C 2013/17, http://www.fao.org/docrep/meeting/027/mf594e.pdf (last visited 17 January 2024); G. Gordillo, 'Food Security and Sovereignty (Base Document for Discussion)' (2013), http://www.fao.org/fileadmin/user_upload/rlc/larc33/FS_base_document_EN.pdf (last visited 17 January 2024); J. Nicastro, 'FAO Accepts to Debate Food Sovereignty', 12 May 2012, https://www.eurasiareview.com/24052012-fao-accepts-debate-food-sovereignty/ (last visited 17 January 2024).

[140] IPC, 'The IPC and FAO Establish Common Priority Themes for a Collaborative Work in the Fight Against Hunger and Food Insecurity', 27 May 2014 http://www.foodsovereignty.org/the-ipc-and-fao-establish-common-priority-themes-for-a-collaborative-work-in-the-fight-against-hunger-and-food-insecurity/ (last visited 17 January 2024); FAO, 'FAO Forges Closer Links with the International Planning Committee for Food Sovereignty', 23 May 2014, https://www.fao.org/partnerships/container/news-article/en/c/233281/ (last visited 17 January 2024).

[141] See FAO, 'FAO Policy and Strategy for Cooperation with Non-Governmental and Civil Society Organizations' (1999), http://www.fao.org/docrep/x2214e/x2214e00.htm (last visited 17 January 2024); FAO, 'FAO Strategy for Partnerships with Civil Society Organizations' (2013), http://www.fao.org/3/a-i3443e.pdf (last visited 17 January 2024). On NGOs needing to legitimize their own work, see McKeon (n. 5) 96.

For example, in 2012 the Committee on World Food Security developed the 'Voluntary Guidelines on Tenure' with significant input from La Vía Campesina and its allies.[142] Later, the NGOs and people's movements came together to develop a 'People's Manual on the Guidelines on Governance of Land, Fisheries and Forests'. This was done with technical assistance from the FAO and with financial assistance from the EU, Oxfam and Brazil's Ministry of Agrarian Development, and the contributions of the organizations participating in and supporting the IPC.[143] In turn, the FAO relied on the People's Manual, continued to work with NGOs and social movements, and co-developed with FIAN (a very prominent right-to-food NGO) the 'Putting the Voluntary Guidelines on Tenure Into Practice: A Learning Guide For Civil Society Organizations'.[144] FIAN, like many NGOs, relies on income from such projects for much of its funding.[145]

## C. Expanding the Movement, 1999–2007

La Vía Campesina successfully established 'unity through diversity' by devoting its first years (1993–1999) to internal consolidation amongst its members despite differences.[146] Food sovereignty as a concept was created and continues to be developed as the ideological framework holding the movement together. Thus, like any product of broad-based solidarity and compromise, it holds within it the defining tensions and paradoxes of the movement.[147]

For instance, there are significant class tensions within La Vía Campesina amongst medium to rich farmers, subsistence farmers, and landless workers.[148] In everyday politics, pastoralists and landowners of all classes often have disputes over land.[149] In fact, La Vía Campesina is dominated by farmers' voices, and others—such as pastoralists, fisherfolk, landless agricultural workers, migrant workers, and forest dwellers—are less prominent.[150] There is also a wide range of ideological

[142] Ibid. 62–65.

[143] IPC, 'People's Manual on the Guidelines on Governance of Land, Fisheries and Forests', 17 June 2016, https://www.foodsovereignty.org/peoplesmanual111/ (last visited 17 January 2024).

[144] FAO, 'Increasing the Use of the VGGT Among Civil Society and Grassroots Organizations', http://www.fao.org/in-action/increase-use-of-vggt-in-civil-society/en/ (last visited 17 January 2024).

[145] FIAN, Annual Report (2017), https://www.fian.org/fileadmin/media/Publications/Annual_Report/FIAN_International_Annual_Report_2017_english_web.pdf (last visited 17 January 2024).

[146] Desmarais, Rivera-Ferre, and Gasco, 'Building Alliances for Food Sovereignty: La Vía Campesina, NGOs, and Social Movements', in D. H. Constance, M.-C. Renard, and M. G. Rivera-Ferre (eds), *Alternative Agrifood Movements: Patterns of Convergence and Divergence, Research in Rural Sociology and Development*, vol. 21 (2014) 89, at 92; Wittman (n. 24) 96–97.

[147] Patel (n. 130).

[148] For a summary on these tensions, see M. Edelman and S. M. Borras, *Political Dynamics of Transnational Agrarian Movements* (2016) 37–60.

[149] M. Rahmanian, 'Food Sovereignty A Critical Dialogue', 21 February 2014, https://www.youtube.com/watch?v=Lgx8cRX1ygc (last visited 14 March 2024).

[150] Edelman and Borras (n. 148) 45.

tendencies that are not inherently linked to class identity and include: (i) radical agrarian populists; (ii) different strands of Marxists, including Maoists; (iii) anarchists; (iv) feminists; and (v) radical environmentalists.[151]

Gender equality is a central tenant of La Vía Campesina and is an organizing principle for its internal governance rules. At first, all elected coordinators were men, but due to feminist struggles within the movement, by 2000 the governance structures were amended to ensure that women and men were equally represented within the movement.[152] Much work, however, remains to be done to use food sovereignty to transform food practices in households, farms, and fields in terms more equitable to women.[153]

Indigenous peoples have had their own histories and politics when it comes to the importance of food in struggles for sovereignty. Many Indigenous peoples also have a different relationship with trade. Moreover, an alliance with a peasant-led movement is not inherently easy for Indigenous peoples who are still in conflict with settler farmers.[154]

Despite these differences, members of La Vía Campesina used food sovereignty to consolidate its transnational peasant movement in complex and dynamic ways.[155] Starting in 1999, it also used the concept to expand its strategic alliances with NGOs and other movements.[156] The process has not been easy or linear, but it has proven to be key to the movement's institutional interventions. In 2002, in preparation for the World Food Summit, La Vía Campesina joined with others to create the International Planning Committee for Food Sovereignty (IPC); this was the point at which one could talk about food sovereignty as a concept and movements that were something more than La Vía Campesina (but with the transnational peasant movement at the core).

The IPC has been a 'network of networks, movement of movements' on a grand scale.[157] It does not act as a singular institutional actor and is instead a decentralized

[151] Ibid. 54.

[152] E. Vivas, 'La Vía Campesina: Food Sovereignty and the Global Feminist Struggle', Pambazuka News, 31 October 2012, https://www.pambazuka.org/gender-minorities/la-campesina-food-sovereignty-and-global-feminist-struggle (last visited 17 January 2024).

[153] Agarwal, 'Food Sovereignty, Food Security and Democratic Choice: Critical Contradictions, Difficult Conciliations', 41 *Journal of Peasant Studies* (2014) 1247; Ellinger-Locke, 'Food Sovereignty Is a Gendered Issue', 18 *Buffalo Environmental Law Journal* (2010) 157; Park, White, and Julia, 'We Are Not All the Same: Taking Gender Seriously in Food Sovereignty Discourse', 36 *Third World Quarterly* (2015) 584; Patel, 'Food Sovereignty: Power, Gender, and the Right to Food', 9 *PLoS Medicine* (2012).

[154] Grey and Patel, 'Food Sovereignty as Decolonization: Some Contributions from Indigenous Movements to Food System and Development Politics', 32 *Agriculture and Human Values; Dordrecht* (2015) 431; Whyte, 'Food Sovereignty, Justice and Indigenous Peoples: An Essay on Settler Colonialism and Collective Continuance', in A. Barnhill, M. Budolfson, and T. Doggett (eds), *The Oxford Handbook of Food Ethics* (2017) 345.

[155] Shattuck, Schiavoni, and VanGelder, 'Translating the Politics of Food Sovereignty: Digging Into Contradictions, Uncovering New Dimensions', 12 *Globalizations* (2015) 421.

[156] Desmarais, Rivera-Ferre, and Gasco (n. 146).

[157] Edelman and Borras (n. 148) 68–70.

network that coordinates members' actions in relationship to governments and international institutions. Since 2003, it has had a formal relationship with the FAO in four priority areas: the right to food, agroecological approaches to food production, local access to and control of natural resources, and agricultural trade and food sovereignty.[158]

The IPC and the FAO agreed to 'establish common priority themes for a collaborative work in the fight against hunger and food insecurity'; this signalled to the public that food sovereignty had some ability to influence the language of decision-making around and within the FAO.[159] While the IPC did gain some ad hoc funding from this arrangement, the arrangement does not include project commissions.[160] Of course, there was always the danger that the FAO would use the enhanced legitimacy granted from working with influential social movements to define and implement the right to food and food sovereignty in ways that did not necessarily benefit the movements (i.e. 'co-optation').

Like many movements of this kind, the IPC holds within it a tension between reformist and radical tendencies.[161] Many in La Vía Campesina were wary of working within the UN system and reforming the FAO in particular; the worry was that this would demand a significant amount of resources that could otherwise be committed to national or regional organizations or to more radical tactics, all without a clear sense of the benefits. At the same time, many of the movement leaders also recognized that they could not cede the FAO to multinational agribusiness.[162] Similarly, in international law, Antony Anghie has often quipped that 'if you don't do international law, international law will do you'. The IPC further complicated this dynamic since it included a fair number of reformist movements and NGOs that were already implicitly comfortable navigating the halls of international institutions.

In the end, the IPC became the vehicle through which La Vía Campesina successfully achieved its slogan of 'globalizing hope and globalizing the struggle'. In light of food sovereignty being taken up by an increasing number of groups, governments, and organizations, La Vía Campesina and others turned to the IPC to ensure that the meaning and goals of food sovereignty were always a product of dialogue and debate and were deeply understood by members of the movement. Along these lines, in 2007 the IPC Secretariat coordinated the International

[158] FAO, 'Evaluation of the FAO Strategy for Partnerships with Civil Society Organizations' (2020) 6, https://www.fao.org/3/cb1636en/cb1636en.pdf (last visited 14 March 2024).

[159] IPC (n. 140).

[160] Ibid: 'Nothing in this agreement implies a financial commitment by either FAO or IPC and any activity undertaken pursuant to this arrangement is subject to the availability of staff and financial resources. FAO and IPC will enter into separate written agreements in relation to any matters which may involve the commitment of funding or other resources.'

[161] See e.g. Eslava and Pahuja, 'Between Resistance and Reform: TWAIL and the Universality of International Law', 3 *Trade, Law and Development* (2011) 103.

[162] McKeon (n. 5) 104.

Nyéléni Forum for Food Sovereignty in Mali. The delegates to the forum produced the most comprehensive definition of food sovereignty to date, the Nyéléni Declaration.[163]

## D. Crisis (Again) and Radical Transformation of the CFS, 2007–2019

The food sovereignty movements were perfectly situated to influence global politics and transform institutional structures when the food crisis of 2007–2008 hit. Governments and international institutions were caught off guard when global food prices rose quickly. According to FAO estimates, by the end of 2008 the average world price for rice had risen by 217 per cent, wheat by 136 per cent, corn by 125 per cent, and soybeans by 107 per cent.[164] People responded by taking to the streets, leading to an unprecedented number of food riots in more than 25 countries all over the world.[165] The absurdity of it all was that food prices were too high for (mainly poor urban) consumers and yet too low for small farmers and farm workers to make a living. Prices spiked again in 2010, once again leading to an increase in poverty, hunger, and social instability.

The politicians' and policymakers' concerns about political and social instability were exacerbated by the 2009 global financial crisis and the second food price spike in 2011–2012. Food security was back on global political agendas in a way that no one had seen since the mid-1970s. Since then, especially against the backdrop of ever-quickening climate change, there has been a consensus that 'food matters'. What transpired—and continues today—is a coming together of the world's leaders to renegotiate the terms of how food matters and on what terms.

Different clusters of power responded to the crisis, each trying to develop the singular plan for governments and international institutions to follow, each jockeying for position to establish the principal site to govern the issue.[166] In April 2008, the UN Secretary-General Ban Ki-Moon named a High-Level Task Force on the Global Food Security Crisis. The primary actors were intergovernmental organizations: 22 UN agencies, the World Bank, IMF, WTO, and OECD. Their main

[163] Declaration of Nyéléni, 27 February 2007, https://nyeleni.org/IMG/pdf/DeclNyeleni-en.pdf (last visited 17 January 2024).

[164] FAO, 'The State of Food Insecurity in the World 2008: High Food Prices and Food Insecurity—Threats and Opportunities' (2008).

[165] Bush, 'Food Riots: Poverty, Power and Protest', 10 *Journal of Agrarian Change* (2010) 119.

[166] J. Duncan, *Global Food Security Governance: Civil Society Engagement in the Reformed Committee on World Food Security* (2015) 63–79; Margulis, 'Global Food Security Governance: The Committee for World Food Security, Comprehensive Framework for Action and the G8/G20', in R. Rayfuse and N. Weisfelt (eds), *The Challenge of Food Security* (2012) 231; Valente and Franco, 'Human Rights and the Struggle Against Hunger: Laws, Institutions, and Instruments in the Fight to Realize the Right to Adequate Food', 13 *Yale Human Rights and Development Law Journal* (2010) 435, at 447–448.

focus was to establish intra-institutional cooperation and coordinate international and national actions without new bureaucratic structures; states and civil society organizations were informally consulted and not direct participants. The High-Level Task Force developed a Comprehensive Framework for Action, which was intended to be updated as a living document.

During that same year, the French President Nicholas Sarkozy, through the G8,[167] proposed the creation of the Global Partnership on Agriculture, Food Security and Nutrition. This effort continued in 2011 at the G20 Summit[168] in Cannes where Sarkozy put food security on the agenda, which led to the G20 Ministers of Agriculture agreeing to an 'Action Plan on Food Price Volatility and Agriculture' and launching the Agricultural Market Information System several months later.[169]

It was, however, the collective efforts of the G77 government leaders, food sovereignty movements, and key international civil servants from within the Rome-based institutions (FAO, IFAD, WFP) that radically reformed the UN Committee on World Food Security (CFS). They pulled the CFS out of irrelevance and obscurity and established it as the most influential intergovernmental policy space on food security to come immediately out of the crisis.

The G77 made the first move and struck a direct blow against the G8/G20 initiatives that left power in the hands of a self-selecting club of states (and granted significant credence to the private sector). The G77 was able to shift global political energy to the CFS. What helped the G77's cause was that the FAO was 'reform ready' before the crisis. The FAO had reached a low point in political relevance and was already in the process of internal reflection and governance reform when the crisis hit.[170]

The G77 wanted ultimate authority to rest with the CFS because it was a forum where it exercised significant formal power, since each state had one vote. The normative argument that won the day was that the CFS was the most legitimate international institution because it was globally representative; at the time, it comprised 123 members, and its membership was (and remains) open to all Member States of the FAO, IFAD, or the WFP and any Member State of the United Nations.[171] The

[167] The G8 is a coalition of national government leaders of the eight largest economies. Its members include Canada, France, Germany, Italy, Japan, Russia, the UK, the United States, and the EU.

[168] The G20 is a forum for world leaders, finance ministers, and national bankers from the world's largest economies who meet regularly. Its members include Argentina, Australia, Brazil, Canada, China, France, Germany, India, Indonesia, Italy, Japan, Mexico, Russia, Saudi Arabia, South Africa, South Korea, Turkey, the UK, the United States, and the EU.

[169] G20, 'Ministerial Declaration—Action Plan on Food Price Volatility and Agriculture', http://www.amis-outlook.org/fileadmin/user_upload/amis/docs/2011-agriculture-plan-en.pdf (last accessed 17 January 2024).

[170] Brem-Wilson, 'Towards Food Sovereignty: Interrogating Peasant Voice in the United Nations Committee on World Food Security', 42 *Journal of Peasant Studies* (2015) 73, at 79.

[171] Valente and Franco (n. 166) 448.

CFS reports to the FAO (which hosts its offices) and to ECOSOC. It receives UN funding in equal parts from the FAO, IFAD, and the WFP.[172]

The CFS was originally created during the 1974 crisis but had never gained any political support. The reforms of 2009 changed that.[173] While the final report that reformed CFS references the UN Comprehensive Framework of Action (para. 6(iii)) and the G8/G20 Global Partnership on Agriculture, Food Security and Nutrition (para. 2), the final vision expands upon (and manoeuvres through) both by stating:

> The reformed CFS as a central component of the evolving Global Partnership for Agriculture, Food Security and Nutrition will constitute *the* foremost inclusive international and intergovernmental platform for a broad range of committed stakeholders to work together in a coordinated manner and in support of country-led processes towards the elimination of hunger and ensuring food security and nutrition for all human beings.[174]

Placing a definite article in front of the CFS was a conscious and contentious political move. As one negotiator from a G20 country explained to Duncan:

> The negotiations between 'the' and 'a'—the foremost' or 'a foremost'—was huge and [some countries] couldn't accept 'the', never. Perhaps they are now saying 'the' just in their speech, but we have moved beyond that because what other platforms are there? There is no alternative unless we work with the institutions we have.[175]

Rich countries lost some ground and had to decide whether to divest from the CFS or remain active. They remained invested in the CFS process because they believed that they could not walk away from global political discussions on food security due to outstanding questions of global and local instability. National leaders in these countries also thought it would be more tactical to influence the progression (or slow things down) at the CFS, while at the same time buttressing initiatives like the World Bank Global Agriculture and Food Security Programme and G20 Agricultural Market Information System.[176]

The reformed CFS had significant doctrinal effects. It re-energized the right to food and further ensured that the right to food was under the jurisdiction of the

[172] Committee on World Food Security, https://www.fao.org/cfs/about-cfs/funding/en/ (last visited 17 January 2024).

[173] CFS, 'Reform of the Committee on World Food Security', 2009/2 Rev.2, 14, 15, and 17 October 2009, http://www.fao.org/3/a-k7197e.pdf (last visited 17 January 2024).

[174] Ibid. para. 4 (emphasis added).

[175] Quoted in Duncan (n. 166) 86.

[176] Ibid. 104–105.

Rome-based food institutions (FAO, IFAD, WFP) and not in the Geneva-based human rights institutions. The last sentence of the vision statement reads:

> The CFS will strive for a world free from hunger where countries implement the voluntary guidelines for the progressive realization of the right to adequate food in the context of national food security.[177]

This evocation of the right to food had two institutional effects. First, it authorized the CFS to spend resources on supporting and advising countries who chose to adopt the 'Voluntary Guidelines for the Right to Food'—this created an incentive for countries to adopt the guidelines since it would grant them access to governance and knowledge-based resources.[178] Second, the CFS redesigned its internal governance structures along the right-to-food principles of participation, transparency, and accountability. CSOs, and more specifically social movements, were granted an unprecedented voice within the new CFS.

The inclusion and definition of the right to food in these terms was a direct result of the food sovereignty's success in its ongoing efforts to reform the FAO. While at first La Vía Campesina was active at FAO conferences on the sidelines, it later shifted its position and used the FAO as a place to influence national government officials.

One criticism against the food sovereignty movements is that as their political agenda has progressed, their definition of sovereignty has become more ambiguous.[179] At first, the movements were very state-centric and articulated food sovereignty as the right of 'nations'.[180] By the 2007 Nyéléni Declaration, however, the focus was on 'peoples', which is a political concept that opens up (or reframes) the question of who is sovereign.[181] This ambiguity, however, has been a strength in how it has reflected the movements' constantly changing dynamics and tactics.[182] It has also allowed the movements to hold governments accountable while also challenging their authority if need be. The open definition allows for each member of the movements to determine their own relationship with different governmental authorities. What does complicate matters is that it also allows the movements themselves to be a space of competing, diverse, and altering sovereignties.[183]

[177] CFS, 'Reform of the Committee on World Food Security' (n. 173).

[178] Ibid. para. 5(iii).

[179] Bernstein, 'Food Sovereignty Via the "Peasant Way": A Sceptical View', 41 *Journal of Peasant Studies* (2014) 1031; Edelman, 'Food Sovereignty: Forgotten Genealogies and Future Regulatory Challenges', 41 *Journal of Peasant Studies* (2014) 959; Hospes, 'Food Sovereignty: The Debate, the Deadlock, and a Suggested Detour', 31 *Agriculture and Human Values* (2014) 119.

[180] La Vía Campesina, 'The Right to Produce' (n. 126).

[181] Edelman (n. 179) 967.

[182] Patel (n. 130).

[183] Schiavoni, 'Competing Sovereignties, Contested Processes: Insights from the Venezuelan Food Sovereignty Experiment', 12 *Globalizations* (2015) 466; Whyte (n. 154).

Nevertheless, this ambiguity allowed the movements to have a direct relationship with international institutions. By laying claim to sovereign power, these broad-based social movements not only held their respective governments accountable but also buttressed their position in dealing with international institutions. Starting in 2002, the food sovereignty movements, through the IPC, had actively engaged with the FAO Secretariat in an effort to transform internal FAO governance and grant peasants access to new sources of influence, knowledge, and resources.

Even though the relationship between the IPC and the FAO ebbed and flowed over the years, the IPC ultimately established itself with FAO civil servants and delegates as a highly credible and resourceful actor. As a result, in those years they developed relationships and friendships with people at the FAO.[184]

When the crisis hit, national leaders and global policymakers were caught off guard, while the food sovereignty movements were at a moment of strong solidarity and established ideas with the Nyéléni Declaration in hand. The series of events begins with the G77 creating the political opportunity. Then, with the sturdy expansion of food-sovereignty solidarity, people from CSOs were able to create successful alliances with key FAO civil servants built around personal friendships and articulated through the right to food. What solidified the food sovereignty movements' success were decisions made by key FAO delegates. All this gave credence to the world leaders who finally agreed to radically reform the CFA. This led to a coalescing and institutionalization of interests that created the current political reality.

In 2009, the CFS Bureau was tasked with commencing the reform process.[185] Many who were part of the process credit the Bureau chair at the time, Maria del Carmen Squeff (Argentina), with the novel creation of a Contact Group which made ample room for CSO participation. Ambassador Squeff was personally committed to broad-based participation and ensured that CSOs, other intergovernmental institutions, and representatives from the private sector had substantive influence in the process. They all had more or less the same degree of access to the process as did Member States. The private sector was not very active, whereas the CSO representatives were key authors of the final reform plan that was approved en bloc by the plenary.[186] Since the IPC had seven years of goodwill amongst many people in the FAO, it was not surprising that its members were the CSOs invited to

[184] N. McKeon, *The United Nations and Civil Society: Legitimating Global Governance—Whose Voice?* (2009).

[185] The Bureau is the executive arm of the CFS responsible for its administration. It is made up of a chairperson and 12 members elected on a regional basis: two from Africa, Asia, Europe, Latin America and the Caribbean, the Near East, and one from both North America and the South-West Pacific.

[186] CFS, 'Reform of the Committee on World Food Security' (n. 173) para. 10. See also J. Brem-Wilson, *The Reformed Committee on World Food Security: A Briefing Paper for Civil Society* (2010); Duncan (n. 166) 91, 99.

be part of the reform process.[187] The reform process was further buttressed by the support of Ambassador Squeff's successor as chair, Noel De Luna (Philippines), and IPC members' continued efforts.[188] The result was a restructuring of the CFS that included unprecedented room and autonomy for CSOs through its Civil Society Mechanism and all non-state actors through its Advisory Group.

The Advisory Group aids the Bureau in advancing the objectives of the CFS and is the interface between stakeholders and governments. The Advisory Group is made up of representatives from five categories: UN bodies,[189] CSOs,[190] international agricultural research bodies,[191] international financial and trade institutions,[192] and private sector/philanthropic foundations.[193]

It is the Bureau's prerogative to allocate the existing number of seats assigned to each category of the Advisory Group. Currently, six seats are assigned to UN agencies and bodies, four to CSOs, one to international agricultural research institutions, one to international and regional financial institutions, and one each to private sector associations and philanthropic foundations.

Studies have described the CFS as a place which hosts a 'discursive turf war' which allows for political give-and-take and not ideological posturing.[194] The consensus is that the CFS is, so far, a unique space that allows people directly affected by the issues in question to have direct influence on global policy coordination. It is inclusive in the sense that it is the result of trying to recalibrate power in more equitable and inclusive terms and not simply a matter of token civil society participation; thus CSOs (and social movements) are granted more seats. It is effective because it is designed to 'facilitate' decision-making and is not intended to represent all organizations involved in food security.

What also makes the CFS unique is that the food sovereignty movements managed to carve out an autonomous space for themselves through the Civil Society Mechanism (CSM).[195] The CSM is an open organization with 'participating

[187] Brem-Wilson (n. 186); I. Gaarde, *Peasants Negotiating a Global Policy Space: La Vía Campesina in the Committee on World Food Security* (2017) 48–49.

[188] Duncan (n. 166) 100.

[189] Food and Agriculture Organisation (FAO), World Food Programme (WFP), International Fund for Agricultural Development (IFAD), Right-to-Food: Special Rapporteur on the right to food, Office of the High Commissioner for Human Rights, UN Standing Committee on Nutrition (SCN), World Health Organization (WHO).

[190] Confederación de Organizaciones de Productores Familiares del Mercosur (COPROFAM); International Women's Alliance (IWA); World Forum of Fish Workers and Fish Harvesters (WFF); Arab Network for Food Sovereignty; Reseau des Organisations Paysannes et de Producteurs de l'Afrique de l'Ouest (ROPPA; Plateforme Regionale des Organisations Paysannes d'Afrique Centrale (PROPAC); National Farmers Union Canada; La Vía Campesina; Coordinadora Latinomericana de Organizaciones Campesinas (CLOC); International Indian Treaty Council.

[191] CGIAR System Organization.

[192] World Bank.

[193] International Agri-Food Network and the Bill & Melinda Gates Foundation. The private sector has its PSM.

[194] Duncan (n. 166) 62.

[195] Participants in the mechanism changed the name to Civil Society and Indigenous Peoples Mechanism in 2021.

organizations' rather than formal 'members'.[196] Any organization that 'belongs to civil society and works on food security and nutrition can join and participate'.[197] To join, interested organizations simply contact the main CSM email address 'expressing their interest in actively joining the CSM through one or more of the working groups'.[198] The CSM then asks for additional information (e.g. website links, annual reports, etc.) to confirm that the organization works on food security and nutrition issues.

Various studies outline the internal functions of the CSM and detail the formal and practical matrix of power and decision-making.[199] Two of the most unique features and evidence of the food sovereignty movements' influence are that the CSM participants organize themselves and social movements are granted privileged representation over NGOs.[200] Thus, the CSM has been the place where social movements convene and directly engage with international institutional decision-making.

Since 2010, the private sector (represented by the International Agri-Food Network) has been more actively involved in the CFS and is lobbying hard to have a number of seats at least equal to CSOs.[201] This interest by the private sector reflects the growing influence and authority of the CFS. The CFS's main purpose is to act as a place to develop global policy and cohesion across international institutions and national governments. It derives its legitimacy in its ability to be accepted by all people, wealthy, poor, or otherwise, whose lives are acutely and directly affected by global food markets.

This increase in private sector involvement puts the food sovereignty movements in a delicate position. Members of the movement want to ensure that the CFS remains the principal site for global food security policymaking because they do not have the resources to influence policymaking spread across a number of international institutions. Also, the FAO, which houses the CFS, remains committed to CSOs. But if the food sovereignty movements do not make the right compromises, the private sector or philanthropic organizations (mainly the Bill and

[196] Civil Society Mechanism for the UN Committee on World Food Security, 'The CSM: What is the CSM?', https://www.csm4cfs.org/what-is-the-csm/ (last visited 17 January 2024).

[197] Ibid.

[198] Teresa Maisano, Programme and Communication Officer for the CSM Secretariat, confirmed by email to the author, 4 April 2018.

[199] Duncan (n. 166) 130–152; Gaarde (n. 187).

[200] Civil Society Mechanism for the UN Committee on World Food Security, 'Terms of Reference for CSO members of the CFS Advisory Group' (2016), http://www.csm4cfs.org/wp-content/uploads/2016/03/terms_of_reference_for_advisory_group_members.pdf (last visited 17 January 2024).

[201] CFS, 'CFS Advisory Group 2018–2019 Composition—Information Note', 6 February 2017, http://www.ipcinfo.org/fileadmin/user_upload/cfs/doclibrary/CFS_Bur_AG_2017_02_06_05_Advisory_Group_2018_2019_Info_note.pdf (last visited 17 January 2024); CFS, 'Evaluation of the Committee on World Food Security—Final Report', 14 April 2017, http://www.fao.org/fileadmin/templates/cfs/Docs1617/Evaluation/CFS_Evaluation_Final_Report__14_April_2017.pdf (last visited 17 January 2024); CFS, 'Implementation of the CFS Evaluation—Recommendation 4', 5 February 2018, http://www.fao.org/fileadmin/templates/cfs/Docs1718/Evaluation/05Feb/CFS_Evaluation_2018_02_05_04_Outcomes%E2%80%8C.FINAL.pdf (last visited 17 January 2024).

Melinda Gates Foundation) will withdraw from the institution, thereby destabilizing its legitimacy; and if CSOs cede too much power, they lose what institutional gains they made. As one La Vía Campesina member stated at the CSM Annual Forum in 2014, at the CFS, '[w]e get to know both our enemies and ourselves better from the engagement'.[202]

Meanwhile, national government leaders are trying to navigate amongst the different stakeholders. Ever since the alter-globalization protests of the 1990s and food riots of the 2000s, national leaders are acutely attuned to the fact that CSOs, especially the food sovereignty movements, can easily activate their network and confront politicians through mass demonstrations in the streets and sustained political campaigns.[203]

In sum, food sovereignty movements have succeeded in making the CFS a political space for debate and negotiation. As the CFS gains credibility through increased participation by private sector actors and philanthropic foundations, the food sovereignty movements have to ensure they maintain what gains they have made while at the same time reconfiguring themselves to ensure that they can still enact parts of their agenda through the CFS—all while the CFS's authority continues to be challenged by other fora and institutions like the G8/G20.

## 5. Looking Ahead

### A. Expanding the Juridical Imagination

La Vía Campesina and its allies have used food sovereignty as the ideological mesh to hold their movement together. They have then deployed the specific tool of the right to food to both broaden their alliance and coordinate their institutional intervention. Thus, the right to food has been key in building transnational solidarity.

Small-holder farmers, food and agricultural workers, pastoralists, fisherfolk, women, youth, and Indigenous peoples have also used the right to food to access autonomous, influential representation at the CSM that is not subservient to national governments, corporations, or NGOs. If one is measuring degrees of ongoing influence within the CFS, then La Vía Campesina is correct in its claim that its work at the CFS has so far been a victory.[204] It has wrangled the meaning of the

[202] Quoted in Gaarde (n. 187) 81.

[203] Brem-Wilson (n. 170) 81; McKeon (n. 132) 51–52.

[204] La Vía Campesina, 'The Committee on World Food Security (CFS): A New Space for the Food Policies of the World, Opportunities and Limitations', 2 November 2012, https://viacampesina.org/en/the-committee-on-world-food-security-cfs-a-new-space-for-the-food-policies-of-the-world-opportunities-and-limitations/ (last visited 17 January 2024). See also Lambek, 'The UN Committee on World Food Security's Break from the Agricultural Productivity Trap', 9 *Transnational Legal Theory* (2018) 415; Wills (n. 7) 94–150.

right to food in novel ways towards practices of communal discourse and popular control.

It is also clear that food sovereignty movements have used the right to food to build and access new international institutional spaces. Through the CFS, the movements have significantly influenced global governance structures and policy. The result is that the CFS is a unique space that can give the right to food meaning and power.[205] This means that the CFS can be a space that reinforces the argument that people's access to and control over adequate food is a political necessity and not a matter of charity or a method of exerting cruel pressure. But these sorts of spaces and the right to food are always the product of undulating matrices of power, authority, and legitimacy. That means that institutional and normative gains and losses are always temporary.

I will conclude by identifying which political challenges may undermine these institutional gains and what sort of legal theoretical agenda may help people in the movements advance their cause. I provide more intervening questions instead of a final summary or argument.

The food sovereignty movements have been successful in part because their understanding of social change is defined by their own ability to organize and not by a theoretical commitment to the right to food or by institutional legitimacy. This understanding includes within it an appreciation that legal and policy wins to any degree do not necessarily turn into the redistribution of resources and reconfigurations of power, as required by the food sovereignty movements' broader agenda.

The implications of the movements' institutional gains remain unclear. The CFS is strictly a normative space with no authority over financial resources; the CFS is not able to provide funds or personnel for implementing any of the global policies. This is left to institutions like the FAO, IFAD, WFP, and national governments. As Ibrahim Coulibaly, President of the Mali organization CNOP (National Coordination of Peasant Organizations/Coordination Nationale des organizations Paysannes), stated at the 37th Session of the Committee on World Food Security (October 2011) at a policy roundtable on food price volatility:

> Instead of responding to the causes of our poverty and of price volatility, we have seen whole catalogues of projects and programmes financed in the name of the agricultural sector, billions of dollars are mobilized every year, but the truth is that more than half of the peasant families in the majority of our countries do not have access to money to buy a plough, a couple of oxen, a cart, or a donkey.[206]

[205] Lambek, 'The Right to Food: Reflecting on the Past and Future Possibilities—Synthesis Paper', 2 *Canadian Food Studies/La Revue Canadienne Des Études Sur l'Alimentation* (2015) 68.

[206] Quoted in Duncan and Barling, 'Renewal Through Participation in Global Food Security Governance: Implementing the International Food Security and Nutrition Civil Society Mechanism to the Committee on World Food Security', 19 *International Journal of the Sociology of Agriculture and Food* (2012) 143, at 157.

If projects are implemented under CFS policies, that alone does not ensure that food producers have access to more resources. Moreover, even if the right to food as defined by the food sovereignty movements were to be accepted and enacted by every country, nothing would guarantee that this would help local producers. Instead, the realization of the right to food in any domestic context depends on the interplay of many social, political, and legal requirements, and its implementation relies on allying with powerful actors or on creating new alliances that reconfigure power. Thus, the process of domestically negotiating the right to food could actually reinforce the interests of the powerful.[207]

This is always the worry about using human rights as well as international law. While human rights provide a powerful platform to articulate one's claim in universal terms, it often curtails agendas aimed at radical reconfigurations of power. This has always been clear to La Vía Campesina, which has 'dealt with both the conceptual and strategic limitations of the human rights framework, in an attempt to keep intact the subversive potential of its rights-based claims'.[208]

Many (including myself) have been preoccupied with the institutionalization question.[209] When social movements take on or infiltrate institutions, the question arises of whether the movement can change the institution or whether the institution will respond to and neutralize the movements' claims. Or even more concerning, whether the institution will coopt the movements' own language against them. Not only can using international human rights restrain one's political agenda, but it also demands some degree of ceding authority to international law itself. The price you pay for using international law—or any law—is losing a bit of yourself to its authority.[210]

So far, however, the food sovereignty movements have deftly navigated these institutional spaces by claiming authority over the right to food. They have adequately overcome the tension of using rights and have defined the right to food to suit their purposes and not the other way around.[211] The institutionalization

[207] Hadiprayitno, 'Who Owns the Right to Food? Interlegality and Competing Interests in Agricultural Modernisation in Papua, Indonesia', 38 *Third World Quarterly* (2017) 97.

[208] Claeys, 'Vía Campesina's Struggle for the Right to Food Sovereignty: From Above or from Below?' in N. C. S. Lambek *et al.* (eds), *Rethinking Food Systems: Structural Challenges, New Strategies and the Law* (2014) 30.

[209] Bellinger and Fakhri, 'The Intersection Between Food Sovereignty and Law', 28 *Natural Resources & Environment* (2013) 45; Claeys (n. 4); A. A. Desmarais, P. Claeys, and A. Trauger (eds), *Public Policies for Food Sovereignty: Social Movements and the State* (2017); Gaarde (n. 187); N. C. S. Lambek *et al.* (eds), *Rethinking Food Systems: Structural Challenges, New Strategies and the Law* (2014). Indeed, this question is endemic to social-movement literature in works by Charles Tilly and Alain Touraine. See also B. Rajagopal, *International Law from Below: Development, Social Movements, and Third World Resistance* (2003).

[210] S. Pahuja, *Decolonising International Law: Development, Economic Growth and the Politics of Universality* (2011) 6.

[211] For other examples in other contexts, see S. Speed, *Rights in Rebellion: Indigenous Struggle and Human Rights in Chiapas* (2008); García-Del Moral, '*Feminicidio*: TWAIL in Action', 110 *AJIL Unbound* (2016) 31.

question will always remain live especially since the movements have and continue to devote much of their energy towards the UN Declaration on the Rights of Peasants.[212]

One of the goals of the food sovereignty movements is to reconfigure global institutions in a way that reduces the power of transnational agribusiness and enhances the power of people who directly make and procure food. This raises the political–economic question of pay-off that accompanies the institutionalization question—that is, does the right to food grant members of the food sovereignty movements access to resources and power? In that regard, the right to food remains untested.

The theoretical corollary to the institutionalization question is the old debate about the relationship between human rights and legal form. Much of human rights practice and theory focuses on the courts and imagines rights only as effective as enacted through the courts. Others try to unmoor human rights theory from law (usually imagined as legislation) as much as possible in an attempt to expand its political and social potential.[213] Taking my inspiration from Upendra Baxi,[214] I want instead to open up the juridical imagination and consider the food sovereignty movements' institutional manoeuvring as an opportunity to reframe the theoretical question. While I have situated the right to food in the specificities of food-making politics, I think this case helps sharpen broader issues. Usually, when human rights are primarily considered as an issue of justiciability, people take the legal form as given. When human rights are treated as something whose ethical and political potential is separate from law, law is interrogated but often in a way that has a narrow theoretical understanding of law.[215] The food sovereignty movements' experience highlights that you cannot avoid fighting over legal forms in these political struggles, that law is too powerful a terrain to ignore or cede. Law, for better or for worse, remains a common form of national and international institutional power to legitimate and implement ideas. The theoretical position that best matches the movements' struggle is not to treat law as natural or limiting but rather as something one is forced to use with some ambivalence and caution.

## B. Converting Institutional Gains into a New Legal Agenda

By observing the struggle of the food sovereignty movements, you can notice the tenuous relationship between the uses of the right to food and any concrete legal meaning and political power that can be derived from it through the work of the

212 Claeys, 'The Rise of New Rights for Peasants. From Reliance on NGO Intermediaries to Direct Representation', 9 *Transnational Legal Theory* (2018) 386.

213 Sen, 'Elements of a Theory of Human Rights', 32 *Philosophy & Public Affairs* (2004) 315.

214 Baxi, 'Amartya Sen and Human Rights', in U. Baxi, *Human Rights in a Posthuman World* (2009) 30.

215 Ibid.

CFS.[216] These movements have made significant institutional gains but what remains unclear is what legal forms would best serve their particular agenda. Can the right to food be used as part of what Honor Brabazon describes as a 'radical legal praxis'?[217] More specifically: can legal arguments be mounted through the right to food to justify something like an occupation of a certain space, hunting or gathering practices not sanctioned by the state, or the disruption or takeover of certain food-production facilities? More constructively: can the right to food underwrite new social relations and protect spaces that maintain an indeterminate relationship to the state? The difficulty is not the marshalling of doctrine and making the legal argument. The hard work is in ensuring that legal tactics always serve the long-term strategy of creating more equitable socio-economic relations amongst beings within the biosphere. I suggest that these are questions that could be explored as the food sovereignty movements continue their struggle.

Most legal arguments take for granted that law is a 'form of social regulation between abstract, formally equal subjects'.[218] The food sovereignty movements' struggle through the right to food can be interpreted in a way that allows us to start taking stock of the plurality of ways in which individuals and communities relate to territory.[219] This would lead to reimagining the right to food's legal form to include the multitude of ways that people socially and politically organize themselves around food along with their concomitant notions of authority and legitimacy—all grounded in the everyday practices around procuring and making food.

With this theoretical sensibility in mind, I want to turn to the food sovereignty movements' institutional gains again, before ending on a political point. Because of the CFS, the right to food grants the food sovereignty movements access to the FAO, IFAD, and (to a lesser degree) the WFP. The question, then, is whether the food sovereignty movement can gain access to institutional resources—prestige, knowledge, and capital—in a way that best serves local producers. One way that FAO (and IFAD) resources have been helpful to people is by reducing the cost of production, either through the funding of local infrastructure projects, skills training, or technical assistance. At the core of all these things is a particular type of knowledge, which thus far has been mostly committed to industrial practices and modernization theories.

[216] My thanks to Nehal Bhuta for pressing me on this point.

[217] Brabazon, 'Occupying Legality: The Subversive Use of Law in Latin American Occupation Movements', 36 *Bulletin of Latin American Research* (2017) 21. See also White and Perelman (n. 7).

[218] Knox, 'Valuing Race? Stretched Marxism and the Logic of Imperialism', 4/1 *London Review of International Law* (2016) 81, at 88. Knox draws from Pashukanis, 'The General Theory of Law and Marxism', in P. Beirne and R. Sharlet (eds), *Pashukanis, Selected Writings on Marxism and Law* (1980).

[219] Rolnik and Brant, 'UN Special Procedures System is "Designed to Be Ineffective"', 11 *SUR—International Journal on Human Rights* (2014) 81, at 83. Rolnick raised this in the context of the right to adequate housing.

The food sovereignty movements have been committed to changing what type of knowledge is supported.[220] The movements are fighting for the experiential knowledge of food producers to be granted priority in all projects and practices. More broadly, they have turned to agroecology which includes the experiences of humans and their relationship with all the parts of the biosphere. Many Indigenous peoples and others would include their relationship to their ancestors or the spirit world as central to this type of knowledge.[221]

Olivier De Schutter, in his capacity as Special Rapporteur to the Right to Food, produced a very convincing report about why agroecology meets the right to food's demands. This, along with similar statements by his successor, Hilal Ever, strengthens the connection between the right to food and food sovereignty.[222] The Special Rapporteur's report provides a succinct description of agroecology:

> As a set of agricultural practices, agroecology seeks ways to enhance agricultural systems by mimicking natural processes. ... The core principles of agroecology include recycling nutrients and energy on the farm, rather than introducing external inputs; integrating crops and livestock; diversifying species and genetic resources in agroecosystems over time and space; and focusing on interactions and productivity across the agricultural system, rather than focusing on individual species. Agroecology is highly knowledge-intensive, based on techniques that are not delivered top-down but developed on the basis of farmers' knowledge and experimentation.[223]

The IPC, in its partnership with the FAO, tried to instil agroecology as a central concept.[224] It has not really gained significant traction—yet. The FAO maintains an Agroecology Knowledge Hub and in 2018 hosted the Second International Symposium on Agroecology, suggesting that some key allies from within and outwith the FAO remain committed to agroecology.[225]

[220] M. P. Pimbert (ed.), *Food Sovereignty, Agroecology and Biocultural Diversity: Constructing and Contesting Knowledge* (2018); Declaration of Güira de Melena: First Global Encounter of La Vía Campesina Agroecology Schools and Formation Processes, 31 May 2018, https://viacampesina.org/en/declaration-of-guira-de-melena-first-global-encounter-of-la-via-campesina-agroecology-schools-and-formation-processes/ (last visited 17 January 2024).

[221] Whyte (n. 154).

[222] O. De Schutter, 'Report on Agroecology and the Right to Food', UN GA A/HRC/16/49, 17 December 2010, https://www2.ohchr.org/english/issues/food/docs/a-hrc-16-49.pdf (last visited 17 January 2024); N. Ahmed, 'UN: Only Small Farmers and Agroecology Can Feed the World', 23 September 2014, https://www.tni.org/en/article/un-only-small-farmers-and-agroecology-can-feed-the-world (last visited 17 January 2024).

[223] De Schutter (n. 222).

[224] McKeon (n. 184) 77–82.

[225] FAO, Agroecology Knowledge Hub, http://www.fao.org/agroecology/en/ (last visited 17 January 2024); FAO, Second International Symposium on Agroecology, 3–5 April 2018, http://www.fao.org/about/meetings/second-international-agroecology-symposium/en/ (last visited 17 January 2024).

If the food sovereignty movements have turned to agroecology as the principal form of knowledge and are looking for opportunities to develop and disseminate this knowledge, what is then the role for the right to food? Can it be used to marshal resources and grant those most affected direct access to those resources? Will agroecology be coopted by those who already hold a lot of power? This is a tactical question that can only be answered by members of the movements. It could be that the right to food's strength will remain a matter of global governance and has nothing else to offer the movements.

The right to food provides states with the legal authority to act. Thus, international institutions and national governments may turn to the CFS as a source of authority to implement new projects. One common way to evoke the right to food's legality is to call for international trade law to submit to the right to food; this approach imagines the right to food in constitutional terms.[226] In fact, a number of countries have actually enacted food sovereignty or the right to food in their constitutions. But if we take our cues from agroecology, the form of legal action will be site-specific, contextual, and diverse. That is to say, we should not claim to know what the right to food's legal form would be in an agroecological future because we have only just begun to explore the legal implications of the agroecological present.[227]

For example, food sovereignty movements are significantly challenging understandings of property; thus, the right to food may very well have to take on fundamental questions and competing understandings of property.[228] If family farms are a central concern, then one has to first understand how law constructs the very notion of what constitutes a family or a household as an economic entity.[229] What we do know is that if agroecology is explicitly a challenge to existing systems of knowledge and an attempt to delegitimize powerful people's tacit assumptions and ensuing policies, then it will bring with it a 'new legal common sense'.[230] What the food sovereignty movements also teach us is that the meaning and internal

[226] Gonzalez, 'International Economic Law and the Right to Food', in N. C. S. Lambek *et al.* (eds), *Rethinking Food Systems* (2014) 165; Narula, 'The Right to Food: Holding Global Actors Accountable Under International Law', 44 *Columbia Journal of Transnational Law* (2005) 691.

[227] For some of the early works in this area, see Gonzalez, 'Climate Change, Food Security, and Agrobiodiversity: Toward a Just, Resilient, and Sustainable Food System', 22 *Fordham Environmental Law Review* (2011) 493; J. W. Head, *International Law and Agroecological Husbandry: Building Legal Foundations for a New Agriculture* (2016); Kameri-Mbote and Cullet, 'Agro-Biodiversity and International Law—a Conceptual Framework', 11 *Journal of Environmental Law* (1999) 257; M. Monteduro *et al.* (eds), *Law and Agroecology: A Transdisciplinary Dialogue* (2015).

[228] Kloppenburg, 'Re-Purposing the Master's Tools: The Open Source Seed Initiative and the Struggle for Seed Sovereignty', 41 *Journal of Peasant Studies* (2014) 1225; Timmermann and Robaey, 'Agrobiodiversity Under Different Property Regimes', 29 *Journal of Agricultural and Environmental Ethics* (2016) 285.

[229] Corcodel, 'The Market and the Family, the Sacred and the Secular in Modern Comparative Law', 7 *Jindal Global Law Review* (2016) 9; Rittich, 'Black Sites: Locating the Family and Family Law in Development', 58 *American Journal of Comparative Law* (2010) 1023.

[230] B. de S. Santos, *Toward a New Legal Common Sense: Law, Globalization, and Emancipation* (2nd ed., 2002).

cohesion of the right to food is not the principal issue. The right to food's progressive power is determined by how well it can be used to enable broad-based popular solidarity built upon principles of equality.

The right to food has created an opportunity for the food sovereignty movements and the FAO to reimagine food markets for the future. The food sovereignty movements have only started articulating their position with regard to markets through the CSM and have not offered new ideas in relation to transnational trade.[231] In the history of the trade regime, they have, at times, privileged freer trade and, at other times, market stability. The unchartered future is a food regime that treats food security as a principal concern, market stability as a (closely linked) secondary matter, and freer trade as tertiary.

The works of James Boyd Orr and B. R. Sen are as good a starting point as any. Also, the 1967 International Wheat Arrangement (aka International Grains Arrangement) is the closest thing to a historical 'proof of concept'.[232] What was remarkable about this treaty was that it was made up of a Wheat Trade Convention, which was a regular ICA for its time that included mechanisms of supply control that were combined with the first-ever Food Aid Convention. This was a rare treaty that prioritized both market stability and food security. Because of the Food Aid Convention, many considered this treaty as a benefit for developing countries since it addressed trade issues related to distinguishing food aid from dumping.[233]

What the history of the FAO tells us is that multilateral trade law and policy do not have to be left to the WTO. In fact, confidence in the WTO, especially regarding agriculture, is at an all-time low from multiple perspectives. Recent bilateral and regional agreements have been narrow in scope and primarily focused on liberalizing agricultural trade amongst a certain number of countries. Elsewhere, I have argued that the WTO Agreement on Agriculture allows governments to negotiate a novel multilateral trade agreement in agriculture under the auspices of any institution.[234] The institutional expression of these ideas and interests might be enacted through the FAO or UNCTAD. It may involve reviving and redesigning ICAs so that they directly address food security instead of their historical focus on market stabilization.

The knowledge necessary to support all of this would be thinking through how to stabilize markets—local and international—so that producers can rationally

[231] CSM, 'Connecting Smallholders to Markets', 29 February 2016, http://www.csm4cfs.org/working-groups/connecting-smallholders-to-markets/ and at https://viacampesina.org/en/connecting-smallholders-to-markets/ (last visited 17 January 2024). See also Burnett and Murphy, 'What Place for International Trade in Food Sovereignty?', 41 *Journal of Peasant Studies* (2014) 1065; Paddock and Smith, 'What Role for Trade in Food Sovereignty? Insights from a Small Island Archipelago', 45 *Journal of Peasant Studies* (2018) 368.

[232] O'Connor, 'Going Against the Grain: The Regulation of the International Wheat Trade from 1933 to the 1980 Soviet Grain Embargo', 5 *Boston College International and Comparative Law Review* (1982) 225.

[233] M. Davies and R. Woodward, *International Organizations: A Companion* (2014) 376.

[234] Fakhri (n. 23).

plan their growing, herding, and hunting, while also adapting to ongoing ecological changes. If production costs are reduced, and people are protected from price shocks, then producers' lives could be supported, if not improved. This type of stability would also be defined by how much it allows people to control how and what they eat.

The implementation of this type of plan requires a significant amount of energy devoted to radically reforming existing institutions and maybe even devising new ones. This energy will have to come from the momentum and victories of the food sovereignty movements. As the movements grow and confront more complex issues, they will need more alliances, friendships, and interface dialogue to enact their ambitions. For the jurist who wants to serve the cunning citizens of the food sovereignty movements, the task ahead may appear daunting, and many questions remain unanswered. But with every day, the choices that lie ahead at the intersection of institutional reconstruction and mass mobilization are becoming clearer.

# 6

# Self-Defence against Non-State Actors and the Myth of the Innocent State

*Eliav Lieblich**

## 1. Introduction

Few recent debates on the international governance of the use of force have been more heated than the argument concerning the existence of, and conditions for, the right of self-defence against non-state actors under international law.[1] As the predominant narrative goes, before the 9/11 attacks, it was clear, at least in theory, that self-defence under international law is strictly limited to inter-state relations. That a state could lawfully invoke self-defence to justify *transnational* strikes against non-state actors was a contradiction in terms. Post 9/11, the story continues, the demonstration of the destructive potential of non-state actors changed the realities of international life. Since then, transnational strikes against non-state actors have become a non-event in international relations.[2]

This narrative, although contested by some, is relatively common.[3] What remains controversial, however, is whether the reality on the ground has also crystalized as an international legal norm which permits such actions. Most states have not expressed a clear stance on this issue, and many others have simply

* This research was supported by the Israel Science Foundation (grant No. 1787/17). I would like to thank Asaf Birger, Widad Elias, Shani Rozenzweig, and Jasmin Wennersbusch for their fantastic research assistance, and Nehal Bhuta, Matthias Goldmann, Claus Kreß, and Adam Shinar for their comments.

[1] For a comprehensive treatment of the debate, see A. Peters and C. Marxsen (eds), *Self-Defence against Non-State Actors: Impulses from the Max Planck Trialogues on the Law of Peace and War* (2017).

[2] Kammerhofer, 'Introduction: The Future of Restrictivist Scholarship on the Use of Force', 29 *Leiden Journal of International Law* (2016) 13, at 13; for a helpful survey of the debate and practice, see C. Gray, *International Law and the Use of Force* (4th ed., 2018) 200–226; see also Kreß, 'Major-Post Westphalian Shifts and Some Important Neo-Westphalian Hesitations in the State Practice on the International Law on the Use of Force', 1 *Journal of the Use of Force and International Law* (2014) 11, at 40–51; see also Reinold, 'State Weakness, Irregular Warfare, and the Right to Self-Defence Post 9/11', 105 *American Journal of International Law* (2011) 244.

[3] Some doubt whether before 9/11 the law on self-defence against non-state actors was as clear as the predominant narrative implies and point out that in the preceding decades there was indeed a contrary position in state practice. See Tams, 'Embracing the Uncertainty of Old: Armed Attacks by Non-State Actor Prior to 9/11', in Peters and Marxsen (n. 1) 53. This view is presented in detail, even before 9/11, in C. Kreß, *Gewaltverbot und Selbstverteidigungsrecht nach der Satzung der Vereinten Nationen in Fällen staatlicher Verwicklung in Gewaltakte Privater* (1995).

Eliav Lieblich, *Self-Defence against Non-State Actors and the Myth of the Innocent State*. In: *Global Rights?* First Edition.
Edited by: Nehal Bhuta and Rodrigo Vallejo, Oxford University Press. 
DOI: 10.1093/oso/9780198940166.003.0006

remained silent. This might be a product of narrow political interests, but can also imply genuine confusion, if not tacit acceptance. Indeed, if there is any consensus on the law on self-defence against non-state actors, it is that the law is nowadays 'in flux'.[4] In such times, it is especially important to think normatively, and to draw a clearer picture of what law *should* be,[5] or—at least—to outline properly what is at stake.

At the heart of the debate on transnational defence lies the position—advanced by the United States and several other (primarily Western) countries—that transnational self-defence is, and should be, lawful when the territorial state is *unwilling or unable* to prevent non-state actors' attacks from its territory.[6] In the last few years, vast literature has addressed this question, and in particular, whether transnational self-defence of this form or the other is part of the *lex lata*.[7] This chapter does not offer another account of *this* particular question. Rather, it inquires into the relevant normative considerations that should inform a standard for self-defence against non-state actors, in particular when no state is at fault for the attacks. Chiefly, it aims to challenge one normative-legal objection to the existence of such right: that when a state is not at fault for an attack by a non-state actor, self-defence would not be permissible in any case, because such a response would entail holding the state accountable for something it did not do.

Although not usually framed this way, the problem of transnational self-defence can be phrased as one that arises in the 'vanishing point' of global governance. This is because this problem becomes acute precisely when conventional mechanisms of global governance are unavailable: collective security mechanisms break down, and bilateral relations are insufficient to resolve the issue. What is left, in such situations, are bare 'diagonal' relations between states and groups of individuals operating beyond their borders, while the inter-state relationship becomes almost incidental. Transnational defence is therefore a radical, residual form of

[4] See Peters, 'The Turkish Operation in Afrin (Syria) and the Silence of the Lambs', EJIL Talk, 30 January 2018, https://www.ejiltalk.org/the-turkish-operation-in-afrin-syria-and-the-silence-of-the-lambs (last visited 2 February 2024); Haque, 'The Use of Force Against Non-State Actors: All Over the Map', 8 *Journal on the Use of Force and International Law* (2021) 278; Modirzadeh and Arrocha Olabuenaga, 'A Conversation Between Pablo Arrocha Olabuenaga and Naz Khatoon Modirzadeh on the Origins, Objectives, and Context of the 24 February 2021 "Arria-Formula" Meeting Convened by Mexico', 8 *Journal on the Use of Force and International Law* (2021) 291.

[5] See Marxsen, 'A Note on Indeterminacy of the Law on Self-Defence Against Non-State Actors', in Peters and Marxsen (n. 1) 79, at 79–80 (emphasizing that the question cannot be resolved by doctrine alone, and that a choice between competing values has to be made).

[6] Security Council, Letter dated 23 September 2014 from the Permanent Representative of the United States of America to the United Nations addressed to the Secretary-General, UN Doc. S/2014/695, 23 September 2014.

[7] See e.g. Starski, 'Right to Self-Defence, Attribution and the Non-State Actor: Birth of the "Unable or Unwilling" Standard?', 75 *Heidelberg Journal of International Law* (2015) 455; T. Christakis (ed.), 'International Law and Practice, Symposium on the Fight against ISIL and International Law', 29 *Leiden Journal of International Law* (2016) 737; Brunée and Toope, 'Self-Defence against Non-State Actors: Are Powerful States Willing but Unable to Change International Law?', 67 *International & Comparative Law Quarterly* (2018) 263.

governance, in which public authority is both challenged and exercised violently across state borders.

What principles should apply to dilemmas beyond this vanishing point? In a different but comparable context, Anne Peters coined the term 'compensatory constitutionalism' to describe the resort to residual basic principles to solve 'de-territorialized problems' that emanate from globalization and state weakness.[8] The approach suggested in this chapter correlates with this strand of thought by seeking to uncover the key interests and rights—both of states and of individuals—that are implicated in the problem of transnational self-defence; and thereafter, by suggesting that the conflicts between them should be resolved by a substantive ordering of rights. This ordering can be seen, in turn, as a residual form of transnational governance, in which individual human rights should override the abstract rights of legal entities.

Indeed, the debate on self-defence against non-state actors under international law has been framed in recent literature as one between restrictivist and expansionist approaches to the international law on the use of force: the former requiring that attacks be *attributable* to states as a precondition for a right to respond in self-defence, while the latter forego such a requirement.[9] Here, I want to recast and theorize the debate as one involving a clash between differing approaches to the basic justification for inflicting harm in self-defence: namely, between that requiring *fault* as a precondition for self-defence—and that which places the emphasis on the victim's *autonomy*—rather than on the perpertrator's *mens rea*—as justifying a forcible response. The intuitions about this question, I argue, have been respectively transposed to the inter-state level by restrictivists and expansionists.

It should be stressed that I do not seek to resolve here the general problem of fault versus autonomy as the constitutive justifications for self-defence between individuals. This issue has been, and likely to remain, very controversial in law and ethics. Rather, this chapter makes a narrower claim, yet one that has significant implications for the global governance of war: that when applied to situations in which on the one hand, the sovereign rights of 'innocent' states would be infringed by a forcible response, and on the other, the basic rights of individuals are jeopardized by an attack by a non-state actor, the mere lack of state fault carries limited normative weight in ascertaining whether there is a just cause for self-defence. This is important, since of all the existing objections to transnational self-defence, the argument on fault is the one that, if accepted, poses an insurmountable barrier

[8] Peters, 'Compensatory Constitutionalism: The Function and Potential of Fundamental International Norms and Structures', 19 *Leiden Journal of International Law* (2006) 580, at 583–584.

[9] See Van Steenberghe, 'The Law of Self-Defence and the New Argumentative Landscape on the Expansionists Side', 29 *Leiden Journal of International Law* (2016) 43; De Hoogh, 'Restrictivist Reasoning on the *Ratione Personae* Dimension of Armed Attacks in the Post 9/11 World', 29 *Leiden Journal of International Law* (2016) 19.

to transnational self-defence against attacks where attribution—or at least a lesser form of responsibility—is lacking.

The underlying argument here is that rather than giving much weight to the question of fault, the problem of self-defence against non-state actors should be addressed by conceiving a proper ordering of conflicting rights, in accordance with their nature and importance. In terms of the nature of rights, it seems that in cases of a clash between abstract rights of states *qua* legal entities (or fictions) and the most basic rights of real-life people, the rights of the latter should prevail. In other words, in such cases, the logic that requires state fault as a precondition for self-defence should be overridden by the logic of individual autonomy. Importantly, this in no way implies that state fault is meaningless in the international law on self-defence. Rather, the argument here offers theoretical support for the view that fault should play a role chiefly in assessing the necessity and proportionality of the response, but not in the question of whether a right to self-defence exists.[10]

Fundamentally, a key problem with the approach that requires state fault as a precondition for self-defence, is that it attributes deontic (overriding) importance to state sovereignty and territory. In effect, this view constructs the problem of self-defence against non-state actors as a crude form of an 'innocent threat' dilemma: the state's territory is being used by the non-state actor—against its will—to stage attacks against other states; but a response against the non-state actor will inevitably violate the innocent state's territory. Therefore, the argument goes, there are overriding grounds to refrain from a response in such cases. As argued here, however, this reasoning harks back, in its essence, to an old anthropomorphism in international law, in which the state was equated to an autonomous individual, and its territory to something akin to a physical body. Indeed, this thought allows assigning great harm to any forcible action on a state's territory. However, it is doubtful whether this particular view can hold, considering recent advances in the ethics of war. Indeed, most contemporary approaches to just war theory generally reject this view. On these *revisionist* views, a state is in essence an organized group of individuals, and therefore, the moral rights of states cannot exceed the aggregate of the moral rights of its individuals. Simply put, individuals, coming together as a state, cannot create an entity that enjoys transcendental rights that they do not possess as individuals. If this is true, the territory of the state cannot be put on the same plane as the physical bodies of individuals harmed by the non-state actor's attack. Rather, the territory of the state is simply an *object*, in relation to which the state *qua* collective enjoys some rights.

This is not to say that the legal rights assigned to faultless states by international law are not important or are not infringed upon when forcible response is undertaken on their territories. To understand the proper ordering between the clashing

[10] See e.g. Akande and Liefländer, 'Clarifying Necessity, Imminence and Proportionality in the Law of Self-Defence', 107 *American Journal of International Law* (2013) 564.

rights in such situations, I employ the 'reductive individualist' method of thinking about questions of just war.[11] This thought experiment reveals that in contrast to the anthropomorphic view of the state, the proper (yet imperfect) analogue to situations in which a non-state actor launches a transnational attack is when someone acts to harm others from within another's property. As rights to 'things' seem generally secondary to the right to life, in such scenarios the former should be overridden, regardless of fault or its absence.

Before moving on, two caveats. First, many objections to transnational self-defence derive from understandable concerns that such doctrines might be abused by powerful states, and otherwise jeopardize the international order.[12] There are, indeed, situations in which one should be especially careful. In particular, the problem of abuse arises when self-defence against non-state actors is conducted preventively, against ill-defined threats and actors, under an *assumption* that a state is unable to prevent such attacks. In the same vein, a problem arises when an attack is *over*, and it is unclear whether a response was at all necessary or was rather a prohibited act of reprisal.[13] The latter problem is particularly concerning, since in most cases, attacks by non-state actors are not continuous like traditional attacks by regular armed forces. The majority of responses, accordingly, would be in the grey area between anticipatory self-defence and reprisals. Moreover, *jus in bello* concerns permeate these scenarios, especially when attacks are conducted in ambiguous situations, in which the substantive, spatial, and temporal boundaries of the alleged armed conflict are unclear; and, as in most contemporary cases, the non-state actor operates in proximity to protected civilians.[14]

The purpose here, however, is not so much to advocate for a broad legal right to self-defence against non-state actors, but rather to test the idea of state fault as a determinative factor in the debate. For the sake of clarity, it is possible to conceive, for the purpose of the analysis here, a 'clean' case in which: (i) a transnational attack by an organized armed non-state actor is taking place and is ongoing; (ii) this attack actually harms individuals (soldiers or civilians) in the attacked state; (iii)

[11] Reductive individualism applies to states the same moral standards that would apply in real life to large groups of people. Since large groups of people have the same moral rights and obligations as individuals, the method of inquiry involves putting forward scenarios involving individuals, and then applying to them to states *qua* collectives (*not* to states *qua* individuals themselves). See McMahan, 'War as Self-Defence', 18 *Ethics and International Affairs* (2004) 75, at 75.

[12] See Moorehead, 'Brazil's Robust Defense of the Legal Prohibition on the Use of Force and Self-Defence', Just Security, 20 April 2018, https://www.justsecurity.org/55126/brazils-robust-defense-legal-prohibition-force/ (last visited 2 February 2024); see O'Connell, 'Dangerous Departures', 107 *American Journal of International Law* (2013) 380, at 384–385; Tzouvala, 'TWAIL and "Unwilling or Unable" Doctrine: Continuities and Ruptures', 109 *American Journal of International Law Unbound* (2015) 266, at 267–268; Lorca, 'Rules for the Global "War on Terror": Implying Consent and Presuming Conditions for Intervention', 45 *New York University Journal of International Law and Politics* (2012) 1.

[13] On this problem in general, see Kretzmer, 'The Inherent Right to Self-Defence and Proportionality in *Jus ad Bellum*', 24 *European Journal of International Law* (2013) 235, at 253–258.

[14] See e.g. Rona and Wala, 'No Thank You to a Radical Rewrite of the *Jus ad Bellum*', 107 *American Journal of International Law* (2013) 386.

the territorial state is unable to stop the attack, either because it admits so or since it is evident from the circumstances; (iv) a forcible response can be proportionate both in the *ad bellum* and *in bello* levels; and (v) the territorial state does not consent to a response, or there is no time to seek consent before an initial response, since lives will be lost in the time spent. This is the paradigmatic case that informs our discussion.

Second, while this approach might result in an expansive view of self-defence against non-state actors in some cases—i.e. when the territorial state's rights clash with individual rights in the defending state—the theoretical approach offered here might also support limitations on the right to self-defence in opposite cases: for instance, when the non-state actor's attack does not implicate individual rights, but only state rights, and on the other hand, a forcible response will harm innocent individuals in the territorial state.[15] While the latter option will not be explored extensively in this chapter, it is important to keep in mind.

The argument proceeds as follows. Section 1 introduces the basic legal problem and outlines the textual uncertainty in the UN Charter that gives rise to doubts on the existence and conditions of the right to self-defence against non-state actors under international law. Section 2 surveys the doctrinal debate on the question. Section 3 focuses on the *Unwilling or Unable* standard and analyses the positions of leading scholars on this test, with special emphasis on their explicit or implied approaches to state fault. Section 4 locates these arguments within the general (philosophical) debate on fault and self-defence. Section 5 reveals that the logic that assigns decisive value to state 'innocence' embraces a particular view of the state *qua* individual, and criticizes this view in light of current thought in just war theory. Section 6 applies this critique to the question of self-defence against non-state actors, demonstrating that at least when state and basic rights of individuals clash, the question of state fault should not be definitive. Rather, we should think of the proper ordering of the clashing rights in such cases. Section 7 suggests conceptualizing the territorial state's rights in regard to its territory as a right to an object, and accordingly, to view the clash that occurs when an attack is launched from an innocent state as one between the right to an object—however defined—and the right to life. Through a series of thought experiments, I argue that since the latter right is more fundamental, it should generally override the former. The conclusion returns to law and makes a preliminary suggestion to rephrase the definition of an 'armed attack' by non-state actors in a manner that reflects these nuances.

[15] In this sense, the argument here might support current critical approaches to the idea of 'national self-defence'. See e.g. D. Rodin, *The Myth of National Self-Defence* (2014); see also McMahan, 'Just Causes for War', 19 *Ethics and International Affairs* (2005) 1; L. May, *The Principle of Just Cause* (2008); for an overview, see H. Frowe, *The Ethics of War and Peace: An Introduction* (2015) 66–68.

## 2. The Space between Articles 2(4) and 51 of the UN Charter

Article 2(4) UN Charter famously prohibits the threat or use of force between states, while Article 51, in turn, recognizes the 'inherent' right to self-defence of states 'if an armed attack occurs'.[16] Yet, an uneasy space exists between the prohibition and its exception: while Article 2(4) clearly addresses the prohibition to states, Article 51 only mentions the defending state's inherent right to defend itself, without mentioning the source of the threat, and is silent on whether state fault is a precondition for the exercise of the right. Therefore, it is unclear whether Article 51 requires that a state, by being at fault, has made itself *liable* to defensive action; or, rather, that self-defence is permissible even when there is *no* fault, simply because the defender's rights override those of the territorial state.[17] Put simply, the basic legal question is whether a violation of Article 2(4) is required for Article 51 to kick in.

First, some clarification of terms is needed. Fault, for our purposes, can mean two things: either that a state is *culpable* for an attack or that it is somehow responsible for it (by action or omission). A state is culpable for an attack when it launches it through its own organs or when the attack can be otherwise attributed to it through the law on state responsibility. Obviously, when a state uses its armed forces to attack another, there is no dilemma. The state is both culpable under Article 2(4) and liable to defensive action under Article 51. Likewise, when the actions of a non-state actor are legally *attributable* to the state—for instance, when the non-state actor is a *de facto* organ of the state, or when it acts under its direction or control—then, in accordance with the international law on state responsibility, it is the state itself which is acting.[18] While the latter situations are difficult to identify, they are unproblematic in legal terms: the state is both in violation of Article 2(4) and liable to defensive action. In other words, in such cases, the space between Articles 2(4) and 51 is inconsequential.

A state can be *responsible* with respect to an attack either by actively contributing to it (in levels that do not amount to attribution) or by failing to act to prevent an attack. In international law, when a territorial state assists such attacks, acquiesces to an attack, or does not exercise 'due diligence' in preventing an attack, it arguably

[16] Article 2(4) UN Charter holds that: 'All Members shall refrain in their international relations from the threat or use of force against the territorial integrity or political independence of any state, or in any other manner inconsistent with the Purposes of the United Nations.' Article 51 provides that 'Nothing in the present Charter shall impair the inherent right of individual or collective self-defence if an armed attack occurs against a Member of the United Nations, until the Security Council has taken measures necessary to maintain international peace and security.'

[17] See Murphy, 'Self-Defence and the Israeli Wall Advisory Opinion: An *Ipse Dixit* from the ICJ?', 99 American Journal of International Law (2004) 62, at 63–64.

[18] For an application of these principles, see e.g. Zimmermann, 'The Second Lebanon War: *Jus ad Bellum, Jus in Bello* and the Issue of Proportionality', in Von Bogdandy and Wolfrum (eds), *Max Planck Yearbook of United Nations Law*, vol. 11 (2007) 99, at 109–115.

accrues state responsibility for a violation of Article 2(4).[19] In all of these cases, we can say that a state is *unwilling* to curtail the attack. Yet even if such acts or omissions amount to a violation of the prohibition on the use of force, they are not necessarily armed attacks by the state itself. In such cases, the space between Articles 2(4) and 51 starts to be consequential: while we do have a violation of Article 2(4), and thus some fault, it is unclear whether the 'unwilling' state can be said to have made itself liable to any defensive action under Article 51.[20]

Last, in some cases, the non-state actor's attack can be clearly against the will of the territorial state; moreover, the state might be actively attempting to prevent these attacks but is not succeeding—either because it lost control over the territory or because of its own military weakness. This is the paradigmatic case of an *unable* state. In such cases, if the state has exercised due diligence in attempt to halt the attacks, it is not violating any international obligation.[21] It is neither culpable, nor responsible, for the attacks emanating from its territory. Therefore, if a violation of Article 2(4) is *not* required for Article 51 to kick in, and a forcible response is undertaken against the non-state actor, the territorial state pays a price although it has done nothing wrong, so to speak.

The problem is that from the point of view of the attacked state, the question whether the territorial state is culpable, responsible, or altogether faultless is immaterial: the harm it might suffer from the non-state actor's attack is completely disconnected from the existence (or level) of fault of the territorial state. Law is trapped in a seemingly intractable clash between two legitimate interests: the territorial state's not to suffer harm when not liable and the attacked state's to defend itself or its citizens. If we look at states as abstract entities, resolving this clash is extremely difficult.

## 3. The Doctrinal Debate

The different views on self-defence against non-state actors have been conceptualized as debates between restrictive and expansionist approaches to the

[19] See GA Res. 2625 (XXV), 24 October 1970, holding that:

> Every State has the duty to refrain from organizing or encouraging the organization of irregular forces or armed bands including mercenaries, for incursion into the territory of another State.
>
> ...
>
> Every State has the duty to refrain from organizing, instigating, assisting or participating in acts of civil strife or terrorist acts in another State or acquiescing in organized activities within its territory directed towards the commission of such acts, when the acts referred to in the present paragraph involve a threat or use of force.

Granted, in order to say that failure to act in due diligence generates a violation of Art. 2(4), we have to say that such failure amounts to *acquiescence* to such an attack. On due diligence obligations, see generally J. Kulesza, *Due Diligence in International Law* (2016) ch. 1.

[20] The ICJ answered this question in the negative. See Section 2.

[21] This is because while international law requires states to exercise due diligence to prevent harmful acts conducted by individuals from their territory, it nowhere obliges them to *succeed*. Corten, 'Regulating Resort to Force: A Response to Matthew Waxman from a "Bright-Liner"', 24 *European Journal of International Law* (2013) 191.

international law on the use of force, divided roughly along the lines of continental and Anglo-American legal cultures, and their respective assumptions on the objectives of the international legal order and the methodology through which international law develops.[22] Others have framed the debate as one between two differing but complementing 'codes' on the use of force: a unilateralist 'state' code and a multilateral 'institutional' code.[23] It can just as well be phrased as a clash between positivist and policy-oriented approaches, or between legal formalist or realist views on the development of international law.[24] Be that as it may, many writers in the field identify a significant change in the practice of (mainly Western) states since 9/11, which reflects their expansive understanding of the right to self-defence against non-state actors. The disagreement between the different camps is not so much on this factual development but rather on whether this practice has crystalized as law.[25]

Indeed, in the post-9/11 practice of the UN Security Council (UNSC), it has become increasingly accepted that (at least) a wide-scale attack by non-state actors can trigger the right to self-defence under international law (rather than being simply a law enforcement problem, to be sorted out peacefully by the relevant states). Importantly, UNSC Resolutions 1368 and 1373 (2001) addressed Al Qaida's attacks on the World Trade Center by reference to 'the inherent right to individual or collective self-defence'.[26] Nonetheless, the position of these Resolutions on the requirement of state fault remains unclear. This is because at hand was a situation in which the territorial state—Afghanistan under the Taliban—was *responsible* by supporting and harbouring the organization.[27] The question remains whether the same logic would apply where the territorial state was not at all responsible.

UNSC Resolution 2249 (2015), addressing the fight against ISIL/ISIS, might imply a further step in widening the understanding of the scope of self-defence against non-state actors. At the time, ISIS operated transnationally from the territory of Syria, against the will of the Syrian government. In fact, it actively *fought* the government. Still, the UNSC labelled ISIS an 'unprecedented threat to

[22] For a helpful account of this divide, see Banks and Criddle, 'Customary Constrains on the Use of Force: Article 51 with an American Accent', 29 *Leiden Journal of International Law* (2016) 67; for a conceptualization of this debate as between 'bright liners' and 'balancers', see Waxman, 'Regulating Resort to Force: Form and Substance of the UN Charter Regime', 24 *European Journal of International Law* (2013) 151, at 163–166; compare with Corten (n. 21).

[23] Hakimi and Katz Cogan, 'The Two Codes on the Use of Force', 27 *European Journal of International Law* (2016) 257, at 257–265, 269–273; see also Hakimi, 'The *Jus ad Bellum*'s Regulatory Form', 112 *American Journal of International Law* (2018) 151, at 187–190.

[24] Compare Banks and Criddle (n. 22) 73.

[25] J. Kammerhofer, *Uncertainty in International Law: A Kelsenian Perspective* (2010) 13; but see again Tams (n. 3) 53–57; and Kreß (n. 3) (challenging the argument that this practice is new and, accordingly, the need to prove that a new rule has emerged).

[26] SC Res. 1368, 12 September 2001, preamble; SC Res. 1373, 28 September 2001, preamble; Murphy (n. 17) 67–68.

[27] Hakimi, 'Defensive Force Against Non-State Actors: The State of Play', 91 *International Law Studies Series US Naval War College* (2015) 1, at 8–12.

international peace and security',[28] noted that ISIS had the capability and intention to carry out attacks,[29] and called upon states to take 'all necessary measures', in compliance with the UN Charter, on the territories under ISIS's control.[30] Indeed, by not invoking Chapter VII, and by referring to the UN Charter as the basis for action, the UNSC could be said to have recognized that a pre-existing right to act against ISIS existed, although, arguably, Syria was not at fault on this specific issue. Yet, the Resolution's wording is so ambiguous that it is difficult to distil a definitive position on whether any form of state involvement is a precondition for self-defence against non-state actors.[31]

The International Court of Justice (ICJ), on its part, has leaned towards the restrictivist view on this question, even in its post-9/11 opinions and rulings. The root of the ICJ's approach can be traced to its *Nicaragua* case, where the Court distinguished between 'less grave uses of force'—which constitute a violation of Article 2(4)—and 'grave uses of force' which also amount to armed attacks, and can therefore be countered by defensive force.[32] Concerning non-state actors, even a high level of state involvement, such as 'organizing, instigating, assisting or participating' in the attacks would only amount to less grave uses of force.[33] An armed attack would only occur if the non-state actor is *sent* by the state, meaning that its actions can be attributed to it.[34] This seems to mean that in all scenarios in which attribution is lacking, no recourse to self-defence is permitted, *even* if the state is responsible for the attacks. In other words, the ICJ seems to adopt the strict view that state *culpability* is needed.[35]

Similarly, in its 2004 *Wall* Advisory Opinion, the ICJ's majority opined that Israel could not rely on Article 51 as justification for building a wall within the occupied West Bank, since the article is relevant only to 'an armed attack by one State against another State'.[36] Since Israel was acting in a territory it occupies, and

28 SC Res. 2249, 20 November 2015, preamble.

29 Ibid. para. 1.

30 Ibid. para. 5.

31 For a helpful analysis, see Akande and Milanovic, 'The Constructive Ambiguity of the Security Council's ISIS Resolution', EJIL Talk, 21 November 2015, https://www.ejiltalk.org/the-constructive-ambiguity-of-the-security-councils-isis-resolution/ (last visited 2 February 2024); see also Hakimi, *Regulatory Form* (n. 23) 188–189.

32 *Case Concerning Military and Paramilitary Activities in and Against Nicaragua (Nicaragua v United States of America)*, Merits, Judgment, 27 June 1986, ICJ Reports (1986) 14, at para. 191.

33 Ibid.

34 Ibid. para. 195.

35 But see the 'substantial involvement' caveat. De Hoogh (n. 9) 25–33; see also Trapp, 'The Use of Force Against Terrorists: A Reply to Christian J. Tams', 20 *European Journal of International Law* (2009) 1049. Moreover, one can distinguish the *Nicaragua* case from our question since that ruling concerned the question of whether support to armed non-state actors that operated *within* the victim state amounted to an armed attack. In such cases, however, the victim state is not completely helpless because it can still act to counter the non-state actor on its own territory. The situation is different when non-state actors operate transnationally, therefore leaving the victim state helpless.

36 *Legal Consequences of the Construction of a Wall in the Occupied Palestinian Territory*, Advisory Opinion, 9 July 2004, ICJ Reports (2004) 136, at para. 139.

did not claim it was subject to an armed attack by a state, Article 51 was deemed irrelevant.[37] In its 2005 ruling in the *DRC v Uganda* case, the Court took a comparable route, holding that Uganda could not invoke Article 51 to justify its attacks against non-state actors in the DRC, since none of the attacks were attributable to the latter.[38] However, several commentators identify significant ambiguity in the ruling, as the Court reserved its judgment on whether self-defence could be justified in response to 'large-scale attacks by irregular forces'.[39] Quite possibly, this implies that the Court has left the crux of the question open. Yet, it is also not unreasonable that this caveat refers to situations when such acts are attributable to the state only.[40] Be that as it may, it is important to note that the majority's restrictive stance was attacked, in each of these rulings, by separate opinions that critiqued this outcome as either unreasonable or incompatible with contemporary practice.[41]

Indeed, in the years between and since these rulings, the transnational use of force against non-state actors, even in cases where attribution was lacking, has been so frequent that some have argued that the restrictivist view has all but disappeared, and that the reality of international relations has settled the question.[42] The legal realist instinct would surely point out that an absolute prohibition against forcible responses to such attacks is so 'out of touch with the operational practice'[43] that it cannot be seriously considered as the final word on the law.[44] Yet, operational practice, in itself, does not constitute the law, nor tells us what the law

[37] Ibid.

[38] *Case Concerning Armed Activities on the Territory of the Congo (Democratic Republic of the Congo v Uganda)*, Judgment, 19 December 2005, ICJ Reports (2005) 168, at paras 146–147.

[39] Ibid. para. 147; Zimmerman (n. 18) 116; Kreß, 'The International Court of Justice and the "Principle of Non-Use of Force"', in M. Weller (ed.), *The Oxford Handbook of the Use of Force in International Law* (2015) 561, at 561, 586; Peters and Marxsen 'Editors' Introduction: Self-Defence in Times of Transition', in Peters and Marxsen (n. 1) 6 (arguing that in *Congo v Uganda* the ICJ explicitly refrained from deciding this very question); see also Trapp (n. 35) 1051–1053.

[40] Hakimi (n. 27) 5.

[41] In the *Wall* case, Judge Higgins, in her Separate Opinion, criticized the majority on the grounds that there was 'nothing in the text of Article 51 that thus stipulates that self-defence is available only when an armed attack is made by a State' (n. 36), Separate Opinion of Judge Higgins, para. 33; Judge Buergenthal viewed this approach as 'formalistic'; ibid., Separate Opinion of Judge Buergenthal, at paras 5–6; Judge Kooijmans argued that UNSC resolutions post 9/11 are a 'new' element that clarify that state attribution is no longer required, even if this was true in the past; ibid., Separate Opinion of Judge Kooijmans, at para. 35; See also *DRC v Uganda* (n. 38) Separate Opinion of Judge Kooijmans, paras 26–29; ibid., Separate Opinion of Judge Simma, paras 7–13. For a similar observation, see Kreß (n. 39) 586.

[42] See e.g. the debate in Kammerhofer (n. 2); Hakimi (n. 27) 7–8; for an analysis of post 9/11 practice, see Reinold (n. 2).

[43] Hakimi (n. 27) 19.

[44] See Schmitt, 'Change Direction 2006: Israeli Operations in Lebanon and the International Law of Self-Defence', 29 *Michigan Journal of International Law* (2008) 127, at 149 (criticizing the ICJ for failing to acknowledge 'that international law is dynamic, that if it is to survive, it has to reflect the context in which it is applied, as well as community expectations as to its prescriptive content'); compare Van Steenberghe, 'The Law of Self-Defence and the Argumentative Landscape on the Expansionists' Side', 29 *Leiden Journal of International Law* (2016) 43, at s. III.

should be.[45] This is especially true, considering—as Monica Hakimi points out—that in the Syria case, for instance, even states that participate in attacks against ISIS on Syrian territory have not coalesced around a unifying legal basis for their operations.[46] Importantly, third party states, too, have not been straightforward on the question. In general, as Hakimi demonstrates, international responses to defensive actions against non-state actors were relatively positive when the latter received the assistance of the territorial state (i.e. when there was at least responsibility) but operations in which fault was completely absent were met (at best) with quiet toleration.[47]

Within the latter cases, one particular standard has drawn significant ire from restrictivists. This approach contends that when a territorial state is 'unwilling or unable' to prevent attacks, the attacked state can respond forcibly even without that state's consent, although a response will 'inevitably constitute the use of force *on* the territorial state' and therefore infringe on its rights.[48] Most notably, this approach was invoked by the United States in order to justify attacks on ISIS in Syria, but several other states share this view.[49]

Three basic claims underline the restrictivist objections to this particular standard.[50] First, they argue, a customary international norm permitting such responses has not crystalized. At most, states were silent towards these actions, and silence in itself is not valid *opinio juris*. Moreover, it is unlikely that such a standard would be accepted as law in the future, given the *jus cogens* status of the law on the use of force—which requires the agreement of 'the international community as a whole' for any modification—and given the fact that states would not endorse a test that could bring about violations of their sovereignty.[51] Second, such a test is prone to abuse and likely to undermine the prohibition on the use of force, and with it international peace and security. As such, it is also against the object and

[45] For a discussion, see I. V. Hull, *A Scrap of Paper: Breaking and Making International Law During the Great War* (2014) 90–92.

[46] Hakimi (n. 27) 25.

[47] Ibid. 8–11. Interestingly, Hakimi points out that the international community was generally positive towards self-defence against non-state actors that operate in areas where states have lost effective control ('ungoverned spaces'). This in itself challenges the approaches that require fault for self-defence, since a state that loses control over its own territory cannot be deemed responsible, much less culpable, for actions emanating from that territory. Restrictivists, however, can respond that loss of effective control over territory generates a certain diminishment of sovereignty over that territory. In these cases, responses directed at that territory constitute a lesser infringement of the territorial state's sovereignty. On ungoverned spaces, see also Reinold (n. 2).

[48] Wilmshurst, 'The Chatham House Principles of International Law on the Use of Force in Self-Defence', 55 *International & Comparative Law Quarterly (ICLQ)* (2006) 963, at 970.

[49] See Hakimi (n. 27) 12.

[50] For a survey of restrictivist arguments against self-defence against non-state actors, both in general and in situations where culpability or responsibility are absent, see De Hoogh (n. 9); for a robust objection by a state, see Brazil's comments in the 2017 ASIL Annual Meeting, summarized in Moorehead (n. 12).

[51] Corten, 'The "Unwilling or Unable" Test: Has it Been, and Could it be, Accepted?', 29 *Leiden Journal of International Law* (2016) 777, at 798; see also O'Connell (n. 12) 380–381; Tzouvala (n. 12) 268–269.

purpose of the UN Charter.[52] And, third, and most interestingly for our purposes, the standard does not require any fault by the territorial state.[53]

All of these objections are significant but have their own weaknesses.[54] It is beyond this chapter to resolve all of these questions or to make a conclusive statement on the policy considerations that should inform the proper legal standard. Importantly, I here leave open the possibility that rule-consequentialist concerns—such as long-term effects on the international system, or potential of abuse or mistake—might lead to restrictions on the right to self-defence in such cases (although this would be a heavy burden to lift, especially when human lives are at stake). Rather, my argument is that in this world of ambiguity, the *third* objection cannot be decisive. At least in some cases, the issue of state fault should not play a determinative role in the existence of a right to self-defence against non-state actors.

## 4. The Unable State and the Problem of Fault

Let us further explore the argument about fault as it appears in this context. Clearly, the *unwilling or unable* standard lumps together two levels of fault: an 'unwilling' state might actively support the non-state actor or be in violation of its due diligence obligations, either because it acquiesces to the attacks or because it opposes

[52] Compare Banks and Criddle (n. 22) 70; see also De Hoogh (n. 9) 23–24.

[53] Corten (n. 51) 792; see also Nolte and Randelzhofer, 'Article 51', in B. Simma *et al.* (eds), *The Charter of the United Nations: A Commentary* (2012) 1397, at 1417, cited in Banks and Criddle (n. 22) 72; O'Connell (n. 12) 384–385; Rona and Wala (n. 14) 386.

[54] Much of the argument on the customary status of such a test revolves around differing views on the method in which customary law develops. On this question, the normative meaning of silence in the development of customary law is contested. See International Law Commission, 'Draft Conclusions on Identification of Customary International Law, With Commentaries' (2018) 140–142 (holding that 'failure to react over time to a practice may serve as evidence of acceptance as law (*opinio juris*), provided that States were in a position to react and the circumstances called for some reaction'). Indeed, while silence by some states, in relation to a specific act by one actor, cannot be considered an agreement to a change in the law, but repeated silence concerning several such acts by different actors might imply an understanding about what the law already is. But see Starski, 'Silence within the Process of Normative Change and Evolution of the Prohibition on the Use of Force: Normative Volatility and Legislative Responsibility', 4 *Journal on the Use of Force and International Law* (2017) 14 (arguing that silence, in the context of reactions to uses of force, can generate normative change only under strict conditions). Pointing out the *jus cogens* nature of the prohibition on the use of force seems to beg the question of whether, considering the open language of Art. 51, this is because of a contested interpretation of the article rather than a 'modification' of the norm as such. Article 53 VCLT; compare Starski, 'A Call for a Turn to the *Meta*-Level of International Law: Silence, the "Interregnum", and the Conundrum of *Ius Cogens*', in Peters and Marxsen (n. 1) 75, 77–78. Some argue, moreover, that *contra* the common narrative, there was no pre-9/11 consensus prohibiting self-defence against non-state actors. See Tams (n. 3). The objection of instability is both empirical and contingent. It is unclear, e.g., whether the recognition of the unwilling or unable standard would generate more instability than sticking to a law which prohibits self-defence in the absence of fault, and potentially incentivizes non-state actors to act transnationally. It is contingent, since it seems mostly concerned with specific abusive policies by states, rather than with the normative justification for this or that standard.

them but does not want to confront the non-state actor for other reasons (other than being unable to do so). In other words, it is legally, and morally, responsible for the threat. An 'unable' state, conversely, is perfectly innocent.[55] Yet, leading proponents of this standard, such as Ashley Deeks, maintain that once it is genuinely established that a state is unable to contain a threat, the *necessity* requirement under *jus ad bellum* has been satisfied.[56] Necessity is thus ultimately judged by reference to the victim's interests, and in the final analysis, these prevail even if the territorial state is at no fault at all. Importantly, most proponents of the *unwilling or unable* standard argue that to fulfil the necessity requirement, the consent of the territorial state should be sought first. However, if consent is denied, or cannot be received in time, this in itself would not block defensive action.[57]

This victim-centric view is consistent in most accounts that support the right to self-defence against unable states. Some view the right to respond in absence of fault as part and parcel of the mere idea of self-defence. For instance, the 2005 Chatham House Principles of International Law on the Use of Force in Self-Defence, drafted by leading UK international lawyers, state explicitly that '[t]he right to use force in self-defence is an inherent right and is not dependent upon any prior breach of international law by the State in the territory of which defensive force is used'.[58] Indeed, the Chatham House experts seem to view the right to respond in absence of fault as part of the *inherent* nature of the right to self-defence.[59]

Some do ascribe importance to fault, but at best, only as a secondary consideration. In Daniel Bethlehem's view,[60] when a state colludes with or harbours the non-state actor, this may be relevant to considerations of the necessity to act in self-defence and the proportionality of such action.[61] Yet, ultimately, even when a state is 'unable to effectively restrain' the non-state actor, the attacked state would possess the right to defend itself, subject to the requirement—at least in some

[55] T. Ruys, *'Armed Attack' and Article 51 of the UN Charter: Evolutions in Customary Law and Practice*, vol. 74 (2010) 488.

[56] Deeks, 'Unwilling or Unable: Toward a Normative Framework for Extraterritorial Self-Defence', 52 *Virginia Journal of International Law* (2012) 483, at 494–495; compare Kreß, 'The Fine Line Between Collective Self-Defence and Intervention by Invitation: Reflections on the Use of Force against "IS" in Syria', Just Security, https://www.justsecurity.org/20118/claus-kreb-force-isil-syria/ (last visited 2 February 2024).

[57] Deeks (n. 56) 519–533; Haque, 'Necessity and Proportionality in the Law of War', in L. May (ed.), *The Cambridge Handbook of the Just War* (2018) 255; some argue that denial of consent even implies fault. Bethlehem, 'Principles Relevant to the Scope of a State's Right to Self-Defence Against an Imminent or Actual Armed Attack by Non-State Actor', 106 *American Journal of International Law* (2012) 1, at principle 12.

[58] Wilmshurst (n. 48) 970.

[59] Arguably, this view—by interpreting 'inherent' not as referring to pre-existing customary law, but as having content in and of itself—seems to assign to states a pre-political right of self-defence. Later on, I argue briefly that this position, too, by assigning inherent rights to states, suffers from the same anthropomorphic predicament that plagues fault-based accounts of self-defence, as applied to states.

[60] A view tellingly informed 'by detailed discussions over recent years with foreign ministry, defence ministry, and military legal advisers from a number of states.' Bethlehem (n. 57) 773.

[61] Ibid. principle 11.

cases—to first seek the consent of the territorial state.[62] Meaning, to Bethlehem, state fault can be an aggravating factor, but lack of fault does not serve as a significant mitigation.

Akande and Liefländer, for their part, do attribute importance to lack of fault as a mitigating factor, but only in terms of the 'burden of justification' of the responding state. To them, when a state attacks another, 'it has rendered itself liable to defensive force'. However, when the territorial state had 'not made itself liable' at all, 'the burden that must be overcome should be greater'. This is because the 'entirely innocent' state must receive some protection under international law.[63] Yet, generally, the burden *can* be overcome, while any contribution by the host state might affect 'the necessity and proportionality calculi'.[64]

Some attempt to solve the problem of fault by drawing a sharp distinction between the faultless state and the culpable non-state actor operating on its territory. Noam Lubell, for instance, joins the former in conceding that even when there is no state fault, self-defence 'does not rest upon the question of a breach of law by the territorial state' but on the mere fact that there is a victim state.[65] Lubell's approach, however, is that forcible responses, if directed exclusively against a non-state actor, are not necessarily attacks *against* the territorial state itself.[66] By bifurcating between the state's organs and its territory, Lubell eases, somewhat, the tension between lack of fault on the one hand, and the right to respond forcibly on the other.[67] Nonetheless, it is doubtful whether except in very limited circumstances an attack against a non-state actor on a state's territory can be said to not involve the territorial state at all. Indeed, its infrastructure can be harmed, and its civilians might

[62] Ibid. principle 12.

[63] Akande and Liefländer (n. 10) 563.

[64] Ibid.

[65] N. Lubell, *Extraterritorial Use of Force Against Non-State Actors* (2010) 40. The logic here is straightforward: whatever the liability structure of the specific case, 'this does not alter the fact that there was an armed attack by a non-state actor ... and that another state was a victim of this armed attack, and therefore has a right to self-defence against the non-state actor.' Ibid. 41. Interestingly, to Lubell, international law does not prohibit infringing the territory of *neutral* states in order to respond to attacks by third states. If this is true, then *a fortiori* a response can be justified when a non-state actor operates from within a 'neutral state'. Ibid. 41–42. Historically, this reasoning evokes the German *Notstand* (emergency) justification, advanced at the outbreak of the First World War, for the violation of Belgian neutrality in order to counter alleged third party threats. See Hull (n. 45) 43–47. We need not accept this reasoning in its entirety, since the analysis here revolves around the prioritization between state rights and individual rights, rather than between state rights of belligerents and neutrals.

[66] By arguing so, Lubell attempts to reconcile this practice of self-defence with the logic of *Nicaragua*: *Nicaragua*, after all, discussed forcible responses by the United States against Nicaragua's organs, ibid. 40. The same reasoning was invoked by Israel in its 2006 conflict with Hezbollah in Lebanon. See Schmitt (n. 44) 138–139.

[67] For a similar view, see on the separation between the state and the non-state actor Trapp, 'Back to Basics: Necessity, Proportionality and the Right of Self-Defence Against Non-State Terrorist Actors', 56 *ICLQ* (2007) 141, at 145; Tom Ruys also suggests the bifurcation between the state and the non-state actor on its territory, citing international practice that approves of this separation. Ruys (n. 5) 493–494. Ruys notes, however, that in this case and in the absence of culpability, the territorial state is itself a victim of the circumstances. Ibid. 488.

be collaterally killed.[68] Still, Lubell makes a significant step towards a more nuanced analysis of the interests implicated when self-defence is undertaken against non-state actors.

Restrictivists reject this reasoning in its entirety. To begin with, leading restrictivists oppose categorically any possible bifurcation between state and territory. Therefore, when forcible response is undertaken on a state's territory absent its consent—even if directed only against a non-state actor—it is the faultless state that is attacked.[69] As Olivier Corten stresses, due diligence requirements under international law oblige states to reasonably *try*, but do not penalize them for a genuine failure to prevent attacks. If a state 'sincerely' tries to put an end to attacks from its territory, it has violated no law. If it is attacked, it is in effect suffering the consequences for 'having not succeeded' to defeat a non-state actor.[70] Indeed, Corten seems to advance a deontic understanding of the rights of the territorial states under current international law: if they have not made themselves liable to attack, their rights cannot be overridden by the subjective necessity of the victim.

Dire Tladi adds much conceptual clarity to this critique by framing it as the *nonconsenting innocent state problem*.[71] The problem, to Tladi, with defensive force on the territory of a faultless state, is that it implies that 'force may be used on the territory of an innocent state without its consent'.[72] Still, while Tladi argues that this proposition is problematic in positive international law, he does not seek to offer a normative defence of the 'innocent state' concept beyond stating that attacks against such states violate principles such as territorial integrity, sovereign equality, and the prohibition on the use of force.[73] Namely, this approach does not explain, beyond pointing to positive law, why the innocence of a state *should* override other competing interests.

The next section uncovers the theoretical underpinnings of the debate on the fault requirement, and in later sections, I inquire whether this distinction is applicable in inter-state relations. This will allow us to situate state innocence in its proper place when conflicting with other rights.

[68] Compare ICRC, 2016 Commentary on Common Article 2 of the Geneva Conventions; Akande, 'Classification of Armed Conflicts: Relevant Legal Concepts', Oxford Legal Studies Research Paper No. 50 (2012) 1.

[69] O'Connell (n. 11) 383 ('attacking NSAs [non-state actors] on the territory of another state is attacking that state as much as the NSAs'); Corten (n. 51) 795–797; compare Hakimi (n. 27) 4.

[70] Corten (n. 51) 792–793.

[71] Tladi, 'The Nonconsenting Innocent State: The Problem with Bethlehem's Principle 12', 107 *American Journal of International Law* (2013) 570.

[72] Ibid. 571.

[73] Ibid. 574. In this context, Ntina Tzouvala advances an interesting argument according to which the category of an 'unable' state reintroduces hierarchy between states into *jus ad bellum* in a manner that invalidates the idea of sovereign equality and replicates the nineteenth-century distinctions between 'civilized' and 'uncivilized' peoples. See Tzouvala (n. 12) 267. The flipside to this argument, however, is that in effect it attributes overriding importance to state sovereignty.

## 5. Fault and the Justification for Self-Defence

How to account for the absence of fault as a strong limiting legal principle for self-defence by and against states? One possible justification is broadly consequentialist: here, the argument goes, exercising self-defence against non-state actors in a faultless state would risk escalating a local situation into a large-scale international conflict, with potential disastrous consequences for the international community. Those holding this position concede that the law might require states to refrain from reacting in such cases, even at the price of exposing their own people to attack. On this view, it is not the primary purpose of Article 51 to guarantee effective protection to individuals in a given situation, but rather to reduce the overall chances for international conflict.[74]

This reasoning has its shortcomings. In essence, it confounds the question on the existence of a just cause to resort to force with the harm–benefit proportionality of the resort to force. It seems to embed a preordained harm–benefit proportionality judgement into the principled question of the existence of a just cause in certain circumstances, while in fact, the proportionality calculus is by nature contingent and heavily fact-dependent. Of course, an argument can be made that because of all-things-considered, rule-consequentialist reasons, it is better to integrate these considerations into a prohibitory legal standard. But when an attack from a non-state actor endangers real individuals, a blanket prohibition on a response because of considerations further down the line would imply that it is possible to sacrifice any number of individuals in real time, for the purpose of achieving uncertain future benefits.

Because restrictivists do not generally subject the prohibition on self-defence on the territory of an innocent state to any exceptions, it seems that a deeper issue is at play here, relating to the most basic justification for self-defence. Indeed, one of the stickiest questions in law and ethics concerns the rationales justifying harm in self-defence, and specifically, the relations between fault and the right to inflict grave harm in self-defence/preservation.[75] Off the bat, it seems odd to apply this reasoning to inter-state relations, since states as juridical entities cannot be physically harmed or killed. Yet, the objections to self-defence against non-state actors that allude to a state's 'innocence' as a decisive factor correspond with this logic. Of course, proponents of the latter view do not think that states can actually be killed

[74] See Kammerhofer, 'Uncertainties of the Law on Self-Defence in the United Nations Charter', 35 *Netherlands Yearbook of International Law* (2004) 143, at 201–202; Nolte and Randelzhofer (n. 53) 1417, cited in Banks and Criddle (n. 22) 70–2.

[75] For leading accounts in law, see Fletcher, 'Proportionality and the Psychotic Aggressor: A Vignette in Comparative Criminal Theory', 8 *Israel Law Review* (1973) 367; Ferzan, 'Justifying Self-Defence' 24/6 *Law and Philosophy* (2005) 711; in ethics, see Thomson, 'Self-Defence', 20 *Philosophy and Public Affairs* (1991) 283; Otsuka, 'Killing the Innocent in Self-Defence', 23 *Philosophy and Public Affairs* (1994) 74. For a helpful overview, see Frowe (n. 15) 13–21.

in self-defence—that would be absurd. But they do seem to view any encroachment of a state's territory as inflicting an especially grave harm. Otherwise, they would not have argued that an innocent state's right not to be subject to such harm so clearly overrides the right of the victim state to respond (even when the rights of individuals in that state are at risk).

So what are the relations between fault and the right to inflict grave harm in self-defence, as these are discussed in ethics and theories of criminal law? Recall that fault can imply culpability or responsibility. In one view ('the culpability account'), it is an attacker's malicious intent to kill or inflict grave harm that drives the permissibility of a forcible response.[76] When malicious intent is absent, there is a deontic prohibition on such a response, even if this would require the victim to suffer grave harm. According to this approach, therefore, self-defence would be prohibited in situations of *innocent threats*: meaning, when people become threatening to others only because they are physically manipulated by a third party or by a force of nature.[77] Now, when restrictivists refer to the overriding rights of innocent states, what is invoked, in practice, is a crude parallel to the moral problem of an innocent threat: the territory of the state—one of its constitutive elements—is used opportunistically, against its will, in order to stage an attack against others.[78]

Importantly, strong versions of the culpability account would deny self-defence even when there is *some* responsibility for the threat, but one that does not amount to culpability.[79] Put simply, contributing to a threat, and even enabling it, is not the same as being culpable for the threat itself. Those who think that even a state that supports or harbours non-state actors, but does not 'send' them, cannot be attacked, seem to endorse this view. The approach in *Nicaragua*, in its differentiation between 'less grave' and 'grave' violations of the prohibition on the use of force, is reminiscent of this type of thinking.[80]

Conversely, those who argue for a right of self-defence against non-state actors in supporting or harbouring states (the *unwilling* state case) seem to embrace the 'responsibility account' of permissible self-defence.[81] On this account, full culpability is not required for the right to materialize, but rather some form of moral

[76] Ibid. 14; Fletcher (n. 75) 377–38.

[77] Thomson (n. 75) 284, 287–289; a related problem is that of the 'innocent aggressor'. See Fletcher (n. 75); see also Frowe (n. 15) 14–16.

[78] The parallel is 'crude' since in the classic innocent-threat scenario it is the person's own body that harms the victim, and here, conversely, the state is merely a cover. Perhaps, the state is used as a 'shield'. But this would not alter our conclusion.

[79] Frowe (n. 15) 14–15; see also Ferzan (n. 75) 677–682.

[80] It seems that, for the same reason, Tladi is reluctant to endorse the view that even the Taliban's Afghanistan support for Al-Qai'da could in itself justify the US attacks against the state. Tladi (n. 71) 575 ('The basis for U.S. action in Afghanistan seems to be some kind of attribution of blameworthiness on the government of the state on which the use of force was to be carried out. Whether or not the international law standard for attribution is met is a different question').

[81] See Hakimi (n. 27) 8–10.

responsibility for the threat.[82] Therefore, in situations in which it is unavoidable that one person will suffer harm, it is morally preferable that the one who is at least *somewhat* responsible for the threat will pay the price.[83] Applied to inter-state relations, the argument is that the territorial state here is 'part of the problem'.[84] Taken to the extreme, this account can also justify attacks against an unable state, if one makes the highly problematic argument that the state is morally responsible for its own inability.[85] Yet, the responsibility account would *not* allow self-defence against a state that is completely innocent.

On the other side of the spectrum, autonomy-based accounts of self-defence shift the gaze to the victim, and the *effects* of the attack on *her*.[86] Autonomy accounts can be roughly split in two. One follows the Hobbesian tradition of self-preservation. To Hobbes, the natural drive of self-preservation is so fundamental that it is not only entirely disconnected from previous wrongdoing but also stands to the wrongdoer against just punishment.[87] On this account, people simply cannot be required, or practically expected, to sacrifice themselves rather than harm someone who threatens them, at fault or otherwise.[88] When Bethlehem, and others, decry the distance between theoretical debates on self-defence and 'operational realities', and call to reshape the law accordingly,[89] they seem to adopt this functionalist line of thought: since no victim can be expected to refrain from acting to preserve herself, law should not require otherwise.

The other strand of the autonomy account seeks to ground self-defence on normative rather than realist grounds. One influential approach (the 'rights-based approach') proceeds from the simple assumption that people have a claim right not to be killed, against which others are under a duty not to kill. When A fails in her duty not to kill V, V's right not to be killed has been violated, and this in itself

[82] McMahan (n. 11); Frowe (n. 15) 20. Compare Haque (n. 57) (contribution vs enabling). Interestingly, there is some support for this standard in the canon of just war: St Augustine argued that just causes for war include situations where the territorial state 'has neglected ... to punish wrongs committed by its own citizens'. Cited in J. Eppstein, *The Catholic Tradition of the Law of Nations* (2008) 74.

[83] The responsibility account is problematic in the sense that it essentially permits killing of those contributing to lethal threats, even if not directly causing them, and that it treats defensive killings as a question of harm distribution rather than a question of rights. See Haque (n. 57) 258–263.

[84] Hakimi (n. 27) 8.

[85] For traces of this position, see Israeli PM Netanyahu's comments on the relations between Lebanon and Hezbollah: 'the fact that the Lebanese army is doing nothing [concerning threats against Israel] means that they are either unable or unwilling or both to do anything about this. *But it doesn't absolve Lebanon's culpability*,' he said. '"My message is: Hezbollah is putting you in great jeopardy"' )emphasis added(. Federman, 'Israel Urges UN to Condemn Hezbollah Over Tunnels', *Washington Times*, 19 December 2018, https://www.washingtontimes.com/news/2018/dec/19/israel-urges-un-to-condemn-hezbollah-over-tunnels/ (last visited 2 February 2024).

[86] Fletcher (n. 75) 378–380.

[87] See Schrock, 'The Right to Punish and Resist Punishment in Hobbes's Leviathan', 44 *The Western Political Quarterly* (1991) 853, at 853. See also S. Uniacke, *Permissible Killing: The Self-Defence Justification of Homicide* (1996) 62.

[88] Ibid. 63.

[89] Bethlehem (n. 57) 4.

generates a right to kill A in self-defence. Significantly, this remains true even if A is not at all culpable or responsible for the threat.[90] This view is strained, since it seems to define, as *violations* of rights, even acts that occur without fault or even moral agency.[91] Nonetheless, the Chatham House Principles allude to this approach when juxtaposing the 'inherent' right to self-defence against any requirement of fault.[92]

In moral terms, the Hobbesian view would probably only provide an excuse for defensive action in the absence of fault, while the rights-based account would also provide moral permission to do so.[93] From a legal point of view, it is less important what version of the autonomy-based account is adopted, as both would support a legal norm which would not require culpability or responsibility for self-defence.[94] It is unnecessary, for our purposes, to decide between these different accounts of the justification for self-defence. Instead, we should ask whether fault-based reasoning is at all applicable to inter-state relations or, rather, if an approach based on the proper ordering of clashing rights is better.

## 6. The *Innocent State* and the Domestic Analogy

Arguably, the approach that gives overriding precedence to state innocence harks back to anthropomorphist tendencies in international law, going as far as the seventeenth century, if not earlier.[95] Under this strand of thought, states are unitary moral persons, perceived to have 'fundamental rights' that resemble those of autonomous individuals ('the domestic analogy').[96] This thinking has also resonated in just war theory, most famously in Michael Walzer's own version of the domestic

[90] See Thomson (n. 75) 289, 299–303; Frowe (n. 15) 15–16.

[91] For these critiques, see Otsuka (n. 75); Rodin (n. 15); debate in Frowe (n. 15) 17–20; Ferzan (n. 75); Fletcher (n. 75) 378.

[92] Wilmshurst (n. 48).

[93] Thomson (n. 75) 284–285.

[94] The account we adopt within the autonomy account might, however, be important for the question whether third parties can support a state that defends a state in collective self-defence. Collective self-defence seems to require a justification rather than an agent-related excuse. Compare Fletcher (n. 75) 375.

[95] See D'Aspremont, 'The Doctrine of Fundamental Rights of States and Anthropomorphic Thinking in International Law', 4 *Cambridge Journal of International and Comparative Law* (2015) 501; see also Dickinson, 'The Analogy Between Natural Persons and International Persons in the Law of Nations', 26 *Yale Law Journal* (1917) 564, at 564–581. Indeed, Andrea Bianchi points out that reification and anthropomorphism are indeed a staple of the traditional thinking on international law. A. Bianchi, *International Law Theories: An Inquiry into Different Ways of Thinking* (2016) 38.

[96] M. Koskenniemi, *From Apology to Utopia* (2005) 89–90, 113, 137; Lauterpacht, 'The Grotian Tradition in International Law', 23 *British Yearbook of International Law* (1946) 1, at 26–28; D'Aspremont (n. 95) 506–507; Knop, 'Re/Statements: Feminism and State Sovereignty in International Law', 2 *Transnational Law & Contemporary Problems* (1993) 293, at 320–331; see also Kalmanovitz, 'Sovereignty, Pluralism, and Regular War: Wolff and Vattel's Enlightenment Critique of Just War', 46 *Political Theory* (2018) 218, at 221–222.

analogy. In Walzer's view, since states 'possess rights more or less as individuals do ... it is possible to imagine a society among them more or less like the society of individuals'.[97] This domestic analogy is 'the fundamental structure for the moral comprehension of war',[98] and aggression, accordingly, can be discussed as the international equivalent of domestic armed robbery or murder.[99] If states are to be treated on the international plane as individuals, and if we adopt a fault account of self-defence, it is clear that absent a breach of international law, no self-defence against an innocent state is justifiable.

Arguably, the attribution of deontic importance to the territory of an innocent state can be traced to an age-old sub-conception of the domestic analogy, which can be called the *organic analogy*. This conception, although no longer popular in international legal discourse, constructed the territory of the state as somehow parallel, in its importance and inviolability, to an organic body.[100] Under this conception, the justification and limits of inter-state self-defence would follow the same considerations that apply to an individual protecting her physical integrity.[101] In the case of the innocent state, the concern would be that the non-state actor uses this fictionalized body for its own purposes. The defending state, therefore, by responding forcefully, inflicts harm somehow akin in its gravity to that inflicted against the body of an innocent human threat. While modern restrictivists do not endorse the organic analogy explicitly, the attribution of decisive, overriding importance to state innocence is reminiscent of this strand of thought.[102]

[97] M. Walzer, *Just and Unjust Wars: A Moral Argument with Historical Illustrations* (1992) 58.

[98] Ibid. 61.

[99] Ibid.

[100] See H. Lauterpacht, *Private Law Sources and Analogies of International Law: With Special Reference to International Arbitration* (1927) 93; see also Knop (n. 96) 322–323. Notably, Walzer himself does not seem to adopt this conception. See Walzer (n. 97) 86.

[101] See D. W. Bowett, *Self-Defence in International Law* (1958) 29 ('the analogy between natural persons and states, drawn by the natural lawyers of the Middle Ages, was used to identify the territory of the state with the body of the individual and thus recognize an assault upon state territory as the clearest example of a situation affording to the territorial state a right of self-defence'); see also Ripstein, 'Property and Sovereignty: How to Tell the Difference', 18 *Theoretical Inquiries in Law* (2017) 243, at 248. Karen Knop has demonstrated how the state–body metaphor figured in feminist critiques of international law. E.g. she shows how violations of territorial integrity invoked the imagery of 'rape'. Knop (n. 96) 323–328. In German law, even the right of *individual* self-defence was developed by analogy to states' absolute right to defend their territories. As Fletcher illustrates: 'if a person's autonomy is compromised by the intrusion, then the defender has the right to expel the intruder and restore the integrity of his domain. The underlying image is that of a state of warfare. An aggressor's violation of our rights is akin to an intrusion of foreign troops on our soil. As we are inclined to believe that any community has the absolute right to expel foreign invaders, any person attacked by another should have the absolute right to counteract aggression against his vital interest'. G. P. Fletcher, *Rethinking Criminal Law* (1987) 860, cited in Kremnitzer and Ghanayim, 'Proportionality and the Aggressor's Culpability in Self-Defence', 39 *Tulsa Law Review* (2004) 875, at 877.

[102] Corten, e.g., warns against the 'splitting the conditions of self-defence' between evaluating the 'armed attack' criterion in relation to the non-state actor and the 'necessity' criterion in relation to the territorial state. This seems to postulate the state as a unitary body. See Corten (n. 52) 796–797. Importantly, this concept finds its flipside in arguments that insist that every incursion into a state's territory—even one that causes no significant harm—can in itself be countered by force. This is because

The persistence of the domestic analogy, in the way international law on self-defence is constructed, is curious, considering that on the jurisprudential level, the essentialist view of the state has been somewhat demystified. To begin with, it is clear that while the domestic analogy might be a convenient way to think about the international system,[103] it certainly does not follow that, in itself, it can or should be a source of transcendental rights. As early as the beginning of the twentieth century, Dickinson pointed out that after all states are 'artificial entities' and that therefore the 'international personal analogy' should be used sparingly.[104] By the mid-twentieth century, Lauterpacht propounded the view of the sovereign state as 'an administrative convenience' meant to promote individual rights, and argued that the domestic analogy should be understood not in the anthropomorphic sense but rather as a recognition that states are composed of human beings.[105] Kelsen famously suggested that the state is nothing more than a 'personification of a legal order', its territory—rather than a body—is merely the 'sphere of validity' of its jurisdiction.[106] Recently, Benvenisti has argued forcefully that the constitutive role of sovereignty is some form of trusteeship or responsibility, rather than a transcendental set of rights.[107] Similarly, in global governance literature, it has become a common view that states are not unitary actors but are instead disaggregated forms.[108]

This shift in international jurisprudence parallels a significant transformation in just war theory, ushered in by the revival of the field in the late twentieth century. Already in the early 1980s, David Luban had decried as 'romantic' the viewing of states, in the context of wars, as 'self-contained ... units of moral regard'.[109] Since

those who invoke states' 'inherent' right to self-defence against any attack, without further nuance, argue on the same logic that invokes the metaphor of state territory as an inviolable construct. Compare D'Aspremont (n. 95) 518; see also May, 'The Principle of Just Cause', in L. May (ed.), *War: Essays in Political Philosophy* (2008) 49, at 55–56. In other words, it is the same metaphor that justifies refraining from self-defence against an innocent state—even if individuals are threatened—that also fuels the idea of 'national self-defence' that justifies self-defence even when *no* individuals are truly threatened. See Rodin (n. 15). Arguably, there are other reasons, beyond state innocence and an inherent right, that might justify national self-defence against such threats. See Frowe (n. 15). It is not my intention to resolve this debate here, but only to point out the arguments that the restrictivist objection to self-defence against faultless states seems to draw from the organic view of the state.

[103] Dickinson (n. 95) 581–582.

[104] Ibid. 583.

[105] H. Lauterpacht, *International Law and Human Rights* (1950) 68, 76–77; Lauterpacht (n. 96) 27; see also Knop (n. 96) 319–320.

[106] H. Kelsen, *Principles of International Law* (2003) 100. At the same time, however, Kelsen endorsed the view that 'the employment of force on the territory of another state is equivalent to the employment of force against the other state; and this is permitted only as a reaction against a violation of international law'. Ibid. 60.

[107] Benvenisti, 'Sovereigns as Trustees of Humanity: On the Accountability of States to Foreign Stakeholders', 107 *American Journal of International Law* (2013) 295; see also E. J. Criddle and E. Fox-Decent, *Fiduciaries of Humanity: How International Law Constitutes Authority* (2016).

[108] See A.-M. Slaughter, *A New World Order* (2009).

[109] Luban, 'The Romance of the Nation-States', 9/4 *Philosophy and Public Affairs* (1980) 394, at 394.

then, in the last three decades, *revisionist* just war theorists have thoroughly questioned the domestic analogy.[110] Revisionists—most notably Jeff McMahan—argue that, in moral terms, states are merely organizations consisting of a (very) large group of individuals. As such, this large group does not enjoy—in itself—moral rights not possessed by each individual separately. This is because to argue that individuals, when working together, possess more rights than each of them has individually would constitute a form of 'moral alchemy'.[111] Revisionism would thus argue that just as individuals cannot create new moral rights simply by acting collectively, they cannot endow a state's territory with transcendental meaning that would necessarily override the rights of other individuals who are threatened from that territory.

Revisionist just war theory, of course, is not immune to critique.[112] Crucially, revisionists themselves usually concede that for pragmatic reasons its effects should remain limited in law.[113] For instance, positive *jus in bello* recognizes the principle of belligerent equality, which holds that all belligerents—just or unjust—enjoy the same legal rights.[114] One of revisionism's main projects is to challenge the morality of this idea, by arguing that aggressors and defenders cannot be morally equal. Even so, most revisionists agree that for structural reasons it is better to leave positive international law as it is.[115] Yet, at least in the context of self-defence against non-state actors, it seems that concerns of this order are not entirely relevant. Applying revisionist reasoning to this issue simply does not raise the same type of problems. Rather, it serves a clarifying purpose by exposing the core of the rights and interests affected, therefore allowing us to strike a proper balance between them. I demonstrate how in the next sections.

## 7. From Fault to an Ordering of Clashing Rights

To illustrate this in our context, consider the following example: an 'innocent' state, I, is unable to prevent a non-state actor from using its territory to launch continuous and deadly attacks against civilians in neighbouring state V. Assume

110 For a helpful survey, see Dill, 'Just War Theory in Times of Individual Rights', in C. Brown and R. Eckersley (eds), *The Oxford Handbook of International Political Theory* (2018) 221.

111 J. McMahan, *Killing in War* (2009) 82.

112 For an overview, see Lazar, 'Introduction', in C. Fabre and S. Lazar (eds), *The Morality of Defensive War* (2014) 1.

113 Ibid.; Dill (n. 110); for approaches that apply revisionism to interpret positive law, see Dannenbaum, 'Why Have We Criminalized Aggressive War?', 126 *Yale Law Journal* (2017) 1242; see also Lieblich, 'Internal *Jus ad Bellum*', 67 *Hastings Law Journal* (2016) 687.

114 Blum, 'On a Differential Law of War', 52 *Harvard International Law Journal* (2011) 163.

115 Simply put, depriving unjust combatants of belligerent rights is unlikely to do any good, chiefly because most combatants believe they are just, and would therefore always deny the rights of their enemies. Compare McMahan, 'The Ethics of Killing in War', 114 *Ethics* (2004) 693, at 730–733.

also, that V can respond against the non-state actor without incidentally harming any of I's civilians. On the domestic analogy, and if we adopt the fault account of self-defence, V should refrain from a forcible response, even at the cost of human life. On the revisionist account, however, whether we adopt the fault approach or otherwise is secondary. First, a state's territory does not have a transcendental value, so it makes little sense to attribute to it deontic prohibitions that would attach, perhaps, to innocent human threats. Second, it is clear that there *is* culpability here, which attaches to the *individuals* comprising the non-state actor; it is *this* culpability which should inform our moral inquiry. On this view, therefore, even if State I can be described as 'innocent', and even if a forcible response by V would infringe its rights, what ensues is simply a transnational clash of rights:[116] between the rights of a legal entity I and the basic rights of real people in V. The key question thus seems to be not one of state fault, but rather of the proper ordering of clashing rights, between those of legal entities and those of individuals.[117]

Therefore, rather than looking at the relations between the territorial state (used by the non-state actor) and defending state as between unitary bodies of moral regard, their relations should be conceived as a transnational clash of rights of differing importance, in which some rights must be overridden by others. Unless we attribute transcendental importance to state rights, it seems that in a clash between a legal entity's fictionalized right not to be harmed while innocent, and a physical person's right not to be killed, the latter should override the former.

Why so? The answer can be found in the realization, highlighted in revisionist just war theory, that state rights cannot exceed the aggregate of individual rights.[118] Even if the revisionist account is not averse to the creation, by individuals, of legal entities that possess certain rights, and even if such entities can be referred to functionally as moral agents, these legal rights cannot relieve individuals of their moral obligations towards other individuals. This, too, would be a form of moral alchemy: assume that A has a claim right against B, C, and D not to interfere if she defends herself against an attack by E, even if A's response against E would harm some lesser interest of theirs. It is obvious that B, C, and D cannot 'contract out' of this

[116] In the classic sense in which Jessup phrased transnational law: 'the law applicable to the complex interrelated world community … beginning with the individual and reaching on up to the so-called "family of nations" and or "society of states"'. P. C. Jessup, *Transnational Law* (1956) 3.

[117] This is not to say that state culpability or responsibility is meaningless. If a state has breached an international obligation, the victim state, in addition to its right to defend itself, would be entitled to reparations in accordance with the international law on state responsibility. ILC, Draft Articles on Responsibility of States for Internationally Wrongful Acts, UN Doc. A/56/10 (2001), ch. 2.

[118] There are many ways to conceive this ordering of rights. One approach would simply posit that the right to life is the 'supreme right', a prerequisite for the enjoyment of all other rights. If this is so, the individual right to life must trump the rights of legal fictions. See HRC, General Comment No. 36 on the International Covenant on Civil and Political Rights, 27 July 2017, Art. 6 on the right to life. Another would distinguish between rights of legal entities as instrumental, while rights of individuals possess intrinsic value. Still another approach distinguishes between legal rights and natural rights, political vs pre-political rights, and so on. It is not necessary here to adopt one account over the other.

duty simply by creating a legal entity—be it a state or any other—to protect their interests (that is, unless that legal entity has transcendental rights of its own).[119]

Before moving on, two possible objections. First, an objection can be made that my example above is too clean. In most cases, forcible responses against non-state actors would also harm innocent civilians. Therefore, a response would not only impinge on the rights of an innocent state *qua* legal entity but also might harm the state's civilians. The latter cannot be presumed to bear any responsibility for the attacks; after all, their state is innocent. But this is beside the point. Whether or not individuals can be incidentally harmed is ultimately not a question of their political responsibility or affiliation. Rather, it is a question of when, if at all, their rights can be justifiably infringed (overridden).[120] Accepting that lack of political responsibility is a determinative factor in restricting the right to self-defence would also carry the dangerous repercussion of allowing *more* collateral damage where political responsibility *is* assumed.

A more challenging objection is that there are indeed cases in which international law favours state rights over individual rights. If this is not an anomaly in other cases, why should it not be so also in our context? A significant example is the relatively broadly accepted position that unilateral humanitarian intervention, absent UNSC authorization, is unlawful under positive international law.[121] Even if we agree with this position (and this question is beyond this chapter), this doesn't necessarily have a bearing on the clash between state and individual rights in situations of transnational defence. This is because, overall, humanitarian intervention (as with interventions at large)—even if it can be morally justified in certain

[119] We can think of this in another way: in our clean example, when decision-makers in Victimia decide *not* to respond on Innocentia's territory, they decide not to save individuals in Victimia; in other words, they choose to let them die. While one can plausibly argue that it is morally preferable to let X innocent people die rather than to kill X innocent people, it seems absurd to argue that it is preferable to let X innocent people die rather than harm an innocent state. Compare A. A. Haque, *Law and Morality at War* (2017) (invoking this asymmetry in the context of *jus in bello* proportionality). Similarly, it seems odd that international law would ascribe deontic importance to the rights of innocent states while not doing the same for innocent individuals. Proportionality under *jus in bello* tolerates incidental harm to innocent individuals, if it is not excessive in relation to a concrete and direct military advantage (Art. 51(5)(b) Protocol Additional to the Geneva Conventions of 12 August 1949, and relating to the Protection of Victims of International Armed Conflicts 1977, 2404 UNTS 261 (hereinafter API)). Tolerating the latter type of harm, while not the former, would result in a system that fetishizes sovereignty—hardly the position to which most restrictivists aspire.

[120] Rights can be said to be justifiably overridden 'when the moral reasons in favour of infringing them outweigh the moral reasons against infringing them'. Haque (n. 119) 7.

[121] See Franchini and Tzanakopoulos, 'The Kosovo Crisis', in T. Ruys and O. Corten (eds), *The Use of Force in International Law: A Case Based Approach* (2018) 594; another example is the law on sovereign immunity, which protects states against the jurisdiction of foreign domestic courts, even concerning grave international crimes. See *Jurisdictional Immunities of the States (Germany v Italy)*, Judgment, 3 February 2012, ICJ Reports (2012) 99. Here, too, international law prioritizes state rights over the individual right to access to justice. Yet, we cannot draw a parallel to our case: (i) access to justice is not as important as the right to life; and (ii) while state immunity does not negate access to justice, say, in the court of the perpetrating state, an ongoing armed attack usually does not offer alternative recourse, or at least not one that can prevent the harm in due time.

cases—[122] presents more structural problems than self-defence against non-state actors.[123] First, in humanitarian interventions, the intervener would usually act directly against the territorial state's organs, rather than only on its territory. In this sense, humanitarian interventions are more intrusive than self-defence against non-state actors. Moreover, as opposed to self-defence against non-state actors—which might also benefit weaker states challenged by transnational violence—humanitarian intervention would usually be available to powerful states only, which seems to heighten the risk of abuse. In addition, the intervener in such cases presumes to act in favour of the rights of 'others', and under severe epistemic limitations both concerning the facts on the ground and the outcome of the intervention. In transnational defence, the defender is better situated to assess both the threat and the prospects of success. These reasons militate in favour of a more cautious legal approach towards intervention than towards self-defence. Last, it is worthwhile noting that even if humanitarian intervention is unlawful, here, too, fault is not a decisive argument. On the contrary, those who argue that humanitarian intervention is prohibited, maintain this position even when the state is *culpable* in grave atrocities. If anything, the example of humanitarian intervention further weakens the role of state fault as a decisive element in the law on the use of force.

Setting aside state innocence as a decisive consideration, and opting for a rights-ordering approach, relieves us of two other problems. First, some argue that if self-defence on the territory of an innocent state were to be permitted, then the latter would be justified in invoking an 'equally valid' self-defence claim against the responding state. A 'vicious cycle' of self-defence and counter-self-defence would ensue.[124] Whether or not real individuals who become innocent threats may defend themselves against a defender's response is an unresolved question in the ethics of killing.[125] But if we understand conflicts on the inter-*state* level as clashes between rights of differing importance, then, arguably, a legal entity's innocence cannot provide it with a right to defend itself against a response that is meant to safeguard rights of greater importance.[126] The 'vicious circle' problem seems to be another consequence of attributing transcendental rights to states.

122 On the morality of humanitarian intervention, see McMahan, 'Humanitarian Intervention, Consent, and Proportionality' in N. Ann Davis, R. Keshen, and J. McMahan (eds), *Ethics and Humanity: Themes from the Philosophy of Jonathan Glover* (2010) 44.

123 On the complexities of interventions, see Doyle, 'A Few Words on Mill, Walzer, and Nonintervention', 23 *Ethics and International Affairs* (2009) 349.

124 See De Hoogh (n. 9) 22; compare Haque, 'Self-Defence Against Self-Defence, In Syria and Beyond', Just Security, 31 May 2018, https://www.justsecurity.org/57223/self-defence-self-defence-syria/ (last visited 2 February 2024).

125 See Frowe (n. 15) 20.

126 This problem can be conceptualized as one of 'double prevention': the territorial state here would attempt to prevent the defending state from preventing harm to individuals. Yet, while arguably individuals can sometimes act to double prevent something when their lives are at stake, the interest the *territorial* state would be protecting here (sovereignty, territory) would be of much less importance than the one it seeks to prevent others from protecting (saving lives). On double prevention in the context of the ethics of war, see Haque (n. 119) 79–80.

Second, and crucially, if state fault were a precondition for self-defence, this would necessarily mean that an attacked state would not be permitted to defend itself *even* against attacks launched by aggressor *states* from territories they occupy (an occupied state being the quintessential 'unable state'). It is certainly true that, in most of these cases, it would be in the interest of the occupied state to consent to a forcible response against its occupier, but it is not difficult to imagine cases where this will not be so.[127] If restrictivists resist the conclusion that in such cases, too, state innocence overrides self-defence, they must offer an explanation as to why state fault matters when non-state actors are involved, but not where third states are the ones taking advantage of an innocent state.

## 8. Territory as Object: Some Thought Experiments

If we reject the domestic analogy, but still concede that forcible responses against non-state actors implicate the rights or interests of the territorial state and its people, how can we best conceptualize the clash of rights in such cases? To do so, we have to say something about territory under international law. While in the past, territory was either perceived as a body, in accordance with the organic analogy, or—later on—as an 'element' of the state, the more accepted perception today conceives state territory as an *object* regarding which the state, as a legal entity, enjoys some form of exclusive rights. These rights are sometimes reminiscent of, but often differing from, property rights. Hersch Lauterpacht called this the 'object theory' of the state.[128]

The methodology of revisionist just war theory can help to shed light on the proper resolution of a clash between territorial rights—conceived as rights pertaining to objects—and individual rights, when a transnational attack by a non-state actor takes place.[129] Recall that war, to revisionists, is not a clash between abstract entities but between groups of individuals. When assessing the right of states to use force, therefore, the method of inquiry is 'reductive individualism': rather than treating the state *qua* individual body, we must ask whether in a certain case, against harm to a certain interest, a real-life *individual* would be permitted to use lethal

[127] Think of a situation in which states A, B, and C distrust one another, where A occupies B and mounts an attack against C. A is unlikely to consent to C's response since it fears that C would just be another occupier.

[128] See Lauterpacht (n. 100) 92, 94–96 ('there is, in fact, no ground for assuming that the science of international law will discard the analogy between territorial sovereignty and property in private law, even if it does not go the length of identifying the two conceptions').

[129] To stress, I am not claiming here that the *lex lata* follows the premises of revisionist just war theory. Indeed, positive international law deviates from these ideas in many respects. Rather, the methodology of reductive individualism is used here to assist in uncovering the moral rights affected in situations of transnational defence, and therefore to expose the normative shortcomings of positions that place overriding importance on state innocence.

force, and then apply this reasoning to the state *qua* group of individuals.[130] On this account, a helpful way to analyse transnational attacks by non-state actors is to draw a crude parallel to situations in which person A attacks person V from B's property, and then to ask ourselves what would be the permissible response by V, or someone entrusted in protecting her. To reiterate: the analogy between state territory and property, as well as the existence of property-like relations between individuals and their state's territory, is much more contested and strained than implied here.[131] For our purposes, it is sufficient to adopt a thin version of this parallel. Ultimately, when a non-state actor uses force from a state's territory, it is using, against its will, an *object* regarding which the state (*qua* collective of individuals) enjoys some form of exclusive rights. At least for the sake of testing the proper ordering of rights—and the role that fault plays in this ordering—this is a close enough parallel.

Consider the following series of thought experiments:

*A breaks into B's house, while B is at work. Standing on the porch, she is now shooting at V, who is pinned down in the street below. O is a police officer, armed with a light weapon. Any response against A would (incidentally) trespass on B's property.*

Can O return fire?[132] Few would object, and few criminal systems would hold O accountable for the ensuing infringement of B's rights if A is engaged, although B is completely innocent. This is because in relation to V's right not to be killed, B's rights against trespass can be justifiably overridden.[133] This situation parallels a transnational attack by a non-state actor, emanating from an innocent state's territory, and risking individuals on the other side, where a response by the state would only incidentally infringe on the territorial state's sovereignty. Quite clearly, we need very strong reasons to conclude that in such cases this type of right would not be overridden by the right of individuals not to be killed. Even if such all-things-considered reasons can be found, it is surely *not* the state's innocence that plays a decisive role.

Assume, however, that:

*A is taking cover behind a window. O's only possibility to defend V would be to sling a hand grenade and incidentally destroy B's living room.*

[130] H. Frowe, *Defensive Killing* (2014) 1–3.

[131] See Ripstein (n. 101). Interestingly, Ripstein argues that sovereignty over territory cannot be equated to property *precisely* because it is closer to a 'body'. He justifies this by invoking 'the familiar moral and legal idea that defensive war can be legitimate to protect the state's territorial integrity'. Otherwise, as Ripstein points out, this right 'would be in tension with the equally familiar idea that potentially lethal force may not be used to protect property'. Ibid. 248. However, in my view, this tension is precisely what needs to be explored.

[132] The example here assumes the contractual 'bodyguard' view of the state, in the sense that the state possesses all, but no more, of the defensive rights which its individuals possess ('other defence'). See Frowe (n. 130) 26–28 for a brief discussion.

[133] Interestingly, in German domestic law, the concept of *Defensivnotstand* also permits defensive actions in the property of others because of the perception that the owner of the property bears an ultimate—fault-independent—responsibility for its property being risk free. I thank Claus Kreß for pointing this out. For a more detailed exploration of this concept, see Kreß (n. 3).

Here, the response would not only trespass on B's property but would also harm it incidentally. And yet it seems that this additional harm would not negate V's right to defend herself or O's derivative permission to do so. This is because B's rights not to suffer trespass or harm to her property are simply not powerful enough to override V's right not to be killed. This example parallels the inter-state scenario earlier, only that in addition to an infringement of sovereignty, the response also incidentally harms objects within the state. Whether or not self-defence would be morally permitted here would be a question of harm–benefit *proportionality* and, in law, mainly a question of *jus in bello* proportionality. Indeed, some infrastructure is of such importance to the survival of many, that harming it incidentally might be prohibited even if some lives are thereby put at risk.[134] Yet, in general, human life is vastly more important than objects. In most cases, the state's rights concerning its infrastructure would be overridden by the rights of individuals not to be killed. Again, state fault would not play a significant part in our judgement.

What if B actively tries to stop A from attacking V? Assume that:

*B has just returned from work, to witness the attack going on. Unarmed, B tries to throw stones at A, but A is well protected.*

It is clear that this in itself cannot affect V's right to defend herself (and O's permission to do so). Quite simply, whether B is fulfilling any responsibility she might have to try to prevent the harm caused from her property is not determinative. The parallel to the *unable* state is clear. Of course, on the inter-state level, there are very good reasons to let the territorial state handle the threat itself, if possible. But these reasons relate chiefly to considerations of necessity (last resort), rather than to the fact that the territorial state is faultless.

Of course, the analysis changes completely, if:

*A holds several hostages in B's house, and they are likely to be killed if O responds.*

In this scenario, O's response would trespass on B's property, incidentally harm her property, and also incidentally kill the hostages. Now, we have a clash between the equal rights of V and those of the hostages not to be killed. Therefore, it is difficult to argue that V's right overrides those of several hostages. Rather, it seems that the hostages' rights override V's.[135] But neither the harm to B's property nor B's innocence seem to play any decisive role in untangling this clash. On the inter-state level, this problem replicates a situation in which the non-state actor operates from a highly populated area but risks only a few individuals in the attacked state. A response in such circumstances might be morally disproportionate if its harms outweigh its benefit, and unlawful if disproportionate under *jus in bello*. But the

134 See API (n. 119) Art. 54.

135 Haque, e.g., argues that due to the asymmetry between killing and letting die, the incidental killing of people can be justified only if it results in saving a much greater number of people. See Haque (n. 119) 175–206.

permissibility of a response does not seem to be affected significantly by the mere existence of harm to the state's territory or by state fault.[136]

So, is fault meaningless? Akande and Liefländer, I think, are right to suggest that fault mainly implicates necessity and proportionality considerations, as these are understood under the law on the use of force.[137] It is here that a distinction between responsibility and culpability makes a difference. If, in our example, O could find a way to stop A without harming B's interests—for instance, by getting some kind of cooperation from B—it seems that the *necessity* (last resort) condition would indeed require O to do so. Assume, however, that B has invited A to her house, visibly does not object to her actions, and does nothing to try to stop her. In such cases, B is responsible for the threat. But, more importantly, the same actions that trigger this responsibility also affect necessity: it seems that if we know that B supports A, our understanding of what 'last resort' means will change. For example, if any attempt at cooperation would surely receive no response and, on the other hand, would enhance the risk to V because of the time spent, it seems unjust to require such a pause. On the inter-state level, the parallel, of course, is situations in which a territorial state supports or harbours the non-state actor. While *jus ad bellum* necessity requirements certainly apply to a response against such an attack—and, naturally, these would be more strenuous as much as there is a pause between attacks—it seems that the territorial state's position in such cases would lower the threshold required to prove necessity. For instance, the extent to which the attacked state would be required to seek and wait for the cooperation of the territorial state before responding would naturally be affected by the involvement of that state in the threat.

Yet, in the latter case, B, albeit being responsible, would not *itself* constitute the threat against V. In legal terms, if O attacked B, we would say that it was disproportionate, in the sense that it was beyond what was needed to halt A's shooting. In fact, O would be punishing B, rather than defending V. If, however, B directed

[136] This example implies that a rights-ordering approach not only serves as an enabling, but also as a constraining, principle. E.g. assume the same scenario as earlier, but that rather than shooting at V, A is shooting at *something belonging* to V. Although this is undoubtedly a grave infringement of V's rights, few would agree that V, or O, would be entitled to respond lethally against A, much less in a manner that would incidentally kill the hostages. This reasoning problematizes the expansionists' automatic invocation of states 'inherent' right to self-defence in order to respond to any attack by non-state actors. This ties in to the wider discussion in the ethics of war on the right to 'national self-defence'. Compare Rodin (n. 15) (arguing that self-defence can only be invoked against threats against vital interests) with Frowe (n. 129) (arguing that aggregation of harm can collapse the distinction). We might accept that in an inter-state scenario, there are good reasons (and a legal basis) to conclude that non-state fighters are liable for transnational defensive killing, even if their attacks only infringe on a state's sovereignty or territory. To me, the best justification in such cases is imminent self-defence against greater harm (but see Rodin (n. 15) on conditional threats). But we would be hard-pressed to argue that these violations of territory, per se, can justify self-defence when such action would infringe the right to life of innocent individuals on the other side. Simply put, the 'innocence' of the victim state, or the fact that its territory is attacked, would not justify overriding the rights of individuals not to be killed.

[137] Akande and Liefländer (n. 10).

A's shooting, she would be *culpable* for the threat. O's response against B, here, would be defensive rather than punitive. On the inter-state level, this would mean that territorial state attribution might make it *proportionate* for the attacked state to target the territorial state's military, or at least the specific units taking part in the non-state actor's attack.

In sum, the examples above demonstrate that in a transnational clash between a state's (*qua* collective) right to an object (territory) and individuals' rights to life, the latter should prevail, while fault would only adjust necessity and proportionality considerations.

## 9. Conclusion

As mentioned earlier, international law on self-defence against non-state actors is in flux. Since the development of law should take into account normative considerations, this chapter suggests that scenarios of transnational self-defence against non-state actors should be conceived as clashes between rights of different orders. Basic rights of physical persons should override rights of 'innocent' legal entities, and the right to life should generally override rights to objects. Under these assumptions, how could positive law reflect the proper ordering of rights? Perhaps—and without exhausting the debate—the key might be the definition of an 'armed attack' by a non-state actor.

At least in the literature, even those who endorse self-defence against non-state actors usually agree that such an attack must cross a certain threshold of gravity. Some argue that, concerning attacks by non-state actors, the attack has to be *more* grave than would constitute an armed attack by a state. The rationale seems to be that by setting the threshold higher, territorial states would have more space to deal with the problem alone, before international escalation ensues. It is unclear whether states actually endorse this specific limitation.[138] Nonetheless, even if non-state actor attacks must cross a higher threshold to be considered 'armed attacks', this threshold still needs to be properly defined.[139]

As a preliminary suggestion, an ordering of rights calls for a test that would mainly ask whether the attack actually threatens or harms individuals or, perhaps, objects essential for their survival.[140] If this view is adopted, what matters for the sake of self-defence is the actual harm, not necessarily the scope of the attack. In this sense, even a low-level attack that puts people at risk might justify an *ad bellum*

[138] For an analysis, see Hakimi (n. 27) 16–17.

[139] This is difficult since both on the inter-state and transnational levels, the 'armed attack' threshold has never been precisely circumscribed. Hakimi and Katz Cogan (n. 23) 271.

[140] Compare Dannenbaum (n. 113) 1270–1278 (highlighting that the criminalization of aggression should be understood first and foremost as protecting individuals, rather than state sovereignty).

and *in bello* proportionate response to halt and repel the attack. Importantly, however, such a standard can also be constraining: for instance, even a wider attack, in terms of scale, might not significantly threaten individuals. One example can be the launch of mortar rounds by non-state actors that hit open areas in another state. In such cases, it is unclear why self-defence on the territory of the territorial state would be *automatically* justified.[141] To sum up this point, it seems that for a non-attributable attack by non-state actors to amount to an armed attack, it should pose a grave and immediate threat to the life and limb of individuals (or harm objects or infrastructure essential for the survival of individuals). Attacks that merely implicate a state's territory should not, in general, be presumed to cross this threshold. In other words, in the preliminary stage of assessing whether an armed attack has occurred, it is the actual type of harm that should be the primary focus.

Of course, even if an attack by a non-state actor crosses this threshold, necessity and proportionality limitations apply. It is here that the question of state fault might be significant. If a state is 'innocent' (unable), the necessity threshold should be higher, *in particular* when the armed attack is not ongoing.[142] Conversely, if the state is *responsible* for the attack, say, by supporting or harbouring a non-state actor, this indeed might implicate our perceptions on the necessity of a transnational response. Beyond that, if the state is *culpable* (the attack is attributable), this can affect the scope of permissible response under proportionality.

Whether or not the standard above is adopted as international law, the crucial point is that demystifying the innocent state is important for untangling the clashing rights and interests that are implicated when non-state actors launch transnational attacks.

[141] Arguably, one can claim that there is a 'law and order' justification to respond here. However, there is a parity between the territorial rights of both states in such cases, and since a forcible response might escalate the conflict and eventually harm individuals, there are good policy grounds to limit self-defence.

[142] E.g. when there is an imminent threat, or when there might be a lull between attacks. Indeed, if the attack is non-recurring and obviously over, there is no necessity to begin with.

# Index

*For the benefit of digital users, indexed terms that span two pages (e.g., 52–53) may, on occasion, appear on only one of those pages.*

The manufacturer's authorised representative in the EU for product safety is Oxford University Press España S.A. of el Parque Empresarial San Fernando de Henares, Avenida de Castilla, 2 – 28830 Madrid (www.oup.es/en or product.safety@oup.com). OUP España S.A. also acts as importer into Spain of products made by the manufacturer.

www.ingramcontent.com/pod-product-compliance
Lightning Source LLC
LaVergne TN
LVHW011753200926
848484LV00003B/696

*9780198940166*